STUDY GUIDE FOR

Dillingham, Skaggs, and Carlson

ECONOMICS
INDIVIDUAL CHOICE AND IT'S CONSEQUENCES

Prepared by

J. Lon Carlson
Illinois State University

Lawrence Gwinn
Wittenberg University

ALLYN AND BACON
BOSTON LONDON TORONTO SYDNEY TOKYO SINGAPORE

A Division of Simon & Schuster, Inc.
160 Gould Street
Needham Heights, MA 02194

ISBN 0-205-13023-2

Printed in the United States of America

10 9 8 7 6 5 4 3 2 1 95 94 93 92 91

CONTENTS

PREFACE

Introduction

Many students view economics as being a very difficult, if not impossible, course to master. However, this perception is, in all likelihood, based on observations of the experiences of other students who did not apply the proper approach to learning economics. In many courses, simple memorization is enough. In economics, we would argue, this is not the case. The nature of economics is such that, while you need to understand the meaning of basic terms and concepts, you also need to be able to apply economic concepts in specific situations. In other words, you need to develop the ability to think like an economist.

You need to remember that economics is a participation sport. You learn economics by doing economics. That is why this study guide has been developed. The study guide contains a wide variety of problems that require you to apply what you have learned and, at the same time, test your under-standing of the material. We cannot stress enough the importance of using the study guide on a regular basis.

Organization of the Study Guide

The material in the study guide has been organized to help you identify the key points in each chapter and test your mastery of the material that is presented in the text. The first section of each chapter consists of an overview that highlights the major topics and points that are presented in the text. The overview has been designed to alert you to the major topics and is not intended to serve, in any way, as a substitute for the material in the text. As you read the overview, be sure you are familiar with the topics being discussed. You should use the overview as your first indicator of topics requiring further study on your part.

The second section of each chapter highlights key graphs and terms that are presented in the text. Once again, the purpose of this discussion is to emphasize the major concepts and, in the case of graphs, alert you to the major factors that affect the relationship being illustrated. In order to be able to use graphs to analyze the effects of changes in key economic variables, you must have a clear understanding of how the determinants of the functions being illustrated in a graph are related. A key element in mastering graphical analysis is the ability to distinguish among factors that cause movements along a particular function, and factors that cause the function to shift.

The third section of each chapter consists of exercises that are designed to test your mastery of basic concepts as well as your ability to apply the analytical tools that have been developed in the text. Questions range from fill-in-the-blank to applications involving graphical and numerical analysis.

The fourth section of each chapter consists of a set of review questions that are organized in a multiple choice question format. The section containing the review questions is intended to serve as self-test, and has been structured to emulate the type of test that is given in many principles of economics courses. As such, you should treat this section as if it were an actual test. Do not use your book or notes (or your friends), and do not consult the answers at the back of the chapter until you have finished the entire section. Using the review questions in this manner is an excellent way to prepare for the "real thing."

The final section in each chapter consists of an answer key for the exercises and the review questions. In the case of the review questions, you are provided with the correct answer, as well as an explanation of why the answer is correct, and in some cases, why the alternative answers are not correct.

Using the Study Guide

We recommend the following approach to studying and learning economics. 1) Read over the material that will be covered in class prior to attending the lecture. The idea is not to master the material being covered but rather to familiarize yourself with the concepts that will be covered. 2) Attend each lecture and take good notes. 3) After the lecture, read the text again, study your lecture notes and begin working in the study guide. Approaching the study of economics in this manner will allow you to get the most out of the course and may actually result in less time spent studying than you might if you resort to "cramming".

With respect to the use of the study guide, remember that the overview and discussions of key graphs and terms are not a substitute for reading the text. Instead that are designed to "flag" key topics and alert you to specific items you may have missed. When completing the exercises and the review questions, we strongly recommend that you avoid using your book or notes to answer the questions on your initial run through. Instead, use the exercises as a way to flag topics that you have not yet mastered. When you get a question wrong, you should take that as a signal to go back and devote more study to the topic in question. Once you have finished going over the material in question, wait for a period of time and then go back and try the question again. In most cases you will see your mistake immediately. You will also have a much better grasp of the material.

Lon Carlson

Larry Gwinn

CHAPTER 1
ECONOMIC THINKING

OVERVIEW

Economics is the science of decision making. Economists recognize that in almost all activities the decision to pursue one alternative requires that other alternatives be foregone. Stated differently, there are always trade-offs! This is true whenever decision makers face a resource constraint. For example, at the individual level we must decide how to allocate scarce resources such as time and income. With respect to production decisions, decisionmakers must determine the amount of resources to devote to the production of various goods and services.

The need to choose among alternatives is the result of scarcity. Specifically, society is faced with the problem of trying to satisfy unlimited wants with a limited supply of available resources--land, labor, capital, and entrepreneurial ability. Because resources are scarce, choices have to be made among competing wants. The choices we make, in turn, force us to incur opportunity costs. Opportunity cost is measured as the highest-valued alternative foregone in selecting a specific alternative when making a choice. For example, the decision to use resources in the production of a specific good requires that society forego the next best alternative that could be produced with those resources.

The Fundamental Premise of Economics states that in all decision making, individuals choose the alternative for which they believe the gains to be the greatest. The gains associated with a given alternative are measured by the net difference between the benefits and costs that would be gained if the alternative were selected. From an economic perspective, the goal of individuals and society is to maximize their total net gains. In this way, the problem of scarcity is minimized.

The concepts of scarcity, opportunity cost, and choice are illustrated by the production possibilities frontier (PPF). The PPF indicates the maximum amount of two goods that can be produced with a fixed set of resources and the existing level of technology. When society produces a combination of goods on the PPF, it is using it's scarce resources efficiently. Production at a point inside the PPF is the result of inefficient use of resources. For example, if people are involuntarily unemployed production will be limited to a point inside the PPF.

The PPF also can be used to illustrate the concepts of constant and increasing marginal costs. Marginal cost is the opportunity cost of producing one more unit of output. When marginal costs are constant the PPF is a straight line. When marginal costs are increasing, the PPF is bowed out (concave to the origin). Increasing marginal costs are the result of the nonadaptability of resources to the production of specific goods.

The PPF indicates the maximum amounts of two goods that can be produced at a point in time. However, the PPF can also be used to illustrate the concept of economic growth, which is depicted by an outward shift of the PPF. Growth occurs whenever we realize an increase in at least one of the factors of production, all else constant. For example, growth will occur as a result of an increase in the stock of capital goods or the level of technology.

The PPF is an example of how economists model an economic problem. Like any other science, economics seeks to understand cause and effect relationships. Examples include the relationships between variables such as unemployment and inflation and the different policies designed to deal with them, the effects of tax changes on investment behavior, and the results of technological innovation on the relative values of productive resources. In order to facilitate an increased understanding of such relationships, models are developed that simplify the problem so that it can be analyzed. Models are also used to evaluate the economic impacts of various courses of action and assist decision makers in performing their job.

KEY GRAPHS AND TERMS

Graphs

The primary model introduced in this chapter is the PPF. The PPF can be used to illustrate a variety of situations in which choices must be made among competing alternatives. These alternatives can take the form of competing uses of one's time, different combinations of goods that could be produced with the same set of resources, and different ways to spend a fixed amount of income to name but a few. The position of the PPF is determined by the amount of each of the resources available to the decision-maker, e.g., the individual in society. For example, the position of the PPF for a given economy is determined by the available quantities of the factors of production--land, labor, capital, and entrepreneurial ability--and current technology.

Production at points inside the PPF are the result of the under-utilization or inefficient use of resources. For example, there may be involuntary unemployment or capital may be sitting idle, such as occurs in a recession. Production at a point on the PPF indicates that society is using its scarce resources efficiently. However, production at a point beyond the PPF is not possible without an increase in at least one of the factors of production or technology. When either of these situations occurs, the PPF will tend to shift out to the right making production beyond the original PPF possible.

Terms

SCARCITY
OPPORTUNITY COST
FUNDAMENTAL PREMISE OF ECONOMICS
CONSTANT MARGINAL COSTS
INCREASING MARGINAL COSTS
PRODUCTION POSSIBILITIES FRONTIER
INVESTMENT
TECHNOLOGY
RESOURCES
ENTREPRENEURIAL ABILITY
LAND
LABOR
CAPITAL

EXERCISES

1. The economic problem of ___Scarcity___ is characterized by ___unlimited___ wants, but ___limited___ resources.

2. When constructing the PPF for an economy, technology, ___LAND___, ___LABOR___, ___CAPITAL___, and ___ENTREPRENEURIAL ABILITY___ are assumed to be fixed in amount.

3. ___OPPORTUNITY___ ___Cost___ is defined as the highest-valued alternative foregone in making a particular choice.

4. The limited amount of time that a person can devote to various activities each day, and the fixed amount of labor available to an economy at a point in time are both examples of a ___RESOURSE POSSIBILITIES___ ___Constraint___.

5. All else constant, an increase in the amount of capital stock will cause the economy's PPF to ___Shift___ ___out___.

6. A set of generalizations intended to explain a set of observed regularities is called a ___Theory___, and the corresponding testable implications are called ___HYPOTHESIS___.

7. ___Positive___ science involves the study of what is, while a ___NORMATIVE___ position is based on a belief of what should be.

Chapter 1, Economic Thinking

Use the following figure, which depicts a hypothetical PPF, to answer questions 3 - 8.

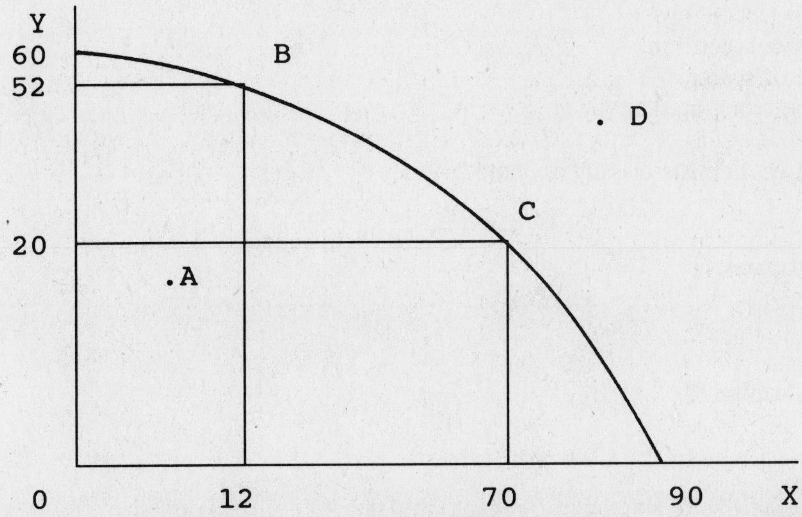

8. The opportunity cost of moving from point C to point B is _58_ units of good _X_.

9. The opportunity cost of production at point B is _8_ units of good Y.

10. List at least 3 possible causes of production at point A. Resources are not fully employed. Redistribution of wealth, reducing the level of satisfaction wealthy people are able to attain. Reducing the level of production of the economy.

11. Is production at point D possible in the current period? _No_ In the future? _Yes_ If so, how? Through Economic Growth.

12. Within the figure, illustrate the effect on the PPF of an increase in the amount of capital that can be used to produce both X and Y. How would your answer change if the increased capital could only be used to produce good Y? Whole PPF shifts out along both axes. PPF would rotate showing that more of Y can be produced when X = 0, but that X still equals 90 when Y = 0.

13. Assume that Good Y represents capital goods and Good X represents consumer goods. At which of the points shown in the figure should the economy operate if it wants grow as rapidly as possible? _B_ Why? Capital Good are a factor of production, consumer goods are not.

REVIEW QUESTIONS

1. Which of the following is the best general definition of the study of economics?

a) Inflation and unemployment in a growing economy.
b) Business decision making under foreign competition.
c) Individual and social choice in the face of scarcity.
d) The most profitable way to invest in the stock market.

2. Which of the following resources would economists classify as "land?"

a) Raw bauxite in a South African mine.
b) Aluminum tubes used to make bicycle frames.
c) A man-made lake.
d) Steel used to make automobiles.

3. What do economists mean by the term "capital?"

a) Certificates of ownership such as stocks.
b) Currency, coins, checks, and credit cards.
c) Man-made factors of production.
d) Naturally occurring factors of production.

4. What implication(s) does resource scarcity have for the satisfaction of wants?

a) Not all wants can be satisfied.
b) We will never be faced with the need to make choices.
c) We must develop ways to decrease our individual wants.
d) The discovery of new natural resources is necessary to increase our ability to satisfy wants.

5. What does rational decision making require?

a) That one's choices be arrived at logically and without error.
b) That one's choices be consistent with one's goals.
c) That one's choices never vary.
d) That one makes choices that do not involve trade-offs.

6. What is the Fundamental Premise of Economics?

a) Natural resources will always be scarce.
b) Individuals are capable of establishing goals and acting in a manner consistent with achievement of those goals.
c) Individuals choose the alternative for which they believe the net gains to be the greatest.
d) No matter what the circumstances, individual choice always involves a trade-off.

7. Which of the following illustrates the concept of opportunity cost?

a) "If I go back to college full time, I will have to give up my $20,000 a year job."
b) "Let's see, should we go to see a movie tonight, or go out for pizza and a beer?"
c) "Increased government spending on the military, will force a reduction in spending on welfare programs."
d) All of the above.

8. If the number of radar-toting highway patrol vehicles increases so that there is a greater probability of being caught speeding, what do you think will happen to the number of drivers exceeding the speed limit?

a) It will increase because costs have increased.
b) It will decrease because costs have increased.
c) It will increase because benefits have increased.
d) It will decrease because benefits have decreased.

9. How is the concept of trade-offs illustrated by the PPF?

a) By a rightward shift of the PPF.
b) By a leftward shift of the PPF.
c) By a movement along the PPF.
d) The concept of trade-offs is not illustrated by the PPF.

10. If the PPF is linear, i.e., a straight line, which of the following is true?

a) As the production of a good increases, the marginal cost of that good rises.
b) As the production of a good increases, the marginal cost of that good falls.
c) There are no increasing marginal costs.
d) The economy is not at full employment when operating on the PPF.

11. Which of the following is an example of the "What" question?

a) "Should we produce ten-speed bicycles or all- terrain bicycles?"
b) "Should we produce New Coke with NutraSweet or cane sugar?"
c) "Is it better to use migrant workers or automated machines to harvest our crops?"
d) "What are we going to do to ensure that we are producing personal computers at the lowest possible cost?"

12. Which of the following is an example of the "How" question?

a) "Should we produce ten-speed bicycles or all- terrain bicycles?"
b) "Is it better to use migrant workers or automated machines to harvest our crops?"
c) "What are we going to do to ensure that the real income of the elderly is maintained?"
d) "How do we determine whether the current distribution of income is fair?"

13. Which of the following is a normative statement?

a) The natural rate of unemployment is 6% of the labor force.
b) Rising prices create a greater burden on those with fixed incomes than on those with incomes rising at the same rate as prices.
c) A 1% increase in national output will reduce unemployment by 0.25%.
d) A 6% rate of unemployment is too high to leave alone.

14. Which of the following is the best statement of the Law of Increasing Costs?

a) As more of a good is produced, the opportunity cost of each additional unit of the good declines.
b) If the economy is at full employment, it must sacrifice some of one good to obtain more of another good.
c) Unemployment is illustrated by the movement from one point to another on the production possibilities frontier.
d) As additional units of a good are produced, the marginal cost of that good rises.

Use the following figure to answer questions 15 - 19.

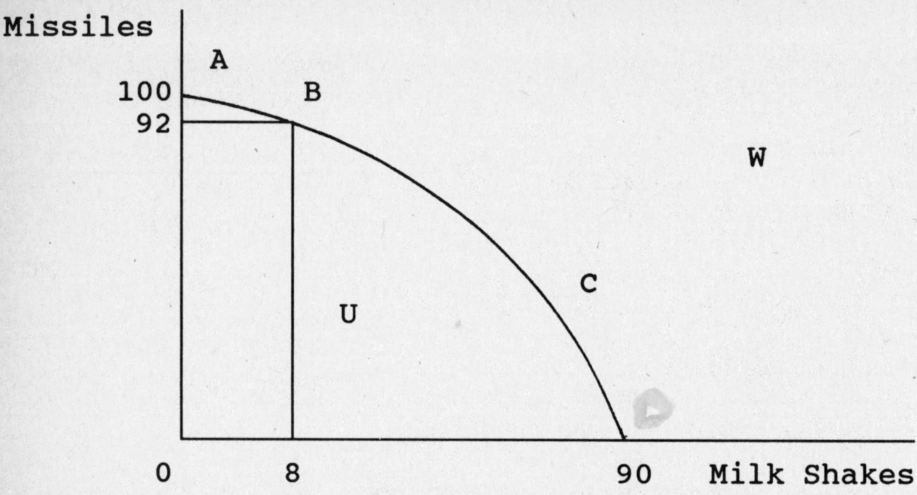

15. Which of the following represents the concept of trade-offs?

a) A movement from point A to point B.
b) A movement from point U to point C.
c) Point W.
d) Point U.

16. Which of the following would NOT move the production possibility frontier for this economy closer to point W?

a) A decrease in the amount of unemployed labor resources.
b) A shift in preferences toward greater capital formation.
c) An improvement in the overall level of technology.
d) An increase in the population growth rate.

17. Moving from point A to point D, what happens to the opportunity cost of producing more milk shakes?

a) It increases.
b) It decreases.
c) It remains constant.
d) It increase up to point B, then falls thereafter.

18. What is the opportunity cost of moving from point A to point B?

a) 100 missiles.
b) 8 milk shakes.
c) 90 missiles.
d) 10 missiles.

19. Unemployment is thought to make society as a whole worse off. This is illustrated in Figure 3 by which of the following?

a) The sacrifice of milk shakes that must be made when moving from point C to point B.
b) The opportunity cost involved in moving from point A to point D.
c) The society employing idle resources as it moves from point B to point C.
d) The zero opportunity cost involved in moving horizontally from point U to the PPF.

20. What is the opportunity cost of greater capital formation?

a) Greater consumption in the current period.
b) Smaller consumption in the current period.
c) Opportunity cost is zero for developed nations.
d) Slower economic growth in the future.

21. How would one illustrate a decrease in unemployment on the PPF?

a) By a movement down along the PPF.
b) By a rightward shift of the PPF.
c) By a movement from a point on the PPF to a point inside the PPF.
d) By a movement from a point inside the PPF to a point on the PPF.

22. Which of the following is a reason for the curvature or bowed-out shape of the PPF?

a) Falling unemployment as we move along the curve.
b) The economy having to produce less of one good in order to produce more of another good.
c) Opportunity costs increase as more of a good is produced.
d) The assumption that technology is fixed.

23. Which of the following is a reason for the negative slope of the PPF?

a) The inverse relationship between the use of technology and the use of natural resources.
b) The sacrifice of one good that must be made when producing more of another good at full employment.
c) Resource specialization.
d) Increasing opportunity costs.

24."If our country does not have the resources to produce what we want then we must learn to do without." What economic principle is this writer ignoring?

a) The principle of increasing cost.
b) The principle of scarcity.
c) The Fundamental Premise of Economics.
d) The principle of constant marginal costs.

25. Often during presidential election campaigns, candidates will promise both more "guns" and more "butter" if they are elected. Assuming unemployment is not a problem, what possible assumption are they making but not revealing to their audience?

a) There will be a sufficient increase in the supply of natural resources used to produce "guns" and "butter."
b) That there will be an improvement in the technology of both "gun" and "butter" production.
c) That there will be an increase in the labor force.
d) All of the above.

26. What is one of the future consequences of an increase in current consumption experienced in the US today?

a) Slower economic growth in the future.
b) Greater economic growth in the future.
c) No change in our economic growth rate.
d) Greater capital accumulation in the future.

27. The President of a Midwestern University was reported to have told the students that "they could have all the fun they wanted without sacrificing their educational goals." Is there anything wrong with her statement?

a) Yes, because it ignores the fact that choices always involve trade-offs.
b) No, because one can party as much as one wants and still do well in school.
c) Yes, because it fails to mention that the advice works only if one stays out of economics classes.
d) No, because the statement is consistent with the Fundamental Premise of Economics.

28. Which of the following is most likely to increase attendance in a given class?

a) Remind the students of the importance of a good education.
b) Schedule the class time for 10:00am rather than 4:30pm.
c) Have the teacher read to the class from her notes.
d) Hold the class in the largest lecture hall on campus.

29. If the University wants to stop students from drinking beer on campus, which of the following policies should it adopt?

a) Lower the drinking age on campus only.
b) Sell beer at the student union.
c) Encourage membership in fraternities.
d) Require immediate dismissal from the University for anyone caught drinking on campus.

30. If the government wished to discourage the illegal dumping of hazardous wastes, which policy would be effective?

a) Subsidize research and development into ways to profitably use previously hazardous wastes.
b) Increase funding to the department required to monitor and enforce dumping laws.
c) Increase the minimum fine and jail term for those getting caught and subsidize legal dumps.
d) All of the above.

31. How does society go about deciding whether to invest some of its resources now or consume them all?

a) By comparing the marginal benefits of current consumption to the marginal cost of slower economic growth.
b) By comparing the marginal benefits of current consumption to the marginal benefits of slower economic growth.
c) By comparing the extra cost of current consumption to the extra cost of slower future economic growth.
d) By comparing the arguments of national politicians.

REVIEW QUESTIONS: APPENDIX

32. What happens to the equation of a positively-sloped straight line when that line shifts parallel to the right?

a) The intercept falls, but the slope remains unchanged.
b) The intercept falls, and the slope decreases.
c) The intercept remains unchanged, but the slope decreases.
d) The intercept rises, but the slope remains unchanged.

33. What happens to a curve when the variable(s) that are normally held constant are allowed to change?

a) The curve flattens out.
b) There is a movement along the curve.
c) The curve shifts.
d) The curve becomes steeper.

34. Assume that the relationship between two variables, X and Y, can be illustrated graphically by a straight line that is upward sloping. Suppose the relationship between X and Y changes so that for every unit change in X there is now a greater change in Y than before. Which of the following changes in the line will occur?

a) The intercept will increase and the slope will remain constant.
b) The intercept will increase and the slope will increase.
c) The intercept will remain the same and the slope will increase.
d) The intercept will remain the same and the slope will decrease

35. Referring to the previous question, and recognizing that Y is the dependent variable, assume a variable that is normally held constant changes so that at every level of X, the amount of Y now increases. How will this change be shown on a graph?

a) The line will shift up and the slope will remain unchanged.
b) The line will shift down and the slope will remain unchanged.
c) The line will shift to the left and the slope will increase.
d) The line will shift to the right and the slope will increase.

36. Referring to the previous question (35), what will happen to the area under the line?

a) It will remain constant.
b) It will increase.
c) It will decrease.
d) Cannot tell.

ANSWER KEY

Exercises

1. scarcity, unlimited, limited
2. land, labor, capital, entrepreneurial ability
3. Opportunity cost
4. resource constraint
5. shift out
6. theory, hypotheses
7. Positive, normative
8. 58 units of good X
9. 8 units of good Y
10. unemployment of anyone of the factors of production (give three specific examples).
11. No. In the future? Yes. Through economic growth.
12. Whole PPF shifts out along both axes. PPF would rotate showing that more of Y can be produced (Y > 6) when X = 0, but that X still equals 90 when Y = 0.
13. B. Capital goods are a factor of production, consumer goods are not.

Review questions

1. c) is the correct answer. While answers a and b are certainly included in the study of economics, only answer c is consistent with the general definition of economics as the study of how people allocate scarce resources to satisfy unlimited wants.

2. a) is the correct answer. In the economists' lexicon, the term "land" refers to all natural resources, such as land, air, water, minerals, forests, fish, etc. Aluminum tubes, water in a man-made lake, and steel are all made by man, hence are classified as "capital" inputs.

3. c) is the correct answer. As noted in question 2, the term "capital" refers to all man-made factors of production.

4. a) is the correct answer. Faced with unlimited wants but only a limited amount of resources to satisfy those wants, we must make choices. Having to make choices implies that all of our wants cannot be satisfied at any one time.

5. b) is the correct answer. One behaves rationally, according to economists, when one sets up goals and makes choices consistent with attaining those goals. One need not behave logically (a la Mr. Spock). One may alter one's choices and still behave rationally.

6. c) is the correct answer. The Fundamental Premise of Economics states that one tends to make choices that add to net benefits, so that the additional benefits of a choice exceed the additional costs of a choice. Answers a, b, and d are true, but they are not the Fundamental Premise of Economics.

7. d) is the correct answer. The concept of opportunity cost draws attention to the fact that all choice involves trade-offs. The opportunity cost of a choice is the value of the next best alternative forgone. In answers a - c, the speaker is recognizing that each choice involves giving up at least one alternative.

8. b) is the correct answer. According to the Fundamental Premise, if the costs of a choice increase,with benefits unchanged, people will make that choice less often. Increasing the number of radar-toting highway patrol vehicles will increase the cost of speeding, with benefits unchanged, and hence will result in fewer people putting the "pedal to the metal".

9. c) is the correct answer. The PPF shows the maximum combination of any two goods that may be produced given the current stock of land, labor, capital, and entrepreneurial talent. Moving along a PPF we see that to have more of one good we must give up some of the other good, ceteris paribus. That is, that a trade-off is involved.

10. c) is the correct answer. If the production possibilities is linear, there are no increasing marginal costs is effect. As the production of a good is increased, the cost of one more unit remains constant. This is illustrated by the constant slope of the PPF. d) is incorrect because the economy is always at full employment when at a point on the PPF.

11. a) is the correct answer. The "What" questions asks "What should be produced?". Only answer a asks that question.

12. b) is the correct answer. The "How" question asks "How shall we produce the goods we've decided on?". Only answer b asks that same question. Answers c and d refer to the "For Whom" question, and answer a refers to the "What" question.

13. d) is the correct answer. Normative statements include value judgments, i.e., what one believes should be. Positive statements consist of facts. Answers a - c are facts relating to the US economy. Answer d is a value judgment that the unemployment rate is "too high".

14. d) is the correct answer. This is a correct statement of the Law of Increasing Costs.

15. a) is the correct answer. Trade-offs result whenever a choice for more of one good implies simultaneously reducing the amount of the other good. Moving along the PPF from A to B is a choice to have more milk shakes, but at the same time to have fewer missiles.

16. a) is the correct answer. Because point W lies outside the PPF, it can only be attained through economic growth, i.e., by a rightward shift in the PPF. The only way the PPF can shift is if the stock of resources (land, labor, or capital) increases or if the technology for producing one or both of the goods improves. A decrease in unemployed resources (labor, land, or capital) moves the economy from a point inside the PPF to a point on or closer to - but not beyond - the PPF.

17. a) is the correct answer. Starting from point A, if we decide to produce one unit of milk shakes, we would transfer our least productive missile-making resources that are easily adaptable to the production of milk shakes. As a result, the production of missiles would drop, but only a little, since the resources transferred were not very productive in the missile industry. But as we decide to produce more milk shakes, we must transfer resources that are increasingly more productive in the missile industry and not easily adaptable to producing milk shakes. Hence we lose increasingly larger amounts of missiles for every unit increase in milk shakes.

18. d) is the correct answer. The opportunity cost of moving from point A to point B is the number of missiles forgone. At point A the country has 100 missiles and 0 milk shakes. At point B the country has 90 missiles and 8 million milk shakes. Therefore, the opportunity cost of producing and additional 8 million milk shakes is 10 missiles.

19. d) is the correct answer. A horizontal movement from the point of unemployment to the curve illustrates an increase in the production of milk shakes without any sacrifice of missiles. Thus the opportunity cost is zero. If we could employ the idle resources, we could have more of one good without sacrificing any of the other good. Full employment is assumed at each point on the curve, so a. and b) are both incorrect. The society does not have any idle resources when on the curve, therefore c) is incorrect.

20. b) is the correct answer. There are always trade-offs. If we want high economic growth in the future, then fewer resources will be available to devote to the production of current consumption goods.

21. d) is the correct answer. A decrease in unemployed resources (labor, land, or capital) moves the economy from a point inside the PPF to a point on or closer to the PPF.

22. c) is the correct answer. The bowed-out shape of the PPF implies that as we move along the frontier we must give up increasing amounts of one good to get more of another.

23. b) is the correct answer. The PPF has two main features--its slope and its curvature. Its negative slope is due to the sacrifice of one good that must be made when producing more of the

other good when on the frontier, ie. when at full employment. d) is incorrect because increasing marginal costs are illustrated by the curvature, rather than the slope, of the frontier. A linear frontier is negatively-sloped, but marginal cost is constant rather than increasing. c) is also incorrect since it is a reason for increasing marginal costs.

24. b) is the correct answer. Attempts to reduce the desire for material possessions does not eliminate the problem of scarcity. It may only succeed in shifting wants from material goods to something else, such as leisure.

25. d) is the correct answer. Having more of both goods requires economic growth, i.e., an rightward shift in the PPF. The sources of economic growth are: increases in the stock of land, labor, or capital; or an improvement in technology.

26. a) is the correct answer. Increased current consumption reduces the amount of capital available for future production. Hence economic growth will be slower in the future.

27. a) is the correct answer. Unfortunately, as every college freshman has observed (or learned first hand), "You can't eat your cake and have it too". In order to choose "all the fun you want" the trade-off is likely to be a reduction in GPA, a change to a less prestigious major, or an increase in the number of years it takes to finish college.

28. b) is the correct answer. To encourage class attendance, one could increase the marginal benefits, or reduce the marginal cost, of going to class. By holding classes earlier in the day, the marginal cost of attending is decreased. (Note: The marginal benefits are unchanged - they are determined by the lecturer and the material.)

29. d) is the correct answer. To discourage beer drinking, one could increase the marginal cost of drinking, or reduce the marginal benefits of drinking. Imposing a severe penalty for getting caught drinking increases the cost and hence is likely to reduce the quantity of beer consumed on campus.

30. d) is the correct answer. To discourage illegal dumping, one could increase the marginal cost of dumping, or reduce the marginal benefits of dumping. Making resale of the waste profitable will increase the cost of dumping; increasing enforcement of the laws raises the probability of being caught, hence increases the cost of dumping; the same result follows from raising the penalty for dumping; reducing the cost of legal disposal reduces the benefits of illegal disposal.

31. a) is the correct answer. All rational choices are made by comparing the extra (marginal) benefits of the choice to the extra (marginal) costs of the choice.

32. a) is the correct answer. Consider a positively-sloped line such as the line drawn in Figure 11 of the text. If that line shifts horizontally to the right, forming a new parallel line, the slope will remain unchanged. Note that the intercept of the vertical axis will fall to some level below the original intercept.

33. c) is the correct answer. For two-dimensional graphs, only two variables are allowed to vary--all others must be held constant. When the variable(s) normally held constant are allowed to change, a curve shifts either to the right or to the left.

34. c) is the correct answer. The slope will increase if there is a greater change in Y for every one unit change in X. This simply restates the definition of slope, i.e., rise over run. The slope represents the specific relationship between X and Y. The intercept will not change because everything else was assumed to stay the same.

35. a) is the correct answer. Since the change causes the value of Y to increase for every value of X, the line will shift up. That is, the intercept will become larger. The change which has occurred in this case has not changed the specific relationship between X and Y. Therefore, the slope remains unchanged.

36. b) is the correct answer. The line will shift up, with the slope remaining constant, so the area under the function will increase. The larger the intercept, given the slope, the greater the area under the line will be.

CHAPTER 2
MUTUALLY BENEFICIAL EXCHANGE

OVERVIEW

In this chapter we examine the relationships among individuals' wants, the value of resources, and economic efficiency. Individuals and societies employ a variety of resources to produce goods and services. In turn, individuals derive satisfaction--utility--from the consumption of goods and services. In each of these situations the problem of scarcity arises. Specifically, we are faced with the problem of satisfying unlimited wants with limited resources.

Resources, in and of themselves, do not possess value. Rather, the value of resources is measured in terms of the goods and services they are be used to produce. Because resources are scarce it is necessary to consider the costs and benefits of committing a resource to a specific use. Once again, the concept of opportunity cost arises. Benefits are measured by the value of the good or service that is produced. Economic efficiency requires that the difference between the benefits and costs, i.e., the net benefits, of using a resource in a specific way be as large as possible. Economic efficiency consists of getting the most total satisfaction out of available resources.

In the context of the production possibilities frontier (PPF) economic efficiency is achieved when we produce the combination of goods most preferred by society. Economic efficiency requires that two conditions be met. First, we must be productively efficient, that is, we must be producing a combination of goods or services on the PPF. The second condition for economic efficiency is allocative efficiency, in which case we are producing that combination of goods most preferred by society.

Economic efficiency works to offset the problem of scarcity. The benefits of economic efficiency can be enhanced further through specialization and trade. In situations where the relative costs of production differ among countries or among individuals, the involved parties can specialize in the production of those goods or services for which opportunity costs are lowest. That is, they can specialize in goods in which they possess a comparative advantage, and then trade the surplus outputs, allowing both parties to consume beyond their respective PPFs. This fact explains why we observe countries specializing in the production of goods, and then trading. It is an example of the Fundamental Premise of Economics at work.

The benefits of trade can also be analyzed in the context of two individuals who have varying tastes for the same good. By comparing the marginal benefits associated with each unit of a good or service consumed we can show that the two individuals can engage in mutually beneficial trade. The result is that by giving up lower-valued goods in exchange for higher-valued goods, each individual can be better off than they would without trade.

Specialization and trade can increase the net welfare of economic agents. However, costs are often incurred. Specialization in production often results in jobs that are monotonous and boring. In addition, specialization in the production of some goods, at the expense of others, will result in lost jobs in those industries where production is cut back. In such cases the issue of individual versus group well-being must be addressed. In particular, the costs incurred by individuals as a result of specialization must be weighed against the benefits of increased consumption enjoyed by society as a whole.

The fact that the pursuit of efficiency entails costs gives rise to an important consideration, i.e., efficiency is only one of many goals that societies try to achieve. Other possible social goals include equity and the provision of a minimum level of well-being to be enjoyed by all. It is quite possible, and indeed is often the case, that a society's goals conflict with one another. A frequent result is the realization of an outcome that is not the most economically efficient but one that simultaneously satisfies each of society's goals to some extent.

KEY GRAPHS AND TERMS

Graphs

The PPF, provides a convenient way to analyze the benefits of specialization and trade between two individuals or countries. An example of the benefits of specialization and trade is found in Figure 5 in the text. Notice that while the opportunity costs of production are constant for both countries (South Korea and the United States), the relative opportunity costs are different. When opportunity costs are constant, as is the case in Figure 5, relative opportunity costs in each country are calculated by forming a ratio of the maximum amount of the two goods that a country can produce. Thus, for South Korea relative opportunity costs are calculated as 150 unit of shoes = 50 units of wheat, which can bereduced to 3 units of shoes = 1 unit of wheat, or 1 unit of shoes = 1/3 unit of wheat. Realtive opportunity costs in the Umited States are calculated in a similar manner. The relative opportunity costs in each country indicate that South Korea has a comparative advantage in shoe production and the United States has a comparative advantage in wheat production.

Because the relative opportunity costs are different, it is possible for each of these countries to consume beyond its respective PPF. For this to occur, each country must specialize in the production of the good for which it possesses a comparative advantage.

Key Terms
NET GAIN
ECONOMIC EFFICIENCY
PRODUCTIVE EFFICIENCY
ALLOCATIVE EFFICIENCY
UTILITY
ABSOLUTE ADVANTAGE
COMPARATIVE ADVANTAGE
TERMS OF TRADE
TRANSACTIONS COSTS

EXERCISES

1. When individuals possess a comparative advantage in the production of different goods, ______________ and ______________ enable them consume beyond their PPFs.

2. In the context of the PPF, ______________ efficiency implies that a country is producing on its PPF, while ______________ efficiency implies that the combination of goods most preferred by society is being produced.

3. An individual who can produce a good at a lower resource cost than other producers is said to have an ______________ advantage, while an individual who can produce a good at a lower opportunity cost than other producers is said to have a ______________ advantage.

4. Assume that with a day's labor John can mow 6 acres of grass or plant 12 acres of sod. In the same amount of time, Jill can mow 8 acres of grass or plant 10 acres of sod. Which person has a comparative advantage in mowing grass? __________ Planting sod? __________ Give an example of mutually beneficial terms of trade between John and Jill.

5. Assume that with a day's labor (8 hours) Ann can produce 4 fish or 12 coconuts while Betty can produce 6 fish or 2 coconuts. Assuming that Ann and Betty decide to specialize and trade, which of the following would be considered mutually beneficial terms of trade?

4 fish = 1 coconut 3 fish = 1 coconut 1 fish = 1 coconut 5 fish = 1 coconut

Chapter 2, Mutually Beneficial Exchange

Use the figures below, which depict the production possibilities frontiers for Fred and George, respectively, to answer questions 6 - 8.

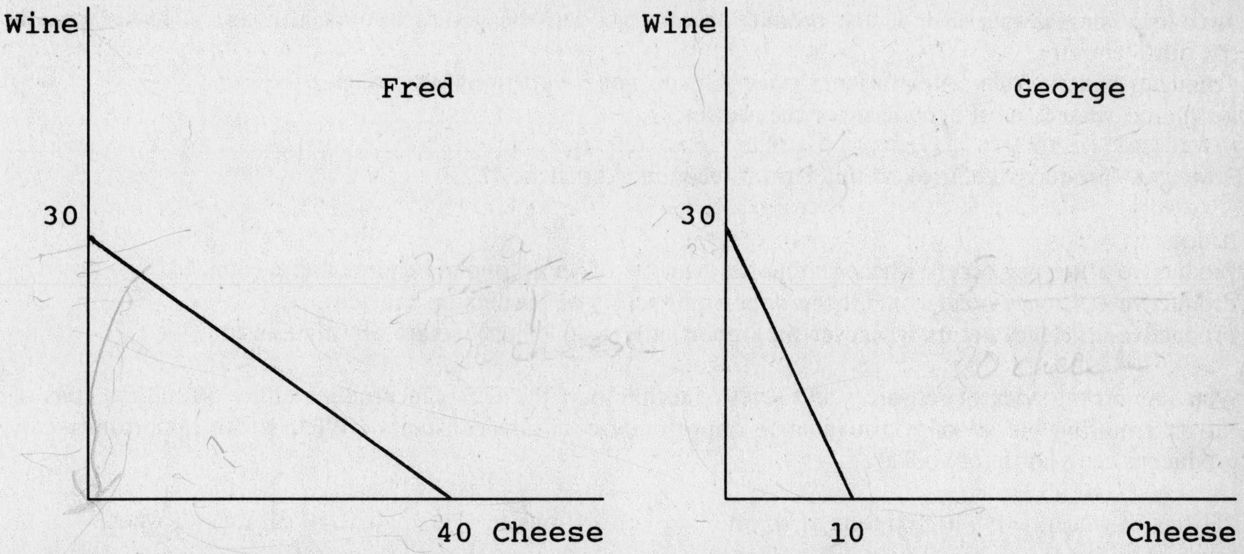

6. Calculate the relative opportunity costs of production incurred by Fred and George.

Fred: ______________________ George: ______________________

7. Based upon your answer to question 6, which individual has a comparative advantage in cheese production? ______________ Wine production? ______________ This suggests that Fred should specialize in the production of ______________ and George should specialize in the production of ______________.

8. According to the principle of comparative advantage, individuals should specialize in the production of those goods for which they possess a comparative advantage and then trade with each other. Assuming that Fred and George specialize and then trade, which of the following would be considered mutually beneficial terms of trade?

2C = 1W   3W = 2C   3W = 5C   3C = 2W

REVIEW QUESTIONS

1. What is meant the phrase "economic efficiency"?

a) Producing the most goods possible with a given stock of resources.
b) Producing goods and services so as to avoid wasting resources.
c) Being able to change the mix of goods one can consume at a zero opportunity cost.
d) Getting the greatest satisfaction from available resources.

2. What is the "Principle of Comparative Advantage"?

a) One's comparative advantage in production tends to increase the more one produces.
b) A country should specialize in the production of a good if the good's opportunity cost is lower than in the other country.
c) Countries benefit from self-sufficiency since they do not have to rely on foreign producers.
d) People do what is most beneficial for themselves.

3. How does "productive efficiency" differ from "economic efficiency"?

a) It doesn't.
b) Productive efficiency occurs whenever the net benefits of any economic choice are maximized.
c) Productive efficiency occurs only if the opportunity costs of production are zero.
d) Productive efficiency occurs whenever the opportunity costs of production are minimized.

4. With its current stock of resources and level of technology, the U.S. can produce either 50 million tons of wheat or 2 million bottles of vodka (assume opportunity costs are constant). What is the opportunity cost of producing each bottle of vodka?

a) 25 tons of wheat. b) 100 tons of wheat. c) 0.4 tons of wheat. d) 52 tons of wheat.

5. In order for two countries to gain from exchange:

a) one country must produce more of one good and less of the other good than the other country.
b) both countries must have goods they don't need.
c) the opportunity costs of production must differ.
d) each country must specialize in producing the good they want the most.

6. For trade to be mutually beneficial, what must the relationship be between the terms of trade and each country's opportunity cost ratios?

a) They must be equal.
b) The terms must be greater than the opportunity cost ratios.
c) The terms must be less than the opportunity cost ratios.
d) The terms must lie between the opportunity cost ratios.

7. What does one's marginal benefit function reveal?

a) The total benefit one obtains from buying stock with borrowed money.
b) The total benefit of consuming all the good one wants.
c) The maximum amount of one good one would be willing to give up to obtain an additional unit of another good.
d) How much of two goods one can produce with a given amount of resources and time.

8. An economy achieves "allocative efficiency" when:

a) resources are employed in their most highly-valued uses.
b) the best resources are employed.
c) the total number of goods produced is greatest.
d) opportunity costs are greatest.

Chapter 2, Mutually Beneficial Exchange

9. Specialization in production can result in increased efficiency. However, specialization also entails certain disadvantages including:

a) the boredom associated with many specialized jobs.
b) a decrease in the interdependence of individuals in the economy.
c) a reduction in the amount of surplus outputs.
d) an increased reliance on the barter system.

10. Which of the following statements is in agreement with the Principle of Comparative Advantage?

a) If the absolute cost of producing a good is cheaper in Country A than in Country B, then Country A should not buy that good from Country B.
b) Countries should specialize in those goods for which the relative costs of production are least.
c) The country with the greatest output will have a relative advantage when it comes to specialization and trade with smaller countries.
d) Countries that tend to increase imports very little as their output increases will have advantage with respect to the benefits of trade.

Use the following figure to answer questions 11 - 13.

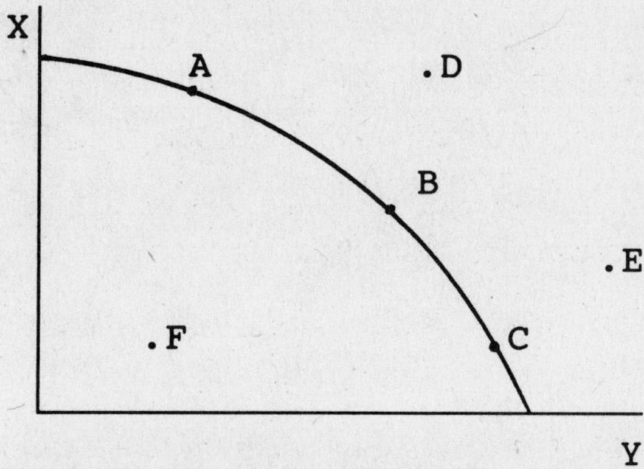

11. Which point on the PPF shows a productively efficient level of output?

a) A   b) B   c) C   d) All of the above.

12. Which point on the PPF shows the allocatively efficient level of output?

a) A
b) B
c) C
d) Cannot be determined without more information.

13. Which of the following represents a movement toward greater economic efficiency?

a) A movement from point A to point B.
b) A movement from point C to point D.
c) A movement from point F to point C.
d) A movement from point E to point B.

14. With its current stock of resources and level of technology, the Soviet Union can produce either 30 million tons of wheat or 10 million bottles of vodka. If the Soviet Union specializes in vodka production, what terms would attract the Soviet Union to trade vodka for wheat from the United States?

a) 1w = 1v   b) 3w = 1v   c) 5w = 1v   d) 1w = 3v

Use the following table to answer questions 15 - 19.

Production per Day

	Lawns Mowed	Pages Typed
Wilson	2.5	25
Xavier	10	50

15. What is the opportunity cost to Wilson of mowing one lawn per day?

a) 0.1 pages typed.
b) 0.1667 pages typed.
c) 6 pages typed.
d) 10 pages typed.

16. What is the opportunity cost to Xavier of typing one page per day?

a) 0.1 lawns mowed.
b) 0.2 lawns mowed.
c) 0.5 lawns mowed.
d) 5 lawns mowed.

17. Wilson has a comparative advantage in:

a) both lawns mowed and pages typed.
b) pages typed.
c) lawns mowed.
d) neither lawns mowed nor pages typed.

18. Xavier has an absolute advantage in:

a) both lawns mowed and pages typed.
b) pages typed.
c) lawns mowed.
d) neither lawns mowed nor pages typed.

19. Under which of the following terms would Wilson specialize in typing and trade typed pages for lawns mowed?

a) If Xavier offered to mow exactly 1/10th of a lawn for each paper Wilson typed.
b) If Xavier offered to mow more than 1/10th of a lawn for each paper Wilson typed.
c) If Xavier offered to mow less than 1/10th of a lawn for each paper Wilson typed.
d) None of the above.

20. Suppose you're considering three different ways to get to a rock concert. It would take you three hours to drive your car there and back, and cost you $12 in gas; two hours to take the University bus there and back, and cost you $8 round-trip; and 30 minutes by plane there and back, and cost you $40 round-trip. If you value your time at $10 per hour, how should you travel?

a) By bus.
b) By plane.
c) By car.
d) By either plane or car.

21. For the above question, what is the opportunity cost of travelling by the least expensive method?

a) $25 b) $28 c) $45 d) $48

22. Assume that with a day's labor (8 hours) Hobbes can produce 12 bottles of wine or 6 pounds of cheese while Ben can produce 6 bottles of wine or 2 pounds of cheese. Based on this information:

a) Hobbes has a comparative advantage in wine production.
b) Hobbes has a comparative advantage in the production of both wine and cheese.
c) Ben has a comparative advantage wine production.
d) Ben has an absolute advantage in the production of both wine and cheese.

23. Given the information in the previous question, which of the following would be considered mutually beneficial terms of trade?

a) 1W = 1C
b) 1C = 3W
c) 5C = 3W
d) 2C = 5W

24. Specialization and exchange often leave a country in the (short run) position of increasing employment in one industry, while increasing unemployment in some other industry. How should a country determine whether this specialization and exchange is really beneficial?

a) If specialization and exchange creates unemployment it is never beneficial.
b) If the country's trading partner benefits, then that country will not benefit.
c) It depends upon whether the benefits to the consumers (who are able to enjoy more of both goods than before trade) outweigh the cost to the workers in the industry experiencing an increase in unemployment.
d) The country may benefit from trade in the short run, but a long run goal of every country should be self-sufficiency.

25. The United States has a number of laws on the books that restrict the quantity of certain goods that may be imported into the country. The argument behind these laws is that they protect the industries that would be put out of business by the imports. Is this defense a good one?

a) Yes, trade is a zero-sum game; one industry may gain only at another's loss.
b) No, trade is a zero-sum game; no one loses in the long run.
c) No, such laws entail trade-offs; the protected industries and workers gain while the consumers and some other industries (and their workers) lose.
d) Yes, passing such laws recognizes the long-term benefits of being self-sufficient.

26. Applied to the world economy, the concepts of comparative advantage and mutually beneficial exchange suggest that:

a) countries with the most productive resources should produce the greatest amount of all outputs.
b) specialization and trade with foreign countries could make U.S. consumers better off.
c) free trade will most likely reduce the well-being of consumers.
d) only a few firms are well suited to operating in the international market for goods and services.

Use the following table to answer questions 28 - 32.

Production per Year

	Good X	Good Y	Good X	Good Y
U.S.	1000 units	500 units	.5	2
U.K.	400 units	100 units	.25	4

27. Which of the following is true if the U.S. and U.K. engage in specialization and exchange?

a) The industry producing X will decline in the U.S.
b) The industries producing both X and Y will decline in the U.S.
c) The industry producing X will decline in the U.K.
d) The industries producing both X and Y will decline in the U.K.

28. If specialization and exchange take place, which of the following will occur?

a) In the U.S., unemployment will increase in the short-run in the industry producing Y.
b) In the U.S., employment will increase in the industry producing Y.
c) In the U.K., unemployment will increase in the short-run in the industry producing X.
d) In the U.K. there will be an increase in unemployment in both industries.

29. Which of the following is true at a terms of trade of 3X = 1Y?

a) The U.S. will be made better off, but the U.K. will be made worse off.
b) The U.K. will be made better off, but the U.S. will be made worse off.
c) Both the U.S. and the U.K. will be made better off.
d) Neither the U.S. nor the U.K. will be made better off.

30. If the U.S. and U.K. specialize and exchange at the terms of trade of 3X = 1Y, which of the following is true?

a) the U.S. will produce and consume outside its PPF.
b) The U.K. will produce, but not consume, outside its PPF.
c) The U.S. will consume, but not produce, outside its PPF.
d) The U.K. will neither produce nor consume outside its PPF.

31. Suppose the U.S. imposes a tariff on its imports. Which of the following will occur?

a) Producers of Good Y will be helped.
b) Consumers of Good Y will be hurt.
c) Producers of Good X will be hurt.
d) Consumers of Good X will be hurt.

Chapter 2, Mutually Beneficial Exchange

ANSWER KEY

Exercises

1. specialization, trade
2. productive, allocative
3. absolute, compatative
4. Jill (grass), John (sod); anything in the range 1.25S < 1G < 2S (or 0.5G < 1S < 0.8G).
5. 1 coconut = 1 fish
6. The relative opportunity cost ratio for Fred is 1W = 4/3C, or 1C = 3/4W. For George, the relative opportunity costs can be written as 1W = 1/3C or 1C = 3W.
7. Fred has a comparative advantage in the production of cheese. George has a comparative advantage in wine production. Fred should specialize in cheese and George should specialize in wine.
8. 3W = 2C

Review Questions

1. d) is the correct answer. Economic efficiency occurs whenever choices are made such that net benefits are maximized. Net benefit is equal to total benefit minus total cost. "Getting the greatest satisfaction out of available resources" is just another way of saying getting the greatest net gain from one's actions.

2. b) is the correct answer. When the opportunity cost of producing a good differs between two individuals or countries, the individual or country with the lower opportunity cost is said to have a "comparative advantage" in producing that good. In the case of international trade the Principle of Comparative Advantage holds that by specializing in the production of the good for which each has a comparative advantage, and trading for the other good, two countries can consume beyond their individual PPFs.

3. d) is the correct answer. Productive efficiency requires producing at the lowest possible cost. Because all costs are ultimately opportunity costs, productive efficiency occurs when opportunity costs are minimized. Productive efficiency is a necessary condition for economic efficiency but is not sufficient by itself; the goods that are produced must also be the most preferred.

4. a) is the correct answer. The opportunity cost of a choice is the value of the next best alternative forgone. The U.S. can <u>either</u> produce 50 million metric tons of wheat <u>or</u> 2 million bottles of vodka with its resources and technology. Thus, for each million bottles of vodka the U.S. produces it must give up 50/2 = 25 million metric tons of wheat.

5. c) is the correct answer. In order for the benefits of specialization and exchange to take place, opportunity costs must differ. If the opportunity costs of production for all goods are the same between two countries, neither has a comparative advantage, hence no net gains will occur from trade.

6. d) is the correct answer. A county's opportunity cost reveals its "internal terms of trade", i.e., how much of X it must give up to get an additional unit of Y without trade. If another country offers to trade it one unit of Y in exchange for <u>less</u> X than it would have to give up to produce the extra Y itself, it is better off with the trade.

7. c) is the correct answer. One's marginal benefit function reveals the most one would be willing to sacrifice(the maximum one would be willing to give up) of one good to get an additional unit of another good.

8. a) is the correct answer. Answer a is the definition of allocative efficiency.

9. a) is the correct answer. Specialization implies that individual concentrate their efforts and develop their skills in a specific area. However, this often results in the same tasks being completed over and over--think of assembly line production. Note that each of the alternative answers are incorrect since specialization results in the opposite of each of the results listed.

10. b) is the correct answer. The Principle of Comparative Advantage holds that countries

should specialize in producing those goods for which the opportunity cost is lowest, i.e., the relative cost of production is least.

11. d) is the correct answer. Productive efficiency requires producing at the lowest possible cost. By definition, any point on the PPF is a least-cost level of production.

12. d) is the correct answer. An allocatively efficient level of output is obtained only when that combination of goods is produced that is most desired. With no knowledge of social preferences for missiles and milk shakes, it is not clear which point on the PPF is allocatively efficient.

13. c) is the correct answer. Economic efficiency requires producing the goods society wants at the lowest possible cost. Point F inside the PPF illustrates an economically inefficient level of output. Therefore movement from point F to any point on the PPF represents a movement toward greater efficiency.

14. c) is the correct answer. The terms of trade must lie between a country's opportunity cost ratio in order for the trade to be beneficial. The opportunity cost ratio for the Soviet Union is 3w = 1v; for every unit of vodka they produce, they must give up 3 units of wheat. If the U.S. offered to trade wheat for vodka on any terms greater than 3w = 1v, e.g., 4w = 1v or 5w = 1v, it would benefit the Soviet Union to specialize in vodka and trade vodka for wheat with the U.S..

15. d) is the correct answer. To Wilson, the opportunity cost of mowing 2.5 lawns per day is the 25 pages she could have typed. Therefore the opportunity cost of mowing 1 lawn is the 25/2.5 = 10 pages.

16. b) is the correct answer. To Xavier, the opportunity cost of typing 50 pages per day is the 10 lawns he could have mowed. Therefore the opportunity cost of typing 1 page is the 10/50 = one-fifth or 0.2 of a lawn he could have mowed in the same amount of time.

	Opportunity Cost of a lawn mowed (pages per day)	Opportunity Cost of a page typed (lawns per day)
Wilson	10	0.10
Xavier	5	0.20

17. b) is the correct answer. Referring to the above table, Wilson has a comparative advantage in that activity which entails the lower opportunity cost. Wilson has the lower opportunity cost for typing. Therefore, she has a comparative in typing. Xavier has the lower opportunity cost, and therefore, a comparative advantage in mowing.

18. a) is the correct answer. Because Xavier can mow more lawns in one day and type more pages in one day than Wilson, Xavier has an absolute advantage in both typing and mowing. However, note that Xavier can still gain from trading with Wilson.

19. b) is the correct answer. For every page Wilson types she must give up 1/10th of a mowed lawn. As long as Xavier offers to mow more than 1/10th of a lawn in exchange for each page Wilson types, the trade would be to her advantage.

20. a) is the correct answer. You would take that method of travel that entails the lowest cost. Driving would cost you $12 in gas and $60 in travel time (don't forget the drive home), for a total of $72; Taking the bus would cost you $8 for a ticket and $40 in travel time, for a total of $48; flying would cost $40 for air fare and $10 in travel time, for a total of $50. Therefore, the cheapest way to travel to the concert is by the University bus.

21. b) is the correct answer. Traveling by bus would cost $8 for the round-trip fare and $20 for the two hours time it would take travelling both ways, for a total of $28.

24. c) is the correct answer. The total gain to consumers should be compared to the losses experienced in the industry in which unemployment occurs. If the gains to consumers is greater than the losses experienced by the unemployed workers, then the country specialize and exchange.

25. c) is the correct answer. Laws that allow some groups to gain while causing other groups to lose are not necessarily in <u>society's</u> best interest.

26. b) is the correct answer. Specialization and trade allows an economy to consume a combina-

tion of goods that lies beyond its PPF (aasuming the realtive costs of production differ across countries. Hence, consumers are made better off than they are in the absence of trade.

27. a) is the correct answer. The U.S. has a comparative advantage in Good Y. Therefore, as the U.S. specializes if Good Y and exchanges Good Y for Good X, industry Y will grow at the expanse of industry X, thus industry X will decline. Similarly, since the U.K. has a comparative advantage in Good X, industry X will grow at the expanse of industry Y.

28. b) is the correct answer. As the U.S. specializes in the good in which it has a comparative advantage, Good Y, the Y industry will expand, increasing employment in that industry. Industry X will expand in a similar fashion in the U.K.

9. c) is the correct answer. 3X = 1Y is a mutually beneficial terms of trade. The U.S. receives 3 units of Good X for every unit of Y it trades to the U.K.(instead of the 2 units it receives if doesn't trade.) The U.K. sacrifices only 3 units of Good X for every unit of Good Y it obtains from the U.S. (instead of the 4 units it sacrifices if it doesn't trade.) Therefore, both countries are made better off at the mutually beneficial terms of trade.

30. c) is the correct answer. When a country trades it can consume outside its PPF. No country can produce outside its PPF. Both the U.S. and the U.K. will consume outside their PPF's, but neither will produce outside their PPF's.

31. d) is the correct answer. When a country imposes a tariff, it is protecting the industry in which the country has a comparative disadvantage. In this case, the U.S. has a comparative advantage in Good Y and a comparative disadvantage in Good X. The tariff raises the domestic price of Good X, thus the consumers of Good X will be hurt.

CHAPTER 3
THE MARKET MECHANISM: SUPPLY AND DEMAND

OVERVIEW

In this chapter we introduce the concept of the market and how it allocates scarce resources among competing wants. Simply put, the forces of supply and demand determine the quantities of various goods and services that will be produced and, in turn, the quantities of the different resources that will be allocated to the production of each good and service. The market price is the "equilibrating mechanism" that equates quantity demanded with quantity supplied.

The term demand refers to the relationship between the price of a good and the quantity that consumers are willing and able to purchase at each price. The law of demand states that there is an inverse relationship between price and quantity demanded, i.e., as price increases, quantity demanded decreases and vice versa. This relationship is influenced by a number of different factors including consumers' incomes, the prices of related goods (substitutes and complements), tastes and preferences, and expectations. For a given demand curve each of these other variables is held constant so that we can focus on the relationship between price and quantity demanded.

There are two types of related goods that are of particular interest in the theory of demand--substitutes and complements. Substitutes are goods that can be consumed in place of each other, such as cars and mass transportation, and Pepsi and Coke. Complements are goods that are consumed jointly, such as tennis balls and tennis racquets, and cake and ice cream. In the case of substitutes, if the price of one good rises (falls), the demand for its substitute will rise (fall). In the case of complements, if the demand for one good rises (falls), the demand for its complement will fall (rise).

The term supply refers to the relationship between the price of a good and the quantity producers are willing and able to supply at each price. According to the law of supply, there is a direct relationship between price and quantity supplied, i.e., as price increases, so does quantity supplied. This relationship is influenced by a number of different factors including input prices (production costs), technology, and the prices of related goods. For a given supply curve each of these other variables is held constant so that we can focus on the relationship between price and quantity supplied.

Market equilibrium occurs when quantity demanded equals quantity supplied at the existing market price. So long as this equality holds, there is no pressure for market price to change. Should supply or demand change, however, disequilibrium will result and price will change to reestablish market equilibrium. In the case where market price is too low (the current price is below the equilibrium price), quantity demanded exceeds quantity supplied and a shortage occurs. In this case, market price will rise, causing quantity demanded to decrease and quantity supplied to increase until market equilibrium is reestablished. In the case where market price is too high, quantity supplied exceeds quantity demanded and a shortage occurs. Market price will fall, causing quantity supplied to decrease and quantity demanded to increase until market equilibrium is reestablished.

A change in supply or demand, ceteris paribus, causes the market equilibrium to change. For example, an increase in supply will result in an increase in equilibrium quantity and decrease in equilibrium price. As another example, a decrease in demand will cause both equilibrium price and quantity to fall. If there is a simultaneous change in supply and demand, the effects are more ambiguous, as described in the next section.

KEY GRAPHS AND TERMS

Graphs

The key model introduced in this chapter is the market model of supply and demand. This simple, yet powerful, model enables us to explore the possible consequences of changes in economic conditions and their effects on the quantities of various goods and services that are produced and exchanged in the economy. In order to be able to effectively use the supply and demand model, it is necessary to master the terminology that accompanies it.

For a particular good, the demand curve is downward sloping, reflecting the law of demand. In a similar manner, the supply curve is upward sloping, reflecting the law of supply. The equilibrium price and quantity correspond to the intersection of supply and demand.

The term "demand" refers to the entire demand curve. Hence, the phrase "change in demand" refers to a shift of the entire demand curve to the left or the right. The term "quantity-demanded" refers to a single point on the demand curve. As such, the phrase "change in quantity demanded" refers to a movement along the demand curve.

In an analogous manner, the term "supply" refers to the entire supply curve. Hence, the phrase "change in supply" refers to a shift of the entire supply curve to the left or the right. The term "quantity-supplied" refers to a single point on the supply curve. As such, the phrase "change in quantity supplied" refers to a movement along the supply curve.

A "change in quantity demanded" or "change in quantity supplied" is caused by a change in the price of the good in question and is shown by a movement along the demand curve or supply curve. A "change in demand" or "change in supply" is caused by a change in a non-price determinant of demand or non-price determinant of supply and is shown by a shift of the entire demand or supply curve. An "increase in demand" is shown by shifting the demand curve to the right. An "increase in demand" implies that at each and every price, quantity demanded is now greater. A "decrease in demand" is shown by shifting the demand curve to the left. A "decrease in demand" implies that at each and every price quantity demanded is now lower. An "increase in supply" is shown by shifting the supply curve to the right. An "increase in supply" implies that at each and every price, quantity supplied is now greater. A "decrease in supply" is shown by shifting the supply curve to the left. A "decrease in supply" implies that at each and every price, quantity supplied is now lower.

In the case where we have only a change in supply or a change in demand, we can deter-mine, with certainty, the effect of the change on both equilibrium price and equilibrium quantity. However, if there is a simultaneous change in supply and demand, depending on the situation, we can only say something with certainty about the effect on equilibrium price or equilibrium quantity. For example, a simultaneous increase in supply and demand will cause equilibrium quantity to increase. However, without more information (i.e., how far does each curve shift?), the effect on equilibrium price is uncertain.

Key Terms

MARKET ECONOMY	PROFIT
COMMAND ECONOMY	MARGINAL COST
MIXED ECONOMY	LAW OF SUPPLY
MARKET PRICE	SHORT RUN
LAW OF DEMAND	LONG RUN EQUILIBRIUM
CETERIS PARIBUS	DISEQUILIBRIUM
MARGINAL BENEFIT	SHORTAGE
SUBSTITUTE GOODS	SURPLUS
COMPLEMENTARY GOODS	

EXERCISES

1. List the three basic questions every economy must answer. 1.) What should be produce? 2.) How should we produce it? 4.) for whom should we produce it?

2. In a MIXED economy, economic decision making is shared by individuals and government.

3. In a market economy, the mechanism use to ration scarce goods is Price.

4. According to the law of demand, an increase in price results in a Decrease in Quantity Demanded.

5. So long as we are focussing on the relationship between price and quantity demanded, a change in market price causes a movement along the demand curve and is referred to as a change

in quanitity Demanded. A change in any of the other determinants of demand causes the demand curve to Shift and is referred to as a change in Demand.

6. An increase in income causes the demand curve to Shift right, and this is referred to as an increase in demand.

7. Assuming that goods A and B are substitutes, an increase in the price of A will cause the demand for B to increase, which is shown by a rightward shift of the demand curve for B. Ceteris paribus, this will cause the equilibrium price of B to increase and equilibrium quantity to increase.

8. Assuming that goods X and Y are complements, a decrease in the supply of X will cause the demand for Y to Decrease. Ceteris paribus, this will cause the equilibrium price of Y to Decrease and equilibrium quantity to DECREASE.

9. The difference between total revenue and the opportunity cost of production is called Profit.

10. According to the law of supply, the quantity supplied of a good is positively related to its price. This reflects the assumption that, in the short run, marginal cost increases as the level of output is increased.

11. So long as we are focussing on the relationship between price and quantity supplied, a change in market price causes a MOVEMENT Along the supply curve and is referred to as a change in quantity Supplied. A change in any of the other determinants of supply causes the supply curve to Shift and is referred to as a change in Supply.

12. Ceteris paribus, an increase in the price of one or more inputs used to produce good D will cause the Supply of D to Decrease. This will cause the equilibrium price of D to increase and the equilibrium quantity to Decrease.

13. Ceteris paribus, an increase in the number of suppliers of a good will cause the equilibrium price of the good to Decrease and the equilibrium quantity to increase.

14. When the price of a good is above the equilibrium price a Surplus develops. In this case, quantity demanded is less than quantity supplied.

15. Assume there is an improvement in the technology used to produce frozen yogurt, and that there is a simultaneous increase in tastes and preferences for frozen yogurt relative to ice cream. These changes will cause the equilibrium quantity of frozen yogurt to increase. However, the effect on equilibrium price is uncertain. In addition, these changes will cause the equilibrium price of ice cream to decrease and the equilibrium quantity to Decrease.

The table below contains hypothetical data on the demand for and supply of oil. Use this information to answer questions 16 - 20. (Note: Quantities are in millions of barrels per day.)

Price	Quantity Demanded	Quantity Supplied
$10	40	--
15	35	--
20	30	0
25	25	10
30	20	20
35	15	30
40	10	40
45	5	50
50	0	60

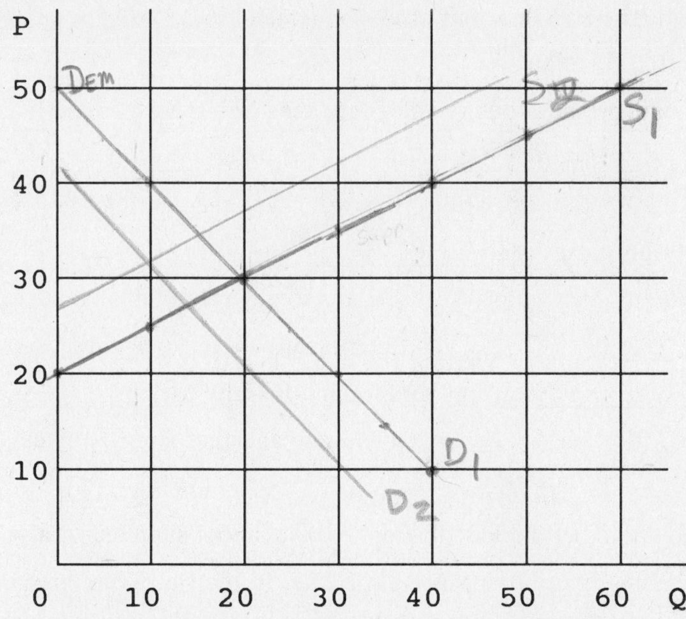

16. Plot the demand curve and supply curve in the space provided. Label them D1 and S1.

17. Based on the table and graph, the equilibrium price is $ 30 /barrel and the equilibrium quantity is 20 barrels/day.

18. In the graph, illustrate the effect of a decrease in the number of countries that are able to produce oil. Label the new supply curve S2. What has happened to the equilibrium price? Increase Quantity? Decreases

19. Now assume that there is also a decrease in the number of buyers of oil. Show this effect graphically in the figure.

20. What can you say, with certainty, about the effects of the changes described in questions 18 and 19 on the equilibrium quantity of oil that is exchanged? fall What about the equilibrium price of oil? uncertain

Use the following table which represents three individuals' demand schedules and a representative firm's supply schedule for god X to answer questions 21 - 25.

Price	Bob Qd	Jean Qd	Carlos Qd	Market Demand	Firm 1 Qs	Market Supply
$1	300	160	250	710	12.5	62.5
2	200	120	200	520	39	195
3	100	80	150	330	66	330
4	0	40	100	140	92.5	462.5
5	0	0	50	50	120	600
6	0	0	0	0	145	725

21. Calculate the market demand for X and plot the demand curve in the figure below.

22. Assume that there are five identical firms that serve the market for X. Calculate the market supply for X and plot the supply curve in the figure as well.

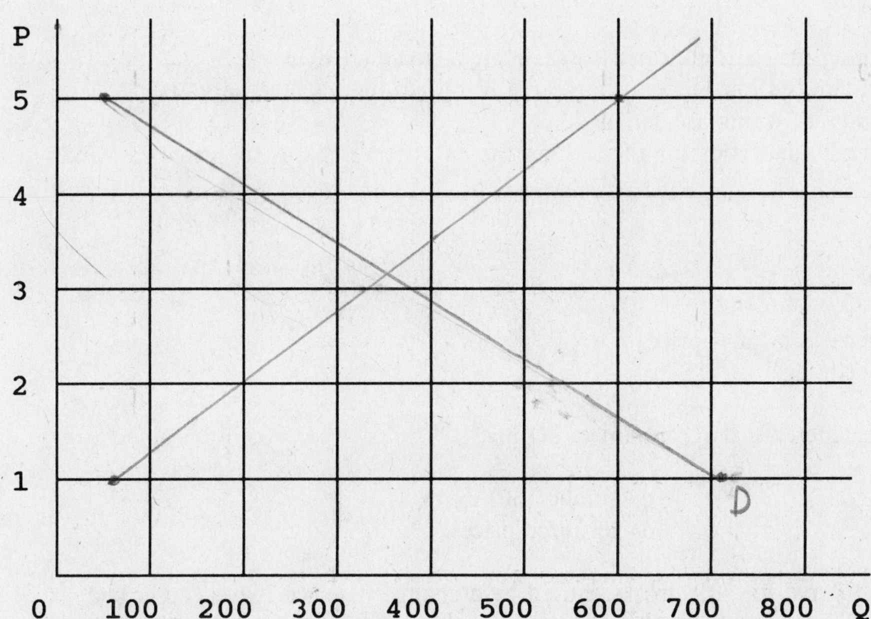

23. What are the equilibrium price and quantity of X? Price = $3 , Quantity = 330 .

24. Ceteris paribus, assume Bob experiences a substantial increase in his income. Illustrate the effect of this in the figure. What has happened to the equilibrium price? increased Quantity? increased

25. Assume instead that there is an increase in the price of good Y, (which is the result of a decrease in the supply of Y), and X and Y are complements. How would this affect the demand for X, and what would happen to the equilibrium price and quantity of X? The demand for X should decrease as would its quantity and equilibrium price due to a left ward shift in the graph

REVIEW QUESTIONS

1. Which of the following is <u>not true</u>?

(a) In economies that rely on centralized decision-making there's no competition for scarce resources.
b) A decentralized economy usually relies on markets as rationing devices.
c) Scarcity leads to competition.
d) When a market transaction occurs, both suppliers and demanders benefit.

2. All of the following are determinants of demand except:

a) tastes and preferences.
b) quantity supplied.
c) income.
d) price of related goods.

3. Which of the following is not true?

a) If resources are allocated efficiently, they are allocated to their highest-valued uses.
b) The primary function of an economic system is to ration scarce resources, goods, and services.
c) If resources are allocated efficiently all wants are satisfied.
d) All economic systems must determine methods for reconciling the competing claims to scarce resources.

4. Markets develop to:

a) Avoid the use of a rationing device.
b) Economize transactions cost.
c) Make sure individuals pay and receive a "fair" price.
d) Prevent marginal benefit from declining.

5. Which of the following is not considered a determinant of supply?

a) technology.
b) taxes and subsidies.
c) number of buyers.
d) resource prices.

6. The movement along the demand curve for soft drinks caused by a change in price is best described as:

a) An increase in demand.
b) A decrease in demand.
c) A change in quantity demanded.
d) A change in demand.

7. Suppose income increases. What occurs at the initial equilibrium price for a normal good which signals market participants that the equilibrium must change?

a) Excess demand.
b) Excess supply.
c) A surplus.
d) The supply function shifts to the right.

8. What is the reaction of suppliers to a change in the incomes of consumers?

a) Suppliers do not react, since income shifts the demand function, not the supply function.
b) The supply function shifts to the right.
c) The supply function shifts to the left.
d) Quantity supplied increases.

9. If video tape movies for home rental and movies seen at a theater are substitutes, and the price of movies seen at a theater rises, what will happen to the equilibrium price and equilibrium quantity for movies on video tape?

a) price up; quantity down
b) price down; quantity down
c) price down; quantity up
d) price up; quantity up

10. Which of the following is not true:

a) Sweden is a mixed economy.
b) In Sweden the government claims more than 50% of the income of its citizens.
c) A democratic society cannot have a mixed economy.
d) The fundamental premise of economics applied to consumption decisions states that consumers try to obtain goods and services that will provide them with the greatest satisfaction.

11. When the price of Pepsi falls relative to the price of Coke and 7-Up, the demand for:

a) coke will fall.
b) 7-Up will fall.
c) coke and 7-Up will rise.
d) coke and 7-Up will fall.

12. Suppose that the supply of cameras increases due to an increase in foreign imports. Which of the following would most likely occur?

a) the equilibrium price of cameras would rise.
b) the equilibrium quantity of cameras exchanged would decrease.
c) the equilibrium price of camera film will decrease.
d) the equilibrium quantity of camera film exchanged will increase.

13. Assume that a recent geological study has resulted in the discovery of huge deposits of oil in the central plains of the U.S. Assume that during the same time there is a shift in consumer preferences toward mass transit, as opposed to personal cars. Based on this information, we can conclude, with certainty, that in the market for gasoline, equilibrium:

a) price will fall.
b) price will rise.
c) quantity will fall.
d) quantity will rise.

14. Assume that consumers' incomes and the number of sellers in the market for good A both decrease. Based upon this information we can conclude, with certainty, that equilibrium:

a) price will increase.
b) price will decrease.
c) quantity will increase.
d) quantity will decrease.

15. Assume that in the market for good Z there is a simultaneous increase in demand and the quantity supplied. The result will be:

Help

a) an increase in equilibrium price and quantity.
b) a decrease in equilibrium price and quantity.
c) an increase in equilibrium quantity and uncertain effect on equilibrium price.
d) a decrease in equilibrium price and increase in equilibrium quantity.

16. Which of the following statements is correct?

a) A change in demand or supply can only be caused by a change in price.
b) A simultaneous decrease in demand and increase in supply will result in an increase in equilibrium price and uncertain effect on quantity.
c) If price is currently above equilibrium, market adjustments will result in a decrease in price and quantity supplied.
d) An increase in supply invariably leads to a shortage in the affected market.

17. Suppose consumers expect a recession to begin in the next few months. They might react by trying to save more in case they are laid-off or have to work reduced hours. Under these circumstances, what would happen to the equilibrium prices and quantities of the goods the consumer usually buy?

a) price up; quantity down
b) price down; quantity down
c) price down; quantity up
d) price up; quantity up

18. As the price of milk rises, what would reasonably be expected to happen to the equilibrium price and equilibrium quantity for cereal? (Milk and cereal are complements.)

a) price up; quantity down
b) price down; quantity down
c) price down; quantity up
d) price up; quantity up

19. Referring to the previous question, what happens at the original equilibrium that signals market participants that the original equilibrium must change?

a) Excess demand.
b) A surplus.
c) A shortage.
d) The supply function shifts to the left.

20. Suppose an auto firm's factories are capable of producing both large and small cars and are operating at full capacity. Suppose the price of large cars rises, due to an increase in demand. What would reasonably be expected to happen to the equilibrium price and equilibrium quantity for the firm's small cars?

a) price up; quantity down
b) price down; quantity down
c) price down; quantity up
d) price up; quantity up

21. Which of the following is not true?

a) Rationing devices exist only in market economies and mixed economies, but not in centralized economies.
b) Rationing may occur on a "first come, first serve" basis.
c) When the President and Congress determine the national budget, they are rationing scarce resources.
d) The market rations goods by individuals' willingness to pay.

22. Which of the following is not true?

a) The fundamental premise of economics, as applied to consumption decisions, says all goods are normal goods.
b) The law of demand says that the quantity of a good demanded and its price are negatively related.
c) One reason demand functions are downward-sloping is that as more of a good is consumed, consumers are willing to pay less for each additional unit.
d) If individuals are to maximize their benefits from exchanging goods, they must know what their alternatives are.

23. Suppose wages paid by a firm increase. What would reasonably be expected to happen to the equilibrium price and equilibrium quantity for the firm's output?

a) price up; quantity down
b) price down; quantity down
c) price down; quantity up
d) price up; quantity up

24. Referring to the previous question, what will the reaction of consumers be?

a) Quantity demanded will fall.
b) Quantity demanded will rise.
c) The demand function will shift to the left.
d) There will be no reaction by consumers, since input prices determine supply, not demand.

25. Suppose the technology for producing personal computers improves and, at the same time, individuals discover new uses for personal computers so that there is greater utilization of personal computers. Which of the following will happen to equilibrium price and equilibrium quantity?

a) price up; quantity cannot be determined.
b) price down; quantity cannot be determined.
c) quantity up; price cannot be determined.
d) quantity down; price cannot be determined.

26. Suppose over a certain period of time the technology for producing compact disk players has improved, and over the same period of time the economy has moved into a recession, causing the incomes of consumers to fall. Which of the following will happen to the equilibrium price and equilibrium quantity for CD players? (Assume CD players are normal goods.)

a) price up; quantity cannot be determined
b) price down; quantity cannot be determined
c) quantity up; price cannot be determined
d) quantity down; price cannot be determined

27. Suppose the cost of production in the U.S. auto industry is rising, and at the same time, the prices of Japanese-made autos are falling. What would reasonably be expected to happen to the equilibrium price and equilibrium quantity for U.S.-made autos?

a) price up; quantity cannot be determined
b) price down; quantity cannot be determined
c) quantity up; price cannot be determined
d) quantity down; price cannot be determined

28. Which of the following most closely describes the influence of advertising on the market for aspirin?

a) The market demand shifts to the right, creating a shortage at the original equilibrium price for aspirin.
b) Individual demand functions shift to the right, but the market demand function remains at its original position.
c) The market supply function for aspirin shifts to the right, creating a surplus at the original equilibrium price.
d) The market supply function for aspirin shifts to the right, causing equilibrium price to fall.

29. If a firm has a fixed amount of factory or office space, which of the following will happen as output expands?

a) Marginal cost increases.
b) The opportunity cost of an additional unit of output falls.
c) The firm will be willing to accept a lower price for an additional unit of output.
d) Worker productivity usually increases as the firm hires more labor.

30. In the previous question, the firm must be operating:

a) In the short-run, because plant size is fixed.
b) In the short-run, because the firm can vary the amount of labor it uses.
c) In the long-run, because the firm can vary some, but not all, inputs.
d) In the long-run, because plant size is fixed.

31. Suppose a firm experiences an increase in the cost of raw materials. Which of the following will occur?

a) The firm's marginal cost function will shift upward.
b) The firm's supply function will shift to the right.
c) The firm's supply function will shift downward.
d) The firm will try to increase its supply.

32. Suppose wages have been increasing over a period of time, but prices have remained the same. Which of the following allows this to be possible?

a) Other input prices, besides wages, have been rising.
b) Demand has been increasing at the same time supply has been decreasing.
c) Demand has been stable while supply has been decreasing.
d) Demand has been stable and technology has been improving.

33. Which of the following is <u>not</u> a characteristic of a competitive market?

a) Many buyers, many sellers.
b) Advertising.
c) Complete, costless information.
d) Trader mobility.

34. Suppose there is a reduction in the shipments of petroleum products due to political tension in the Persian Gulf. Which of the following does <u>not</u> happen?

a) Oil companies "ration" their supplies of gasoline by raising price.
b) There is a shortage of the original equilibrium price.
c) Quantity demanded will decrease.
d) The demand curve will shift to the left.

35. Consider the information given in the above question. In the market system, which consumers will get the reduced supplies of gasoline?

a) The consumers that value gasoline the most.
b) Wealthy consumers.
c) Lower income consumers.
d) Who gets the gasoline would be a random process. Those who arrive at the service station first will get the gasoline, regardless what its price is.

36. Suppose the auto market is initially in equilibrium with imports from Japan taking up a significant share of the market. Suppose a quota on imports of Japanese cars is established. What happens at the initial equilibrium price to signal to market participants the change that has taken place?

a) Excess supply.
b) A surplus.
c) A shortage.
d) The demand function shifts to the left.

37. Consider the information given in the previous question. What will happen to the equilibrium price and quantity for cars?

a) They will stay the same as domestic producers replace the cars once imported.
b) The shortage will cause the equilibrium price to rise and equilibrium quantity will fall.
c) The surplus will cause equilibrium price to fall and equilibrium quantity to rise.
d) The shift in the demand function will cause equilibrium price to rise and equilibrium quantity to rise.

38. Speculation that is profitable is:

a) destabilizing because speculators take advantage of consumers by selling when price is high.
b) destabilizing because speculators try to both buy and sell when price is low.
c) stabilizing because speculators sell when consumers place a high value on an additional unit of the good.
d) stabilizing because speculators buy when consumers place a high value on an additional unit of the good.

39. Ceteris paribus, if the market for diet soft drinks is initially in equilibrium and a new brand of diet soft drink is then introduced into the market, this will cause:

a) a decrease in equilibrium price and quantity.
b) an increase in equilibrium price and quantity.
c) a decrease in equilibrium price and increase in equilibrium quantity.
d) an increase in equilibrium price and decrease in equilibrium quantity.

40. A change in the relative amounts of the factors of production would most likely result in:

a) A change in product prices and a movement along the PPF.
b) A change in product prices and no movement along the PPF.
c) A movement along the PPF, but no change in product prices.
d) No change in product prices and no movement along the PPF.

ANSWER KEY

Exercises
1. 1) what to produce, 2) how to produce, 3) for whom to produce
2. mixed
3. price
4. decrease, quantity demanded
5. movement along, quantity demanded, shift, demand
6. shift right, increase, demand
7. increase, rightward shift, increase, increase
8. decrease. decrease, decrease
9. profit
10. positively, rises
11. movement along, quantity supplied, shift, supply
12. supply, decrease, increase, decrease
13. decrease, increase
14. surplus, less,
15. quantity, increase, price, decrease, decrease

16. The demand curve is downward-sloping straight line passing through the points P = $10, Q = 40; and P = $50, Q = 0; as well as all intermediate points between these two pairs. The supply curve is an upward-sloping straight line passing through the points P = $20, Q = 0; and P = $50, Q = 60; as well as all intermediate points between these two pairs.
17. Equilibrium price = $30, equilibrium quantity = 20 million bbl/day.
18. The supply curve will shift left. Equilibrium price increases, equilibrium quantity decreases.
19. The demand curve will shift left.
20. Equilibrium quantity will fall. The effect on equilibrium price is uncertain.
21., 22

Price	Bob Qd	Jean Qd	Carlos Qd	Market Demand	Firm 1 Qs	Market Supply
$1	300	160	250	710	12.5	62.5
2	200	120	200	520	39	195
3	100	80	150	330	66	330
4	0	40	100	140	92.5	462.5
5	0	0	50	50	120	600
6	0	0	0	0	145	725

23. Equilibrium price = $3, equilibrium quantity = 330 units
24. An increase in Bob's income will shift the demand curve to right. Equilibrium price and quantity will both increase.
25. The increase in the price of Y will cause the demand for X to decrease, i.e., the demand curve for X will shift left, resulting in a decrease in the equilibrium price and quantity of X.

Review Questions

1. a) is not true. b, c, and d are true. Centralizing the decision-making for an economy does not eliminate the basic economic problem of scarcity. It is scarcity which leads to competition. For example, in centralized economies current consumption goods and capital goods compete with one another for scarce resources.

2. b) Quantity supplied refers to a point on the supply curve and only tells how much output producers are willing to supply at a given price.

3. c) is not true. Even if resources are allocated efficiently (that is, to their highest-valued uses) all wants cannot be satisfied. Human wants are unlimited. All an economic system can do is develop ways of ranking the competing alternative uses of the scarce resources, but it cannot completely eliminate the problem of scarcity.

4. b) is the correct answer. Market participants, acting in their self-interest, want to make the best trade possible. But they can do this only if they know the available trading opportunities, such as: who has goods for trade, what kinds of goods, what are their prices, etc. Obtaining such information is costly--it requires time and effort. Markets develop to reduce the time and effort required to make transactions.

5. c) is the correct answer. The number of buyers in market is a determinant of market demand and has no effect on supply.

6. c) is the correct answer. A movement along a single demand function due to a change in price is known as a change in quantity demanded, not a change in demand, which refers to a shift in a demand function.

7. a) is the correct answer. Refer to Figure 3-10 in the text. An increase in income causes the demand function to shift to the right. This causes excess demand or a shortage to occur at the initial equilibrium price. This signals market participants that equilibrium price must rise.

8. d) is the correct answer. A shift to the right in the demand function results in a movement along the supply function. This is described as an increase in quantity supplied. The shortage that

results from the increase in demand causes price to rise. As price rises, quantity supplied increases.

9. d) is the correct answer. As the price of movies shown in a theater increases, consumers substitute video-taped movies to rent and watch at home. That is, consumers buy more video-taped movies and watch them at home rather than go out to a movie theater. Thus, the demand curve for video tapes shift to the right. The result is a higher equilibrium price and quantity.

10. c) is not true. In fact most democratic societies are mixed economies in which some economic decisions are made by the government and some are made by individuals. Both Sweden and the U.S. are mixed economies, for example. But in Sweden the government spends a much bigger proportion of national income than in the U.S.

11. d) is the correct answer. Assuming Pepsi is a substitute for Coke and 7-Up, as the price of Pepsi falls relative to the prices of its substitutes some consumers will switch over to the now less expensive good. In this case there is a decrease in the number of buyers of Coke and 7-Up, i.e., a change in non-price determinant of demand.

12. d) is the correct answer. Ceteris paribus, an increase in supply causes an increase in equilibrium quantity and a decrease in equilibrium price. Since cameras and camera film are complements, the decrease in price will cause the demand for film to increase, resulting in an increase in the equilibrium price and quantity of film.

13. a) is the correct answer. In this case, there is a simultaneous increase in supply--the supply curve shifts right--and decease in demand--the demand curve shifts left. Thus, with certainty the equilibrium price will fall. However, because we don't know how far each curve is shifting, the effect on equilibrium quantity is uncertain.

14. d) is the correct answer. Income is a non-price determinant of demand. The number of sellers is a non-price determinant of supply. Thus, in this case we have a simultaneous decrease in supply and demand--both curves shift left. Equilibrium quantity will fall, but the effect on price is uncertain since we don't know the relative magnitude of the shifts.

15. d) is the correct answer. An increase in demand means the demand curve has shifted right. An increase in quantity supplied implies a movement down the supply curve (which in turn is the result of an increase in demand). Hence, equilibrium quantity increases and equilibrium price falls.

16. c) is the correct answer. Changes in demand or supply are caused by changes in their respective non-price determinants, A simultaneous decrease in demand and increase in supply will result in a decrease in equilibrium price, and an increase in supply initially creates a surplus that is eventually eliminated by market forces.

17. b) is the correct answer. In order to increase their savings, consumers must reduce spending on goods and services. Therefore, the demand for goods and services falls and the demand function shifts to the left. This results in both equilibrium price and equilibrium quantity falling.

18. b) is the correct answer. As the price of milk rises, the demand for cereal will fall because the more expensive milk makes consuming the cereal more expensive, since milk and cereal are complementary goods and are consumed together. The demand curve for cereal would shift to the left, so that equilibrium price and equilibrium quantity both fall.

19. b) is the correct answer. In the previous question, there was a decrease in demand for cereal due to an increase in the price of a complement. This change in market conditions creates a surplus at the original equilibrium price of cereal, signaling to market participants that there should be a decrease in price.

20. a) is the correct answer. If the firm's factories can produce both large and small cars, then they are substitutes in production. As the price of large cars rises, the firm wants to produce more. But in order to produce more large cars, the firm must produce less small cars. Therefore, the supply curve for small cars shifts to the left, so that equilibrium price rises and equilibrium quantity falls.

21. a) is not true. Rationing exists in any economic system. It exists because of scarce resources, not because of the particular economic system.

22. b) is false. The fundamental premise of economics as applied to consumption decisions says consumers attempt to acquire goods and services that provide them with the maximum satisfaction.

23. a) is the correct answer. Wages are input prices. As input prices rise, the supply function shifts to the left--the firm will offer less on the market at each price. A leftward shift in supply cause equilibrium price to rise and equilibrium quantity to fall.

24. a) is the correct answer. Even though the demand function does not shift, demanders react to the change in market conditions. This reaction is shown by the slope of the demand function. As price rises, quantity demanded falls as the equilibrium point changes along the demand function.

25. c) is the correct answer. As technology improves, the supply curve shifts to the right. As tastes shift toward personal computers, the demand curve shifts to the right. Refer to Figure 3-13 in the text. These two shifts reinforce one another with respect to the change in equilibrium quantity, since they both cause it to rise. They counteract each other with respect to a change in equilibrium price.

26. b) is the correct answer. As the technology for producing CD players improves, the supply curve shifts to the right. As consumers' incomes fall, the demand for CD players shifts to the left. These shifts are the opposite of the shifts shown in Figure 3-14 in the text. These two shifts reinforce each other with respect to a change in equilibrium price, since they both cause price to fall. They counteract each other with respect to equilibrium quantity.

27. d) is the correct answer. The increase in the cost of production causes the supply for U.S. autos to fall, i.e., shift to the left. The fall in Japanese car prices causes the demand for U.S. cars to fall, i.e., shift to the left. These two shifts reinforce one another in terms of their effects on equilibrium quantity. Both shifts cause equilibrium quantity to fall. The two shifts counteract one another in terms of their effects on equilibrium price. Price therefore cannot be determined.

28. a) is the correct answer. Advertising is intended to shift individual demand functions to the right. Since the market demand consists of a summation at every price of the individual demand functions, it also shifts to the right, creating a shortage at the original equilibrium price. This enables the producer to raise price.

29. a) is the correct answer. If the firm has a fixed plant and increases its output by adding more labor, for example, each additional unit of labor has less of the fixed input with which to work and, therefore, is less productive. This causes the cost to the firm of one more unit, the marginal cost, to rise.

30. a) is the correct answer. The short-run is defined as the period of time over which the firm's capital stock is fixed. In this case, the firm's plant size is fixed. Answer b) is incorrect because the firm usually can vary the amount of labor it uses in both the short- and long-runs.

31. a) is the correct answer. The cost of raw materials is an input price. As input prices rise, the marginal cost function shifts up. This is because as input prices rise, the cost of producing each additional unit is higher. The competitive firm's marginal cost function is also its supply function, so when marginal cost shifts up, the supply curve shifts up (or to the left). That is, supply decreases. Therefore, b), c), and d) are incorrect.

32. d) is the correct answer. The improvement in technology can offset the increase in wages, so that the cost of production does not increase as wages rise. In this case, labor productivity has risen(due to the improvement in technology) at the same rate as the increase in wages. Thus, the supply function does not shift and price remains the same.

33. b) is the correct answer. Advertising is not a characteristic of a competitive market. This is

due to another characteristic of competitive markets--products should be nearly identical. Under such circumstances, advertising is useless, unless consumers are ignorant about the products being sold, which violates the "good" or accurate information characteristic.

34. d) does not happen. The reduction in the supply of gasoline causes a shortage at the original equilibrium price. (The supply shifts to the left.) Oil companies ration their smaller gasoline supplies to consumers by raising price. The increase in price causes quantity demanded to decrease, but the demand curve does not shift.

35. a) is the correct answer. Consumers that value an additional unit of the good most highly obtain that unit in the market system. This may or may not be wealthy consumers. For example, a middle income individual that has to drive to get to work may place a very high value on an additional tank of gasoline, while the wealthy, retired individual that drives only for pleasure, may place a very low value on an additional tank of gasoline and curtail spending.

36. c) is the correct answer. The quota causes the supply function, which includes both foreign-produced and domestically-produced cars to shift to the left as the supply of foreign cars is restricted. This creates a shortage at the original equilibrium price which signals the change in market conditions (imposition of the quota) to market participants.

37. b) is the correct answer. The shortage caused by the shift to the left in the supply function results in the equilibrium price rising. This causes quantity demanded to fall, therefore equilibrium quantity falls. Domestic producers increase quantity supplied as price rises but only partially replace the units that were previously imported from Japan. See Figure 3-12 in the text.

38. c) is the correct answer. In order to make a profit, speculators buy a good when its price is low, i.e., when consumers place a relatively low value on additional units of the good and sell the good when its price is high, i.e., when consumers place a relatively high value on additional units of the good. The additional amount of the good purchased when price is low causes demand to shift to the right and equilibrium price to rise. The additional amount of the good offered on the market when price is high causes the supply to shift to the right and equilibrium price to fall.

39. c) is the correct answer. The introduction of a new brand is equivalent to an increase in the number of sellers, which results in an increase in supply. Thus, equilibrium price will fall while equilibrium price increases.

40. a) is the correct answer. A change in the relative amounts of the factors of the production implies a change in supply in one or more resource markets. This will, in turn, cause the equilibrium price of one or more resources to change--production costs will change. This, in turn, implies a change in supply in output markets and therefore a change in equilibrium quantities. Overall, input prices, quantities of outputs, and therefore the combination of outputs will change.

CHAPTER 4
ECONOMIC EFFICIENCY: A MEASURE OF MARKET PERFORMANCE

OVERVIEW

In this chapter we identify the conditions necessary for a market equilibrium to be economically efficient. We also consider how to measure the net gains from consumption in production. The effects of price floors and price ceilings on economic efficiency are also considered. We conclude the chapter with a discussion of why society might choose to be inefficient in specific situations.

Starting with the assumptions that the market demand curve represents the social benefits from consumption and the market supply curve represents the social costs from production, we can measure the net social benefit--the net gain--that results from the production and consumption of a good. Net social benefits can be decomposed into two components--consumers' surplus and producers' surplus. Consumers' surplus is measured as the difference between consumers' total willingness to pay for a given quantity of a good and the total amount actually spent. Producers' surplus is measured as the difference between the total revenue received from selling a given quantity of a good and the minimum total amount that producers would be willing to receive.

In order for a market equilibrium to be economically efficient, several conditions must be met. In particular, the market must be characterized by a high degree of competition, all social benefits and social costs must accrue to the individuals participating in the market, and there must be economic stability. When any one of these conditions is not met, market failure can occur. When market failure occurs, inefficiency is the result.

Assuming that the conditions necessary for an economically efficient outcome to occur are met, a divergence of market price and the equilibrium price will result in inefficiency. A classic source of such inefficiency is the use of price controls--price floors or price ceilings--that prevent price from reaching its equilibrium level. Examples of price floors include agricultural price support programs and minimum prices that are set by firms that work together to artificially raise the market price of their product. Examples of price ceilings include rent controls and interest rate caps.

From society's perspective, economic efficiency is only one of a number of different goals that are considered desirable. Policymakers are also concerned with the degree of equity associated with many outcomes, such as the price and quantity exchanged of certain goods. However, efficiency and equity are often at odds with one another, i.e., the efficient outcome is often viewed as being inequitable. As a result of this trade-off, society often chooses to forego efficiency in pursuit of equity. Programs that reflect this willingness to accept something less that the economically efficient result include income redistribution programs, agricultural support programs, and some forms of business regulation.

KEY GRAPHS AND TERMS

Graphs

In this chapter, the model of supply and demand is used to illustrate the concept of the net benefits from exchange--the sum of consumers' and producers' surplus. This model is also used to illustrate the effect of price controls on the net social benefits from production and consumption in a particular market.

In Figure 3, which illustrates the market for ground beef, the equilibrium price and quantity are Pe and Qe. However, the demand curve indicates that for each unit of ground beef between 0 and Qe, consumers would be willing to a pay a price that is greater than Pe. The supply curve indicates that producers would be willing to supply each unit of ground beef between 0 and Qe at a price below Pe. (Note that as we approach Qe, these differences get progressively smaller.) The difference between the maximum price consumers are willing to pay and the minimum price producers are willing to accept for a unit of ground beef is a net gain to society. In Figure 3, the total net gain to society is the triangle ABE.

This net gain consists of two parts, the part accruing to consumers--consumer surplus--and the part accruing to producers--producers' surplus. Total consumers' surplus is equal to the area of the triangle PeBE. Total producers' surplus is equal to the area of the triangle APeE.

The efficiency effects of price controls--price ceilings and price floors--are illustrated in Figures 5 and 6. Such policies have the effect of reducing the net social benefits of production and consumption. If a price floor is set above the market equilibrium price, producers will supply more of the good than consumers are willing to buy at the going price; a surplus will result. Moreover, producers will produce a level of output that is greater than the efficient level--marginal cost exceeds marginal benefit, and there is an overallocation of resources.

In the case of a price ceiling that is set below the market equilibrium price, just the opposite occurs. A shortage will result, implying an underallocation of resources.

Terms
CONSUMERS' SURPLUS
PRODUCERS' SURPLUS
COMPETITION
PROPERTY RIGHTS
MEDIUM OF EXCHANGE
VALUE OF MONEY
PRICE FLOOR
PRICE CEILING

EXERCISES

1. The difference between the total willingness to pay for a quantity of a good and the total amount actually spent is referred to as Consumer Surplus.

2. Assuming that there are no external costs or benefits, the net gain from producing and consuming a given quantity of a good is calculated as the difference between Total Social benifits and Total Social Cost. In addition, net gains are maximized by producing the level of output at which the marginal Social Benifits and the Marginal Social Cost of the last unit of output are equal.

3. The net gain from production and consumption in a market is equal to the sum of Consumer's Surplus and Producer's Surplus.

4. List three conditions that must be met for market outcomes to be economically efficient. 1.) High degree of competition. 2) all social benifits and social costs are incorporated into decision making. 3.) the economy is relatively stable.

5. The situation in which one or more of the conditions for economic efficiency is not met is referred to as Market failure.

6. A price floor that is set Above the equilibrium market price will result in a surplus, while a price ceiling that is set below the equilibrium market price will result in a shortage.

Answer questions 7 - 9 using the figure on the following page.

7. Total consumer surplus is 900. Total producer surplus is $600. The net social gain is 1500.

8. Assuming that a price ceiling of $20 is imposed in the market, the resulting loss in social welfare will be 375. What is the new net social gain? 1125

9. Assume instead that a price floor is set at $25. In this case, what are the equilibrium price and quantity?

Price = 30. Quantity = 60. Do not change

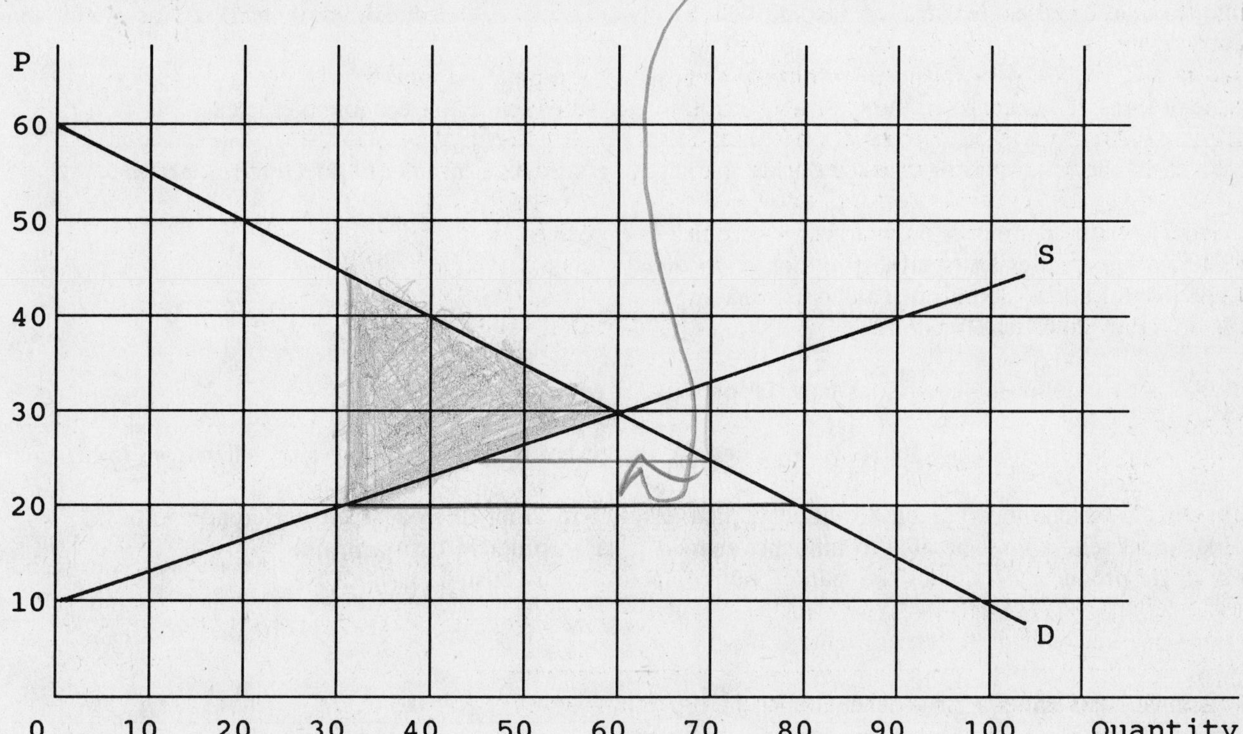

REVIEW QUESTIONS

1. Which of the following is not true? At the equilibrium price and quantity for computers:

a) the outcome is efficient.
b) every computer for which the marginal benefit is greater than the marginal cost is produced.
c) firms will produce a computer for which marginal benefit is less than marginal cost only if they can increase their profits.
d) net social benefits are maximized.

2. Which of the following conditions is not required for market equilibrium to be economically efficient?

a) Competition.
b) The demand curve reflects all social benefits.
c) A stable system of property rights exists.
d) The supply curve reflects only private costs.

3. If more than the equilibrium quantity of a good were produced, which of the following would occur?

a) marginal benefit would not equal the change in total benefit divided by the change in quantity.
b) marginal benefit would be greater than marginal cost.
c) marginal benefit would be less than marginal cost.
d) none of the above.

4. Which of the following statements is not correct?

a) In many cases there is a tradeoff between economic efficiency and equity.
b) Policies designed to redistribute income will have no effect on the outcomes in markets for goods and services.
c) economic efficiency is a positive concept, as opposed to a normative concept.
d) unemployment insurance in the U.S. tends to have a negative effect on economic efficiency.

5. Which of the following is not a reason the market is an attractive means of allocating resources?

a) Under certain conditions, the market yields efficient outcomes.
b) The market ensures an equal distribution of income.
c) The market allows decentralized decision-making.
d) It preserves individual freedom.

6. Which of the following conditions must be present for competition to exist?

a) The number of buyers and sellers is large enough to prevent an individual buyer or seller from influencing market outcome.
b) Individual buyers must be able to influence market price in order to make their preferences known.
c) Individual sellers must be able to influence market price in order to earn a profit.
d) A single producer dominates the market, but competes by advertising heavily.

7. For a market outcome to be efficient:

a) marginal coats and marginal benefits must be 0.
b) there can be no external costs or benefits.
c) marginal benefits and marginal costs must be equal.
d) Total benefits and total costs must be equal.

8. Consumer surplus is defined as the difference between:

a) the total amount spent on a good and the total cost of producing it.
b) the total willingness to pay for a good and the amount actually spent.
c) the total willingness to pay for a good and the total cost of producing it.
d) the total amount spent on a good and 0.

9. Which of the following is not true?

a) National security is cited as a reason some societies may choose to be inefficient.
b) In its efforts to promote equity, a society may produce economically inefficient results.
c) If a firm is running an economic loss, the market is signaling that the firm needs to attract more resources form other industries to become economically efficient.
d) The high cost of adjustment in declining industries sometimes leads to government engaging in economically inefficient policies.

10. Which of the following conditions are required for the market equilibrium to be economically efficient?

a) Individuals must be well-informed about consumption alternatives.
b) Firms must not be required to pay the full cost of production.
c) The government must be able to expropriate property to correct unequal income distributions.
d) Private costs must be lower than social costs.

11. When the market "fails," which of the following does not hold true?

a) Government has the opportunity to improve the allocation of resources.
b) Some rationing device, other than the market, may be used to improve economic efficiency.
c) Since the market outcome is inefficient, government intervention assures an improved social outcome.
d) Marginal social benefits and marginal social costs are not equal at the equilibrium point.

12. Which of the following is not true?

a) In an efficient market, trading at the equilibrium price results in the largest possible net gain to society.
b) Economic efficiency is the achievement of the greatest possible difference between benefits and costs.
c) A demand curve indicates the minimum amount the consumer will pay for a particular quantity of a good.
d) It is possible for self-interested market decision-making to be consistent with the maximization of society's well-being.

13. A measure of the total social benefits derived from the consumption of 100 personal computers at an equilibrium price of $1200 is:

a) $1200
b) $1200 X 100 units
c) the area under the demand curve up to price = $1200 and quantity demanded = 100 units.
d) the area under the demand curve, above the equilibrium price of $1200, and up to quantity demanded of 100 units.

14. The supply curve for a producer represents:

a) the most the producer will accept to offer an additional unit of output on the market.
b) the producer's marginal opportunity cost of production.
c) the additional benefit received by consumers for each additional unit of output.
d) combinations of price and quantity supplied for which marginal cost exceeds price.

15. The total social cost of producing 100 personal computers at an equilibrium price of $1200 each is:

a) $1200
b) $1200 X 100 units
c) the area above the supply function but below price = $1200.
d) the sum of the marginal costs up to 100 units of output.

16. A price floor that is set below the equilibrium market price will:

a) result in a shortage.
b) result in a surplus.
c) have no effect on the market outcome.
d) have an indeterminate effect on the market outcome.

17. Which of the following is not true?

a) If the total cost of producing 3 cameras is $360, then the marginal cost of the third camera is $120.
b) Marginal cost is the change in total cost divided by the change in output (when the change in output is small).
c) Total cost equals the sum of the marginal costs.
d) Marginal cost of the 20th unit is the difference between the total cost of producing 20 units and 19 units.

18. Marginal cost equals:

a) total cost divided by quantity. (Quantity must be small.)
b) the change in total cost divided by the change in quantity. (The change in quantity must be small.)
c) total cost divided by quantity. (Quantity must be large so a more representative number of units is used.)
d) the change in total cost divided by the change in quantity. (Quantity must be large so that a more representative number of units are used.)

Use the following table to answer questions 19 - 22

COSTS AND BENEFITS OF PRODUCING AND CONSUMING COMPUTERS

No. of Computers	Total Cost	Marginal Cost	Total Benefit	Marginal Benefit
0	$ 0	---	$ 0	---
1	$1,000	$1,000	$2,000	_____
2	$2,200	_____	$3,500	_____
3	_____	$1,500	_____	$4,500

19. The marginal cost of the second computer is:

a) $200
b) $1,000
c) $1,200
d) $2,200

20. What is the total cost of producing the first three units output? (You need to use the answer from the previous question to answer this question.)

a) $3,700
b) $3,200
c) $2,200
d) $1,500

21. What is the total benefit associated with the consumption of one computer?

a) $0
b) $1,000
c) $2,000
d) $5,500

22. What is the marginal benefit of consuming the second computer?

a) $1,000
b) $1,500
c) $2,000
d) $3,500

23. Which of the following is not true of consumers' surplus?

a) It is the area below the demand function and above equilibrium price.
b) It is the area between the demand and supply functions up to equilibrium quantity.
c) It is the difference between what consumers would be willing to pay and what they actually have to pay.
d) It is the difference between what the consumer receives in terms of marginal benefit and what the consumer has to pay for a good.

24. Assume that in the market for good X, the equilibrium price is $10, equilibrium quantity is 100, quantity demanded is 0 at a price of $25, and quantity supplied is 0 at a price of $5. Based on this information, producer surplus is:

a) $250.
b) $500.
c) $750.
d) $1,000.

25. Referring to the previous question, the net social gain from consuming good X is:

a) $250.
b) $500.
c) $750.
d) $1,000.

26. Suppose a ceiling price on apartment rents is set above the equilibrium price for apartment rents. Which of the following will occur?

a) The amount of apartments actually rented will be greater than the equilibrium quantity.
b) The amount of apartments actually rented will be less than the equilibrium quantity.
c) The equilibrium price and quantity will continue to prevail.
d) There will be a shortage of apartments.

36. Which of the following is true of the distribution of income?

a) The best distribution of income is determined by positive economic considerations.
b) The most equitable distribution of income is the most efficient distribution.
c) Markets may be efficient if the income distribution is quite unequal.
d) Given the efficiency of markets, an economist can determine what the income distribution should be.

28. Which of the following is true of agricultural marketS?

a) In the U.S., agricultural programs are designed to improve the efficiency of agricultural markets.
b) Higher food prices created by agricultural support programs disproportionately harm low-income consumers.
c) Financially-troubled farmers benefit the most from agricultural programs in the U.S.
d) Farm programs cost consumers more, but do a good job of redistributing income from high-income individuals to low-income individuals.

29. Which of the following is not true?

a) Policies designed to redistribute income distort the demands of consumers and supplies of producers.
b) Policies designed to redistribute income drive the market price away from the equilibrium that would have existed prior to intervention.
c) The more efficient the economy, the more income there is to redistribute.
d) The efficient market equilibrium results in the best distribution of income.

30. In 1990, Congress increased the minimum wage to $4.25 per hour. However, many critics of the minimum wage law argued that this would simply result in increased unemployment. Which of the following arguments could be used to support this assertion?

a) An increase in the minimum wage causes labor supply to increase.
b) An increase in the minimum wage reduces the demand for labor.
c) The minimum wage acts like a price floor set above equilibrium.
d) The minimum wage acts like a price ceiling set below equilibrium.

Use the following figure, which illustrates the market for bicycles, to answer questions 31 - 35.

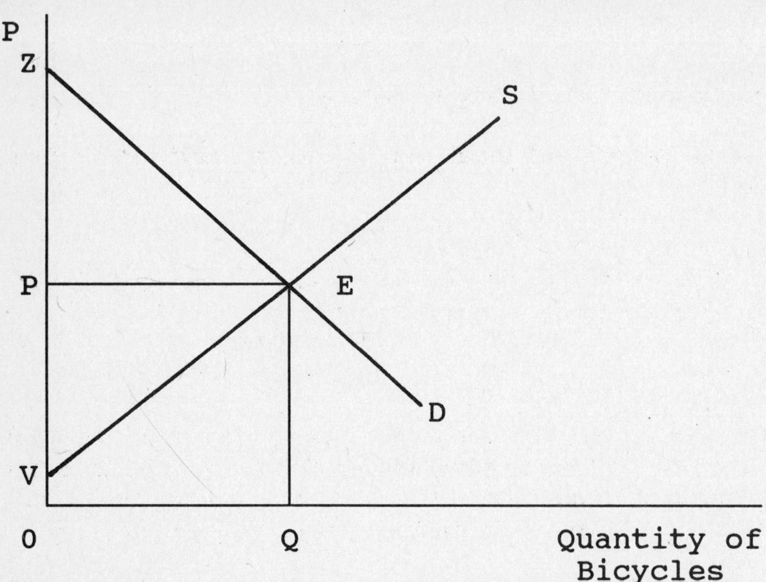

31. The total benefit to society from consuming quantity Q bicycles is area:

a) ZEP
b) PEV
c) PEQO
d) ZEQO

32. The total cost to society from producing Q bicycles is:

a) ZEP
b) PEV
c) EQOV
d) PEQO

33. The net benefit to society is shown by area:

a) ZEP
b) ZEV
c) ZEQO
d) PEQO

34. Consumers' surplus is equal to what area?

a) ZEP
b) PEV
c) ZEQO
d) ZEV

35. What area represents producers' surplus?

a) ZEV
b) PEV
b) PEQO
d) EQOV

36. Suppose the government sets an effective floor price for wheat. Which of the following is not true?

a) Private demanders will continue to buy the original equilibrium quantity of wheat.
b) There will be a surplus of wheat at the floor price.
c) Suppliers will offer more wheat on the market at the floor price than at the original equilibrium price.
d) The floor price will be above the equilibrium price.

Chapter 4, Economic Efficiency

ANSWER KEY

Exercises

1. consumer surplus
2. total social benefits, total social costs. marginal social benefit, marginal social cost
3. consumers' surplus, producers' surplus
4. 1) High degree of competition, 2) all social benefits and social costs are incorporated into decision making, 3) the economy is relatively stable.
5. market failure.
6. above, below.
7. $900, $600, $1500
8. $375, $1125
9. $30, 60

Review Questions

1. c) is not true. If marginal benefit is less than marginal cost, firms will not make a profit and, therefore, will not produce the good.

2. d) is not required. In fact, just the opposite is the case. The supply function must include all social costs. For example, if a firm is polluting the air and paying no penalty, all social costs are not reflected in the supply function and the markets outcome will be inefficient.

3. c) is the correct answer. Since the supply function is above the demand function for quantities greater than the equilibrium quantity, marginal cost is greater than marginal benefit. Answer (a) is incorrect because it denies the definition of marginal benefit.

4. b) is the correct answer. When income is redistributed it alters the composition of demand for different goods and services--demands increase, others decrease. The result is a change in market equilibria.

5. c) is not a reason. Answers a), b), and d) are all reasons the market is an attractive means of allocating resources. The market system does not allocate resources so that everyone receives an equal share.

6. a) is the correct answer. For competition to exist, neither individual buyers or sellers can be able to influence market price, i.e., market outcome. This requires a large number of both buyers and sellers.

7. c) is the correct answer. This is the condition for economic efficiency. A movement in either direction, i.e, an increase or decrease in the level of output will cause net gains to decline.

8. b) is the definition of consumer surplus. See the text.

9. c) is not true. If a firm is running an economic loss, the market is signaling that output should fall in that industry and that resources in the industry could be used more efficiently elsewhere.

10. a) is the correct answer. Consumers and producers must be well"informed about alternatives or their choices may not maximize benefits or minimize costs. If pollution occurs, private costs are less than social costs and the market outcome is not efficient. Therefore b) and d) are incorrect. Individuals must be assured that they will enjoy the benefits of their property if they are to engage in innovative, but risky, types of activities. Therefore c) is incorrect.

11. c) is not true. Government intervention may improve the allocation of resources and provide an improved social outcome, but it won't necessarily accomplish this. Answers a), b), and d) are all true of market failure.

12. c) is not true. The demand curve indicates the maximum amount consumers will pay for a particular quantity of a good. For example, if price = $10 and quantity demanded = 50 units, this indicates that consumers are willing to pay at most $10 for the 50th unit.

13. c) is the correct answer. The amount the consumer is willing to pay at each quantity represents the social benefit at that quantity. Summing the amounts consumers are willing to pay at each quantity up to the equilibrium quantity yields the area underneath the demand function up to that quantity. Answer d) indicates net benefits (= marginal benefit - equilibrium price) at each quantity.

14. b) is the correct answer. The supply curve relates the marginal opportunity cost of production at various quantities. Therefore, the supply curve represents the least producers will accept for an additional unit of the good. Along the supply curve price must equal or exceed marginal cost.

15. d) is the correct answer. The sum of the marginal costs is the area under the supply function up to 100 units of output. This is because price represents marginal cost along the supply function. Answer b) would be correct only if marginal cost were constant. Answer c) refers to the net benefit to producers.

16. c) is the correct answer. A price floor only sets a limit on how low price can go. So long as the equilibrium price is above the price floor, the price floor has no effect in the market.

17. a) is not true. This answer refers to the average cost of production. The cost of the third camera, the marginal cost, will be different than the cost of the second camera, unless marginal cost is constant. Answers b) and d) are correct definitions of marginal cost. Answer c) is also correct.

18. c) is the correct answer. Marginal analysis always refers to the change in one variable due to a change in another variable. The change in quantity must be fairly small, such as a one unit change.

19. c) is the correct answer. Marginal Cost equals the change in total cost due to producing an additional computer (in this case the second computer.) The change in total cost is $2,200 - $1,000 = $1,200.

20. a) is the correct answer. We know from the previous question that the marginal cost of the 2nd computer is $1,200. Total cost equals the sum of the marginal costs. Thus, total cost in this case equals $1,000 + $1,200 + $1,500 = $3,700.

21. c) is the correct answer. If the marginal benefit for the first unit is consumed is $2,000, then the total benefit at that level of consumption is also $2,000. Remember total benefit equals the sum of the marginal benefits.

22. b) is the correct answer. From the previous question the total benefit of consuming the first computer is $2,000. The total benefit from consuming the first and the second computer is $3,500. Since marginal benefit equals the change in total benefit, it is $3,500 - $2,000 = $1,500.

23. b) is not true. The area between the demand and supply functions represents the net social benefit from producing and consuming a good. It includes not only consumers' surplus, but also producers' surplus.

24. a) is the correct answer. Producers' surplus is the area bounded by the supply curve, the price line and the vertical axis, or, in this case, [($10 - $5) x 100]/2 = $250.

25. d) is the correct answer. The net social gain is the sum of producers' surplus and consumers' surplus. Consumers' surplus is the area bounded by the demand curve, the price line and the vertical axis, or, in this case [($25 - $10) x 100]/2 = $750. Producers' surplus plus consumers' surplus is therefore $250 + $750 = $1,000.

26. c) is the correct answer. A ceiling price above equilibrium price will have no effect on the market. The equilibrium price is legal in this case and so equilibrium price and quantity will continue to prevail. If the existing equilibrium price is declared to be legal, there will be no effect in the market.

27. c) is the correct answer. The distribution of income does not determine whether markets are efficient or not. Markets might also be efficient with a relatively equal distribution of income. Therefore answer b) is incorrect. Answer a) is incorrect because the best distribution of income

is determined by normative considerations. Answer d) is therefore incorrect. Positive economics cannot determine what the distribution should be.

28. b) is the correct answer. Since low income consumers spend a relatively large share of their income on food, the higher food prices created by agricultural support programs harm low income consumers dispropor-tionately. Answer a) is incorrect since agri-cultural programs make market less efficient. Answer c) is incorrect because, according to the text, the most financially-troubled farmers are not helped. Farm programs therefore do not redistri-bute income, so answer d) is also incorrect.

29. d) is not true. The "optimal" distribution of income is determined by normative considerations rather than market efficiency. Answers a) and b) are correct because changing the distribution of income distorts the preferences of demanders and the decisions of suppliers. This, in turn, affects the equilibrium price and quantity. Answer c) is correct because the more efficient the allocation of resources, the more productive those resources, and the greater the income generated by them.

30. c) is the correct answer. The minimum wage is an example of price floor. When a price floor is set above the equilibrium price, quantity demanded declines--there is a movement up the demand curve. In this case, to the extent that the minimum wage exceeds the market equilibrium wage, less labor will be employed, i.e., unemployment will increase.

31. d) is the correct answer. Each point on the demand curve represents the marginal benefit to society of consuming one more unit. The summation of the marginal benefits up to the quantity produced, Q, yields the total benefit to society of consuming Q bicycles. ZEQO is the area under the demand curve up to quantity Q.

32. c) is the correct answer. Each point on the supply curve represents the marginal cost of production. That is, each point indicates the least firms will take to produce the additional unit at that point. The summation of the marginal costs at each quantity up to the equilibrium quantity, Q, is the total cost of producing Q, area EQOV.

33. b) is the correct answer. At each quantity, the corresponding price on the demand function represents the marginal benefit associated with that unit and the corresponding price on the supply function represents the marginal cost of producing that unit. Therefore, the difference between the demand and supply functions at each unit represents the difference between the marginal benefit and marginal cost for that unit, i.e., the net marginal benefit. Summation of the net marginal benefits for the units up to quantity, Q, yields the total net benefit of consuming Q units of bicycles.

34. a) is the correct answer. Consumers surplus at any quantity is the difference between what the consumer would be willing to pay, which is represented by the point on the demand function at that quantity, and what the consumer has to pay, which is the equilibrium price. The summation of these differences for all units up to the equilibrium quantity is shown by area ZEP.

35. b) is the correct answer. Producers' surplus is the difference between the price suppliers would accept and what they actually get, i.e., the equilibrium price. The supply function represents the marginal cost of production at each unit. This is the minimum price producers would accept. The difference between the minimum price producers would accept for each unit and the equilibrium price, summed up to the equilibrium quantity, Q, is the area between the supply function and the equilibrium price, PEV.

36. a) is not true. Private demanders will buy less than they did at the original equilibrium price because the price rises to the floor price level, causing quantity demanded to fall. b) and c) are correct because at the floor price there will be a surplus. d) is correct. To be effective a floor price must be greater than the equilibrium price.

CHAPTER 5
DECISION MAKING IN AN IMPERFECT WORLD

OVERVIEW

In this chapter we continue our analysis of how markets work to allocate society's scarce resources to the production of goods and services. We begin by examining the manner in which markets answer three fundamental questions--what to produce, how to produce, and for whom to produce. We then go on to consider various types of market failure and how they affect the efficiency of market outcomes. We conclude the chapter with a discussion of the potential for successful government intervention designed to address market failure.

For markets to be efficient, certain conditions must be met. When one or more of these conditions is violated, market failure occurs. A lack of effective competition is one of the main sources of market failure. The usual result of a lack of competition is higher prices and lower levels of output than would occur under competitive conditions.

Externalities, or spillovers, also result in market failure. External costs are costs resulting from a market exchange that are borne by some third party who is not part of the original transaction. In a similar manner, external benefits are benefits resulting from a market exchange that are borne by some third party. Examples of external costs include environmental pollution, and the noise from cars with faulty exhaust systems. Examples of external benefits include the benefits an orchard owner receives when a bee keeper locates on adjacent property, and the side benefits of flu vaccination programs. In order for market outcomes to be efficient, external costs or benefits must be factored into the decision making processes of firms and consumers.

Public goods also result in market failure. Unlike private goods, public goods cannot be divided up for sale to individual consumers. In addition, individuals cannot be excluded from consuming public goods. The result is a tendency for people to free ride, i.e., consume public goods without helping to bear the costs of their provision. As such, the market does not have an incentive to produce public goods. Examples of public goods include national parks, national defense, and police protection.

A lack of economic stability can also result in market failure. Sources of economic instability include poorly-defined property rights, and widely fluctuating economic conditions such changes in the price level, interest rates, and the levels of employment and output.

In general, market failure suggests that there is a role for the government to play in the workings of the economy. However, government intervention may or may not improve economic conditions. On the one hand, failed efforts by the government may be attributable to an inadequate understanding of the complex workings of the economy. Alternatively, unsuccessful government policies may be the result of politically-motivated behavior by policymakers. According to the economics of public choice, public decision making is motivated by the desire for re-election. The effect of such factors as the power of special interests, the shortsightedness of political decision making, the inability of voters to select a candidate who's views are totally consistent with those of the voter, and voters' pursuit of individual interests all make it unlikely that government actions will be efficiency enhancing.

KEY GRAPHS AND TERMS

Graphs

The model of supply and demand is used in this chapter to illustrate the effects of externalities on the efficiency of market outcomes. Referring to Figure 1, in the case of external costs, there is a divergence between private costs--those directly borne by the producer--and social costs which include the full opportunity costs of production. The difference between private costs and social costs is the external costs, i.e., costs borne by third parties. Assuming there are external costs (for example, resulting from pollution), the market supply curve understates the full opportunity costs of production. Adding together private costs and social costs yields the true social supply curve. When a negative externality exists, in the absence of government intervention the level of output will be too high. In other words, there is an overallocation of resources to production of the good in question. Failure to include external costs in the decision making process reduces society's net gain.

Referring to Figure 2, in the case of external benefits, there is a divergence between private benefits--those directly borne by the consumer--and social benefits which include the benefits accruing to third parties. The difference between private benefits and social benefits is the external benefits, i.e., benefits borne by third parties. Assuming there are external benefits, the market demand curve understates the full benefits to society. Adding together private benefits and social benefits yields the true social demand curve, which lies to the right of the private demand curve. When an external benefit exists, in the absence of government intervention the level of output will be too low. In other words, there is an underallocation of resources to production of the good in question.

Terms

COLLUDE
MICROECONOMICS
EXTERNALITIES
EXTERNAL COST
EXTERNAL BENEFIT
PRIVATE GOOD
PUBLIC GOOD
FREE RIDE
FREE RIDER PROBLEM
CENTRAL BANK
MONETARY POLICY
MACROECONOMICS
FISCAL POLICY
ECONOMICS OF PUBLIC CHOICE
SPECIAL-INTEREST GROUP

EXERCISES

1. List the three questions that must be addressed by every economy. 1) What to produce 2) How to produce it 3.) For whom to produce it.

2. The process by which efforts to increase individual well-being also increase society's well-being is referred to as the Invisible Hand.

3. In general, the effects of a reduction in the level of competition in a market are a lower level of output and higher prices.

4. In the case where production of a good results in external costs, the market-determined level of output is too high. As such, there is an overallocation of resources to the good in question. In the case where production of a good results in external benefits, the market-determined level of output is too low. As such, there is an underallocation of resources to the good in question.

5. A Public Good is a good whose use by one person does not reduce its availability for use by other people.

6. People who intentionally understate their willingness to pay for a public good in the hope of being able to enjoy the benefits of the good without having to bear the cost of providing it are referred to as Free Riders.

7. The study of the economy as a whole is called MACROECONOMICS

8. FISCAL Policy refers to the use of the government's powers to tax and spend to affect the level of economic activity.

9. The application of economic principles to the study of political behavior is known as the Economics of Public Choice.

Chapter 5, Decision Making in an Imperfect World

Use the following figure, which illustrates the market for good X, to answer questions - .

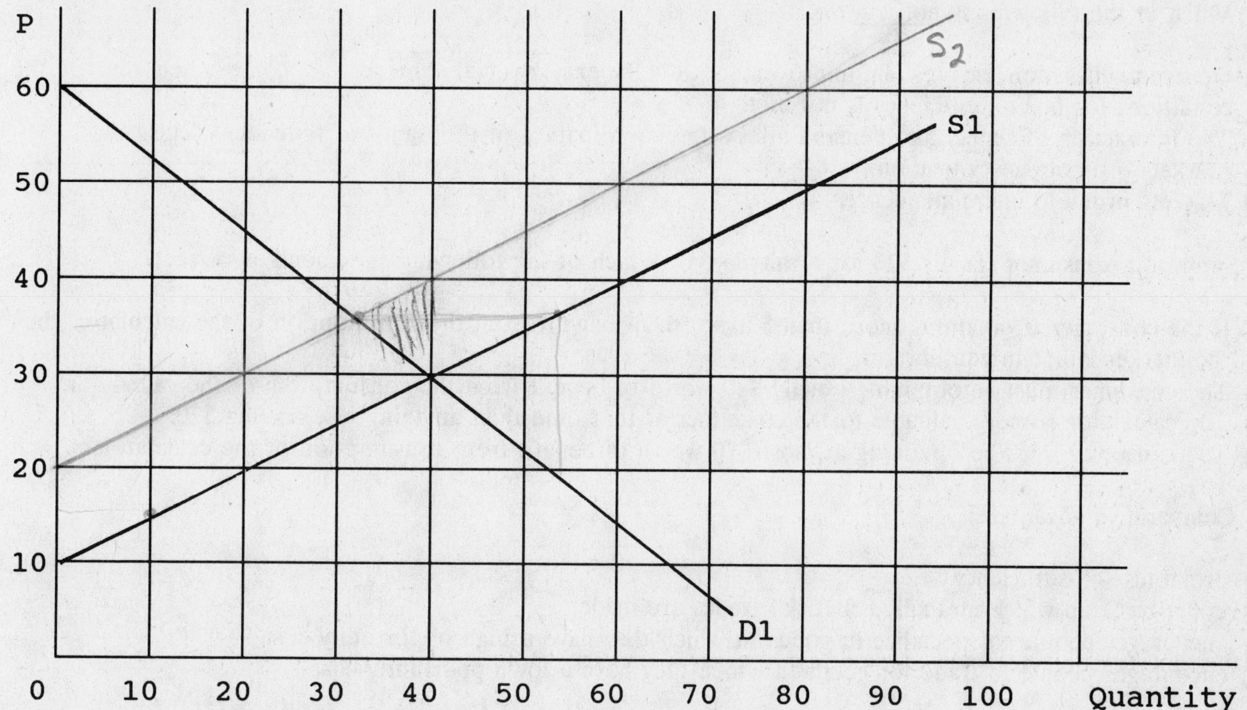

10. According to the figure above, what are the current equilibrium price and quantity?

Price = $30 Quantity = 40

11. Assume that production of X results in a large amount of pollution, but that the supply curve labeled S1 only reflects the private costs of production. Is the current level of output efficient? No

12. A group of economists and other experts has determined that the marginal external costs of the pollution are $10 per unit. Use this information to plot the true social supply curve in the figure and label it S2.

13. Based on your answer to #12, what are the new equilibrium price and quantity of X?

Price = $36 Quantity = 32

14. Assuming that firms are forced to account for the full social costs of production, what is the net social gain from the production and consumption of X? $640 (32 · 40 · ½)

15. Calculate the welfare loss (reduction in net social gain) that will occur in the absence of government intervention in the market for X. $40

16. Alternatively, assume that supply curve S1 reflects the true social costs of producing X, but that there are external benefits from the consumption of X, and that these marginal external benefits are estimated to be $15 per unit of output. In this case, the socially efficient price and level of output are $36 and 52 units of output. As such, allowing the market to continue to operate without intervention will result in a welfare loss of $90.

REVIEW QUESTIONS

1. Which of the following is not true?

a) Government action ensures an improvement in efficiency over the market outcome when one of the conditions for market efficiency is not met.
b) The interaction of supply and demand allows the coordination of thousands of individual decisions.
c) Markets promote specialization.
d) Markets promote interdependence.

2. Suppose a consumer spends $20 for a calculator. Which of the following statements is correct?

a) If the consumer is obtaining more than $20 worth of benefit from the consumption of the calculator, then the market is not in equilibrium.
b) The consumer must be obtaining exactly $20 worth of benefit from the consumption of the calculator.
c) The calculator is more valuable to the consumer at that time than anything else costing $20.
d) The consumer must be obtaining at most $20 worth of benefit from consumption of the calculator.

3. Comparative advantage:

a) promotes self-sufficiency.
b) is the basis on which mutually-beneficial trades are made.
c) encourages people to specialize in goods in which they have a high opportunity cost.
d) encourages people to trade for goods in which they have a low opportunity cost.

4. Which of the following is not a means by which the market solves the problem of "What to produce"?

a) Consumer sovereignty.
b) Consumers are free to consume those goods they find beneficial.
c) Producers have an incentive to produce goods at the highest possible cost, so that they can maximize profits by charging consumers the highest possible price.
d) Dollar votes.

5. Why do producers operating in the market system have an incentive to incorporate technological changes into their production techniques?

a) Because they have to compete for consumers with other firms that will incorporate new technologies which lower cost and price.
b) So that costs will remain high and thus the firm will be able to charge the consumer a higher price.
c) So that consumers do not have as much of an opportunity to cast their dollar votes and prices can be maintained at a higher level.
d) So that ability to pay will not be determined by the consumer's income.

6. "Economic stability" is thought to be required for the market to generate an efficient outcome. Which of the following is the best example of economic stability?

a) Government loans which ensure that large firms such as Chrysler and Lockheed will not go out of business.
b) Government using its taxing and spending powers to redistribute income.
c) Government enforcement of private property rights.
d) The government engaging in stable policies in which it does not intervene and allows inflation and recession to run their natural courses.

7. Which of the following statements is <u>not true</u>?

a) Macroeconomics is the study of the behavior of the firms in an industry.
b) One of the problems with centralized decision-making is the amount of information that is needed to improve upon the efficiency of the market outcome.
c) The government can provide macroeconomic stability by smoothing out the business cycle.
d) In its attempts to provide macroeconomic stability, the government might actually implement policies that destabilize the economy.

8. Adam Smith's "Invisible Hand":

a) rationalizes government intervention into the market system in a secretive or invisible manner.
b) suggests that the pursuit of self-interest is consistent with social well-being.
c) suggests that income redistribution is the primary goal of the market system.
d) is applied to markets in which economic efficiency cannot be achieved.

9. Which of the following conditions is <u>not</u> necessary for the market to generate an efficient outcome?

a) There must be many producers so that each producer is limited in its ability to raise price and profits.
b) There must be positive externalities from the production or consumption of the good.
c) There must be no negative externalities.
d) Private and social costs must be the same.

10. In a market system, firms have an incentive to avoid competition, resulting in:

a) a greater quantity sold to consumers, so that the firm can increase its profits.
b) consumers paying a higher price for a unit of the good and receiving less of the good.
c) consumers paying a lower price for a unit of the good and receiving less of the good.
d) consumers paying a higher price for a unit of the good and receiving more of the good.

11. Suppose the production of paper towels exhibits an external cost, such as water pollution. Which of the following will be true of the paper-towel market equilibrium outcome?

a) Equilibrium quantity will be greater than the economically-efficient level.
b) Equilibrium quantity will be less than the economically-efficient level.
c) Equilibrium price will be less than it would be at the efficient level.
d) Resources are "under allocated" toward the production of paper towels.

12. Referring to the example given in the previous question, which of the following is correct?

a) The social supply function is below the private supply function.
b) The social supply function is above the private supply function.
c) The social demand function is below the private demand function.
d) The social demand curve is above the private demand function.

13. Suppose there are external benefits associated with the provision of education by the private market. Which of the following is <u>not correct</u>?

a) Social benefits are greater than private benefits.
b) Less than the economically-efficient quantity is provided by the market.
c) The market equilibrium price is less than the price that would exist at the economically-efficient quantity.
d) The social demand curve is below the private demand curve.

Use the following figure to answer questions 14 and 15.

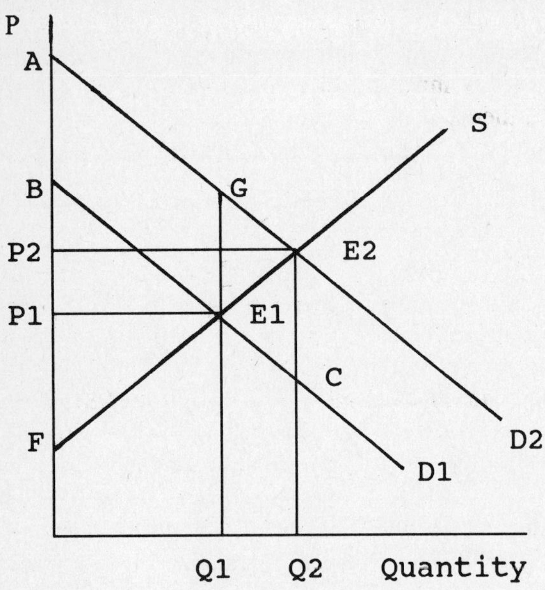

14. In the above graph, suppose D1 represents the private demand curve and D2 represents the social demand curve. Which of the following statements is correct?

a) The external benefit per unit is shown by the difference between P1 and P2.
b) The external benefit per unit is shown by the distance E1G.
c) Private benefit exceeds social benefit in the market pictured.
d) Pollution of a river is consistent with the market pictured.

15. Referring again to the above graph, if the external benefits were taken into account:

a) The equilibrium price would be P1.
b) Society would gain area BE1F.
c) Society would gain area GE2E1
d) Society would gain area BE1P1.

16. Which of the following is not a way government can improve on the market outcome when there are external costs?

a) Assign property rights.
b) Encourage greater production so that the market moves closer to its efficient level.
c) Internalize the externality.
d) Engage in policies which equalize private and social costs.

17. Which of the following is true of private goods?

a) If used by one consumer there are less of them available for others to use.
b) They cannot be efficiently allocated by the market.
c) Once provided, others cannot be excluded from their benefits.
d) Consumers will not reveal their true preferences about them.

18. Which of the following is not true concerning public goods?

a) They can be consumed by one person without reducing the amount available for consumption by others.
b) Once provided, others cannot be excluded from their benefits.
c) The market mechanism is of considerable help in determining how much of them to provide.
d) Consumers will not willingly reveal their true preferences for them.

19. Which of the following is the best example of the Free-Rider Problem?

a) Only buying items of clothing when they are on sale.
b) Taking advantage of a shortage of gasoline by raising price.
c) Refusing to contribute to public TV.
d) Paying more rent for an apartment than a ceiling price legally allows.

20. Which of the following is not required for the market to generate an economically efficient outcome?

a) Many buyers and many sellers.
b) The existence of external benefits.
c) The absence of external costs.
D) A stable system of property rights.

21. Which of the following is not true of the market economy?

a) The distribution of income is unequal.
b) Ability to pay is determined by one's income.
c) High income individuals will always be able to outbid low-income individuals for goods.
d) The is an incentive to supply resources to their most productive employment in order to maximize income.

22. Suppose there is a shift in tastes toward polka-dot neckties. The market will react to this in which of the following ways?

a) The price of polka-dot ties will fall so that consumers can take advantage of the change in tastes.
b) Producers of neckties will withhold production to the greatest extent possible so that the price of polka-dot ties will rise and profits will be maximized.
c) The government will have to provide incentives for the production of polka-dot neckties, otherwise resources will continue to be used for the production of other styles of neckties.
d) The price of polka-dot neckties will rise, allocating resources to their production as producers try to maximize profits.

23. Suppose the government forces a firm to stop polluting a river. Which of the following statements is correct?

a) The government will probably have a good idea of the benefits of reducing the pollution.
b) If the cost of reducing the pollution is borne by the firm, it will influence neither social benefits nor social costs.
c) The market outcome will remain the same if the firm bears the cost of reducing the level of pollution.
d) It is possible that the government will not improve on the efficiency of the market outcome if the cost of reducing the pollution is great and the benefit is small.

24. The government provision of safety through OSHA indicates:

a) The government believes the social demand curve for safety is above the private demand curve for safety.
b) The government believes safety is overvalued by the private market.
c) The government favors a market solution to the problem of safety in the work place.
d) OSHA's primary method for increasing safety in the work place involves taxing firms for injuries which occur on the job.

25. If voters act as consumers of goods and services provided by the government:

a) The outcome will be efficient as it is in the case of the market.
b) Voters cannot unbundle the goods provided by the government.
c) Voters are able to vote for only those specific government goods and services they want.
d) Voters express their preferences for particular goods with more force than they do in the private market.

26. Which of the following statements is <u>not true</u>:

a) Government answers the "For Whom" question when it redistributes income.
b) It may be argued that if a worker accepts a risky job, the worker has demonstrated that the income from the job is greater than the risk of injury associated with the job.
c) A rational worker would never choose to increase the risk of personal injury in return for income.
d) Public Choice Theory evaluates public decision-making on the same terms as market decision-making.

27. Which of the following is a big problem which is associated with government provision of goods and services:

a) Consumers must necessarily sacrifice more for government-provided goods than for goods provided by the market.
b) Consumers cannot vote on the provision of specific government-provided goods and must vote for groups of them.
c) Consumers are able to express such strong preferences for individual government-provided goods, that it is impossible to determine what to produce.
d) Since goods and services provided by the government do not use scarce resources, the government tends to provide them in quantities that are "too great."

28. It may be rational to be uninformed about political decisions because:

a) Consumers can readily unbundle goods that are provided by the government.
b) The benefits from political decisions are frequently quite large for the consumers of government goods and service.
c) The cost of acquiring information about the issues which political candidates address is now quite low, with the importance of television in elections.
d) The cost of collecting information about political decisions could be greater than the perceived benefit.

29. Special interests can influence politicians to make decisions which are not in the public interest because:

a) the benefits of acquiring information about special interests are greater than the costs.
b) the cost to each individual voter is large.
c) the resources allocated to special interests are not considered to be scarce resources by society.
d) the costs are spread out over a large number of taxpayers.

Chapter 5, Decision Making in an Imperfect World

ANSWER KEY

Exercises

1. 1) What to produce, 2) how to produce, and 3) for whom to produce
2. invisible hand
3. lower, higher
4. high, overallocation, low, underallocation
5. public good
6. free riders
7. macroeconomics
8. Fiscal policy
9. economics, public choice
10. $30, 40 units
11. No
12. The supply curve would shift up by a vertical distance of $10 per unit, and pass through the points P = $20, Q = 0; and P = $40, Q = 40.
13. price is approximately $36, and quantity is approximately 32 units.
14. approximate amount of net social gain is $640.
15. approximate value of welfare loss is $40.
16. socially efficient equilibrium price and quantity are approximately $36 and 52 units. Approximate value of welfare loss is $90.

Review Questions

1. a) is not true. Government action has the potential for improving efficiency, but it will not necessarily do so.

2. c) is the correct answer. The fact that the consumer bought the calculator indicates that at that time there is nothing else costing $20 that would provide greater benefit to the consumer. A review of consumers' surplus from the last chapter will show that answers a), b), and d) are not true.

3. b) is the correct answer. Comparative advantage is the basis on which mutually-beneficial trades are made. The explanation for this lies in the notion that people produce goods in which they have a low opportunity cost and trade those goods for other goods in which they have a high opportunity cost. Thus, answers c) and d) are incorrect. Comparative advantage promotes trade, which is associated with specialization. Therefore, it does not promote self-sufficiency, at least in an economic sense.

4. c) is the correct answer. In order to maximize profits, producers have an incentive to minimize costs, not maximize costs. Given the price, the lower the cost of production, the more profit the producer will earn.

5. a) is the correct answer. In a competitive market, the firm has to compete with other firms for a limited amount of consumers. Thus, if another firm incorporates a new technology into their production process, then any other firm in the industry must do the same or lose consumers. There is a strong incentive to incorporate new technology to hold costs down.

6. c) is the correct answer. In order for the market to provide the efficient outcome, market participants must be assured that their personal wealth will not be confiscated. Otherwise they will refuse to invest and take risks. Therefore, it is an important function of government to enforce property rights. Answer is not correct because one of the aspects of economic stability is the avoidance of periods of severe inflation or recession.

7. a) is not true. The behavior of firms in an industry is studied in microeconomics. Macroeconomics deals with the economy as a whole.

8. b) is the correct answer. The "Invisible Hand" suggests that the most attractive feature of the market system is that the pursuit of self-interest creates an unintended socially-beneficial outcome-

-resources are allocated to their most productive uses. This occurs without the intervention of any central authority, such as the government. However, the invisible hand works only in markets that are reasonably efficient.

9. b) is the opposite of the condition that needs to exist in order for the market to generate an efficient outcome. If private and social benefits are to be the same, then there can be no externalities, either negative or positive.

10. b) is the correct answer. Competition can be prevented if new firms find it difficult to enter the market to take advantage of high profits. Expensive costs which need to be paid for large-scale production facilities is an example of this. Under these circumstances the market may be dominated by one or a few large firms. In this case, the firm will restrict supply so that there are higher prices than there would have been in a competitive market.

11. a) is the correct answer. If the production of paper towels exhibits external costs, resources are "overallocated" toward paper towels. Private costs are less than social costs. If private producers had to pay the external costs, supply would decrease, resulting in a higher equilibrium price and lower equilibrium quantity. When there are external costs, which are not paid by the firm, the market equilibrium quantity is greater than the efficient quantity.

12. b) is the correct answer. Refer to Figure 5-1 in your text. If there are external costs associated with the production of a good, the social supply curve is above the private supply curve by the amount of the external cost per unit.

13. d) is not correct. If there are external benefits, the social demand curve is above the private demand curve by the amount of the marginal external benefit per unit. Answers a), b), and c) are all correct statements about a market in which there are external benefits.

14. b) is the correct answer. The external benefit per unit is shown by the vertical distance between the private and social demand functions.

15. c) is the correct answer. If external benefits were taken into account, the market price would be P_2 and the equilibrium quantity would be Q_2. Note that between Q_1 and Q_2 the social demand function is above the supply function. Summing the vertical distance between the social demand and supply functions from Q_1 to Q_2 yields area GE_2E_1.

16. b) is not a way the government can improve the market outcome. If there are external costs, the market outcome results in more being produced than the efficient amount of the good. Therefore, the government would not want to encourage additional production.

17. a) is the correct answer. If one consumer buys a personal computer, there are less personal computers available for other consumers, for example. Answers b), c), and d) are all correct for public goods.

18. c) is not true of public goods. The market mechanism is of little help in determining how much of a public good to produce, since consumers will not voluntarily reveal the benefits they receive, since they cannot be excluded from consumption of the public good.

19. c) is the best example of the Free-Ride problem. Once public TV is provided to one household in an area, it is provided to all households. Since consumers are not excluded from the benefits of public TV if they do not contribute, many will not voluntarily pay for the value of the true benefits they receive.

20. b) is not required. In fact, the existence of no external benefits is required for the market outcome to be economically efficient. Answer a) describes a situation in which competition is likely to exist.

21. c) is not true. Income determines ability to pay. Having a greater ability to pay does necessarily mean an individual will be able to outbid any other consumer with a lower ability to pay. This is because the lower income consumer may have a great willingness to pay and thus be able to outbid others for a good.

22. c) is the correct answer. The rising price of polka-dot neckties will signal producers to allocate resources to their production. Producers will offer more polka-dot neckties on the market in an effort to maximize profits. The increase in quantity supplied will moderate the rise in price. These changes are brought about by individuals who are acting in their own self-interest.

23. d is correct. If the cost of reducing pollution is greater than the benefit, then reducing pollution results in an outcome that is less efficient than the market outcome. Measuring costs and benefits is frequently quite difficult in such cases, so answer a) is not correct.

24. a) is the correct answer. The existence of OSHA suggests that firms and workers undervalue safety, so the government believes that the private demand curve is below the social demand curve as it would be for a public good. If this is true, a market solution leads to an inefficient result. The government is using rules rather than taxes which raise the cost of injuries to the firm, so answers c) and d) are not correct.

25. b) is the correct answer. When voters make a choice among politicians, they do not make a choice about particular goods but about bundles of goods being promised by the politician. These bundles cannot be decomposed into their separate component goods. This leads to inefficiency in the government's provision of goods and services.

26. c) is <u>not true</u>. The statement in answer b) is correct and refutes answer c) If a worker takes a job which is associated with a certain level of risk, this indicates that the worker values the income from the job more highly than the cost associated with the increased level of risk which the worker is experiencing.

27. b) is the correct answer. Politicians offer a bundle which is composed of many goods and services. In voting for a politician, consumers cannot "unbundle" the goods, that is, break them down into their components and vote only for the goods they want. This is why consumer preferences for individual government-provided goods is weakly expressed relative to the expression of preferences in the market.

28. d) is the correct answer. The cost of obtaining information about the promises of politicians can be very large. If the benefits that are likely to accrue to an individual voter are low, the voter is rational to remain uninformed. For the voter to become informed under these circumstances, the additional cost would exceed the additional benefit.

29. d) is the correct answer. While the benefits of special interest legislation frequently accrue to a narrow group of individuals, politicians may nevertheless have an incentive to support special interest legislation. One reason for this is that the additional taxes paid by each individual taxpayer for special interest legislation may be quite small, although in the aggregate the tax bill or other cost may be large. Under these circumstances, individual taxpayers may show little concern for special interest legislation.

CHAPTER 6
THE ELASTICITY OF DEMAND

OVERVIEW

In this chapter we address the question of how responsive quantity demanded is to a change in price, i.e., the price elasticity of demand. We also identify a number of factors that influence the price elasticity of demand. We then analyze the way in which the relationship between prices changes and changes in total revenue is influenced by elasticity. We conclude the chapter with a brief discussion of additional measures of elasticity.

The responsiveness, or sensitivity, of quantity demanded to a change in price is measured by the price elasticity of demand, which is expressed as the ratio of the percentage in quantity demanded to the percentage in price. This ratio is referred to as the coefficient of the price elasticity of demand. Because the price elasticity of demand is usually calculated over an interval, the average price and the average quantity over the interval are used in calculating the percentage in price and quantity. This approach ensures consistency in the manner in which arc, or range, elasticity is calculated.

As a technical matter, the coefficient of the price elasticity of demand is a negative number. However, conventional practice is to drop the negative sign. As such, the coefficient of elasticity can vary between 0 and infinity. In the case where the elasticity coefficient is zero, demand is said to be perfectly inelastic, and the demand curve appears as a vertical line. At the other extreme, when the coefficient is infinity, demand is said to be perfectly elastic, and the demand curve appears as a horizontal line. When the price elasticity coefficient is between 0 and 1 the percentage change in quantity demanded is less than the percentage change in price, and demand is said to be inelastic. When the coefficient is between 1 and infinity, the percentage change in quantity demanded is greater than the percentage change in price, and demand is said to be elastic.

Price elasticity of demand varies across goods and services. The major determinants of the price elasticity of demand include the number of available substitutes, the cost of a good relative to the consumer's total income, and the time period in question. An increase in any one of these three factors results in an increase in the price elasticity of demand.

Price elasticity of demand is particularly useful in predicting the effect of a change in price on the total revenue received from the sale of a good or service. In particular, when demand is price inelastic, the percentage change in price is greater than the percentage change in quantity demanded. Since total revenue is the product of price and quantity, the price effect dominates in this case and therefore total revenue moves in the same direction as price (and the opposite direction of quantity demanded). On the other hand, when demand is price elastic the percentage change in quantity demanded is greater than percentage change in price, and the quantity effect dominates. In this case, total revenue moves in the same direction as quantity demanded (and the opposite direction of the change in price).

Additional measures of elasticity include the income elasticity of demand which measures the percentage in quantity demanded (holding price constant) resulting from a percentage change in income, the cross price elasticity of demanded which measures the percentage change in quantity demanded (holding price constant) resulting from a percentage change in the price of a related good, and the price elasticity of supply.

KEY GRAPHS AND TERMS

Graphs

There are no new models or graphs in this chapter. However, it is strongly recommended that you refer back to the figures in the chapter to reinforce your understanding of how the change in quantity demanded resulting from a given change in price can vary (Figure 1), and the shapes of perfectly inelastic, perfectly elastic, and unit elastic demand curves (Figure 2). In addition, be sure you understand the difference between the slope of a demand curve, and the price elasticity of demand.

Terms

PRICE ELASTICITY OF DEMAND
COEFFICIENT OF ELASTICITY
PERFECTLY INELASTIC DEMAND
PERFECTLY ELASTIC DEMAND
UNITARY ELASTIC DEMAND
INELASTIC DEMAND
ELASTIC DEMAND
ARC ELASTICITY
POINT ELASTICITY OF DEMAND
TOTAL REVENUE
PRICE DISCRIMINATION
INCOME ELASTICITY OF DEMAND
CROSS PRICE ELASTICITY
PRICE ELASTICITY OF SUPPLY

Exercises

1. The coefficient of elasticity is measured as the ratio of the ___Percent___ ___Change___ in ___Quantity___ ___Demanded___ to the ___Percentage___ ___Change___ in ___Price___.

2. ___Arc___ elasticity of demand refers to the elasticity of demand between two points on a demand curve.

3. When demand is elastic, the percentage change in quantity demanded is ___greater___ than the percentage change in price. When demand is inelastic, the percentage change in quantity demanded is ___Less___ than the percentage change in price.

4. If we observe that when the price of a good is increased, the total revenue received from the good decreases, we can conclude that demand is ________________. In a similar fashion, if we observe that when the price of a good is increased, the total revenue received from the good increases as well, we can conclude that demand is ________________.

5. As we move down a linear demand curve, the price elasticity of demand ________________.

6. Assume that, for a particular demand curve, when price is $60, quantity demanded is 130, and when price is $50, quantity demanded is 175. As such, over this range, demand is ________________.

7. Firms that rely on the practice of charging different prices to different customers of the same good or service, which is called ________________ ________________, can increase their revenues by charging a ________________ price to customers for whom demand is inelastic and a ________________ price to customers whose demand is elastic.

8. List three factors that influence the price elasticity of demand. ________________________________

____

9. As the number of different brands of blue jeans on the market increases, the elasticity of demand for any single brand will ________________.

10. If the cross price elasticity of demand between two goods, A and B, is negative, we can conclude that A and B are ________________.

Chapter 6, The Elasticity of Demand

Use the following figure, which illustrates the market for good Y, to answer questions 11 - 15.

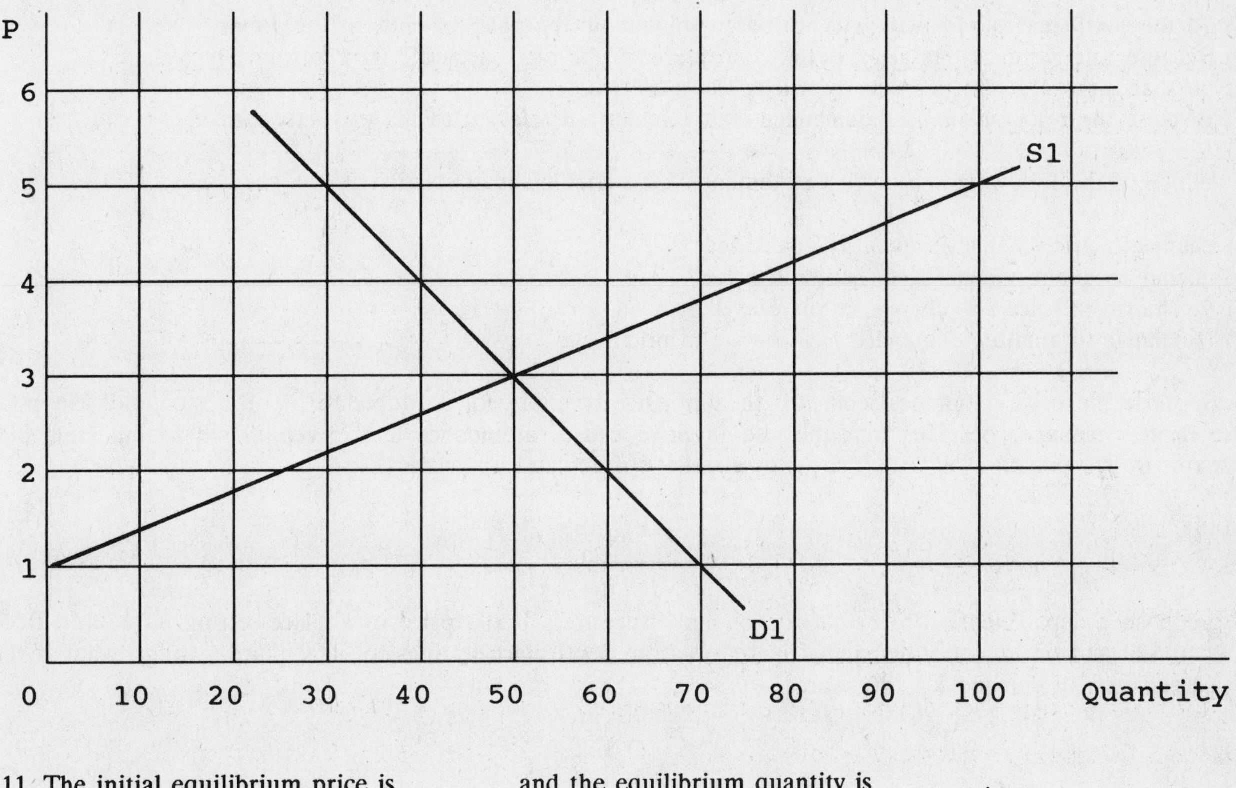

11. The initial equilibrium price is _______ and the equilibrium quantity is _______.

12. Assume that the government imposes a tax of $1.00 per unit on suppliers of Y. Draw a new supply curve to reflect the effect of the tax and label it S2. As a result of the tax, the new equilibrium price is _______, and the new equilibrium quantity is _______.

13. How much of the per unit tax is paid by producers? _______. By consumers? _______.

14. Calculate the coefficient of the price elasticity of demand between 40 and 50 units. _______

15. In general, the more (elastic, inelastic) the demand for a particular good is, the greater is the amount of a tax that can be passed on to consumers.

REVIEW QUESTIONS

1. The definition of the price elasticity of demand is:

a) The responsiveness of price to changes in quantity demanded.
b) The responsiveness of quantity demanded to changes in price.
c) The responsiveness of price to changes in income.
d) The responsiveness of quantity demanded to changes in income.

2. Why is the price elasticity of demand a relative measure? That is, why is elasticity measured in percentage terms rather than in absolute terms?

a) So the coefficient of elasticity will not be dependent on the physical units of the good.
b) Because relative measures are generally considered to be more accurate than absolute measures.
c) So that the coefficient of elasticity will not be negative.
d) Because the price or quantity demanded of a product is irrelevant to the elasticity measure.

3. Which of the following is a correct statement of the coefficient of elasticity?

a) change in price/change in quantity demanded.
b) change in quantity demanded/change in price.
c) % change in price / % change in quantity demanded.
d) % change in quantity demanded / % change in price.

4. Suppose the price of movies seen at a theater rises from $12 for a couple to $20 for a couple. Suppose the theater manager observes that the rise in price causes attendance at a given movie to fall from 300 persons to 200 persons. What is the price elasticity of demand for movies?

a) .5
b) .8
c) 1.0
d) 1.2

5. Suppose a department store has a sale on its silverware. If the price of a place-setting is reduced from $30 to $20 and the quantity demanded increases from 3000 place-settings to 5000 place-settings, what is the price elasticity of demand for silverware?

a) .8
b) 1.0
c) 1.25
d) 1.50

6. Suppose a discount store has a special offer on compact disk players and lowers their price from $150 to $100. Suppose the store manager observes that the quantity demanded increases from 600 disk players to 1000 disk players. What is the elasticity of demand for compact disk players?

a) .8
b) 1.0
c) 1.25
d) 1.50

7. If the local pizzeria raises the price of a medium pizza from $6 to $10 and quantity demanded falls from 700 pizzas a night to 100 pizzas a night, the price elasticity of demand for pizzas is:

a) .67
b) 1.5
c) 2.0
d) 3.0

8. Suppose a car dealer wants to get rid of the stock of last year's model. Assume that the dealer knows from past experience that the price elasticity of demand for cars is unitary(= 1). If the price of the cars is currently $20,000 and the dealer wants to increase the quantity demanded from 30 units to 50 units, what must the new price be if the dealer is to sell the 20 additional cars?

a) $10,000
b) $12,000
c) $16,000
d) $18,000

9. Which of the following best describes a perfectly inelastic demand function?

a) The quantity demanded is completely insensitive to changes in price.
b) Price is completely insensitive to changes in quantity demanded.
c) When price changes by a certain %, quantity demanded changes by the same %.
d) The demand function is horizontal at the given price.

10. Which of the following is not true of a perfectly elastic demand function?

a) Consumers will purchase all of the good offered on the market at one price.
b) Consumers will not purchase any of the good at a higher price.
c) The slope of the function is equal to infinity.
d) It represents the demand function faced by an individual farmer.

11. If electricity demand is inelastic, and electric rates increase, which of the following is likely to occur?

a) Quantity demanded will fall a relatively large amount.
b) Quantity demanded will fall a relatively small amount.
c) Quantity demanded will rise in the short-run, but fall in the long-run.
d) Quantity demanded will fall in the short-run, but rise in the long-run.

12. Suppose the demand for meals at a medium-priced restaurant is elastic. If the management of the restaurant is considering raising prices, what should it expect to result?

a) A relatively large fall in quantity demanded.
b) A relatively large fall in demand.
c) A relatively small fall in quantity demanded.
d) A relatively small fall in demand.

13. Point elasticity is useful for which of the following situations?

a) The bookstore is considering doubling the price of notebooks and wants to know the sensitivity of quantity demanded.
b) A restaurant is considering lowering the price of its most expensive dishes by 50%.
c) An auto producer is interested in determining the response of consumers to the price of cars being lowered by $100.
d) An insurance company raises the health insurance premiums it charges by 30%.

14. The ______________ the price along a linear demand function, the ______________.

a) higher; more sensitive consumers are to a change in price
b) higher; the lower the coefficient of elasticity
c) lower; the more sensitive consumers are to a change in price
d) lower; the higher the coefficient of elasticity

15. An decrease in price will result in an increase in total revenue if:

a) the % change in quantity demanded is less than the % change in price.
b) the % change in quantity demanded is more than the % change in price.
c) demand is inelastic.
d) the consumer is operating along a linear demand function at a point at which the price is very low and the quantity demanded is very high.

16. An increase in price will result in an increase in total revenue if:

a) the % change in quantity demanded is less than the % change in price.
b) the % change in quantity demanded is more than the % change in price.
c) demand is elastic.
d) the consumer is operating along a linear demand function at a point at which the price is very high and the quantity demanded is very low.

17. An increase in price will result in no change in total revenue if:

a) the % change in price is large enough to cause quantity demanded to fall to zero.
b) the coefficient of elasticity is equal to zero.
c) the % change in quantity demanded is equal to the % change in price.
d) if the demand function is perfectly elastic.

18. If the demand for a good is ______________, the imposition of an excise tax on that good will result in consumers bearing a ______________ amount of the tax burden.

a) inelastic; small
b) represented by a vertical demand function; small
c) elastic: large
d) represented by a very flat demand function; small

19. If the demand for a good is inelastic, the consumer will bear:

a) a large part of the tax burden, since they have few alternatives.
b) a large part of the tax burden, because they are sensitive to changes in price.
c) a small part of the tax burden, since they have few alternatives.
d) a small part of the tax burden, because they are not sensitive to changes in price.

20. In the long-run elasticity is ______________ than in the short-run because ________________.

a) smaller; consumers have more time in which to make adjustments to price changes.
b) smaller; the % change is measured over a larger amount of time.
c) larger; consumers have more time in which to make adjustments to price changes.
d) larger; firms have more time to shift the burden of the tax forward to consumers.

21. If an airline is engaging in price discrimination it will:

a) raise fares for families going on vacation, since they have an elastic demand.
b) lower fares for families going on vacation, since they have an elastic demand.
c) raise fares for business travelers, since they have an elastic demand.
d) lowers fares for business travelers, since they have an inelastic demand.

22. Which of the following is a plausible reason that restaurants offer "Senior Citizen Discounts":

a) Senior citizens tend to have elastic demands for restaurant meals.
b) Senior citizens tend to have inelastic demands for restaurant meals.
c) Senior citizens are not very sensitive to changes in price.
d) Senior citizens are easily fooled by "come-ons" and are therefore frequently victims of price discrimination.

Chapter 6, The Elasticity of Demand

23. A good will tend to have an elastic demand if it exhibits which of the following characteristics:

a) It represents a small part of the consumer's income.
b) The good has many substitutes available.
c) It is addictive.
d) There is little time for the consumer to adjust to the price change.

24. A good will tend to have an inelastic demand if it exhibits which of the following characteristics:

a) The good has many substitutes.
b) The good is not addictive.
c) The good is a small part of the consumer's income.
d) There is a great deal of time for the consumer to adjust to the change in prices

25. If the consumer has a great deal of time to adjust to an increase in the price of gasoline, which of the following is correct:

a) Quantity demanded will be sensitive to a change in price.
b) The % change in quantity demanded will be quite small relative to the % change in price.
c) The % change in price will be quite large relative to the % change in quantity demanded.
d) Demand will tend to be unitary elastic as it is for most goods in the long-run.

26. Advocates of legalization or decriminalization of drugs argue that reducing the supply of drugs:

a) actually lowers the price of drugs along a relatively elastic demand function.
b) actually lowers the price of drugs along a relatively inelastic demand function.
c) has little effect on the quantity demanded for drugs since the demand for drugs is quite inelastic.
d) has little effect on the quantity demanded for drugs, since goods that are addictive tend to have elastic demands.

27. If the purchase of a good can be moved up or postponed:

a) it tends to exhibit a perfectly inelastic demand.
b) its demand function is vertical.
c) the % change in quantity demanded is less than the % change in price for the good.
d) the % change in quantity demanded is greater than the % change in price for the good.

28. Suppose a consumer's income increases from $30,000 to $33,000. As a result, the consumer increases the purchases of compact disks from 25 to 30 disks. What is the consumer's income elasticity of demand for compact disks?

a) 0.5
b) 1.0
c) 1.5
d) 2.0

29. Coffee and tea have:

a) positive income elasticities of demand with respect to each other.
b) negative income elasticities of demand with respect to each other.
c) a positive cross price elasticity of demand.
d) a negative cross price elasticity of demand.

30. Cereal and milk have:

a) positive income elasticities of demand with respect to each other.
b) negative income elasticities of demand with respect to each other.
c) a positive cross price elasticity of demand.
d) a negative cross price elasticity of demand.

ANSWER KEY

Exercises

1. percentage change, quantity demanded, percentage change, price
2. Arc
3. greater, less
4. elastic, inelastic
5. decreases
6. elastic
7. price discrimination, higher, lower
8. 1) Availability of substitutes, 2) cost of the good as a percentage of total income, and 3) the time period in question.
9. increase
10. complements
11. $3, 50 units
12. Supply curve shifts up by a vertical distance of $1. S2 passes through P = $2, Q = 0; and P = $4, Q = 50. The new equilibrium price is $3.75 (approximate), and the new equilibrium quantity is 42 units (approximate).
13. Producers pay $0.25 of the tax, while consumers pay $0.75 of the tax.
14. 0.78
15. inelastic

Review Questions

1. b) is the correct answer. The price elasticity of demand is defined as the sensitivity or responsiveness of the quantity demanded to a change in price.

2. a) is the correct answer. The reason for using relative or percentage measures is to obtain a consistent coefficient of elasticity, no matter what units are used to measure the quantity of the product being demanded at the various prices. Answer d) is incorrect because the initial size of the price and quantity are important. That is in fact why a relative measure is needed.

3. d) is the correct answer. The coefficient of elasticity is the % change in quantity demanded divided by the % change in price. Answer a) is the slope of the demand function, answer b) is the reciprocal of the slope, and answer c) is the reciprocal of the coefficient of elasticity.

4. b) is the correct answer. The % change in quantity demanded is 100/250 = 40%. The % change in price is 8/16 = 50%. 40%/50% = .8. This suggests that demand for movies is somewhat inelastic.

5. c) is the correct answer. The % change in quantity demanded is 2000/4000 = 50%. The % change in price is $10/$25 = 40%. Therefore, the price elasticity of demand is 50%/40% = 1.25.

6. c) is the correct answer. The % change in quantity demanded is 400/800 = 50%. The % change in price is $50/$125 = 40%. Therefore, the price elasticity of demand is 50%/40% = 1.25.

7. d) is the correct answer. The % change in quantity demanded is 600/400 = 150%. The % change in price is $4/$8 = 50%. The price elasticity of demand is 150%/50% = 3.

8. b) is the correct answer. We know from the definition of elasticity that the % change in quantity demanded desired by the car dealer is 20/40 = 50%. We must now solve the coefficient of elasticity formula for the change in price when the initial price is $20,000. The % change in price must be 50%, since the % change in quantity demanded is 50% and the coefficient of elasticity is 1. If X is our unknown, the new price, then we know that ($20,000 - X)/[(X + $20,000)/2] = 50%. So we simply solve this equation for X. X = $12,000.

9. a) is the correct answer. Along a perfectly inelastic demand function, quantity demanded does not change at all as price changes. A drug addict who is willing to pay any price(at least over some range) to obtain more of a drug is an example of an individual who might have a perfectly inelastic demand function.

10. c) is not true. While the coefficient of elasticity is equal to infinity, the slope of the perfectly elastic demand function is equal to zero. That is, the perfectly elastic demand function is horizontal. This points up the difference between elasticity and slope.

11. b) is the correct answer. If demand is inelastic, then an increase in price will cause quantity demanded to fall a relatively small amount. c) and d) are incorrect because elasticity generally becomes greater in the long-run.

12. a) is the correct answer. Since demand is elastic, the management should expect quantity demanded to fall a relatively large amount due to the rise in price. b) and d) are incorrect because elasticity refers to the sensitivity of quantity demanded, not demand, which refers to a shift in the entire demand function.

13. c) is the correct answer. Point elasticity is useful for <u>small</u> changes in price, such as a change in the price of autos by only $100. All of the other responses refer to relatively large changes for which arc elasticity would be more appropriate.

14. a) is the correct answer. The higher the price along a linear demand function, the greater the elasticity coefficient. The greater the elasticity coefficient, the more sensitive consumers are to a change in price.

15. b) is the correct answer. A decrease in price will result in an increase in total revenue if demand is elastic, that is if the % change in quantity demanded is greater than the % change in price.

16. a) is the correct answer. An increase in price will result in an increase in total revenue if demand is inelastic, that is, if the % change in quantity demanded is less than the % change in price.

17. c) is the correct answer. An increase or decrease in price will result in no change in total revenue if the price elasticity is equal to 1(unitary elasticity). In order to have unitary elasticity, the % change in quantity demanded must be equal to the % change in price.

18. d) is the correct answer. Consumers will pay a small part of the tax burden if demand is elastic and a large part of the tax burden if demand is inelastic. Demand is relatively elastic if it is represented by a flat demand function.

19. a) is the correct answer. If demand is inelastic, it is frequently because there are few substitutes and therefore consumers have few alternatives to purchasing the good. Under these circumstances, firms can shift the tax burden forward to consumers.

20. c) is the correct answer. The longer the period of time over which elasticity is measured, the more of a chance consumers have to adjust, for example search for substitutes, and therefore the greater the sensitivity to a change in price.

21. b) is the correct answer. In order to increase total revenue, a firm which is engaging in price discrimination will raise prices to consumers with inelastic demands and lower prices to consumers with elastic demands. Vacationers tend to have elastic demands for airline tickets since they are able to shop around and need not buy a ticket on short notice as business travelers frequently must.

22. a) is the correct answer. Senior citizen discounts are an example of price discrimination.

Prices are lower for senior citizens because they tend to have a more elastic demand for meals in restaurants. This is because they are frequently retired and therefore have time to search for the best price.

23. b) is the correct answer. If there are many substitutes available for a good, then an increase in the price of that good causes consumers to buy one of the substitutes. Thus, consumers are very sensitive to changes in price in this case.

24. c) is the correct answer. If a good is a small part of the consumer's income, a given percentage change in its price is not very important to the consumer. On the other hand, if the good is a large part of the consumer's budget, such as housing, then the consumer will consider a price change to be very important and quantity demanded will be very sensitive to a change in price.

25. a) is the correct answer. If the consumer has a great deal of time to adjust to an increase in the price of gasoline, the consumer will be able to find substitutes and conserve. In general, the longer the period of time over which elasticity is measured, the greater the coefficient of elasticity for a particular good.

26. c) is the correct answer. Advocates of legalization of drugs argue that reducing supply, which drives up price, has little effect on quantity demanded, since drugs exhibit inelastic demands.

27. d) is the correct answer. If a good is durable, that is if its purchase can be moved up or postponed, then it exhibits an elastic demand. If the good exhibits an elastic demand, the % change in quantity demanded is greater than the % change in price.

28. d) is the correct answer. The income elasticity of demand is the % change in quantity demanded divided by the % change in income. In this case, the % change in quantity demanded is 20% and the % change in income is 10%. Therefore, income elasticity is 2.0.

29. c) is the correct answer. If coffee and tea are substitutes, the cross price elasticity of demand is positive. For example, if the price of coffee rises, the quantity demanded for tea rises, as consumers substitute tea for coffee.

30. d) is the correct answer. If cereal and milk are complements, the cross price elasticity of demand is negative. For example, an increase in the price of milk will result in a decrease in the quantity demanded for cereal, since it is now more expensive to consume cereal.

CHAPTER 7
THE THEORY OF CONSUMER BEHAVIOR

OVERVIEW

In this chapter we examine the consumer's decision-making problem, and develop an explanation for why demand curves are downward sloping. We also consider how such factors as information costs and mobility costs influence the decision making process.

The central assumption of the theory of consumer behavior is that individuals seek to maximize their well being, in part, through the consumption of goods and services. The benefits, or satisfaction, that individuals receive from consumption is referred to as utility. According to the theory of consumer behavior, individuals consume a combination of goods and services that maximizes their total utility. However, the maximum level of utility achievable by an individual is usually constrained by her budget--the amount of money she has available to spend, and the prices of goods and services.

In order to be able to identify the utility maximizing combination of goods for an individual, it is necessary to distinguish between total utility and marginal utility. Marginal utility refers to the additional utility received from consuming one more unit of a good. This can be thought of as the marginal benefit from consumption. The price of an additional unit of a good is the marginal cost of consumption. Hence, the consumer compares marginal benefits and marginal costs in deciding which goods to consume. By considering the ratio of marginal utility to price, one can determine the marginal benefits per dollar spent on each good. Comparing these ratios across all available goods tells the consumer which goods to consume. This leads logically to the rule for utility maximization: consume the combination of goods for which MU/P is equal across all goods consumed.

The fact that demand curves are downward sloping can be shown by considering the effect of a decrease in the price of a good, ceteris paribus. Assuming that the consumer was initially in equilibrium, MU/P would now be greater for the good in question. Hence, the consumer will consume more of the good (and possibly others) to once again reach equilibrium. This adjustment process can be decomposed into two parts--the substitution effect and the income effect.

According to the substitution effect, a decrease in the price of a good causes its relative price to fall. Hence, consumers will now substitute more of the good for other, relatively more expensive goods. The income effect refers to the effect of a price change on the consumer's total purchasing power. Ceteris paribus, a decrease in the price of a good causes total purchasing power to increase. Thus, is the price of a good falls, a consumer will react to the price change by consuming more of the good (and possibly other goods as well).

In practice, consumers' decisions are influenced by more than simply the market prices of the goods and services they consume. In particular, transactions costs, such information costs, mobility costs, and decision-making costs all increase the full opportunity cost of consumption.

KEY GRAPHS AND TERMS

Graphs

Figure 1 in the text illustrates graphically the difference between total utility and marginal utility. Note even as marginal utility declines, at least up to a point, total utility continues to increase. Figure 2, which depicts Jane's demand curve for sky diving jumps, once again illustrates the law of demand--price and quantity demanded are inversely related.

Terms

UTILITY
MARGINAL UTILITY
LAW OF DIMINISHING MARGINAL UTILITY
MARGINAL UTILITY PER DOLLAR
CONSUMER DECISION MAKING RULE
CONSUMER EQUILIBRIUM
SUBSTITUTION EFFECT
INCOME EFFECT
TRANSACTIONS COSTS
INFORMATION COSTS
MOBILITY COSTS
DECISION-MAKING COSTS

EXERCISES

1. _________________ _________________ refers to the additional benefit a consumer receives from consuming one more unit of a good or service.

2. When the price of a good falls, the _________________ _________________ prompts a consumer to buy more since its relative price is now lower, while the _________________ _________________ prompts him to buy more because of the resulting increase in purchasing power.

3. Transactions costs include _________________ costs, _________________ costs, and _________________-_________________ costs.

4. Assume that a consumer has $46 in total income and that he is buying only two goods, X and Y. Utilizing the information in the following table, complete the table and answer questions 5 - 7.

GOOD X				GOOD Y			
# of Units	TUx	MUx	MUx/Px	# of Units	TUy	MUy	MUy/Py
1	60	_____	_____	1	100	_____	_____
2	80	_____	_____	2	180	_____	_____
3	98	_____	_____	3	252	_____	_____
4	112	_____	_____	4	312	_____	_____
5	124	_____	_____	5	360	_____	_____
6	126	_____	_____	6	396	_____	_____

5. Initially, if the price of X is $2 per unit and the price of Y is $12 per unit, how much X will this consumer purchase? _____. How much Y? _____.

6. Assume that the price of Y falls to $6 per unit. Now how much X will the consumer purchase? _____. How much Y? _____.

7. Using the information in questions 5 and 6, plot the demand curve for good Y in the figure below.

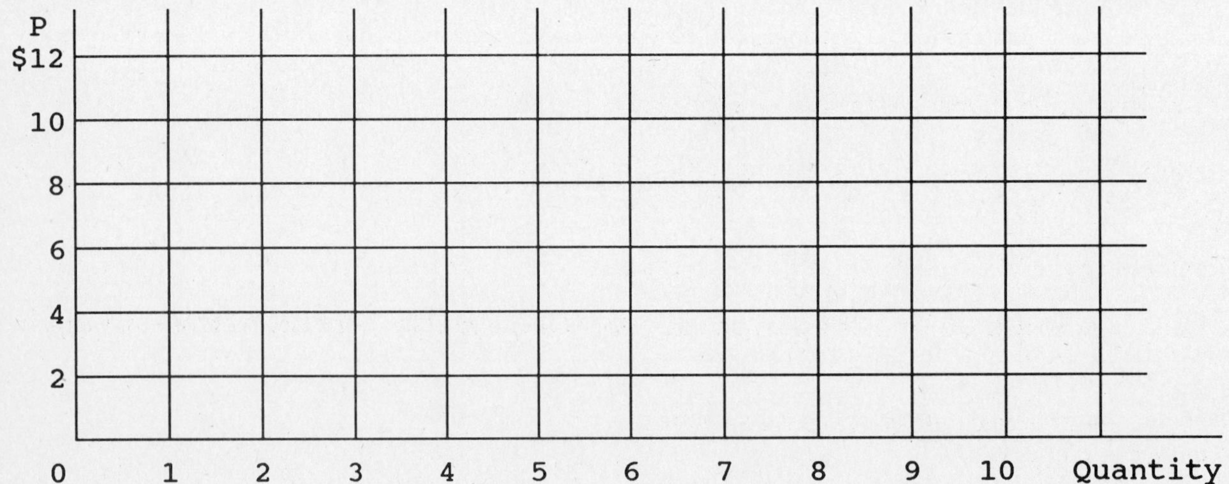

Chapter 7, The Theory of Consumer Behavior

REVIEW QUESTIONS

1. Consumers seek to ______________ utility, subject to ______________.

a) equalize; a fixed amount of total utility
b) equalize; a limited amount of income
c) maximize; a limited amount of income
d) maximize; a limited amount of marginal utility

2. Suppose we say that Individual A says she obtains 20 units of utility from the consumption of one slice of pizza and Individual B says he obtains 25 units of total utility from one slice of pizza. Which of the following is a correct statement?

a) Individual B enjoys pizza more than Individual A.
b) Individual B is willing to pay more for one more slice of pizza than Individual A.
c) Individual A has probably eaten more slices of pizza than Individual B.
d) We cannot compare Individuals A and B because utility is subjective.

3. Marginal Utility is defined correctly by which of the following:

a) The change in total utility due to the consumption of one more unit of a good.
b) The utility due to the consumption of a certain number of units of a good.
c) Total utility divided by the total number of units consumed.
d) That measure of utility which is not subjective.

Use the following table answer questions 4 - 6.

Number of Compact Disks	Total Utility	Marginal Utility
0	0	----
1	15	_____
2	_____	13
3	35	_____

4. What is the marginal utility of the first compact disk?

a) It cannot be determined, since utility is subjective.
b) 13 units of utility.
c) 15 units of utility.
d) 28 units of utility.

5. Referring to the table from the previous question, what is the total utility associated with the consumption of two compact disks?

a) It cannot be determined, since utility is subjective.
b) 13 units of utility.
c) 15 units of utility.
d) 28 units of utility.

6. What is the marginal utility of consuming the third compact disk?

a) 35 units of utility.
b) 28 units of utility.
c) 15 units of utility.
d) 7 units of utility.

7. Which of the following is a correct statement of the Law of Diminishing Marginal Utility?

a) As an individual consumes more of a good, the extra utility associated with each extra unit of the good falls.
b) As an individual consumes more and more of a good, at some point, total utility diminishes.
c) As units of a variable input are added to units of a fixed input, additions to total utility fall.
d) As less of a good is consumed, marginal utility diminishes for that good.

8. Which of the following is not true?

a) The Law of Diminishing Marginal Utility is a "law" because it is considered to be such an accurate representation of consumer behavior that the Congress has made it part of the U.S. legal system.
b) The Law of Diminishing Marginal Utility is a "law" because it is accepted by economists as a generalization about consumer preferences.
c) The Law of Diminishing Marginal Utility is based on the premise that consumers have a "hierarchy of wants" which they want to satisfy.
d) In general, the first unit of a good that consumers buy is used to satisfy their most important wants.

9. The market price of a good:

a) is usually higher than consumers are willing to pay for the last unit of the good, due to the Law of Diminishing Marginal Utility.
b) represents the opportunity cost of consumption of the good for consumers.
c) is not useful in utility analysis, since utility is a subjective concept and price is not.
d) is low if consumers derive little total utility from consumption of the good.

10. Consider the following hypothetical numerical example:

	Personal Computers	Compact Disk Players
Price	$1200	$200
MU	2400 units	600 units

What should the consumer do in this case to maximize total utility?

a) Buy more personal computers, since marginal utility per dollar is higher for PC's than it is for CD players.
b) Buy more CD players, since marginal utility per dollar is higher for CD players than it is for PC's.
c) Buy more personal computers, since marginal utility is higher for PC's than it is for CD players.
d) Lower the price of personal computers.

11. Referring to the information in the previous question, which of the following changes will occur as the consumer adjusts her consumption bundle to maximize total utility?

a) The price of personal computers will rise.
b) The price of CD players will rise.
c) The marginal utility of personal computers will rise.
d) The marginal utility of CD players will rise.

12. Again referring to the information given in the two previous questions, which of the following changes will occur as the consumer adjusts her consumption bundle to maximize total utility?

a) The price of personal computers will fall.
b) The price of CD players will fall.
c) The marginal utility of personal computers will fall.
d) The marginal utility of CD players will fall.

13. Consider the following hypothetical numerical example:

	Compact Disks	Tapes
Price	$12	$7
MU	24 units	14 units

What should the consumer do to maximize total utility?

a) Buy more compact disks.
b) Buy more tapes.
c) Raise the price of tapes.
d) Nothing; the consumer is already in equilibrium.

14. Referring to the information given in the previous question, suppose the price of compact disks falls to $10, due to improvements in the technology for producing them. What should the consumer do to maximize total utility?

a) Buy more compact disks.
b) Buy more tapes.
c) Raise the price of tapes.
d) Nothing; the consumer is already in equilibrium.

15. Referring to the information given in the previous two questions, what will occur as the consumer adjusts to maximize total utility at the new price of compact disks?

a) The marginal utility of tapes will fall.
b) The marginal utility of compact disks will fall.
c) The consumer's total utility will fall.
d) The price of tapes will rise.

16. Referring to the information from the three previous questions, which of the following will occur as the consumer adjusts to maximize total utility at the new price of compact disks?

a) The marginal utility of tapes will rise.
b) The marginal utility of compact disks will rise.
c) The consumer's total utility will fall.
d) The price of tapes will rise.

17. Which of the following statements is true when the consumer is in utility-maximizing equilibrium?

a) The marginal utility of the last dollar spent is maximized.
b) The prices of the goods in question must be equal.
c) The total utility the consumer receives from every good consumed must be the same for all goods.
d) The marginal utility of the last dollar spent must be the same for all goods the consumer buys.

18. Which of the following best describes the Income Effect?

a) As the price of a good rises, the consumer's real income rises.
b) As the price of a good rises, the consumer's purchasing power falls.
c) As the price of at least one good rises, the consumer will be able to buy more of all other goods, due to a rise in the consumer's purchasing power.
d) As the price of at least one good falls, the consumer will not be able to buy as much of all other goods, due to a decline in the consumer's purchasing power.

19. The market price of buying a textbook at the student bookstore is:

a) less than the full opportunity cost of the book.
b) more than the full opportunity cost of the book.
c) equal to the full opportunity cost of the book.
d) none of the above--price has nothing to do with opportunity cost.

20. Suppose a service station is having a sale on gasoline, charging $0.90 a gallon. Suppose there is a line of consumers waiting to purchase gas at the station and a you calculate that it will take you half an hour to fill your ten-gallon tank. Suppose a second service station is charging $1.10 per gallon and you can immediately fill your tank there, with no wait. If you calculate the opportunity cost of your time to be $10 per hour, what should you do?

a) Buy gas at the lower-priced station, since you save $2.00.
b) Buy gas at the higher-priced station.
c) Fill half of your tank at the higher priced station and half at the lower priced station.
d) Fill one-third of your tank at the lower priced station and two-thirds at the higher priced station.

21. Use the information from the previous question, but suppose the sale price of gasoline at the lower priced station is $0.60 per gallon. In this case, as a rational consumer, you would do which of the following?

a) Buy gas at the lower-priced station.
b) Buy gas at the higher-priced station.
c) Fill half of your tank at the higher priced station and half at the lower priced station.
d) You would be indifferent between the two stations.

22. Consumers are not fully informed about many of the products they buy. This is rational behavior because:

a) unless the product is expensive, the cost of acquiring the additional information may not be worth the additional time.
b) under competitive conditions consumers need not be fully informed, since competition will ensure that the products will be of uniform quality.
c) transactions costs and information costs are not the same.
d) consumers cannot use the same benefit-cost calculation that they apply to the goods themselves for choices about information costs.

23. Which of the following is not true?

a) The time needed for travel to a market is included in transactions costs.
b) Time is considered to be a scarce good.
c) The cost of gasoline needed to drive to buy groceries is not included in transactions costs, since the gasoline is purchased in a separate market.
d) The cost of making a decision is included in transactions cost.

24. Which of the following statements is correct with respect to charitable contributions?

a) They are different from the purchase of a consumer good in that the person making the contribution receives no benefits.
b) While the consumer receives satisfaction from making a charitable contribution, this is not the same as the satisfaction received from the purchase of a consumer good.
c) The individual making the contribution compares the marginal benefit of the contribution to its marginal cost.
d) The rational consumer will make the donation even if the marginal benefit of the contribution to the contributor is less than the marginal cost to the contributor.

25. Under which of the following circumstances will a private contribution be made?

a) When the marginal utility of the contribution is maximized.
b) When the marginal utility of a dollar spent on the contribution is greater than the cost of the dollar itself.
c) When the marginal utility of the contribution is greater to the recipients than it is to the donor.
d) When the recipients make a sacrifice at least equal to the cost of the contribution.

26. Which of the following arguments can be made to justify government assistance rather than private contributions to alleviate problems of poverty?

a) Taxpayers feel they have a great deal of control over the causes to which their payments go.
b) The beneficiaries of the government payments are viewed as making considerable sacrifice themselves.
c) The government is in a position to identify the individuals who are in the greatest need of assistance.
d) The distribution of funds through a single distribution point makes it impossible to compare the benefits of providing assistance to alternative groups.

REVIEW QUESTIONS: APPENDIX

27. If utility is held constant and the consumer gets gets more or one good, the amount of the other good the consumer is willing to sacrifice:

a) becomes larger and larger.
b) becomes smaller amd smaller.
c) remains the same if total utility is held constant.
d) cannot be determined, since utility is a subjective concept.

28. Which of the following is not true? At the point of tangency between the budget constraint and the indifference curve:

a) the consumer has acheived the highest possible level of total utility, given the budget constraint.
b) the marginal utilities of the two goods are equal.
c) the marginal rate of substitution equals the price ratio.
d) the ratio of the marginal utilities equals the price ratio.

29. An indifference curve is negatively-sloped because:

a) utility is a subjective concept.
b) as the consumer gets more and more of one good, the consumer is willing to sacrifice less and less of the other good.
c) in order to remain on the same level of utility, if an individual gets more of one good, he must sacrifice some of the other good.
d) marginal utility is constant along an indifference curve and increases in the consumption of one good cause the price of that good to fall.

30. Consider an indifference curve drawn for movies and pizzas. Which of the following statements is not true about this indifference curve?

a) As an individual consumes more pizzas, the amount of movies the consumer is willing to give up for an additional pizza increases.
b) If the individual consumes more pizzas, the amount of movies consumed must fall if the consumer is to stay on the same indifference curve.
c) The indifference curve will be convex to the origin, that is, bowed-out toward the origin.
d) If the consumer gets more of both movies and pizzas, total utility will increase, but the consumer will be on a new indifference curve that is farther from the origin than the orignal indifference curve.

31. Which of the following is not true?

The marginal rate of substitution:
a) is the ratio of the marginal utilities of the two goods.
b) is the rate at which the consumer is willing to trade one good for another.
c) is the slope of the indifference curve.
d) is constant along an indifference curve.

32. The slope of the budget constraint:

a) changes as the marginal rate of substitution changes.
b) is the ratio of the prices of the two goods.
c) is the ratio of the budget to total utility.
d) equals one, since the consumer can purchase any combination along the budget constraint.

Chapter 7, The Theory of Consumer Behavior

ANSWER KEY

Exercises

1. marginal utility
2. substitution effect, income effect
3. information, mobility, decision-making
4.

GOOD X

# of Units	TUx	MUx	MUx/Px
1	60	60	30
2	80	20	10
3	98	18	9
4	112	14	7
5	124	12	6
6	126	2	1

GOOD Y

# of Units	TUy	MUy	MUy/Py
1	100	100	8.33
2	180	80	6.67
3	252	72	6
4	312	60	5
5	360	48	4
6	396	36	3

5. 5 units of X, 3 units of Y
6. 5 units of X, 6 units of Y
7. The demand curve will pass through the points P = $12, Q = 3 and P = $6, Q = 6.

Review Questions

1. c) is the correct answer. Consumers seek to maximize total utility subject to a limited amount of resources. Usually this constraint is reflected in a limited amount of income.

2. d) is the correct answer. Economists say we "cannot make interpersonal comparisons of utility." This means that the utility measurement is subjective and is relevant for only one individual. In other words, Individual A's unit of utility is not the same as Individual B's.

3. a) is the correct answer. Marginal utility is the change in total utility due to the consumption of one more unit of a good. It is the change in total utility due to the a change in consumption of one more unit of a good. b) defines total utility. All utility measures are subjective.

4. c) is the correct answer. Marginal utility is the change in total utility due the consumption of one more compact disk. In this case, total utility changes from 0 units of utility to 15 units of utility, a difference of 15 units.

5. d) is the correct answer. Total utility in this case is the amount of utility obtained from the consumption of 2 compact disks. It is also the sum of the marginal utilities. We know that the marginal utility of the first compact disk is 15 units of utility. If the marginal utility of consuming the second compact disk is 13 units of utility, then the sum, 15 + 13 = 28 units of utility is the total utility associated with consuming 2 compact disks.

6. d) is the correct answer. The marginal utility of the third compact disk is the difference in total utility of consuming the second and third unit. This is 35 - 28 = 7 additional units of utility.

7. a) is the correct statement of the Law of Diminishing Marginal Utility. As more of a good is consumed, the additional utility associated with additional units of the good(the marginal utility) falls.

8. a) is the statement which is not true. b) is the actual reason that the Law of Diminishing Marginal Utility is considered a "law."

9. b) is the correct answer. The market price of a good is the opportunity cost of the consumption of the good, because it represents the amount of other goods the consumer will have to give up. d) is incorrect, because price is related to marginal utility, not total utility--as the text's example of water points out.

10. b) is the correct answer. The rule the consumer uses to maximize total utility is to set marginal utility per dollar higher for all goods. If MU per dollar is higher for CD players than it is for other goods, then the consumer should substitute CD players for other goods. Thus, the consumer should buy more CD players to maximize total utility.

11. Since the consumer is buying less personal computers to maximize utility, the marginal utility of an additional PC will rise. This helps to move the consumer to the equilibrium in which marginal utility per dollar is the same for both goods.

12. Since the consumer is buying more CD players, the marginal utility of an additional CD player will fall. Combined with the effect described in the previous question, the consumer moves in the direction of equilibrium by purchasing more CD players and less PCs.

13. d) is the correct answer. Since MU per dollar is the same for both goods, the consumer is already in equilibrium, so the consumer can make no changes which will increase total utility.

14. a) is the correct answer. The fall in the price of compact disks causes the consumer to move out of equilibrium, and the consumer must make some adjustments to move back into equilibrium. In this case, the MU per dollar is now greater for compact disks than it is for tapes. So the consumer should buy more disks and less tapes.

15. b) is the correct answer. As the consumer buys more compact disks, the marginal utility of CDs will fall.

16. a) is the correct answer. As the consumer buys more compact disks, she must buy less tapes. As less tapes are consumed, the marginal utility of tapes rises. Combined with the falling marginal utility of CDs, this change moves to the consumer to a new utility-maximizing equilibrium.

17. d) is the correct answer. The marginal utility of the last dollar spent must the same for all goods. This is equivalent to saying that the marginal utility per dollar is the same for all goods.

18. b) is the correct answer. The Income Effect suggests that if there is an increase in the price of a good, the consumer's real income will fall. This means that the consumer will buy less of the good for which the price has risen, and less of other goods as well.

19. a) is the correct answer. Due to the existence of transactions costs, the full opportunity cost of buying the book is more than the price of the book. For example, the cost time a student would have to take to go to the bookstore and stand in line to purchase the book is an example of a transaction cost that is over and above the price of the textbook.

20. b) is the correct answer. You should buy gas at the higher price station. If you buy gas at the lower priced station, you will save $0.20/gallon times 10 gallons = $2.00. But you will lose one-half hour, which is worth $5.00 to you at an opportunity cost of time of $10.00 per hour. Therefore, you would actually lose $3.00 if you bought gas at the lower priced station.

21. d) is the correct answer. You would save $5.00 by purchasing gas at the lower priced station, but you would lose $5.00 in transaction costs. Therefore, you would be indifferent between the two stations.

22. a) is the correct answer. Consumers are not fully informed about many of the products they buy, because the cost of acquiring the additional information is greater than the perceived benefit.

23. c) is the answer which is not true. The cost of gasoline needed to drive to the grocery store would be included in transactions costs, as would the time required to go to the grocery.

24. c) is simply a statement of what the contributor will do when determining whether to make a contribution or how much to contribute. If the marginal benefit of the contribution is greater than the marginal cost of the contribution, then the individual will make the contribution.

25. b) is the correct answer. When making contributions, consumers behave just as they do when purchasing any consumer good. If the

marginal utility of the contribution is greater than the opportunity cost of the contribution, then the contribution will be made.

26. c) is the correct answer. The government may have more information available to it about which groups are most in need of assistance and thus may have an advantage over private individuals in the distribution of assistance.

27. b) is the correct answer. If utility is held constant, as it is along an indifference curve, and the consumer gets more and more of one good, the consumer will be willing to give up less and less of the other good. As an individual receives more of one good, additional units of that good are worth less to the consumer, it terms of other goods.

28. b) is not true. The marginal utilities need not be equal at the tangency between the budget constraint and the indifference curve, consumer equilibrium. The ratio of the marginal utilities to the prices must be the same for both goods, but the marginal utilities would be equal only if the prices of the two goods were exactly the same.

29. c) is the correct answer. If the consumer is to remain on the same level of total utility, an increase in the consumption of one good must be accompanied by a reduction in the consumption of the other good. If this were not so, total utility would increase, since it is assumed that more is preferred to less.

30. a) is the answer that is not true. In order for this statement to be true, it would have to read: "... the amount of movies the consumer would be willing to give up for an additional pizza decreases.

31. d) is the answer that is not true. As we move along an indifference curve, the MRS usually changes. In the text's example of jeans and shirts, as the consumer gets more jeans, the amount of shirts she is willing to sacrifice for one more pair of jeans falls.

32. b) is the correct answer. The slope of the budget constraint is the ratio of the prices of the two goods.

CHAPTER 8
ENTREPRENEURIAL BEHAVIOR

OVERVIEW

In this chapter we begin our analysis of the decision making of firms. We start by discussing alternative methods that can be used to categorize firms. We then go on to define the concept of profit as it is used in economic analysis. We conclude the chapter with a discussion of the short-run versus the long run in the context of production costs.

In order to analyze the behavior of firms, it is necessary to have some method we can use to group firms together, and thereby simplify the problem somewhat. The three methods considered here are grouping firms 1) by the industry in which they operate, 2) according to their legal structure--sole proprietorship, partnership or corporation--and 3) according to the structure of the market in which they operate. Of these three methods, the last is most useful for understanding how firms answer such questions how much output to produce and what price to charge.

Market structure is closely related to the degree of competition in the market. Highly competitive markets are referred to as perfectly competitive. At the other extreme we can have that case where there is only one firm in the market, and hence no competition. This situation is referred to as monopoly. Between these two extremes are monopolistic competition and oligopoly.

An overriding assumption of the analysis in this and subsequent chapters is that firms are in business to make a profit, and that the objective of each firm is to maximize the amount of profit it earns. However, there is an important distinction between the usual definition of profit--accounting profit--and the economist's definition of profit--economic profit. This distinction arises from the way in which explicit and implicit costs are treated in each case. Explicit costs are out-of-pocket expenses such as payments for raw materials and labor. Implicit costs are opportunity costs for which no payment is made, such as rent foregone by an entrepreneur who uses a building they own in their own business.

Accounting profit is the difference between total revenues and explicit costs. Implicit costs are considered in the calculation of accounting profit. Economic profit, on the other hand, is calculated as the difference between total revenues and total economic costs, where total economic costs are the sum of explicit costs and implicit costs including a normal profit--the amount of money just sufficient to keep the owner/entrepreneur in business. Note that, as such, economic profit is that amount of revenue that is left over after the full opportunity costs of production have been accounted for.

The firm must make a number of different decisions in the course of attempting to maximize profits. As we shall see in subsequent chapters, it is often convenient to group decision on the basis of the time frame in which they take place. In particular, the length of time in question is an important determinant of the range choices available to the firm.

For convenience, decisions can be grouped according to whether they are short-run decisions or long-run decisions. A short run decision involves a constraint that limits the decision makers choices. Generally, the constraint takes the form of one or more factors of production (inputs) that are fixed in amount. The fixed factor is usually capital and/or technology. Long-run decisions, on the other hand, are not constrained by any of the inputs employed by the firm. Instead, the firm is free to vary the levels of all of the inputs it uses in its efforts to minimize production costs.

KEY GRAPHS AND TERMS

Graphs

There are no new graphs in the chapter.

Terms

ENTREPRENEUR
INDUSTRY
SOLE PROPRIETORSHIP
FINANCIAL CAPITAL
PARTNERSHIP
CORPORATION
SHARES OF STOCK
DIVIDENDS
RETAINED EARNINGS
BOND

MATURITY
SECURITY
SECURITIES MARKETS
MARKET STRUCTURE
PROFIT
COSTS OF PRODUCTION
EXPLICIT COSTS
IMPLICIT COSTS
DEPRECIATION
NORMAL PROFIT
ECONOMIC PROFIT
ACCOUNTING PROFIT
NATIONAL INCOME
LONG-RUN DECISION
SHORT-RUN DECISION
SUNK COST
LABOR-INTENSIVE PRODUCTION TECHNIQUES
"CAPITAL" INTENSIVE PRODUCTION TECHNIQUES

EXERCISES

1. A person who organizes, manages, and assumes the risks of a business enterprise is called an _______________.

2. Sole proprietorships and partnerships are similar to the extent that the owners of each face _______________ liability. In contrast, the owners of a corporation face _______________ liability.

3. An advantage of the corporate form of business organization is the corporation's ability to obtain _______________ capital. List the three sources from which a corporation can acquire funds to support growth and expansion. ____
____

4. The portion of a firm's profits that is reinvested in the business is called _______________ _______________.

5. The length of time for which a bond is issued is called its _______________.

6. An industry consisting of a single firm is called a _______________.

7. In economic analysis it is generally assumed that the objective of all firms is to _______________ _______________.

8. The payment for raw materials and rent on a building are examples of _______________ costs. The interest foregone on retained earnings that are invested in a firm are an example of _______________ costs. The total costs of production represent the full _______________ costs of production and are equal to _______________ plus _______________ costs.

9. The minimum payment required to compensate an entrepreneur for her risk-taking and the use of her financial capital is called _______________ _______________.

10. _______________ profit is the difference between total revenue and total explicit costs, while _______________ profit is the difference between total revenue and the sum of explicit and implicit costs.

11. _______________ _______________ is the total annual income paid to all owners of resources; it is the sum of _______________, _______________, _______________, and _______________.

12. In the ________________ ________________, at least one of the firm's productive inputs in fixed in amount, while in the ________________ ________________ all inputs are variable.

13. Costs that have been incurred in the past and can no longer be recovered are called ________________ ________________.

14. Florence is considering going into business for herself, and has developed the following estimates of monthly costs and revenues to aid her in her decision making process. She has decided to house the business in a building that she already owns, although she could rent the building to someone else for $1,000 per month. Estimated payment for utilities (electricity, natural gas, water, and telephone) are $475 per month. She will hire one employee at a total cost of $1,100 per month. Inventory is estimated to cost $2,800 per month. Finally, Florence earns $3,000 a month in her current job.

a. How much monthly revenue would Florence have to take in to earn a normal profit? __________

b. Assume that Florence has estimated her monthly revenue to be $9,000. In this case, Florence would earn an accounting profit (loss) of ________________, and an economic profit (loss) of ________________.

c. Assume instead that Florence does not own a building, and that she will have to rent a building for $1,000 per month (all other estimates remain the same). In this case (assuming estimated monthly revenue is still $9,000), Florence would earn an accounting profit (loss) of ________________, and an economic profit (loss) of ________________.

REVIEW QUESTIONS

1. Which of the following is not true?

a) There is an element of riskiness that is present in consumption decisions, but absent in production decisions.
b) Firms take advantage of the benefits of specialization.
c) Both firms and consumers choose among the available alternatives to maximize well-being.
d) Firms exist mainly to maximize profit.

2. Which of the following is true of the risk that firms must incur in their production decisions?

a) It is smaller than the risk incurred by consumers, since firms usually have much greater financial assets available than consumers.
b) It is due in part to the fact that firms must incur costs before they generate revenue.
c) It generally disappears after the firm becomes well-established in an industry.
d) It is usually not incurred by entrepreneurs, who only organize and manage the firm.

3. Which of the following is not true?

a) A set of firms which are grouped according to the products they produce is called an industry.
b) The firms in an industry face similar market conditions.
c) The firms in an industry generally use similar production processes.
d) Based on employment, the services industries in the U.S. have been shrinking over the last thirty years.

4. Which of the following is not a characteristic of sole proprietorships?

a) Unlimited liability for the owner
b) Control over all business decisions
c) Fairly easy access to financial capital
d) Small and numerous firms

5. Why do sole proprietorships tend to be small?

a) It is easy for the proprietorship to raise financial capital, so there is no reason to grow.
b) Sole proprietors are usually not in business to make a profit as corporations and partnerships are.
c) The proprietor is responsible for all the debts incurred by the firm.
d) The sole proprietorship can issue common stock to raise financial capital so large size is not necessary.

6. Which of the following is not true of a partnership?

a) Each partner is responsible only for the money he or she has invested in the partnership.
b) It is usually easier for a partnership to raise financial capital than it is for a proprietorship.
c) Decision-making is more complicated than for a proprietorship.
d) Partnerships tend to be larger than proprietorships.

7. Suppose you own common stock in Mastodon, Inc. and it goes out of business. Which of the following situations is true?

a) You will receive a payment for the value of your stock before any of the other creditors of Mastodon are paid off.
b) You are responsible for the debts incurred by the partners in Mastodon, but not any of the other debts of the firm.
c) You are responsible only for the value of the common stock you own in Mastodon.
d) You are liable to sued by the creditors of Mastodon for the funds they are owed by Mastodon.

8. Which of the following is not an important source of financial capital for a corporation?

a) The sale of stock by the firm.
b) The retained earnings of the firm.
c) Borrowing from financial institutions.
d) The personal assets of the managers.

9. Which of the following is not true?

a) According to their charter, corporations must return all of their profits to the owners of common stock in the form of dividends.
b) The owners of common stock gain not only from the payment of dividends, but also from the possibility that their ownership shares will appreciate in value.
c) Owners of common stock participate in the decisions of the firm only very indirectly.
d) If retained earnings are high, the stockholders may benefit from the increase in the price of their common stock.

10. Which of following is true about corporate borrowing?

a) Corporations usually find it less expensive to borrow from a financial institution than to borrow by issuing corporate bonds.
b) Corporations usually borrow from financial institutions for long-term needs.
c) The secondary market allows corporations to borrow less expensively than they otherwise could.
d) The owner of a bond can legally force a corporation to repay the face value of a bond before it matures.

11. Which of the following is not true?

a) Most of the average corporation's borrowed funds are obtained by issuing bonds.
b) The primary market refers to the sale of new securities.
c) A market structure which is characterized by a competitive industry consists of a few large firms.
d) A monopoly is an industry consisting of only one firm.

12. Which of the following is not true?

a) Economic profit is the difference between total revenue and the full opportunity cost of all the resources used in production.
b) Economic profit is the difference between total revenue and explicit costs.
c) Profit is the payment to the resources owned by the firm.
d) The owners of a firm must be compensated for the use of their funds, because those funds have alternative uses.

13. Which of the following is an example of an explicit cost?

a) The wages a proprietor could have made by working as an employee of a large firm.
b) The income that could have been earned in alternative uses by the resources owned by the firm.
c) The payment of wages by the firm.
d) The normal profit earned by a firm.

14. Which of the following is an example of an implicit cost?

a) The interest that could have been made on retained earnings that are used by the firm to finance expansion.
b) The payment of rent by the firm for the building in which it is housed.
c) The interest payment made by the firm for funds borrowed from a bank.
d) The payment of wages by the firm.

15. Which of the following is the best example of depreciation?

a) An individual worker becoming tired at the end of an eight-hour work-day.
b) The notion that individuals obtain less utility from paying taxes than from giving to charitable organizations.
c) A truck which is used by a pizzeria to make deliveries being worth less at the end of the year than at the beginning.
d) A rise in prices depreciating the value of consumers' real income.

16. Suppose that a sole proprietorship is earning total revenues of $100,000 and is incurring explicit costs of $75,000. If the owner could work for another company for $30,000 a year, we would conclude that:

a) the firm is incurring an economic loss.
b) implicit costs are $25,000
c) the total economic costs are $100,000.
d) the individual is earning an economic profit of $25,000.

17. If the economic profits for a firm are positive, but small, which of the following is true?

a) accounting profits could be zero or negative.
b) the firm will leave the industry, since its resources could earn more elsewhere.
c) the resources owned by the firm are earning more than their opportunity costs.
d) economic costs are less than accounting costs.

18. Which of the following is not true?

a) Economic costs include the opportunity costs of the resources owned by the firm.
b) Accounting costs include only explicit costs.
c) Economic profit will always be less than accounting profit if the firm's resources have any opportunity costs.
d) Accounting profit is equal to total revenue less implicit costs.

19. To economists, the main difference between the short-run and the long-run is that:

a) in the short-run all inputs are fixed, while in the long-run all inputs are variable.
b) in the short-run the firm varies all of its inputs to find the least cost combination.
c) in the short-run, at least one of the firm's input levels is fixed.
d) in the long-run, the firm is making a constrained decision about how to use existing plant and equipment efficiently.

20. Which of the following is the best example of a sunk cost?

a) The increase in total costs that a firm will experience if it hires more labor in order to expand output.
b) The interest that could be earned if a firm uses its retained earnings to purchase government bonds rather than buy new machinery.
c) The cost of the first three years of college, when a student is considering whether to complete his senior year.
d) The increase in property taxes that a firm will need to pay if it builds a new plant.

Chapter 8, Entrepreneurial Behavior

ANSWER KEY

Exercises

1. entrepreneur
2. unlimited, limited
3. financial, 1) Sale of ownership shares in the business, 2) its own profits, and 3) borrowing from financial institutions or individuals
4. retained earnings
5. maturity
6. monopoly
7. maximize profits
8. explicit, implicit, opportunity, explicit, implicit
9. normal profit
10. Accounting, economic
11. National income, rent, wages, interest, profit
12. short run, long run
13. sunk costs
14. a. $8,375 b. $4,625, $625 c. $3,625, $625

Review Questions

1. a) is not true. It is exactly the opposite. Firms incur risks that are generally not incurred by consumers. This is because firms must pay costs before generating revenue and firms are not guaranteed that consumers will demand the product which is being produced.

2. b) is the correct. One of main sources of risk for the firm is from the time lag between the need finance production and the sale of outputs.

3. d) is not true. The service industries in the U.S. have been growing over the last thirty years, when measured by employment. The agriculture sector has been shrinking, when measured by employment.

4. c) is not a characteristic of sole proprietorships. It is difficult for proprietorships to raise financial capital for growth. This is because borrowing opportunities are constrained by the fact that loans to a proprietorship must be secured by the personal assets of the owner.

5. c) is the correct answer. Because proprietors know that if their firm fails they will be personally responsible for the debts of the firm, up to the point of selling their personal property, so they are very careful about borrowing.

6. a) is not true of a partnership. Each partner is not only responsible for their investment in the partnership, but they are also personally responsible for the debts incurred by the other partners.

7. c) is the correct answer. Since Mastodon has issued common stock we know that it is a corporation. The owners of the corporation are liable only for the value of the part of the corporation they own, in other words, the value of the common stock they own. If Mastodon goes completely out of business you will only lose the value of your common stock.

8. d) is not an important source of financial capital for the corporation. Corporations are not dependent on the personal assets of those who run the firm, as proprietorships and partnerships are. a.), b.), and c) are the important sources of corporate borrowing.

9. a) is not true. Corporations may retain some of their profits and therefore not pay those as dividends. However, these retained earnings may also benefit stockholders, since if the retained earnings are used to help the firm grow, the value of the firm and thus the value of the common stock increases.

10. c) is correct. The existence of a secondary market allows the initial owners of corporate bonds to sell the bonds before they mature. Thus, if an individual who owns a corporate bond may

be able to sell it on the secondary market if the individual needs cash.

11. c) is not true. A competitive industry consists of a large number of small firms. Each firm is too small to influence the industry price.

12. b) is not true. Economic profit is the difference between the firm's total revenue and all opportunity costs, both implicit and explicit.

13. c) is the correct answer. The payment of wages is the only explicit cost listed. Labor is purchased in the market. The other payments in the question are to resources that have not been purchased in the market.

14. a) is the correct answer. The interest payments that could have been made on retained earnings that the firm uses for its own expansion are an implicit cost. This implicit cost is due to income that could have been earned in some alternative use by a resource which is owned by the firm.

15. c) is the correct answer. The depreciation of the truck is the loss of value due to its use in the production of a service, namely, the delivery of pizzas. Depreciation is the loss of value of capital equipment due to its use in production.

16. a) is the correct answer. Since the owner could earn $30,000 working for another company, we know that implicit costs are at least $30,000. Therefore, the firm's total costs are at least $75,000 + $30,000 = $105,000. Therefore the firm is running an economic loss of at least $5,000. This illustrates the difference between economic profits and accounting profits.

17. c) is the correct answer. If economic profits are positive, even if they are small, the resources owned by the firm are earning more than they could in any other alternative use. That is, the resources are earning more than their opportunity cost--what they could be earning in the next best alternative.

18. d) is not true. Accounting profits are equal to total revenue less explicit costs. This is an important point, since accounting profits are what people normally consider to be profits, whereas the economist is interested in economic profits.

19. c) is the correct answer. In the short-run at least one of the firm's inputs is fixed. In fact, this is the distinction between the short and long-run to the economist. In the long-run, all inputs can be varied.

20. c) is the correct answer. When a student is deciding whether or not to complete his senior year, the cost of the first three years is a sunk cost. This is because it cannot be recovered and is therefore irrelevant to the current decision.

CHAPTER 9
PRODUCTION COSTS, REVENUES, AND PROFIT MAXIMIZATION

OVERVIEW

In this chapter we consider the relationship between the firm's production function and the costs of production. In particular, we focus on the various types of costs a firm incurs, and the relationship between production costs and the time horizon in question. We also derive the rule that all firms follow in identifying the profit maximizing level of output.

We have assumed that the objective of firms is to maximize profits. Profit, once again, is simply the difference between total revenue and total costs. Revenue is the product of price and quantity sold. Costs, on the other hand, are determined by the types and quantities of inputs used in the production process, and their per unit prices.

A firm's production function is the technical relationship between the quantities of inputs needed to produce a good and the amount of output produced. In the short run, at least one of the inputs to the production function (e.g., capital) is fixed in amount. One of the many decisions a firm must make is the selection of the production function that will minimize its production costs. A short-run production function typically reflects the law of diminishing marginal returns, which states that at some point, as additional units of the variable input(s) are added to the production function, the additional output--marginal product--attributable to each additional unit of variable input declines.

A firm's production costs are directly related to its production function. Total fixed costs are equal to the per unit price of the fixed input multiplied by the number of units employed. Total variable costs are measured in a similar manner. Total costs are equal to the sum of total fixed and total variable costs. Dividing each of the total cost functions by the level of output yields a set of average cost functions--average fixed cost, average variable cost, and average total cost. In addition, marginal cost is calculated as the change in total cost associated with the production of an additional unit of output. The relationship between the firm's short-run production function and short-run cost function can be seen by examining the marginal product curve and the marginal cost curve. In particular, when marginal product rises, marginal cost falls; when marginal product falls, marginal cost rises.

Because at least one input, usually capital, is fixed in the short run, the firm's productive capacity is limited. However, over the long run a firm can vary all of its inputs, including capital. It can therefore vary the size, or scale, of its productive capacity. A firm's long-run average cost curve is generated by allowing the scale of the firm to increase and observing the effect on short-run average total costs. Economies of scale refers to the situation where an increase in capacity results in lower short-run average total costs. Diseconomies of scale are encountered when an increase in productive capacity causes short-run average total costs to increase. In the long run, a firm minimizes its total costs by selecting that scale of plant associated with the minimum of the long-run average total cost curve.

In order to identify the level of output at which profits are at a maximum, a firm must compare the marginal cost and marginal revenue of each additional unit of output it produces. So long as marginal revenue exceeds marginal cost, the firm will earn additional profit by producing the additional unit of output. Profits are at a maximum when marginal revenue and marginal cost are equal. The profit maximizing rule--produce the level of output at which MR = MC--holds for all firms, regardless of whether they are price takers or price searchers.

KEY GRAPHS AND TERMS

Graphs

The key models and their associated graphs introduced in this chapter include the short-run production function, the short-run cost function, the long-run cost function and the revenue functions for price-taking and price-searching firms. These models enable us to illustrate the process by which firms identify their profit maximizing level of output in the short run and the long run.

Figure 4 in the text illustrates a representative set of short-run cost functions for a typical firm. A number of points should be noted. First, the vertical distance between the average total cost curve and the average variable cost curve at each level of output is equal to average fixed cost. Hence, the AFC curve can be left out without loss of information. Second, the ATC, AVC, and MC curves are U-shaped, reflecting the law of diminishing returns. Marginal cost is at a minimum when marginal product is at a maximum. In addition, so long as marginal cost is less that average total cost, average total cost will continue to fall. Only when marginal cost exceeds average total cost, will the average total cost increase. The same holds true for the relationship between marginal cost and average variable cost. The result is that the marginal cost curve intersects the average total cost curve and the average variable cost curve at their respective minimum points.

Figure 6 in the text illustrates the long-run cost curve for a typical firm. The long-run cost curve is constructed by drawing a curve that is just tangent to each of the short-run average cost curves. Recall that each SRATC curve is associated with a different level of capacity. As we move from left to right, the firm's capacity is increasing. The LRAC curve illustrates the effects of economies of scale and diseconomies of scale on the average costs of production.

Figures 9 and 10 illustrate the profit-maximizing level of output for a price-taking firm and a price-searching firm. In each case profits are maximized by producing the level of output at which MR = MC. What distinguishes the two situations is the firms marginal revenue functions and the price they are able to charge. As its name indicates, a price-taking firm treats the market-determined price as given--it charges the same per unit price for its output, regardless of the level of output produced. Consequently, marginal revenue is constant and the marginal revenue curve appears as a horizontal line that intersects the horizontal axis at the prevailing market price. In contrast, when a price-searching firm increases its output, it moves along a downward-sloping demand curve. This results in declining marginal revenue and the marginal revenue curve therefore lies below the firm's demand curve.

Terms

PRODUCTION FUNCTION
MARGINAL PHYSICAL PRODUCT
LAW OF DIMINISHING MARGINAL RETURNS
AVERAGE PRODUCT
TOTAL COST OF PRODUCTION
FIXED COST
VARIABLE COST
AVERAGE TOTAL COST
AVERAGE VARIABLE COST
AVERAGE FIXED COST
MARGINAL COST
SHORT-RUN CAPACITY
LONG-RUN AVERAGE COST CURVE
ECONOMIES OF SCALE
DISECONOMIES OF SCALE
CONSTANT ECONOMIES OF SCALE
PRICE-TAKING FIRM
PRICE-SEARCHING FIRM
AVERAGE REVENUE
MARGINAL REVENUE

EXERCISES

1. The maximum quantity of output that can be produced from a given quantity of inputs is determined by a firm's ________________ ________________.

2. The change in total output resulting from the employment of an additional unit of a variable input is called the input's ________________ ________________ ________________.

3. In the short run, at least one of the firm's inputs is ________________ in amount.

4. The change in total cost associated with the production of an additional unit of output is called ________________ ________________.

5. When marginal product is rising, _________________ cost is _________________, and when marginal product is falling, _________________ cost is _________________.

6. The MC curve intersects the ATC and AVC curves at their respective _________________ points.

7. A firm's short-run _________________ is defined as the level of output at which total cost is minimized.

8. Assume that a firm experiences an increase in the per unit price of labor. This would cause the firm's short-run cost curves to _________________ _________________, resulting in _________________ production costs at each level of output.

9. The situation in which an increase in a firm's capacity causes the average total costs of production to decrease is called _________________ _____ _________________.

10. Assume that a firm is currently employing 10 units of capital and 20 units of labor. The cost of capital is $50 per unit, and the cost of labor is $10 per unit. The marginal product of the last unit of labor is 30 units and the marginal product of the last unit of capital is 100 units. Is this firm employing the cost minimizing combination of inputs? _________ If not, what should the firm do to reduce its production costs?

11. In order to maximize profits, a fir should produce the level of output at which _________________ _________________ equals _________________ _________________.

12. In the case of a price taking firm, as output increases, marginal revenue _________________ _________________.

13. A firm is contemplating increasing its output from 100 units to 110 units. The firm's total revenue from selling 100 units is $15,000 and total revenue from selling 110 units is $15,500. Total costs of producing each level of output are $13,500 and $14,200. Should the firm go through with the increase?_______ If it does, what will happen to total profit? _________________________________

14. Complete the table below which represents the production costs for a typical firm. (Round numbers to the nearest tenth.)

TP	TFC	TVC	TC	AFC	AVC	ATC	MC
0	$20	$ 0	$__	---	---	---	--
1	___	27.5	___	$__	$__	$__	$27.5
2	___	46.8	___	___	23.4	___	___
3	___	63.3	___	___	___	___	___
4	___	82.5	___	5.0	___	___	___
5	___	106.7	126.7	___	___	___	___
6	___	139.7	___	___	___	___	___
7	___	181	___	___	___	28.7	___

15. Use the information from the table to graph ATC, AVC and MC in the space provided.

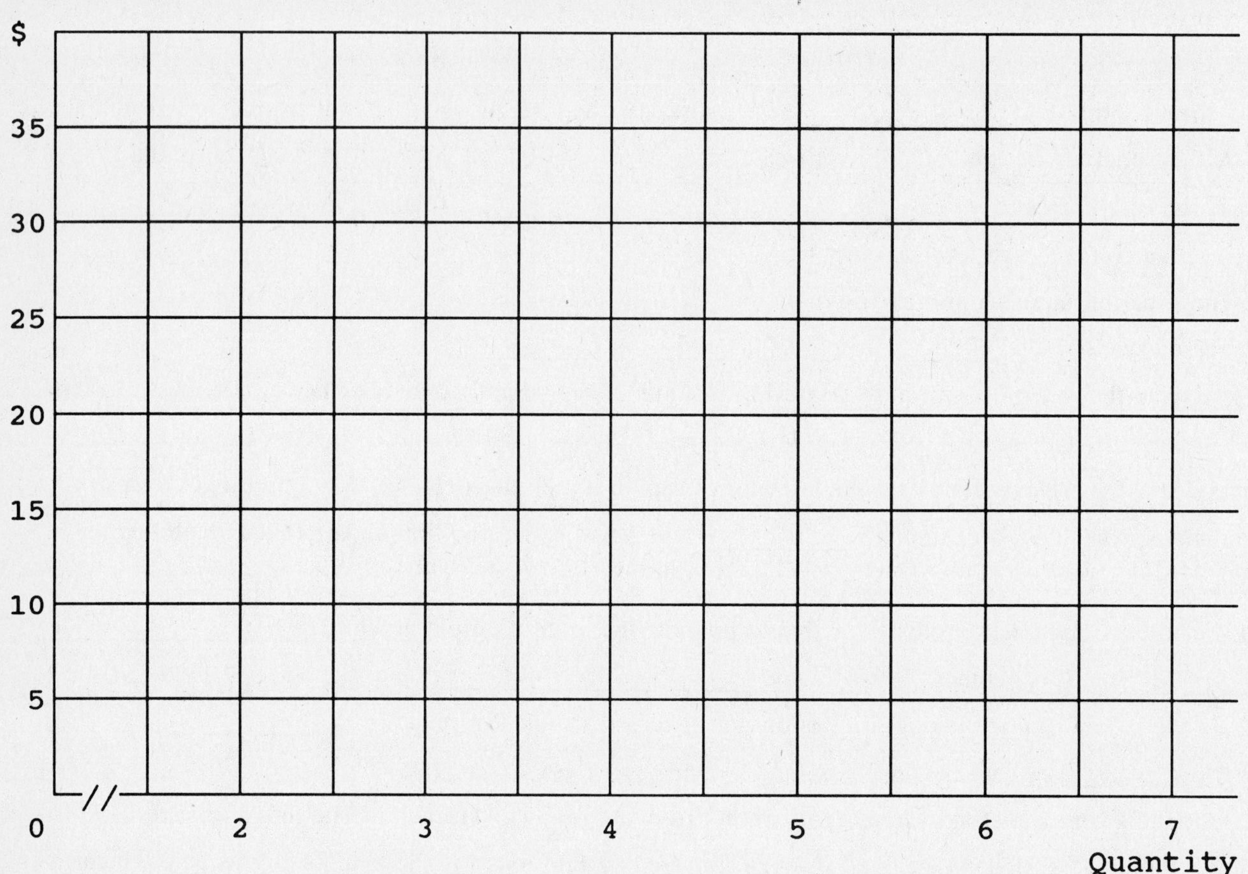

16. At what level of output do diminishing returns set in? _______ How do you know? _______________

____

17. Complete the following table which represents a price searcher's demand curve.

Quantity Demanded	Price	Total Revenue	Marginal Revenue
0	$50	$ 0	$ 0
1	45	_____	_____
2	40	_____	_____
3	35	_____	_____
4	30	_____	_____
5	25	_____	_____

18. From the table we can see that when the demand curve is downward sloping, marginal revenue is almost always (greater, less) than price.

Chapter 9, Production Costs, Revenues, and Profit Maximization

REVIEW QUESTIONS

1. Which of the following is the best definition of the production function?

a) The relationship between market price and quantity supplied.
b) The relationship between the firm's total revenue and the cost of production.
c) The relationship between the quantity of inputs needed to produce a good and the level of output.
d) The relationship between the quantity of inputs and the firm's marginal cost of production.

2. In the mathematical formulation of the short-run production function:

a) the quantity is usually assumed to be fixed.
b) the level of capital is usually assumed to be fixed.
c) both labor and capital are usually assumed to be fixed.
d) both labor and capital must be allowed to vary so that output can vary in the short-run.

Use the following information to answer questions 3 and 4.

Hours of Labor	Total Output	Marginal Product
0	- -	
1	100	100
2	___	80
3	240	___

3. What is the total output when 2 units of labor are being used?

a) 80
b) 100
c) 180
d) 200

4. What is the marginal product of the third hour of labor?

a) 60
b) 80
c) 100
d) 240

5. What is the average product of the first three hours of labor?

a) 60
b) 80
c) 100
d) 240

6. The "Law of Diminishing Returns applies to:"

a) the short run, but not the long run.
b) the long run, but not the short run.
c) both the short run and the long run.
d) neither the short run nor the long run.

7. Diminishing returns occurs:

a) as units of a variable input are added to a fixed input and total product falls.
b) as units of a variable input are added to a fixed input and marginal product falls.
c) as the size of the plant is increased in the long-run.
d) as the quantity of the fixed input is increased and returns to the variable input fall.

8. Which of the following is not a determinant of the firm's cost function?

a) The production function
b) The price of labor
c) Taxes
d) The price of the firm's output

9. Which of the following relationships between the firm's total cost functions is correct?

a) TC = TFC - TVC
b) TVC = TFC - TC
c) TFC = TC - TVC
d) TC = TVC - TFC

10. Suppose output increases in the short-run. Total cost will:

a) increase due to an increase in fixed costs only.
b) increase due to an increase in variable costs only.
c) increase due to an increase in both fixed and variable costs.
d) decrease if the firm is in the region of diminishing returns.

Use the following data to answer questions 11 - 13.

Output (Q):	0	1	2	3	4	5	6
Total Cost (TC):	$24	$33	$41	$48	$54	$61	$69

11. The average fixed cost of 2 units of output is:
a) $8.00
b) $8.50
c) $12.00
d) $20.50

12. The marginal cost of the sixth unit of output is:
a) $1.33
b) $7.50
c) $8.00
d) $45.00

13. Diminishing marginal returns starts to occur between units:

a) 2 and 3.
b) 3 and 4.
c) 4 and 5.
d) 5 and 6.

14. Marginal cost is defined correctly by which of the following statements?

a) The change in total cost due to a one unit change in output.
b) Total cost divided by output.
c) The change in output due to a one unit change in input.
d) Total product divided by the quantity of input.

15. The upward-sloping part of the short-run marginal cost function is due to:

a) marginal product rising as units of a variable input are added to a fixed input.
b) marginal product falling as units of a variable input are added to a fixed input.
c) the change in total product rising as units of a variable input are added to a fixed input.
d) the upward-sloping part of the production function.

16. Which of the following is true of the relationship between the marginal cost function and the average cost functions?

a) If MC is greater than ATC, then ATC is falling.
b) ATC intersects MC at minimum MC.
c) MC intersects AVC at minimum AVC.
d) If MC is smaller than AVC, then AVC is rising.

17. Which of the following is true of the relationship between the average cost functions?

a) ATC = AFC - AVC
b) AVC = AFC + ATC
c) AFC = ATC + AVC
d) AFC = ATC - AVC

18. Suppose there is an increase in sales taxes. Which of the following will result for the firm's cost functions?

a) The marginal cost function will shift up and the average total cost function will shift down.
b) The marginal cost function will shift down and the average total cost function will shift up.
c) Both the marginal and average cost functions will shift up.
d) Both the marginal and average cost functions will shift down.

19. Assume that there is an improvement in technology that increases the marginal product of each unit of labor. This would have the effect of:

a) reducing the average total cost, average variable cost, and marginal cost of production.
b) increasing the average total cost, average variable cost, and marginal cost of production.
c) reducing the average variable cost, and marginal cost of production, but average total cost would be unchanged.
d) reducing the average total cost and average variable cost of production, but marginal cost would be unchanged.

20. Which of the following is true in the short-run, but not in the long-run?

a) The firm's decisions are planning decisions.
b) The firm is free to vary all of its inputs.
c) The firm makes decisions by attempting to predict future product demand and technological developments.
d) The firm is "stuck" with the existing amount of capital.

21. Suppose a firm finds that demand is higher than it predicted when it made its long-run planning decision about the amount of capital it would need. Which of the following will occur?

a) The firm will experience lower costs than it anticipated, due to overutilization of its existing plant.
b) The firm will experience higher costs than it anticipated, due to overutilization of its existing plant.
c) The firm will experience lower costs than it anticipated, due to underutilization of its existing plant.
d) The firm will experience higher costs than it anticipated, due to underutilization of its existing plant.

22. Assume that a firm produces 500 units of a good by using two inputs, capital and labor, whose per unit prices are $10 and $4. If the marginal physical product of the last unit of capital is 30 and the marginal physical product of the last unit of labor is 10, to minimize costs this firm should employ:

a) the existing combination of resources.
b) more labor and less capital.
c) more capital and less labor.
d) both more labor and more capital.

23. In the previous question, what will change to move the firm to a new cost-minimizing equilibrium?

a) The marginal product of capital will fall.
b) The marginal product of labor will fall.
c) The price of labor will rise.
d) The price of capital will rise.

24. Suppose that initially the firm is in its cost-minimizing equilibrium and there is an increase in the marginal product of labor due to improved training techniques. Which of the following will occur?

a) The firm will employ less labor, since each unit of labor is now more productive.
b) The firm will employ more capital in order to take advantage of the increase in labor productivity.
c) The firm will substitute labor for capital in its production process.
d) The firm will be able buy more of both labor and capital.

25. In the previous question, the increase in the productivity of labor will move the firm temporarily into a disequilibrium with respect to its cost minimization condition. Which of the following will occur as the firm adjusts to this new situation to move the firm to a new equilibrium?

a) The marginal product of capital will rise.
b) The marginal product of capital will fall.
c) The price of capital will rise.
d) The price of labor will fall.

26. Which of the following is <u>not</u> true of the long run average cost curve?

a) It represents the least-cost input combination for producing each level of output.
b) It consists of a series of short-run average cost functions.
c) The cost function at the minimum point of the long-run average cost function is the least cost plant size for all levels of output.
d) As output increases, the amount of capital employed by the firm increases along the curve.

27. The negatively-sloped part of the long-run average total cost curve is due to which of the following?
a) Diseconomies of scale
b) Diminishing returns
c) The difficulties in coordinating the many activities of a large firm.
d) Specialization

28. The positively-sloped part of the long-run average total cost function is due to which of the following?

a) Diseconomies of scale
b) Diminishing returns
c) The firm being able to take advantage of large-scale production techniques as it expands its output.
d) Specialization

29. Which of the following is not a characteristic of a "price taker"?

a) TR = P x Q
b) AR = Price
c) Negatively-sloped demand
d) Marginal Revenue = Price

30. Marginal Revenue is equal to which of the following?

a) The change in price divided by the change in quantity.
b) The change in quantity divided by the change in price.
c) The change in P x Q due to a one unit change in quantity.
d) Price, but only if the firm is a price searcher.

31. Which of the following is not true for a price searcher?

a) Average Revenue = Price
b) The demand function is downward sloping.
c) Price must be lowered to sell more.
d) Marginal Revenue = Price

32. Assume that when price is $20, quantity demanded is 9 units, and when price is $19, quantity demanded is 10 units. Based on this information, what is the marginal revenue resulting from an increase in output from 9 units to 10 units?

a) $20
b) $19
c) $10
d) $1

33. Suppose a firm is producing a quantity at which MR > MC. What should the firm do to maximize its profits?

a) The firm should do nothing--it wants to maximize the difference between MR and MC in order to maximize its profits.
b) The firm should hire less labor.
c) The firm should reduce output.
d) The firm should increase output.

34. Referring to the previous question, if the firm is a price taker, what will happen to move the firm to its profit-maximizing equilibrium?

a) Marginal revenue will rise.
b) Marginal revenue will fall.
c) Marginal cost will rise.
d) Marginal cost will fall.

35. How would your answer to the previous question have been different if the firm had been a price searcher instead of a price taker?

a) Marginal cost would have remained constant.
b) Marginal cost would have decreased.
c) Marginal revenue would have remained constant.
d) Marginal revenue would have decreased.

REVIEW QUESTIONS: APPENDIX

36. Which of the following statements is not true of isoquants?

a) They show the combinations of two inputs that result in the same level of output.
b) They are usually convex to the origin.
c) They show the combinations of two inputs that yield the same cost of production.
d) They represent higher levels of output the farther they are from the origin.

37. Which of the following is a correct about the marginal rate of technical substitution?

a) The MRTS is equal to the price ratio at all points along an isoquant.
b) The MRTS is equal to the ratio of the marginal utilities of the two goods.
c) The MRTS is equal to the ratio of the marginal products of the two inputs.
d) The MRTS remains constant as we alter the combinations of the two inputs.

38. Why is the isoquant negatively-sloped?

a) Along a single isoquant, if the firm increases the use of capital it must reduce the use of labor.
b) Diminishing marginal productivity.
c) Because the farther the isoquant is from the origin, the higher the level of output.
d) Because price and quantity demanded are inversely-related.

39. Why is the isoquant convex to the origin?

a) The Law of Diminishing Marginal Utility
b) The assumption of the diminishing marginal productivity of each input.
c) As less capital is used, its marginal productivity falls.
d) As more labor is used, its marginal productivity rises.

40. Which of the following is true of the slope of the isocost line?

a) It changes as the combination of labor and capital is altered by the firm.
b) It is equal to the ratio of the marginal productivities at all points along the isocost line.
c) It is equal to the negative of the ratio of the prices of the outputs.
d) It is equal to the negative of the ratio of the prices of the inputs.

ANSWER KEY

Exercises

1. production function
2. marginal physical product
3. fixed
4. marginal cost
5. marginal, falling, marginal, rising
6. minimum
7. capacity
8. shift up, higher
9. economies of scale
10. no. hire more labor and less capital
11. marginal revenue, marginal cost

12. stays constant
13. No, total profit will decrease.
14.

TP	TFC	TVC	TC	AFC	AVC	ATC	MC
0	$20	$ 0	$20	---	---	---	--
1	20	27.5	47.5	$20	$27.5	$47.5	$27.5
2	20	46.8	66.8	10	23.4	33.4	19.3
3	20	63.3	83.3	6.7	21.1	27.8	16.5
4	20	82.5	102.5	5	20.6	25.6	19.2
5	20	106.7	126.7	4	21.3	25.3	24.2
6	20	139.7	159.7	3.3	23.3	26.6	33
7	20	181	201	2.9	25.9	28.7	41.3

16. Between 3 units and 4 units of output. This is the point at which marginal costs begin to increase.
17.

Quantity Demanded	Price	Total Revenue	Marginal Revenue
0	$50	$ 0	$ 0
1	45	45	45
2	40	80	35
3	35	105	25
4	30	120	15
5	25	125	5

18. less

Review Questions

1. c) is the correct answer. The production function is a technical relationship between the amount of inputs required to produce a good and the quantity of output produced.

2. c) is the correct answer. Usually capital is assumed to be fixed in the short-run production function. In particular, capital goods such as the plant itself and machinery that takes a long time to install are considered fixed.

3. c) is the correct answer. Marginal product is 80 units of output. Therefore total output changes by 80 units, from 100 to 180 units of output.

4. a) is the correct answer. We know from the previous question that the total output for 2 hours of labor is 180 units of output. Therefore, the change in total output due to a one unit change in the labor input is from 180 to 240, a change of 60 units of output.

5. c) is the correct answer. The average is total product divided by the number of units of input. In this case that is 240 units of output divided by 3 units of input, which equals an average of 80 units of output.

6. a) is the correct answer. The Law of Diminishing Returns occurs when one of the inputs is fixed. This can only occur in the short-run, since all inputs are variable in the long-run.

7. c) is the correct answer. Diminishing returns occurs because as more and more of the variable input is combined with the fixed input, at some point there is little of fixed input with which each unit of the variable input can work. At this point, total product or total output does not necessarily fall, but the addition to total product, ie., marginal product falls.

8. d) is not a determinant of the firm's cost function. The price of the firm's output will not have a direct effect on the firm's costs which are dependent on the production function, the prices of inputs, and taxes.

9. c) is the correct answer. Total fixed cost is equal to the difference between total cost and total variable cost. This is why we can pay little

explicit attention to the fixed cost function, since it is already embodied in the total and variable cost functions.

10. c) is the correct answer. An increase in output in the short-run is accomplished by increasing the use of the variable inputs. Of course the fixed inputs remain the same and therefore do not contribute to the increase in total costs.

11. d) is the correct answer. Average cost is equal to total cost divided by the quantity of output. $41 / 2 = $20.50.

12. c) is the correct answer. Marginal cost is the change in total due to a one unit change in output. When output increases from five to six units, total cost changes from $61 to $69, a change of $8.

13. c) is the correct answer. Diminishing returns first occur between units 4 and 5, because this is where marginal cost starts to rise. When diminishing returns occur, marginal cost is rising.

14. a) is the correct answer. Marginal cost is the change in total cost due to a one unit change in output or the change in total cost divided by a one unit change in output.

15. c) is the correct answer. As the firm moves into diminishing returns, the marginal product of the variable input falls. Therefore, it takes more of the variable input to produce an extra unit of output and thus the cost of the extra unit(the marginal cost) rises.

16. c) is the correct answer. MC intersects both ATC and AVC at their minimum points. When MC > ATC, ATC must be rising. When MC < ATC, ATC must be falling. Therefore, when MC = ATC, ATC is neither rising nor falling--it is at its minimum point.

17. d) is the correct answer. AFC + AVC = ATC since TFC + TVC = TC. Therefore, AFC = ATC - AVC.

18. c) is the correct answer. When there is an increase in taxes, there is an increase in the firm's cost of production. That is, at each quantity of output, the firm will have higher costs due to the necessity of paying the tax. Therefore, the cost functions will shift up.

19. a) is the correct answer. An improvement in technology will increase the marginal product of labor and thus less labor will be needed for each unit of output. This causes both the average cost and the marginal cost functions to shift down. At each quantity of output, the total cost of production will be lower and for any one unit change in the total product the change in total cost will be lower.

20. d) is the correct answer. In the long-run the firm is not stuck with the existing amount of capital, since all inputs are variable.

21. c) is the correct answer. The firm will overutilize the capacity of its plant which exists in the short-run. This will move the firm up the SRATC function and raise the firm's costs.

22. c) is the correct answer. The firm should employ more capital and less labor, since the marginal product per dollar is higher for capital than it is for labor.

23. a) is the correct answer. As the firm substitutes capital for labor, the marginal product of capital will fall due to the Law of Diminishing Returns. The marginal product of labor will similarly rise.

24. c) is the correct answer. The firm will buy more labor and less capital due to the increase in the productivity of labor.

25. a) is the correct answer. As the firm adjusts, it will buy more labor and less capital. According to the Law of Diminishing Returns, the marginal product of capital will rise as the firm employs more of it.

26. c) is not true of the LRATC curve. Each of the short-run average cost functions represents the least cost method for producing the level of output at which the SRATC curves are tangent to the LRATC curve.

27. d) is the correct answer. The negatively-sloped part of the LRATC curve is due to

economies of scale. One of the primary reasons for economies of scale is specialization, as the firm employs more of both labor and capital to expand output.

28. a) is the correct answer. The positively sloped part of the LRATC curve is due to diseconomies of scale. These are due mainly to the problems of managing a very large plant, in which many activities are taking place under one roof.

29. c) is not a characteristic of a price taker. Price takers have horizontal demand functions and sell all they can produce as long as it is at the market price.

30. c) is the correct answer. P x Q is total revenue. Marginal revenue is the change in total revenue due to a one unit change in output.

31. d) is not true for the price searcher. Since price searchers have a downward sloping demand curve, they must lower price in order to sell more. When price is lowered it is not only for the extra units which will be sold, but it is for all the previous units of output as well. Therefore price and marginal revenue are not the same.

32. c) is the correct answer. Marginal revenue is the change in total revenue due to a change in output of one unit. At an output of 9 units, TR = 9 x $20 = $180. At an output of 20 units, TR = $190. Thus the change in TR due to a one unit change in output is $10.

33. d) is the correct answer. The firm should increase its output to take advantage of those units on which MR is greater than MC. This will increase the firm's profits. The firm should continue to produce more until MR is equal to MC.

34. c) is the correct answer. As the firm moves to its profit maximizing equilibrium, it will increase output. As this occurs, marginal cost will rise. The price taker should continue to produce more units of output until MC rises to equal MR, at which point there are no longer any units of output on which the firm can increase its profits.

35. d) is the correct answer. In addition to the rise in marginal cost, the price searcher would also have experienced a decrease in marginal revenue due to its need to lower price in order to sell more.

36. c) is the statement about isoquants that is not true. Cost is not constant along an isoquant, only output is constant. Cost is constant along the isocost line.

37. c) is the correct statement of the MRTS. It is the ratio of the marginal products of the two inputs. It generally changes as the combinations of the two inputs are changed. The MRTS is equal to the price ratio only at equilibrium.

38. a) is the correct answer. As we move along a single isoquant, output is constant. If we increase the use of capital, then we must reduce the use of labor. Otherwise, the level of output would increase.

39. b) is the correct answer. As more of either input is used, the input's marginal productivity is assumed to fall. This is what gives the isoquant its "bowed" shape or what makes the isoquant convex to the origin.

40. d) is the correct answer. The slope of the isocost line is equal to the negative of the ratio of the prices of the inputs. If capital is measured along the vertical axis and labor is measured along the horizontal, the slope of the isocost line is the negative of the price of labor divided by the price of capital.

CHAPTER 10
THE PERFECT COMPETITION MODEL

OVERVIEW

In this chapter we develop the model of a perfectly competitive market. We begin by describing the characteristics of this type of market, and then go on to show how to calculate profits and losses. Next, we consider possible short-run equilibria for perfectly competitive firms. We then analyze the adjustment to long-run equilibrium when demand or supply conditions in the market change. The efficiency properties of long-run equilibrium in a perfectly competitive market are also considered.

A perfectly competitive market is characterized by the following conditions: 1) individual firms are small relative to the market in which they operate, 2) firms produce a homogeneous product, and 3) entry and exit are costless. As a result of these conditions firms take market price as given, and earn zero long-run economic profits (i.e., they earn a normal profit). In addition, because of the highly competitive nature of such markets, firms are forced to produce at minimum short-run and long-run average total cost.

As we saw in the last chapter, to maximize profits, firms produce the level of output at which marginal revenue equals marginal cost. When price is greater than the minimum of average total cost, firms will earn positive economic profits. If price is between the minimum of average total cost and the minimum of average variable cost, firms will incur a loss but will continue to operate in the short run. So long as price (marginal revenue) is greater than the minimum of average variable cost, firms will be able to earn enough revenue to pay all of their variable costs and at least part of their fixed costs. However, when price falls below the minimum of average variable costs, firms will minimize their losses by shutting down and simply paying their fixed costs out of pocket.

Profits and losses are the incentives that cause firms to enter and leave perfectly competitive markets. Economic profits attract new firms into the market, causing supply to increase, and market price, and therefore economic profits, to fall. Entry will continue until economic profit is driven to zero. In a similar manner, losses cause firms to leave the market. In this case, exit results in a decrease in market supply and market price rises. The increase in market price causes losses to disappear. Exit continues until all losses are eliminated and the remaining firms in the market are earning a normal profit.

Changes in market demand, or factors such as technology that influence market supply, set in motion the process of adjustment to a new market equilibrium. A change in demand causes a change in market price which then results in economic profits (increase in demand) or losses (decrease in demand). This, in turn, leads to entry or exit, depending on the specific situation. A change in supply resulting from such factors as a change in technology or a change in input prices also results in a change in market price and therefore the profits or losses of firms in the market.

In the long run, the equilibrium in a perfectly competitive market is economically efficient. This is the result of two characteristics of the market equilibrium. First, firms end up operating at the minimum of the short-run and long-run average total cost curves. Hence, they are using their productive capacity efficiently. Also, price (the value of the output to society) and marginal cost (the value of the additional resources used) are equal for the last unit of output produced. This condition is referred to as allocative efficiency.

As we will see in later chapters, this model is especially important since it provides a benchmark we can use to assess the efficiency of outcomes in the types of markets that we observe in the real world. Although very few markets can be considered perfectly competitive, the model of perfect competition provides us with many useful insights to how markets work.

KEY GRAPHS AND TERMS

Graphs

The model of a perfectly competitive market and a representative firm is illustrated in Figure 1. It is important to remember that the firm takes market price, which is determined by the interaction of market supply and demand, as given. Figures 2 - 4 illustrate a series of possible short-run equilibria for perfectly competitive firms. As these figures show, so long as price is greater than the minimum of the AVC curve, the firm will maximize profits (price greater than the minimum of the ATC curve) or minimize losses (price between the minimum of the ATC curve and the minimum of the AVC curve) by producing the level of output at which MR = MC. However, if price falls below the minimum of average variable cost, the firm minimizes its losses by shutting down.

As Figure 5 illustrates, because the firm always produces the level of output at which MR = MC (for P > AVC), the MC curve above the minimum of the AVC curve traces out all the possible output levels for the firm--it is the firm's short-run supply curve.

Figures 6 and 7 illustrate the adjustment process that occurs when long-run equilibrium is disturbed by a change in demand. In a similar manner, Figures 10 and 11 illustrate the long-run adjustment to a change in a determinant of supply. Be sure you are able to work through the steps illustrated in these figures. A good exercise is work through the analysis for alternative scenarios, e.g., a decrease in demand.

Figures 8 and 9 illustrate the derivation of the long-run supply curve in the case of a constant-cost industry and an increasing-cost industry. The key here is what happens to the firm's short-run cost curves when the level of output changes as a result of a change in the level of demand. If costs are unaffected, the industry is characterized by constant costs and the long-run supply curve is perfectly elastic. If costs increase as output increases, the industry is experiencing increasing costs and the long-run supply curve is upward sloping.

Terms

PERFECTLY COMPETITIVE MARKET
BREAKEVEN POINT
SHUTDOWN POINT
CONSTANT-COST INDUSTRY
INCREASING-COST INDUSTRY
CONSUMER SOVEREIGNTY
ALLOCATIVELY EFFICIENT FIRMS
PARTIAL EQUILIBRIUM ANALYSIS
GENERAL EQUILIBRIUM ANALYSIS

EXERCISES

1. List the three major characteristics of a perfectly competitive market. ______________________________

____

____

2. Firms in a perfectly competitive market are price ________________.

3. In terms of the perfectly competitive firm's revenue functions, market price, ________________ revenue and ________________ revenue are all equal and constant so long as market conditions do not change. In addition, the firm's marginal revenue curve is also its ________________ revenue curve and its ________________ curve.

4. So long as market price is greater than the firm's minimum average ________________ cost, the firm will earn an economic profit.

5. If market price falls below the minimum of average ________________ cost, the firm should shut down. By doing so, it will limit its losses to its total ________________ costs.

6. The perfectly competitive firm's short-run supply curve is its ________________ ________________ curve above the minimum of the ________________ ________________ ________________ curve.

7. Assume a perfectly competitive market is initially in long-run equilibrium. In the short run, a decrease in the number of buyers will cause the market price to ________________. As a result, the profits of existing firms will ________________. However, over the long-run, this will cause the number of firms in the market to ________________, and market price will ________________ until firms once again earn a ________________ ________________.

8. In a ________________-________________ industry, input prices are invariant to the level of output. As such the long-run supply curve for the industry is ________________ ________________.

9. In an ________________- ________________ industry, input prices are an increasing function of the level of output. As such, over the long run, an increase in demand in this type of industry will cause the equilibrium market price to ________________.

10. The ability of consumers' preferences to influence the level of output in competitive markets is called ________________ ________________.

11. In long-run equilibrium, a perfectly competitive firm is operating at the ________________ of its short-run and long-run average total cost curves, implying that the firm is using its capacity ________________. In addition, price equals ________________ ________________ for the last unit of output produced. This latter condition is referred to as ________________ ________________.

12. Assume a perfectly competitive market is initially in long-run equilibrium. In the short run, a decrease in raw materials prices will cause the firm's average costs to ________________. As a result, the profits of existing firms will ________________. However, over the long-run, this will cause the number of firms in the market to ________________, and market price will ________________ until firms once again earn a ________________ ________________.

13. Assume that goods X and Y are complements and are produced in perfectly competitive, constant-cost industries. Ceteris paribus, a decrease in demand for X will cause the number of firms that produce X to ________________, and the market price of Y to ________________ in the short run.

14. ________________ equilibrium analysis is concerned with the relationships across markets and the conditions necessary for equilibrium in all markets simultaneously, while ________________ equilibrium analysis focuses on the conditions necessary for equilibrium in a particular market.

15. Assume that a perfectly competitive firm is currently producing 5,000 units of output, and is earning $10,000 in total revenue. The marginal cost of the 5,000th unit of output is $3. Is this firm producing the profit maximizing level of output? ____________. How do you know?

____

Use the following figure, which illustrates the costs for a hypothetical perfectly competitive firm to answer questions 16 - 22.

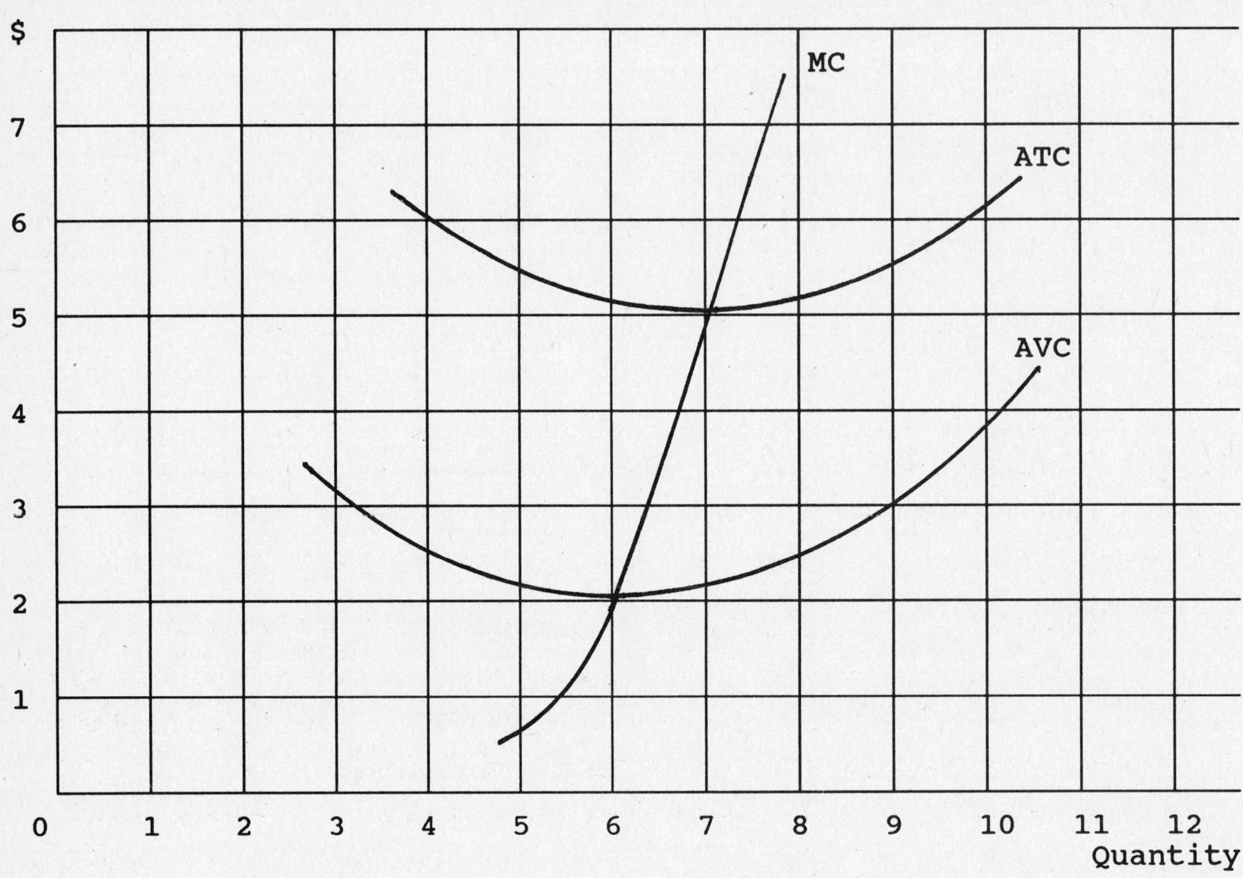

16. Assume that initially the market price is $7.00. Draw the firm's demand curve in the figure and label it D1 = MR1. Is this firm making an economic profit? ______. If so, what is the approximate amount of the firm's economic profit? ______.

17. What is the long-run equilibrium price for the firm? _____. Draw the long-run demand curve for this firm in the figure and label it D2 = MR2. (Assume the firm operates in a constant cost industry.)

18. What are the shutdown price and quantity for the firm? Price = _____, Quantity = _____.

19. Indicate the firm's short-run supply curve with a heavy black line.

20. According to economic theory, firms in any industry will maximize profits or minimize losses by producing the level of output at which ___________.

21. In the short run, a firm should continue to produce output so long as it can pay all of its (fixed, variable) costs. Why?

22. In one sentence, why is the demand curve faced by the individual firm in a perfectly market assumed to be perfectly elastic?

Chapter 10, The Perfect Competition Model

Use the following figure to answer questions 23 - 26.

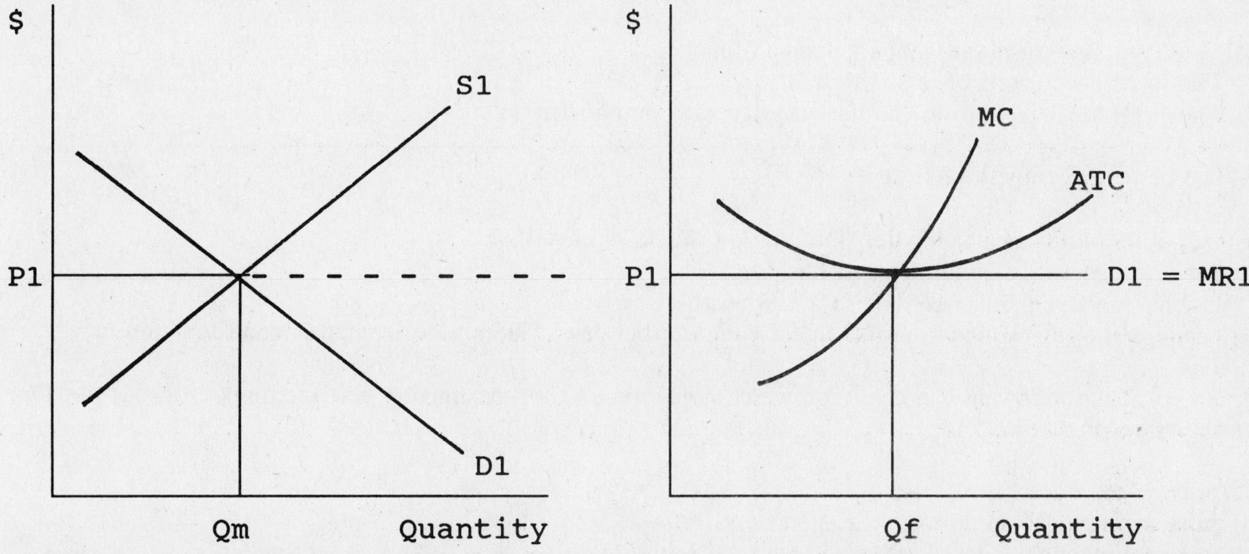

23. Note that the perfectly competitive industry depicted in this figure is initially in long-run equilibrium with price equal to P1. Assume now that there is an increase in market demand for the good produced in this market. Draw a new industry demand curve that illustrates this change and label it D2. Also, draw the new demand curve for the firm and label it MR2 = D2. Is the firm now making economic profit? ______.

24. Given the change in demand described in question 23, over time what will happen to the number of firms in the industry? ____________________. As this change takes place, what will happen to the industry supply curve?______________________________. Assuming that this is a constant cost industry, draw the new industry supply curve that is consistent with long-run equilibrium in the market and label it S2.

25. After the market has once again adjusted to long-run equilibrium, market price is ______ and economic profit for the firm is equal to _____.

26. If instead this was an increasing cost industry, how would your answers to questions 24 and 25 change?

REVIEW QUESTIONS

1. Which of the following is not a characteristic of perfect competition?

a) Large number of firms in the industry.
b) Outputs of the firms are perfect substitutes for one another.
c) Firms face downward-sloping demand functions.
d) No barriers to entry or exit.

2. Perfectly competitive firms are said to be "small." Which of the following best describes this smallness?

a) The firms must lower price in order to sell more, causing prices to be lower than in imperfectly competitive industries.
b) The firms face downward-sloping demand functions.
c) The firms have assets of less than $2M.
d) The firms are unable to affect market price with output decisions.

3. The perfectly competitive firm:

a) makes its profit-maximizing decision only on the basis of output.
b) faces a downward-sloping demand function.
c) can influence market price only in a downward direction.
d) cannot earn any economic profits in the long-run because it faces a horizontal demand function.

4. Which of the following is a condition which holds for a profit-maximizing perfect competitor, but not for an imperfect competitor?

a) price = average revenue
b) price = marginal revenue
c) marginal revenue = marginal cost
d) total cost = average total cost x quantity

5. Which of the following statements is definitely true when average revenue is less than average cost for the perfectly competitive firm operating in the short-run?

a) The firm is running a loss in an accounting sense, so that total revenue is less than total explicit costs.
b) The firm will minimize its losses by shutting down.
c) The firm will be earning negative total revenue.
d) The firm is running an economic loss.

6. Suppose a perfectly competitive firm that is operating in the short-run finds that market price is less than average total cost, but greater than average variable cost. Which of the following statements is correct?

a) The firm should shutdown in order to minimize its losses.
b) The firm should set marginal revenue equal to marginal cost in order to minimize its losses.
c) The firm should move its resources to another industry.
d) The firm should raise its price enough to cover its losses.

7. When a perfectly competitive firm's price is below average variable cost, it should:

a) produce where marginal revenue equals marginal cost if it is operating in the short-run.
b) produce where marginal revenue equals marginal cost if it is operating is the long-run.
c) shutdown, since it will lose nothing in that case.
d) shutdown, since it cannot even cover its variable costs if it stays in business.

8. The shutdown point occurs where:

a) average total cost is at its minimum point.
b) average variable cost is at its minimum point.
c) average fixed cost is at its minimum point.
d) marginal cost is at its minimum point.

9. Fixed costs:

a) are sunk costs in the short-run.
b) are sunk costs in the long-run.
c) cannot be ignored by the firm in the short-run.
d) are almost always higher than total revenue in the short-run.

10. The perfectly competitive firm's supply curve:

a) coincides with its perfectly elastic demand curve.
b) is perfectly inelastic at the market price.
c) is the firm's marginal cost curve above the minimum point on the AVC curve.
d) is the firm's average total cost curve above the shutdown point.

11. Suppose a perfectly competitive firm is in long-run equilibrium and there is an increase in demand. Which of the following will happen in the short-run?

a) The firm will decrease its output in order to increase market price.
b) The firm will experience economic profits.
c) The firm will earn less than then normal level of profits.
d) The firm will reduce output in order to maintain profits at their normal level.

12. Referring to the previous question, which of the following will <u>not</u> happen in the long-run?

a) New firms will enter, causing market price to fall.
b) The market will move to equilibrium when profits return to their normal level.
c) Price will be higher at the new long-run equilibrium if the firm is operating in a constant cost industry.
d) The firms that were already in the industry will return to their original level of output.

13. Suppose a perfectly competitive firm is operating in long-run equilibrium and there is a <u>decrease</u> in demand. Suppose the firm is in an <u>increasing</u> cost industry. Which of the following will occur at the new long-run equilibrium?

a) Price will be lower than it was at the initial long-run equilibrium.
b) Price will be the same as it was at the initial long-run equilibrium.
c) Price will be higher than it was at the initial long-run equilibrium.
d) The industry supply function will shift to the right.

14. Suppose that there is an increase in demand in a perfectly competitive industry that was initially in long-run equilibrium. Which of the following statements is <u>not true</u>?

a) Consumers have shown that they now consider the good to be more valuable.
b) In the short-run, profits will be lower than normal.
c) Resources from other industries will be attracted.
d) The industry supply function will shift to the right.

15. Suppose that a perfectly competitive firm is in long-run equilibrium and there is a decrease in demand. Which of the following will occur?

a) Existing firms will maintain the original level of output, but they will shift their cost functions down in the short-run.
b) Existing firms will raise price to cover the reduction in quantity demanded and maintain total revenue in the short-run.
c) Existing firms will reduce output in the short-run.
d) Market price will be above its original level if the firms are operating in a constant cost industry.

16. We have said that perfectly competition results in an efficient allocation of resources. Which of the following conditions indicates this efficiency?

a) MC = MR
b) Economic profits > 0
c) Price = AR
d) Price = MC

17. What is the "most efficient capacity" for the firm?

a) The plant size at which LRATC is at its minimum.
b) The plant sizes at which any of the SRATC curves are tangent to the LRATC curve.
c) The plant size at which MR = MC.
d) The plant size for which Price = AR.

18. So long as a perfectly competitive firm continues to operate and follow the rule for profit maximization, it will be:

a) allocatively efficient in the long run, but not the short run.
b) allocatively efficient in the short run, but not the long run.
c) allocatively efficient in both the long run and the short run.
d) allocatively efficient in neither the long run nor the short run.

19. Suppose that the price of bicycles is greater than the marginal cost of bicycles. From the point of view of the well-being of society, what should happen to the output of bicycles?

a) We cannot tell from the information provided, since nothing is specified about the level of economic profits in the industry.
b) The output of bicycles should be increased.
c) The output of bicycles should be decreased.
d) The government should place a tax on bicycles.

20. Suppose a perfectly competitive firm experiences an increase in the wages it must pay its employees. In the short-run which of the following will occur?

a) ATC will shift up and MC will shift down.
b) ATC will shift down and MC will shift up.
c) The firm will initially experience economic losses.
d) The resulting change in supply will cause consumers to eventually bid market price down.

21. Assume that there is an improvement in the technology used by firms in a perfectly competitive constant cost industry. After all adjustments have taken place, we would expect to see:

a) a decrease in equilibrium price and an increase in quantity.
b) an increase in equilibrium price and a decrease in quantity.
c) a decrease in equilibrium price and quantity.
d) an increase in equilibrium price and quantity.

22. Suppose there is an increase in the demand for bicycles. Assume that bicycles are produced in a perfectly competitive, increasing cost industry. As a result, which of the following will happen other industries?

a) They will experience increases in demand as well.
b) The will experience an excess supply of workers wanting jobs.
c) Their MC and ATC curves will shift down.
d) Their MC and ATC curves will shift up.

23. "Consumer sovereignty" refers to the:

a) obligation of the government to protect consumers from harmful and defective products.
b) notion that the decision of what to produce must be responsive to consumers' demands.
c) idea that the pursuit of self interests will ultimately prove to be in society's interest.
d) fact that resource prices tend to be high relative to product prices in capitalist economies.

24. Industry Y is a perfectly competitive constant cost industry. Assume that as a result of changes in <u>other markets</u> there is a twenty percent increase in the price of variable inputs used by firms in industry Y. After all adjustments have taken place, we would expect the equilibrium market price in industry Y to:

a) decrease and the number of firms to increase.
b) increase and the number of firms to increase.
c) decrease and the number of firms to decrease.
d) increase and the number of firms to decrease.

25. If all markets are perfectly competitive and are in long-run equilibrium, which of the following will <u>not</u> occur?

a) Prices are equal to the minimum unit cost of production.
b) Economic profits are equal to zero.
c) Allocative efficiency has been acheived.
d) The distribution of income is equal across society.

26. Which of the following is <u>not true</u>? Free trade:

a) Harms the U.S. society as a whole if it causes unemployment in any industry.
b) Results in a more efficient use of the world's resources.
c) Creates more competition in domestic markets.
d) Drives the equilibrium prices of traded goods lower.

27. Which of the following is not true. In a perfectly competitive market:

a) those consumers obtain goods who are willing to pay the highest price for them.
b) goods are produced at the minimum opportunity cost.
c) inputs are allocated to their highest-valued uses.
d) cooperation among individuals is unnecessary due to the influence of the invisible hand.

28. Which of the following is an important reason to study perfect competition?

a) It is fairly common in U.S. society.
b) It shows the inconsistency between individual self-interest and social welfare.
c) It rests on assumptions that are close approximations of the behavior we observe in the "real world."
d) It creates an ideal against which we can compare other markets.

29. Which of following is a key assumption that, when relaxed, means that competition may not result in an efficient allocation of resources?

a) The assumption that price equals average revenue.
b) The assumption that the MR = MC condition results in profits being maximized.
c) The assumption of resource mobility.
d) The assumption that total revenue equal P x Q.

30. If farmers operating in the competitive wheat industry are running losses, and are not kept in business with government subsidies, which of the following will result?

a) Price and quantity produced will both increase in the long-run.
b) Resources will reallocated out of the wheat industry into more productive uses.
c) Farmers will run economic losses indefinitely, if they are rational.
d) The supply of wheat will fall to near zero and the U.S. will become dependent on foreign suppliers of food.

Chapter 10, The Perfect Competition Model

ANSWER KEY

Exercises

1. 1) Firms are small relative to the size of the market, 2) firms produce a homogeneous product, 3) the market is characterized by freedom of entry and exit.
2. takers
3. marginal, average, average, demand
4. total
5. variable, fixed
6. marginal cost, average variable cost
7. decrease, fall, decrease, increase, normal profit
8. constant-cost, perfectly elastic
9. increasing-cost, increase
10. consumer sovereignty
11. minimum, efficiently, marginal cost, allocative efficiency
12. decrease, increase, increase, decrease, normal profit
13. decrease, decrease
14. General, partial
15. No, Price is $2 ($10,000/5,000) and therefore MR = $2 as well. As such, MR < MC.
16. Firm is making an economic profit of approximately $13.95 (Q = 7.75 and ATC = $5.2).
17. Long-run equilibrium price = $5.
18. Price = $2. Quantity = 6.
19. MC above the minimum of the AVC curve.
20. MR = MC.
21. variable costs. If the firm cannot cover all of its variable costs, losses will be greater than simply the fixed costs. Therefore, the firm will minimize losses (equal to fixed costs) by shutting down.
22. The firm can sell as much or as little output as it wants to at the market price without affecting market price.
23. yes.
24. Number of firms will increase. This will cause industry supply curve to shift right.
25. Market price is again P1 and economic profit = 0.
26. Market supply would not shift as far to the right. New long-run market price would be higher than P1. Economic profit = 0.

Review Questions

1. c) is not a characteristic of perfect competition. The perfectly competitive firm faces a perfectly elastic demand function, not a downward sloping demand function.

2. d) is the correct answer. "Small" refers to the firm being unable to influence the market price. This means that the perfect competitor faces a horizontal demand function at the market price.

3. a) is the correct answer. The perfectly competitive firm cannot influence market price and therefore it can only change output to the profit-maximizing level.

4. b) is the correct answer. It is true for the perfectly competitive firm that price = marginal revenue. This derives from the perfectly elastic demand function that exists for perfect competition. Since the imperfectly competitive firm has a downward sloping demand function, it must lower price in order to sell more and this means that price and marginal revenue are not equal.

5. d) is the correct answer. The one thing we can say definitely, given the information presented in the question, is that the firm is running an economic loss. That is, the firm is earning less than the normal level of profit. The firm may or may not be running an accounting loss and it may or may not shutdown.

6. b) is the correct statement. The firm should not shutdown and will minimize its losses by setting MR = MC. As long as price is above average variable cost, the firm is covering its variable costs and has revenue left over to cover its some of its fixed costs.

7. d) is the correct answer. The firm will lose more on each unit it produces if it stays in business. In order to minimize losses, the firm should shutdown, in which case it loses only its fixed costs.

8. b) is the correct answer. The shutdown point occurs where AVC is at its minimum point. If the market price falls below this level, the firm cannot cover its variable costs and it will minimize its losses by producing nothing and paying its fixed costs.

9. a) is the correct answer. Fixed costs are sunk costs in the short-run and are therefore ignored by the firm in the short-run. The perfectly competitive firm makes its short-run output decision based only on variable costs.

10. c) is the correct answer. As market price changes, the perfectly competitive firm will set marginal revenue(= price) equal to marginal cost. Thus the profit-maximizing quantity at various prices will be determined at the points along the the marginal cost curve. If price falls below AVC the firm will shutdown and the quantity supplied will be zero.

11. b) is the correct answer. The firm will experience economic profits in the short-run. This will induce the firm to produce more in the short-run.

12. c) will not occur in the long-run. If the firm is operating in a constant cost industry, the market price will return to its original level. This answer would be correct for an <u>increasing</u> cost industry.

13. a) is the correct answer. In an increasing cost industry, the changes in the industry demand for inputs has an effect on the prices of those inputs. Since the fall in demand for the output of the industry will cause the demand for inputs to fall as firms drop out of the industry and firms remaining in the industry get smaller, the prices of inputs will fall. This shifts the cost functions for the competitive firms down, so that the price at the new long-run equilibrium will be lower than it initially was.

14. b) is not true. In fact, profits will be higher than normal if there is an increase in demand. This is what attracts resources from other industries.

15. c) is the correct answer. In the short-run firms will respond to the reduction in demand and the fall in market price by reducing their output. These firms will also run economic losses in the short-run.

16. d) is the correct answer. Price = MC is the condition necessary for allocative efficiency. This means that the value to consumers of the last unit purchased(price) equals the value of the additional resources used to produce the last unit of the good produced(MC).

17. a) is the correct answer. The most efficient capacity or scale of the plant is the minimum point on the LRATC curve. This is the plant size that will produce the good at the lowest unit cost.

18. c) is the correct answer. Allocative efficiency means that price equals marginal cost. This holds for the perfectly competitive firm in both the short-run and the long-run.

19. b) is the correct answer. If P > MC then consumers would benefit more from consuming one more bicycle than it costs to produce one more bicycle. Thus, society would be made better off with an increase in bicycle production.

20. c) is the correct answer. As long as the market price stays at its original level, the firm will experience an economic loss.

21. a) is the correct answer. An improvement in technology causes the firms' MC and ATC curves to shift down. This causes existing firms to produce more and attracts new firms to the industry. Therefore, the industry supply shifts to the right. There is an increase in quantity and a decrease in price.

22. d) is the correct answer. The bicycle industry must obtain the additional labor it needs to produce more bicycles from somewhere. It will come from other industries. The increase in the demand for labor will drive up wages. Therefore, other industries will experience increases in cost and their cost functions will shift up.

23. b) is the correct answer. Consumers determine what will be produced by the prices they are willing to pay for goods. If consumers have a strong preference for a good, they are willing to pay a high price and this will induce producers to provide the good.

24. d) is the correct answer. The increase in costs in industry Y will result in firms running losses in the short-run. Some of these firms will drop out of the industry. This causes a reduction in supply and an increase in price. This process will continue until economic losses disappear and the industry is in long-run equilibrium.

25. d) will not occur. The perfectly competitive world would result in efficiency, but not necessarily an equal distribution of income.

26. a) is not true of free trade. While it is true that free trade will cause unemployment is some U.S. industries, it nevertheless makes the society as a whole better off, since it results in a more efficient allocation of resources.

27. d) is not true. Actually, the invisible hand promotes cooperation among individuals to the extent that specialization and trade are important for individuals who are trying to maximize their self-interest.

28. d) is the correct answer. Perfect Competition creates a "benchmark" against which we can evaluate other markets and judge them in terms of efficiency.

29. c) is the correct answer. If resources are mobile, firms cannot easily enter an industry in response to economic profits and cannot easily exit an industry in response to economic losses.

30. c) is the correct answer. Resources will be reallocated out of the wheat industry because other industries in which economic profits are normal or positive will be able to bid those resources away from the wheat industry. The losses will cause some farms to leave the wheat industry, the supply of wheat will fall and the price of wheat will rise. This process will continue until profits in the wheat industry return to normal.

CHAPTER 11
SMALL FIRM BEHAVIOR: THE IMPERFECT COMPETITION MODEL

OVERVIEW

In this chapter we develop the model of a monopolistically competitive market. After describing the characteristics of this type of market structure, we consider possible short-run equilibrium positions, and identify the characteristics of the long-run equilibrium. We also discuss the use of product differentiation and government regulation as means to escape the pressures of competition.

Monopolistically competitive markets are characterized by a large number of firms that are small relative to the market, ease of entry and exit (resource mobility), and product differentiation. It is the latter characteristic that is the monopoly element in the market. In effect, each firm faces a downward-sloping demand curve for its output. The result of these characteristics is that monopolistically competitive firms are price searchers. In other words, they select the output-price combination that maximizes their profits.

In the short run, monopolistically competitive firms can earn economic profits, incur a loss, or break even. However, over the long run the pressures of competition and the incentives effects of profits and losses, combined with the assumption of resource mobility, drive economic profits to zero. In the situation in which firms are earning short-run economic profit, new firms will enter the market, causing the demand curve faced by each existing firm to shift left and become more elastic. Entry will continue until economic profits are driven to zero. If firms are incurring a loss, some firms will exit the market, causing the demand curve faced by each remaining firm to shift right and become less elastic. Exit will continue until losses are eliminated and firms once again earn a normal profit.

In the long run, firms in a monopolistically competitive market earn a normal profit. However, unlike the case of a perfectly competitive market, the long-run equilibrium position of a monopolistically competitive firm is not economically efficient. In particular, each firm is allocatively inefficient since price is greater than marginal cost for the last unit produced, and the firm is not at the minimum of its average total cost curve.

In their efforts to earn short-run profits, monopolistically competitive firms compete on the basis of both price and non-price characteristics. Firms rely on the use of product differentiation--either real or imagined--to distinguish their output from that of their competitors. Real product differentiation consists of actual differences across goods that result from the use of different qualities of inputs or production processes. Imagined product differentiation occurs when what are, in fact, identical products are perceived as being different. Imagined product differentiation is often the result of advertising, although advertising also is used to highlight real product differentiation. Viewed from the perspective of economic efficiency, it is not clear whether advertising is in fact beneficial.

Government regulation has also been relied on as a means to escape the pressures of competition. In this case, regulation has the effect of restricting entry into a particular market. Although the regulation is usually intended to serve some other goal, such as an improvement in social welfare, it nonetheless has the effect of benefiting existing firms that face a reduced threat of competition from potential new entrants into the market.

KEY GRAPHS AND TERMS

Graphs

The model of a monopolistically competitive firm in long-run equilibrium is illustrated in Figures 2a and 3 in the text. Note that price is equal to average total cost at the profit maximizing level of output. Hence, the firm is earning a normal profit. If demand were to increase, the firm would earn short-run profits. A decrease in demand would result in an economic loss. Because enrty and exit are assumed to be costless, profits and losses lead to a change in the number of firms in the market. Profits act as an incentive for additional firm to enter the market, causing the demand curve of each existing firm to shift left. Losses have the opposite effect. Some firms leave the market, causing the demand curves of the remaining firms to shift right.

Terms
PRODUCT DIFFERENTIATION
MONOPOLISTIC COMPETITION
NONPRICE COMPETITION
REAL PRODUCT DIFFERENTIATION
IMAGINED PRODUCT DIFFERENTIATION

EXERCISES

1. List the three major characteristics of a monopolistically competitive market. ____________________

____

____

2. Firms in a monopolistically competitive market are price ____________.

3. Assume a monopolistically competitive market is initially in long-run equilibrium. In the short run, an increase in the number of buyers (assume the increase is spread across the firms in the market) will cause the demand curve faced by each existing firm to ____________ ____________. As a result, the profits of existing firms will ____________. However, over the long run, this will cause the number of firms in the market to ____________. As such, the demand curve faced by each individual firm will ____________ ____________ and become ____________ elastic. This process will continue until each firm is once again earning a ____________ ____________.

4. In long run equilibrium a monopolistically competitive firm operates at a point on its ATC curve that is (greater than, less than, equal to) its minimum average total cost. Hence, the firm is using its capacity ____________. Moreover, price is ____________ than marginal cost for the last unit of output produced. Hence, the firm is ____________ ____________ as well.

5. Activities such as product differentiation and advertising are referred to as ____________ ____________.

6. ____________ product differentiation refers to the situation in which similar products differ as a result of actual characteristics. ____________ product differentiation refers to the situation in which products that are in fact identical are perceived as being different.

7. Government regulation of monopolistically competitive markets can benefit existing firms by restricting ____________ into the market, thus enabling firms to earn ____________ economic profits over the long run.

8. The assumption of a high degree of ____________ ____________ ensures that in the long run, monopolistically competitive firms will only earn a normal profit.

Use the following figure, which depicts the situation faced by a monopolistically competitive firm, to answer questions 9 - 12.

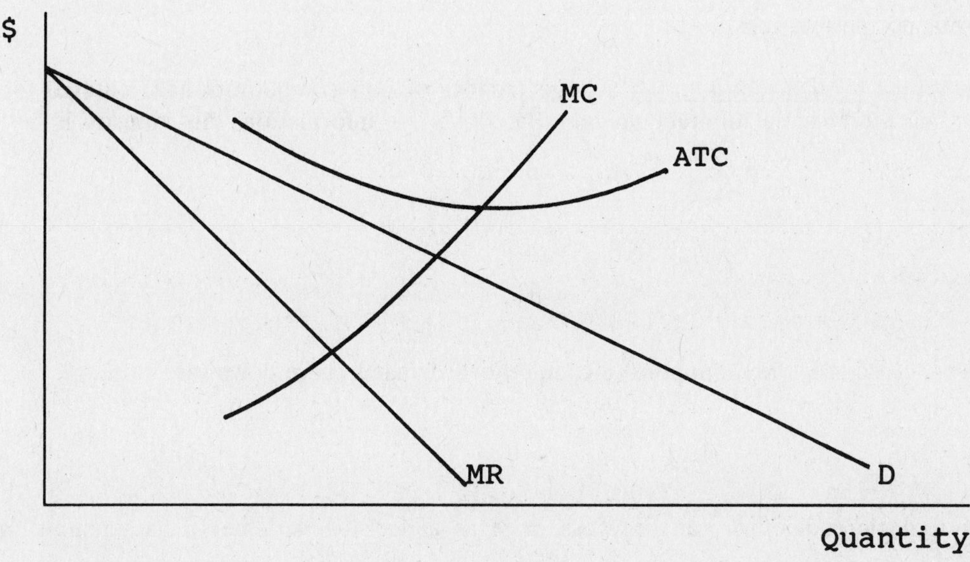

9. Identify the firm's profit-maximizing output level price and label them Q1 and P1.

10. Is this firm earning an economic profit, breaking even, or incurring a loss?

____

11. Shade in the area represents the firm's profit or loss and label it in an appropriate manner.

12. Over the long run, the demand curve faced by this firm will shift __________________ and become __________________ elastic.

<u>REVIEW QUESTIONS</u>

1. For which of the following reasons may prices be different in different locations?

a) Resource immobility
b) Demand functions which are perfectly elastic
c) Consumers having different tastes
d) a) and c), but not b)

2. Which of the following is <u>NOT</u> a characteristic of monopolistic competition?

a) ease of entry into the industry.
b) product differentiation.
c) a relatively large number of sellers.
d) a homogeneous product.

3. Which of the following is a characteristic of monopolistic competition, but not of perfect competition?

a) many firms in the market
b) easy entry into the market
c) easy exit from the market
d) firms producing close, but not perfect substitutes

4. According to an article in the Wall Street Journal, a large number of new competitors have entered the market for mountain bikes, each offering a different model. Based on this information, this industry is best characterized as:

a) perfectly competitive.
b) a monopoly.
c) monopolistically competitive.
d) an oligopoly.

5. For which of the following reasons is the monopolistic competitor's demand curve downward-sloping?

a) Ease of entry and exit
b) Product differentiation
c) Homogenous output
d) The fact that the monopolistic competitor can only use price as a decision variable in its attempts to maximize profits.

6. The monopolistically competitive seller's demand curve will tend to become more elastic the:

a) smaller the number of sellers.
b) greater the degree of product differentiation.
c) larger the number of close competitors.
d) more significant the barriers to entering an industry.

7. Suppose the firms in a monopolistically competitive industry are earning economic profits. Which of the following will not occur?

a) The firms' economic profits will be reduced.
b) New firms will enter
c) Demand for the existing firms' output will become more inelastic.
d) The number of substitutes available in the industry will increase.

8. All of the following are characteristics of long-run equilibrium for firms in a monopolistically competitive market EXCEPT:

a) price equals marginal cost.
b) price equals average total cost.
c) marginal cost equals marginal revenue.
d) price exceeds the minimum of average total cost.

9. Long-run equilibrium occurs for the monopolistic competitor where:

a) MR = Price
b) LRATC = Price
c) Economic Profits > 0
d) Minimum LRAC = LRMC

10. Excess capacity:

a) exists in monopolistic competition because firms do not produce where their SRATC curve is at its minimum.
b) exists to a greater extent the more elastic the monopolistic competitor's demand function.
c) suggests the monopolistic competitor has an incentive to minimize costs.
d) disappears in long-run equilibrium in monopolistic competition.

11. Suppose the firms in a monopolistically competitive market are running a short-run economic loss. In the long-run adjustment, which of the following will occur?

a) The firms' demand functions will become more elastic.
b) The firms' demand functions will shift to the right.
c) More close substitutes will appear in the market.
d) a) and c), but not b)

12. Referring to the previous question, what will happen to move the market to its long-run equilibrium?

a) More close substitutes will appear in the market until economic profits are zero.
b) The firms that dropped out of the market will reenter once the level of economic losses is zero.
c) Firms will continue to exit the market until economic losses are equal to zero.
d) The demand functions of all the firms remaining in the market will become relatively more elastic.

13. In equilibrium, a monopolistically competitive firm is:

a) allocatively efficient and price equals LRATC.
b) allocatively efficient, but price does not equal LRATC.
c) allocatively efficient, but price does not equal MC.
d) not allocatively efficient.

14. There will be less inefficiency in a monopolistically competitive industry:

a) the more elastic the demand curves are for the individual firms.
b) the less elastic the demand curves are for the individual firms.
c) the fewer firms there are in the industry.
d) if advertising makes entry into the industry difficult.

15. In comparing the long-run equilibrium outcome in a perfectly competitive market versus a monopolistically competitive market, it is observed that:

a) the outcome in perfect competition is efficient, while the outcome in monopolistic competition is not. However, monopolistic competition has the advantage of offering consumers a greater range of choices.
b) firms in both market structures are allocatively efficient, but monopolistically competitive firms also make positive long-run economic profits.
c) monopolistic competition leads to significantly greater economies of scale than are possible under perfect competition.
d) there are no differences in the long-run equilibrium conditions for each market structure.

16. If all aspirin is the same chemically, advertising to promote particular brands of aspirin is an example of:

a) excess capacity.
b) a lack of nonprice competition.
c) imagined product differentiation.
d) real product differentiation.

17. Which of the following is not true?

a) Both monopolistic and perfect competitors rely on nonprice competition.
b) Advertising is used in monopolistically competitive markets to highlight product differentiation.
c) There is an incentive for firms to attempt to escape from competition.
d) Competition eliminates economic profits.

18. Which of the following is not cited in the text as a way that monopolistic competitors attempt to reduce competition?

a) government regulation
b) licenses to enter the industry
c) advertising which emphasizes product differentiation.
d) attempts to make the demand curve relatively more elastic.

19. Which of the following is a reason that licenses reduce competition?

a) They promote advertising.
b) They result in price being closer to the minimum point on the LRAC curve.
c) They limit entry into the market.
d) They never can be resold.

20. Regulating the taxi cab market in New York City did not have which of the following effects?

a) It reduced the incentive for black markets to develop.
b) It limited entry into the industry.
c) It increased the profits of the existing firms in the taxi industry.
d) It created excess demand for taxi service.

Chapter 11, Small Firm Behavior: The Imperfect Competition Model

ANSWER KEY

Exercises

1. 1) A large number of small firms, 2) ease of entry and exit (resource mobility), and 3) product differentiation
2. searchers
3. shift right, increase, increase, shift left, more, normal profit
4. greater than, inefficiently, greater, allocatively inefficient
5. nonprice competition
6. Real, Imagined
7. entry, positive
8. resource mobility (ease of entry and exit)
9. see figure below
10. incurring a loss
11. see figure below
12. right, less

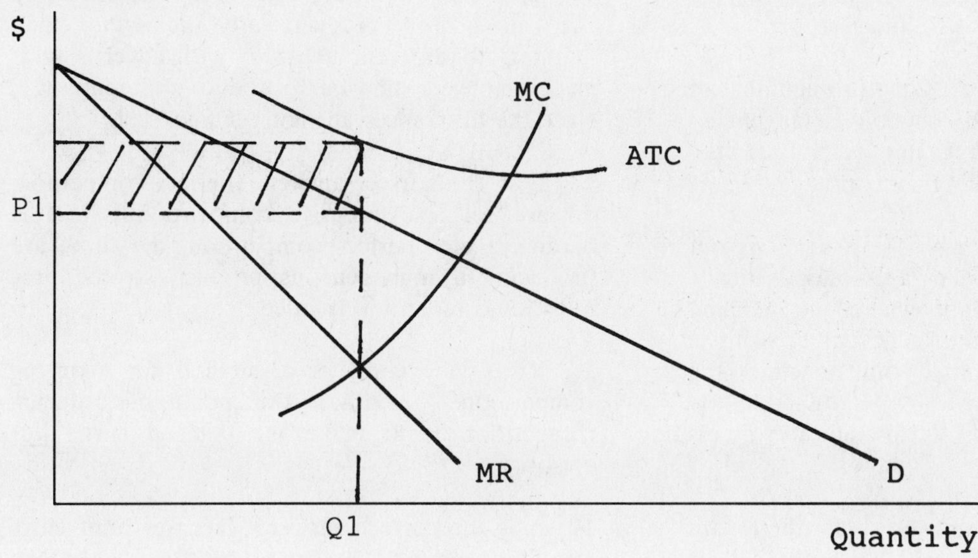

Review Questions

1. d) is the correct answer. One reason prices may be different in different locations is the immobility of resources which prevents free entry into markets in which prices are high and free exit from markets in which prices are low. Another reason is differing consumer tastes which allows firms to charge different prices for particular characteristics their product offers.

2. d) is not a characteristic of monopolistic competition. In fact it is the opposite of product differentiation, which is the characteristic that distinguishes monopolistic competition from perfect competition.

3. d) is the correct answer. This characteristic is another way of describing product differentiation, which exists for monopolistic competition, but not for perfect competition. The output of perfectly competitive firms is homogenous.

4. c) is the correct answer. If a large number of firms are operating and each is producing a somewhat different product, we have two of the main characteristics of monopolistic competition.

5. b) is the correct answer. It is product differentiation that causes the monopolistically competitive firm to face a downward-sloping

demand function. Thus the firm is a price searcher.

6. c) is the correct answer. The more competitors there are in the industry, each producing close substitutes, the closer monopolistic competition will approximate perfect competition.

7. c) is the correct answer. As new firms enter to take advantage of the economic profits, the market will offer more close substitutes. This will make the demand for the existing firms' output become more elastic.

8. a) does not occur in long-run equilibrium under monopolistic competition. Price is greater than marginal cost, since the firm will not be at the minimum point of the LRATC function.

9. b) is the correct answer. Long-run equilibrium occurs where the demand function is tangent to the LRATC function, but this is not at the minimum point on the LRATC curve.

10. a) is the correct answer. In long-run equilibrium, the firms in a monopolistically competitive market produce where the demand function is tangent to the LRATC curve. This is to the left of the minimum point on either the LRATC function or the SRATC function on which the firm is operating. This indicates excess capacity.

11. b) is the correct answer. If there are economic losses, firms will exit the market. This will mean each of the firms that are left in the market will have a larger market share. Thus, the demand curve will shift to the right.

12. c) is the correct answer. Firms will drop out of the market and the demand curves of the remaining firms will shift to the right until the economic losses are eliminated and economic profits and losses are equal to zero.

13. d) is the correct answer. Under monopolistic competition, price does not equal marginal cost, therefore monopolistic competition is not allocatively efficient.

14. a) is the correct answer. The more elastic the demand curve is for the individual monopolistic competitors, the closer the market is to perfect competition and the less economic inefficiency there is.

15. a) is correct. While it is true that monopolistic competition is not economically efficient, it allows the consumer the benefits of greater variety in making choices among products.

16. c) is the correct answer. If it is actually true that all aspirin products are the same, then attempts to differentiate them with advertising is an example of imagined product differentiation, since the differences are not genuine.

17. a) is the correct answer. Perfect competitors do not rely on nonprice competition. This is because under perfect competition, the firms are producing a homogeneous product, so the only basis for competition is price.

18. d) is not cited as a method for reducing competition. In fact, the point of reducing competition is to make the demand curve less elastic.

19. c) is the correct answer. Licenses limit entry into the market by firms that want to take advantage of economic profits that exist. Thus, the economic profits may persist.

20. a) is not an effect that regulation of the taxi industry has. Regulation increases the incentive for illegal markets to develop, since individuals who are prevented from legally entering the taxi industry to take advantage of the economic profits do so illegally.

CHAPTER 12
LARGE FIRM BEHAVIOR: THE IMPERFECT COMPETITION MODEL

OVERVIEW

In this chapter we develop the models of monopoly and oligopoly. These models are presented together because of the high degree of similarity between the two market structures. We begin by developing the monopoly model, focusing on how barriers to entry affect the long-run equilibrium. We also discuss the special case of a natural monopoly and its implications for economic efficiency. Our discussion of oligopoly focuses on the interdependence of the firms in such markets and the implications of this characteristic for firm behavior.

A monopoly market consists of a single firm, and is the result of one or more barriers to entry. Such barriers include control of essential resources, patents on production processes or goods, and economies of scale which enable a single firm to produce at a lower average cost than two or more firms serving the same market. The primary effect of entry barriers is to lessen, or eliminate, the pressures of competition from other firms. In the case of a monopoly, there is no competition. One important result is that monopolists are able to earn economic profits in both the short run and the long run. Recall that in perfectly competitive and monopolistically competitive markets, it is the pressure of competition that eliminates economic profits in the long run.

A natural monopoly refers to the situation in which an industry is characterized by economies of scale over the relevant range of output. In this case, production costs can be minimized by allowing a single firm to serve the entire market. However, the firm's desire to maximize profits will result in an economically inefficient level of output since price is greater than marginal cost at the output level at which marginal revenue and marginal cost are equal. Policymakers have responded to this dilemma by allowing natural monopolists to operate in certain markets subject to regulation. For example, in the case of energy services--electricity and natural gas--a single firm is granted a franchise to serve a specified territory. However, price is set on the basis of rate-of-return regulation, which is intended to limit the firm's profit to a normal return on its investment.

An oligopoly market is characterized by the presence of two or more firms, but where a very few firms control the majority of the market. Like monopoly, oligopolies are characterized by a high degree of resource immobility. Concentration ratios are used to measure the extent to which a market is dominated by a small number of firms. The high degree of concentration in oligopolies results in considerable mutual interdependence, i.e., the price and output decisions of one firm have a significant effect on the decisions of other firms in the market. The effect of mutual interdependence is to encourage firms to seek alternatives to competition on the basis of price. Such alternatives usually consist of some form of collusion.

Collusion refers to the act of firms working together to set the price and level of output in a particular market. Examples of collusive behavior include explicit agreements such as OPEC, price leadership, and secret agreements. The degree to which collusion is successful depends, in large part, on the extent to which firms can cheat on the agreement. Other obstacles to successful collusion include the degree of product differentiation in the market, the extent to which costs differ across firms that are parties to the agreement, the number of firms involved, and the availability of substitutes for the good or service in question.

Government regulation can also enable firms in an oligopoly to avoid the pressures of competition. To the extent that government regulation restricts entry and controls price setting behavior, existing firms can continue to operate without worrying about the threat of losing market share to competitors. Mergers--vertical, horizontal, and conglomerate--also reduce the degree of competition in a market by reducing the number of existing firms.

KEY GRAPHS AND TERMS

Graphs

Figures 1 - 3 illustrate alternative short-run equilibria for a monopolist. It is important to recognize that because there is competition, the short-run equilibrium is also the long-run equilibrium, ceteris paribus. It is also important to note that economic profits are not guaranteed in the case of monopoly. In fact, it is quite possible for a monopolist to incur an economic loss.

Figure 4 summarizes the efficiency characteristics of a monopoly market. Note that monopoly is allocatively inefficient, producing a level of output that too low since P < MC. Note also that monopoly results in a deadweight loss in the form of lost consumer and producer surplus.

Figures 5 - 7 illustrate the situation of a natural monopoly and alternative approaches to regulating the pricing and output decisions of such firms. An important feature of natural monopoly is the potential trade-off between productive efficiency (producing at lowest average total cost) and allocative efficiency.

Figure 8 illustrates the mutual interdependence of oligopolistic firms. It is important to follow the order of the changes that occur to understand the graphs.

Terms

BARRIER TO ENTRY
PATENT
MONOPOLY
NATURAL MONOPOLY
RATE-OF-RETURN REGULATION
REVENUE REQUIREMENT
BLOCK PRICING
PRICE DISCRIMINATION
OLIGOPOLY
MUTUAL INTERDEPENDENCE
CONCENTRATION RATIO
COLLUSION
CARTEL
PRICE LEADERSHIP
HORIZONTAL MERGER
VERTICAL MERGER
CONGLOMERATE MERGER
THEORY OF CONTESTABLE MARKETS

EXERCISES

1. List four potential barriers to entry into a market. ____

____

____

2. A ______________ entitles its owner to exclusive rights to a production process for a period of seventeen years.

3. List the two major characteristics of a monopoly market. ______________________________

____

4. In long-run equilibrium an unrestricted profit-maximizing monopolist will produce the level of output at which MR = MC. However, because the firm's demand curve is downward sloping, price is ______________ than marginal cost, indicating that the firm is ______________ ______________.

5. The situation in which the long-run average cost curve is downward sloping over the relevant range of output is called a ______________ ______________. In such a case, the average costs of production will be minimized by having ______________ firm(s) serve the entire market. However, left unregulated, the market-determined outcome will be ______________ inefficient.

6. Assume that a firm's pricing and output behavior is governed by a regulatory commission on the basis of rate-of-return regulation. The firm's operating expenses are $2 million per year, its rate base is $20 million,

and the allowable rate of return has been set at 12 percent. What is the firm's revenue requirement?

____

7. Assume that a monopolist is able to engage in perfect price discrimination, i.e., each unit of output is sold at the highest price consumers are willing to pay. In this case, the monopolist will maximize its profits by producing the level of output at which ____.

8. The primary characteristic of an oligopoly is the ________________ ________________ of the firms in the market. The other major characteristics of an oligopoly include: ________________________________

____

9. A ________________ ________________ is used to measure the extent to which one or a few firms control the level of production in an industry.

10. If one of the firms in an oligopoly decides to lower its price in an effort to attract new customers and increase its profits, the most likely result will be a ________________ in the profits of all of the firms in the market.

11. ________________ refers to the act of firms working together to establish the price and level of output in a particular market.

12. The situation in which one firm in an industry establishes the market price and the remaining firms in the industry follow suit is called ________________ ________________.

13. List five potential obstacles to successful collusion. ________________________________

____

____

14. A merger between Ford and General Motors would be an example of a ________________ merger, while a merger between a poultry producer and Kentucky Fried Chicken would be an example of a ________________ merger. A merger between Coca-Cola and Levi Strauss would be an example of a ________________ merger.

15. In one or two sentences, summarize the implications of the theory of contestable markets. ____________

____

____

Use the figure below which represents the situation faced by a monopolist to answer questions 2 - 5.

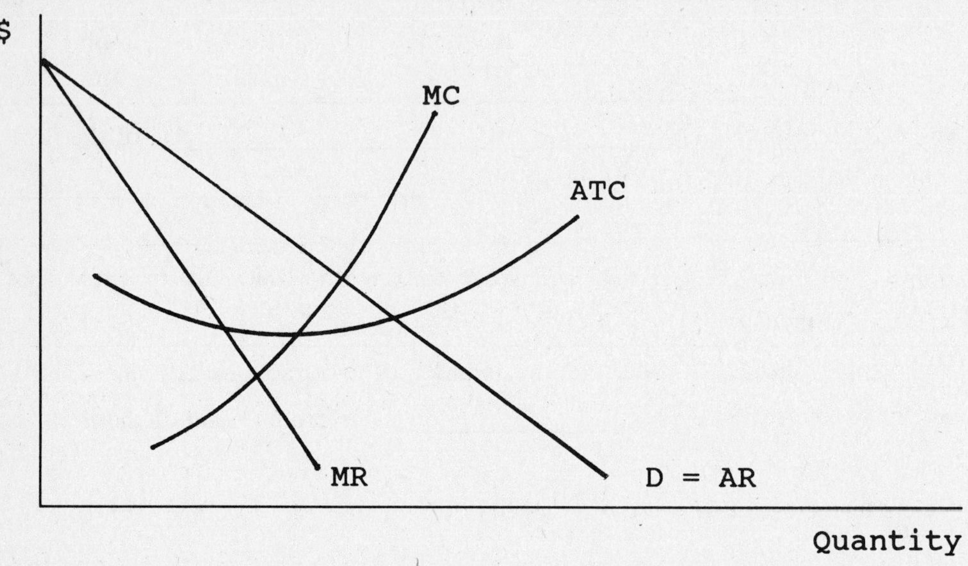

16. In the figure, indicate the profit maximizing price and output level and label them P1 and Q1.

17. Shade in the area that represents the firm's economic profit (or loss).

18. Using a different type of shading, indicate the area (if any) that represents the deadweight loss to society.

19. If this firm wished to discourage entry by other firms it could produce the output level at which it earns only a normal profit (zero economic profit). Indicate the price and output level associated with a normal profit and label them P2 and Q2.

20. Indicate the allocatively efficient price and output level by P3 and Q3. If the firm is forced to produce at this output level will it make an economic profit or loss? ____________________

21. If a firm is a monopolist, it will always be able to make an economic profit. True or False? Why?

22. Because the profit-maximizing monopolist produces the level of output at which MR = MC, the following results hold:

a. price will be ____________ than the marginal cost of the last unit produced, and hence

b. too (many, few) resources will be devoted to the production of the good.

Chapter 12, Large Firm Behavior: The Imperfect Competition Model

REVIEW QUESTIONS

1. All of the following statements about barriers to entry are true except:

a) They restrict the entry into industries in which there are above normal profits being made.
b) They are somewhat eased by the existence of patents.
c) They may be due to legal impediments such as licenses.
d) They may be due to a single firm controlling the access to a natural resource or production process.

2. If an industry is characterized by economies of scale:

a) barriers to entry are usually not very large.
b) long-run unit costs of production increase as the quantity the firm produces increases.
c) capital requirements are small due to the efficiency of the large-scale operations.
d) the costs of entry into the market are likely to be substantial.

3. If there are barriers to entry, it is possible for the existing firm(s) to earn economic profits. All of the following explain this except:

a) New firms cannot enter to take advantage of the profits.
b) Resource immobility.
c) It is possible for a firm in this situation to charge any price it wants and thus preclude anyone else from entering.
d) Competition does not erode profits the way it would under perfect competition.

4. Viewed from the perspective of economic efficiency, which of the following barriers to entry is the best justification for monopoly?

a) a patented production technique.
b) unfair competition.
c) ownership of an essential raw material.
d) significant economies of scale.

5. All of the following are characteristics of a monopoly EXCEPT:

a) there is a single firm.
b) the firm is a price taker.
c) the firm produces a unique product.
d) the existence of some advertising.

6. Which of the following statements is true of a monopoly?

a) The marginal revenue curve is the same as its demand curve.
b) It sets marginal revenue equal to marginal cost.
c) It sets price equal to marginal cost.
d) It will always earn economic profits in both the short-run and the long-run.

7. A pure monopolist will:

a) always realize an economic profit.
b) realize an economic loss if MC intersects the negative portion of the MR curve.
c) realize an economic profit if ATC > MR at equilibrium output.
d) realize an economic profit if P > ATC at equilibrium output.

8. In comparing monopoly to a perfectly competitive industry, which of the following is correct?

a) Price will be higher under perfect competition.
b) Quantity will be higher under perfect competition.
c) Social welfare will be higher under monopoly.
d) Employment will be higher under monopoly.

9. Which of the following is not true of monopoly in long-run equilibrium?

a) Social welfare would be improved if less resources were allocated to the industry in which the monopoly operates.
b) Price > MC
c) Price > ATC
d) Price = Average Revenue

10. Consider the trade-off that occurs when comparing monopoly to perfect competition. Monopoly profits are higher than those that would occur under perfect competition, but they are at the expense of consumer surplus. Which of the following statements is true about this trade-off?

a) The monopoly profits are greater than the reduction in consumer surplus.
b) The monopoly profits are less than the reduction in consumer surplus.
c) The monopoly profits are equal to the reduction in consumer surplus.
d) The monopoly causes consumer surplus to fall to zero.

11. A "natural" monopoly refers to the situation where:

a) an industry is characterized by having many close substitutes.
b) all potential competitors have left due to regulation.
c) there is enough demand to support only one producer.
d) a single firm owns the essential factors of production.

12. Which of the following is a characteristic of a natural monopoly?

a) MC intersects LRATC to the right of the demand curve.
b) Economic profits are less than zero in the short-run if the firm is unregulated.
c) Economic profits are less than zero in the long-run if the firm is unregulated.
d) It has control over the access to some natural resource that is essential to production in an industry.

13. If a market is characterized as a "natural monopoly," economic efficiency would be increased by having:

a) a single firm operating in the market.
b) two or three firms operating in the market.
c) a large number of competing firms operating in the market.
d) an indeterminate number of firms operating in the market.

14. If a natural monopoly is forced to produce at the economically efficient level of output:

a) it will be earning economic profits.
b) price will be greater than LRATC.
c) price will equal LRATC.
d) price will be less than LRATC.

15. If the government regulates the natural monopoly by making it produce where price equals long-run average cost:

a) the natural monopoly will be making zero economic profits.
b) the natural monopoly will be making less than normal profits.
c) the natural monopoly will be running an economic loss.
d) the natural monopoly will be operating at minimum LRATC.

16. The key characteristic of an oligopoly is the:

a) presence of long run economic profits.
b) fact that in all cases, firms produce a standardized product.
c) mutual interdependence of the firms in the market.
d) near total absence of advertising.

17. Oligopolistic industries are characterized by:

a) a few dominant firms and substantial barriers to entry.
b) a few large firms and no entry barriers.
c) a large number of small firms and no entry barriers.
d) one dominant firm and low entry barriers.

18. Assume that the four-firm concentration ratio in industry X is 75% and that firms produce a differentiated product. Industry X would be characterized as:

a) perfect competition.
b) monopolistic competition.
c) monopoly.
d) oligopoly.

19. Suppose an oligopoly consists of two firms. Firm A lowers price and Firm B responds by lowering price the same amount. Which of the following will occur, if average costs and industry output remain the same.

a) the profits of the two firms will increase.
b) the profits of the two firms will decrease.
c) the profits of the two firms will remain the same.
d) barriers to entry will come tumbling down and new firms will enter.

20. Why is the prisoner's dilemma useful in studying oligopoly behavior?
a) Because oligopolies make out like bandits.
b) To illustrate the problems caused by making decisions under uncertainty.
c) To show that oligopolies behave as monopolists in the long-run and earn economic profits.
d) To illustrate how barriers to entry lead to economic profits.

21. Which of the following would make it easier to maintain an effective collusive agreement in a cartel?

a) a decrease in the number of potential entrants into the industry.
b) an increase in the elasticity of demand for the cartel's product.
c) an increase in the number of substitutes for the product produced by the cartel.
d) a new method of pricing that makes it more difficult for each firm to monitor the prices that the other firms in the cartel are charging.

22. Price leadership:

a) has rarely occurred in recent U.S. history.
b) is illegal in the U.S.
c) is usually the result of a dominant firm in the industry.
d) usually results in the smaller firms in the industry running economic losses.

23. If a firm cheats on a cartel agreement it would engage in which of the following:

a) it would raise price above the agreed level.
b) it would lower price below the agreed level.
c) it would sell less than its agreed quota.
d) it would force buyers to make secret payments over and above the agreed price.

24. Firms have tried a number of different strategies to reduce the negative effects of competition on their ability to earn economic profits. Which of the following strategies is most desirable from the viewpoint of economic efficiency?

a) collusion.
b) price leadership.
c) formation of cartels.
d) research on and development of technological innovations.

25. A merger between McDonald's and Burger King would be an example of a:

a) horizontal merger.
b) conglomerate merger.
c) vertical merger.
d) geographic merger.

26. Cartels:

a) are difficult to maintain because firms cheat by raising price above the agreed price.
b) restrict industry output in order to raise price.
c) are stable, since oligopolistic firms rarely change price.
d) are relatively easy to establish since the cost functions of each individual firm is irrelevant.

27. Which of the following best characterizes an oligopolistic market?

a) a large number of firms producing close, but not perfect substitutes.
b) a small number of dominant firms facing perfectly elastic demand functions.
c) a small number of dominant firms facing downward-sloping demand functions.
d) firms that are able to easily enter the market, but cannot easily exit the market.

28. Suppose an oligopolistic firm raises price. The firm's demand function will be relatively ___________ if the other dominant firms in the market _____________.

a) elastic; also raise price
b) inelastic; also raise price
c) flat; also raise price
d) steep; maintain price

29. The auto industry can best be described as:

a) an oligopoly.
b) a monopoly.
c) perfectly competitive.
d) monopolistically competitive

30. When we describe the firms in an oligopoly as being "mutually interdependent," we are saying that each firm:

a) must consider the reactions of its competitors when it sets the price for its output.
b) produces a product that is similar but not identical to the products of its competitors.
c) produces a product that is identical to the products of its competitors.
d) faces a perfectly elastic demand curve for its product.

ANSWER KEY

Exercises

1. 1) Control of resources, 2) control of production processes and product, 3) economies of scale, and 4) legal barriers
2. patent
3. 1) A single firm, 2) barriers to entry
4. greater, allocatively inefficient
5. natural monopoly, one, allocatively
6. $4.4 million
7. the marginal cost curve intersects the demand curve
8. mutual interdependence, a small number of dominant firms, barriers to entry, a homogeneous or differentiated product
9. concentration ratio
10. reduction (decrease)
11. Collusion
12. price leadership
13. 1) Cheating, 2) degree of product differentiation, 3) extent of cost differences among firms, 4) number of firms involved, and 5) availability of substitutes produced outside the industry
14. horizontal, vertical, conglomerate
15. So long as entry and exit are costless, firms will produce at minimum cost and earn no economic profits. Hence, the number of firms in the industry does not have to be large to ensure a competitive outcome.

16 - 19. See figure below

20. See figure below, profit
21. false, the firm's price setting power is restricted by the demand curve. If the ATC curve lies to the right of the demand curve, there is no output level the firm can produce that will not result in a loss.
22. a. greater, b. few

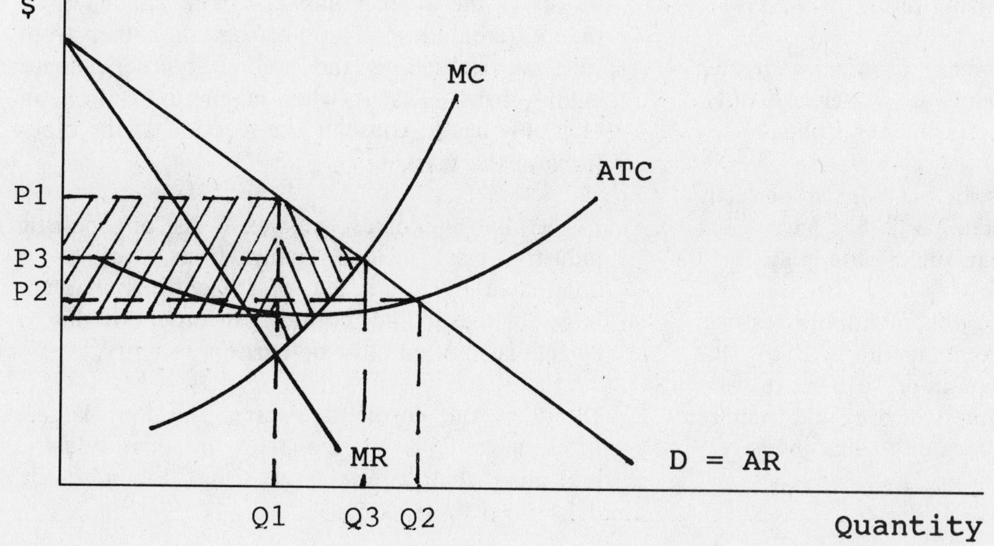

Review Questions

1. b) is not true. Patents do not ease barriers to entry, patents create barriers to entry just as licenses and exclusive franchises do.

2. d) is the correct answer. Industries that are characterized by economies of scale are also usually characterized by large capital requirements. This capital requires substantial funding, which presents a significant barrier to entry.

3. c) is not a correct explanation of barriers to entry. A monopoly cannot "charge any price it wants." It must be on the negatively-sloped demand curve. As it raises price quantity demanded falls.

4. d) is the correct answer. A trade-off exists when there are economies of scale in an industry. On the one hand, a large firm can produce the output at a lower cost than smaller, more competitive firms can. On the other hand, the large firm will not have the pressure of competition to hold down prices and economic profits.

5. b) is the exception here. The monopoly is certainly not a price taker, it is a price searcher, moving along the demand function to find the price and quantity combination that will maximize profits.

6. b) is true of a monopoly. It will set MR = MC in order to maximize profits. This condition holds for all profit-maximizing firms.

7. d) is the correct answer. If price is greater than ATC then total revenue is greater than total cost and there are positive economic profits.

8. b) is the correct answer. Under a perfectly competitive industry, price will be lower and quantity will be higher than under monopoly.

9. a) is not true. Since the monopoly restricts supply relative to perfect competition, P > MC, and society's welfare would improve if more were produced in that industry, which would require that more resources be allocated to that industry.

10. b) is the correct answer. The monopoly profits are less than the reduction in consumer surplus. This is why there is a deadweight loss associated with monopoly.

11. c) is correct. A natural monopoly is an industry in which demand is insufficient to support any more than one firm. Therefore, the long-run average costs of production are declining over the relevant range of output.

12. a) is correct. If you refer to the diagrams of natural monopoly in the text, you will see that there are several characteristics that make it unique. MC = LRATC to the left of the demand function, which is another way of saying that the demand function intersects the LRATC where LRATC is falling.

13. a) is correct. Since the LRATC curve is downward-sloping over the relevant range of production, the larger the firm, the lower the unit cost will be.

14. d) is correct. If the natural monopoly is forced to produce where price = MC, price will be less than LRATC and the firm will run an economic loss.

15. a) is correct. If price is set where LRATC intersects the demand function, price = LRATC and economic profits = 0.

16. c) is the correct answer. The characteristic that differentiates oligopoly from the other types we have studied, is the mutual interdependence among firms. That is, when making a decision, an oligopoly has to consider the reaction of the other firms in the market.

17. a) is the correct answer. As oligopolistic industry may include many firms, but it is dominated by just a few of these firms that are large relative to the industry. In order for this to be the case, there must be barriers to entry.

18. d) is the correct answer. The four largest firms have 75% of the sales in this industry, indicating that a few large firms dominate the

industry. Oligopolies can have either homogenous or differentiated products.

19. b) is the correct answer. The two firms will experience a decrease in profits. This illustrates the difficult decisions an oligopolist faces due to the possible reactions of rival firms.

20. b) is the correct answer. Game Theory is useful in the study of oligopoly because it analyzes strategic behavior when there is uncertainty.

21. a) is the correct answer. One of the problems with a cartel agreement is that the economic profits created by the colluding firms(that are acting as a monopoly) attract potential entrants to the industry. Usually these entrants are turned away by the barriers to entry. But the fewer of them there are, the easier it will be for the cartel to maintain its monopoly position.

22. c) is the correct answer. Price leadership frequently results from a dominant firm in the industry. The dominant firm benefits because there is little threat from competition and the presence of smaller firms shields the dominant firm from charges of monopoly power.

23. b) is the correct answer. If a firm is cheating on a cartel agreement, it will lower price below the agreed price in order to increase its share of the profits.

24. d) is the correct answer. Some economists have argued that large firms can afford to engage in research activities which lead to technological innovations and further economies of scale which benefit consumers with lower prices.

25. a) is the correct answer. A horizontal merger is a merger between two firms which produce the same or similar products.

26. b) is the correct answer. Cartels restrict supply to a level below what it is in the oligopoly situation in order to raise price. This is an effort to reduce the tendency of competition to erode economic profits and to reduce to uncertainty that exists under oligopoly.

27. c) is the correct answer. Oligopoly is characterized by a few large firms that each face downward-sloping demand functions. There may or may not be a number of smaller peripheral firms.

28. b) is the correct answer. If the firm raises price and other firms also raise price, as in the case of price leadership, the firm will experience a relatively small decline in quantity demanded. Therefore, the demand function will be relatively inelastic or relatively steep.

29. a) is the correct answer. The main characteristic of oligopoly is that it must consider the reaction of other firms in the market when making pricing or any other decisions. The answer to the previous question emphasizes this problem--if the firm raises price it may not be sure whether its rivals will also raise price or try to maintain their prices at the original level.

30. a) is the correct answer. The auto industry is an oligopoly because there are a few dominant firms that are mutually interdependent, that is, they must take account of the reaction of their rivals when making decisions.

CHAPTER 13
THE REGULATION OF BUSINESS BEHAVIOR: POLICY IN TRANSITION

OVERVIEW

In Chapters 11 and 12 we saw how a lack of competition can result in economic inefficiency. In this chapter we consider three alternative approaches--direct ownership of business, the use of anti-trust legislation, and direct regulation--government can use to address market failure that results from a lack of competition. The second half of the chapter examines the recent move toward deregulation of many previously regulated industries.

Businesses that are owned by government are referred to as public enterprises. Examples include publicly-owned utilities and the U.S. Postal Service. The primary objectives of government ownership of business are to provide the good or service at a competitive price, maintain minimum product quality standards, and ensure adequate availability of the good or service. However, government ownership amounts to a monopoly. As such, it is possible for same types of problems to arise. In addition, government ownership of business allows political pressures to be brought to bear on the firm's management. The result is that it is not at all clear whether government ownership results in a more efficient outcome than would occur otherwise.

Antitrust legislation consists of a body of law that restricts the extent to which individuals can exercise various property rights. Beginning with the Sherman Antitrust Act, which was passed in 1890, lawmakers have undertaken efforts to limit the extent to which firms can acquire monopoly power and reduce or eliminate competition from other firms. A number of different laws have been passed that limit anti-competitive behavior such as the use of price discrimination and tying contracts, false advertising, and the use of merger to consolidate market power.

One of the interesting features of the enforcement of antitrust legislation concerns the courts' views regarding whether the size of a firm or its behavior is the correct determinant of whether the firm is in violation of the antitrust laws. In the early 1900s, courts developed the rule of reason, which maintained that behavior was considered the key determinant. However, in 1945, the Supreme Court found ALCOA to be in violation of the Sherman Act on the basis of its size. Since the ALCOA case, courts have slowly come back to focus on behavior as the key factor.

The policy on mergers has also moderated over time. Early on, many mergers were blocked on the grounds that they would severely lessen the degree of competition in the affected market. However, since 1973, the government's attitude toward mergers has been much more relaxed. This shift toward a more lenient attitude was reinforced by the Justice Department's adoption of a new set of guidelines in 1982 for use in reviewing proposed mergers.

The third approach to market failure associated with a lack of competition--direct regulation--was discussed at some length in Chapter 12. The key points to note here are that although direct regulation is intended to improve the level of economic efficiency, it can also have the effect of protecting affected firms from competitive pressures. In addition, direct regulation raises a number of unresolved issues including the possibility of regulatory capture, the problem of obtaining reliable information from affected firms, evidence from empirical studies suggesting that direct regulation has no appreciable affect on market outcomes, the extent to which there is actually market failure in specific instances, and the legal cartel theory of regulation.

Since the late 1970s, a number of different industries--e.g., airlines, banking, natural gas, and ground transportation--have been subject to various degrees of deregulation. Efforts to deregulate certain industries have come as a result of observed adverse effects of regulation and predictions about the possible beneficial effects of such efforts. In most cases, deregulation appears to have had a generally positive effect.

KEY GRAPHS AND TERMS

Graphs

There are no new graphs or models introduced in this chapter. However, you should be sure you understand the process of cross subsidization illustrated in Figure 2.

Terms
MARKET FAILURE
PROPERTY RIGHTS
ANTITRUST LEGISLATION
TRUST
THE RULE OF REASON
DEREGULATION
CROSS SUBSIDIZATION

EXERCISES

1. A lack of competition that results in long-run inefficiencies is referred to as ________________ ________________.

2. List three different alternatives government can use to influence economic activity and the level of efficiency associated with specific market outcomes. ____
____

3. The term "________________ ________________" refers to the legally sanctioned control that an individual exercises over a collection of goods, resources, and services.

4. Match up the following antitrust statutes with the descriptions that follow. (Place the letter preceding the statute name in front of the phrase that best describes it basic intent.)

A. Sherman Antitrust Act
B. Clayton Act
C. Federal Trade Commission ACt
D. Robinson-Patman Act
E. Wheeler-Lea Act
F. Celler-Kefauver Act

____. Focused on unfair or deceptive practices, in particular, false advertising
____. Created the agency responsible for investigating anti-competitive practices
____. Prohibited the formation and operation of trusts
____. Disallowed vertical and conglomerate mergers that resulted in a substantial lessening of competition
____. Broadened restrictions on price discrimination
____. Outlawed practices such as price discrimination and the use of tying contracts

5. The rule of reason, which stated that only business practices that are considered ________________ or ________________ should be considered unreasonable, focused on the ________________ of firms rather than solely on their ________________.

6. Since the early 1970s, the government's view toward mergers has become much (more, less) lenient.

7. List the five major issues discussed in the text that are raised in the debate over whether direct regulation results in greater economic efficiency.

8. The practice of charging different prices to different groups of customers and using profits from one group to cover the losses generated by another group is called ______________ ______________. This practice results in an (efficient, inefficient) level of output in each affected market.

9. Briefly summarize some of the basic arguments made by the proponents of deregulation.______________

____

____

____

____

____

REVIEW QUESTIONS

1. All of the following are true of market failure except:

a) It has been viewed as being closely related to the number of firms in the market.
b) It suggests that while monopolies tend to produce less than the optimal amount, oligopolies tend to produce more than the optimal amount.
c) An example of market failure is monopolies producing where price in greater than marginal cost.
d) It has been a greater concern of policymakers with respect to monopoly and oligopoly than with respect to monopolistic competition.

2. Which of the following statements is not true?

a) U.S. policymakers have traditionally not engaged in regulation that controls the property rights exercised by producers.
b) Direct government ownership is one alternative method of the government influencing economic activity in the U.S.
c) In a capitalist economy, an individual has a property right to their own labor skills.
d) Property rights can be sold or exchanged.

3. Government-owned business:

a) is more widespread in the U.S. than in most other economies.
b) is known as a trust.
c) includes such examples as water and sewage treatment facilities in some communities.
d) a) and b), but not c)

4. All of the following are policy objectives of public enterprises except:

a) ensuring that the good is provided at a competitive price.
b) ensuring that the good meets quality standards.
c) earning profit for the sake of government revenues.
d) making substantial capital outlays that private industry is unwilling to make.

5. The Sherman Antitrust Act:

a) prevents the military from using armored vehicles on the public streets.
b) prohibits conspiracies in restraint of trade.
c) allows the formation of trusts as long as they are public enterprises.
d) allows a group of firms to form a trust only if it is done to take advantage of economies of scale.

6. The Clayton Act:

a) was passed in 1985 over the objections of President Reagan.
b) outlaws racial discrimination in the practice of business.
c) outlaws the ownership of stock by the U.S. government unless it is in public enterprises.
d) outlaws price discrimination unless based on cost differences.

7. Which of the following is not true?

a) Horizontal mergers are addressed by the Clayton Act.
b) The "rule of reason" suggested that it was reasonable to price below competitors for the purpose of driving them out of business.
c) In the case of ALCOA, the Supreme Court ruled that the mere size of a firm could constitute a violation of the Sherman Act.
d) The Supreme Court ruled that Du Pont's domination of the cellophane market did not constitute an unlawful restraint of trade due to the existence of substitutes.

8. Which of the following is a reason the Justice Department changed its guidelines for the effects of vertical and horizontal mergers on concentration in an industry?

a) The theory of contestable markets.
b) Because they lost almost every case they brought before the Supreme Court.
c) Firms made very few attempts to merge during the 1980's.
d) Because firms could charge monopoly prices anyway, even if there was considerable competition in the market.

9. All of the following are true of direct regulation except:

a) Direct regulation has mainly been associated with natural monopoly.
b) Direct regulation is used to attempt to get the firm to produce the efficient level of output.
c) Direct regulation has been used frequently to increase competition in monopolistically competitive markets.
d) Rate-setting for utilities by the state government is an example of direct regulation.

10. All of the following are important issues of direct regulation except:

a) Reliance on information provided by the regulated industry.
b) Regulatory staffs that consist of former employees of the regulated firms.
c) Studies which have shown that regulated industries have prices that are much lower than their unregulated counterparts.
d) The existence of substitutes and the true degree of monopoly power.

11. Monopolies may not have the market power which has traditionally been attributed to them for which of the following reasons?

a) The notion of contestable markets.
b) The existence of viable substitutes.
c) The fact that there are never any potential entrants into a monopolized market.
d) and b.), but not c.)

12. Which of the following best illustrates the notion of contestable markets for the cable TV industry?

a) Cable TV is one of the few unregulated monopolies in existence.
b) The entry of direct broadcast satellites into the market.
c) Members of Congress contesting the way in which cable TV programs are allocated.
d) Cable TV having to negotiate rate changes with thousands of localities when there is any change in programming.

13. Regulated air fares led to which of the following in the airline industry?

a) Nonprice competition
b) A large number of entrants into the airline industry.
c) A gain in consumer surplus, but losses for the airlines themselves.
d) b) and c), but not a)

14. The regulation of the airlines caused a redistribution of consumer surplus from ____________ to ____________.

a) Passengers flying on routes for which $P < MC$ to passengers flying on routes for which $P > MC$.
b) Passengers flying on routes for which $P > MC$ to passengers flying on routes for which $P < MC$.
c) Passengers flying on routes for which there is low demand to passengers flying on routes for which there is high demand.
d) Low income passengers to high income passengers.

15. The problem of cross subsidization in the regulation of the airlines suggests that:

a) The optimal level of air travel is provided in the heavily traveled routes, but not in the lightly traveled routes.
b) The optimal level of air travel is provided in the lightly traveled routes, but not in the heavily traveled routes.
c) The optimal level of air travel is provided in both the heavily traveled and the lightly traveled routes.
d) The optimal level of air travel is provided in neither the heavily traveled nor the lightly traveled routes.

16. Why have some policymakers concluded that too much competition is undesirable for consumers in some industries?

a) Because competitive firms are unable to stay in business even though consumers want the products.
b) Because too much competition eventually results in only one producer remaining in the industry.
c) Quality may suffer in the attempts to minimize costs.
d) Firms will produce more in a regulated market.

17. Which of the following is an actual result of airline deregulation?

a) Most of the airlines withdrew service from the most heavily traveled routes.
b) Prices fell on the most heavily traveled routes.
c) Airline safety plummeted.
d) Fares were less closely related to costs than they were before regulation.

18. All of the following are true of the history of airline regulation except:

a) Regulation started in the 1930's.
b) It was argued that competition led to a lack of attention to safety during the 1930's.
c) The CAB allowed free entry of major airlines into the industry.
d) Fares tended to exceed competitively-determined levels.

19. The market pricing of landing slots at airports would have which of the following effects?

a) Increase congestion at the desirable landing times, such as 4:00 P.M.
b) Increase the cost of a ticket on a flight landing at a desirable time.
c) Increase the cost of a ticket on a flight landing at an undesirable time, such as 3:00 A.M.
d) a) and c), but not b).

20. In which of the following cases would efficiency be best served by placing a limit on the exercise of property rights?

a) additional competition will drive economic profits to zero.
b) the developer of a new product has a monopoly on the production of the product.
c) the production of a good is generating substantial external costs.
d) a private firm offers to provide trash collection in a city where the service traditionally has been provided by the government.

Chapter 13, The Regulation of Business Behavior

ANSWER KEY

Exercises

1. market failure
2. 1) Direct government ownership of business, 2) the use of antitrust legislation, and 3) direct regulation of firm behavior.
3. property rights
4. E, C, A, F, D, B
5. unfair, illegal, behavior, size
6. more
7. 1) The possibility of regulatory capture, 2) the information problem, 3) the evidence from empirical studies of the issue, 4) questions about the true degree of monopoly power in specific instances, and 5) the legal cartel theory of regulation.
8. cross subsidization, inefficient
9. Proponents of deregulation argue that regulation can have a number of undesirable effects, including an emphasis on costly nonprice competition, redistribution of income, and a reduction in the efficiency of regulated markets.

Review Questions

1. b) is not a correct statement. Both monopolies and oligopolies tend to produce less than the optimal amount of the good, i.e., where P = MC.

2. a) is not true. In fact, there have been many government attempts to alter market outcomes by limiting or regulating the property rights of firms.

3. c) is the correct answer. Local water and sewage treatment plants are common examples of public enterprises. This type of market intervention is less widespread in the U.S. than in most other countries.

4. c) is not one of the reasons cited in the text for government ownership of business. The other three answers are three of the main reasons policymakers prefer government ownership to private ownership in some industries.

5. b) is the correct answer. The Sherman Antitrust Act outlaws trusts or any conspiracy "in restraint of trade."

6. d) is the correct answer. The Clayton Act also outlawed tying contracts and interlocking directorates.

7. b) is not true. Pricing to drive a competitor out of business was considered to be "unreasonable" and a restraint of trade.

8. a) is the correct answer. the theory of contestable markets suggests that if there are potential entrants into a market, existing firms are deterred from charging monopoly prices and making long-run economic profits.

9. c) is not true of direct regulation. Actually, direct regulation has been used to lessen competition in monopolistically competitive industries, by creating barriers to entry.

10. c) is not an important issue. In fact, studies have shown that there is not much difference between the prices charged by regulated industries and by their unregulated counterparts.

11. d) is the correct answer. Both the idea of contestable markets(which says there are potential entrants for a monopolized market) and the existence of substitutes are reasons to doubt the power traditionally attributed to monopolies.

12. b) is the correct answer. The theory of contestable markets suggests that there are potential entrants ready to enter any monopolized market and that, therefore, the monopoly is deterred from charging prices that allow it to earn long-run economic profits.

13. a) is the correct answer. In their search for profits, the regulated airlines competed on the basis of such nonprice variables as service, on-time performance, etc.

14. b) is the correct answer. The passengers flying on routes for which $P > MC$ are paying more than the cost of the resources needed to carry one more passenger. The passengers flying on routes for which $P < MC$ are paying less than the cost of the resources needed to carry one more passenger on that route.

15. d) is the correct answer. More than the optimal amount of air travel is provided for the lightly traveled routes and less than the optimal amount of air travel is provided for the heavily traveled routes.

16. c) is the correct answer. For example, some policymakers argue that the airlines should be re-regulated because safety has suffered as firms scramble to keep costs low and profits high.

17. b) is the correct answer. With deregulation, the airlines competed on the most heavily traveled routes; prices then fell on these routes.

18. c) is the not true of the period of regulation of the airlines. In fact, the CAB allowed no entry of major airlines into the industry in this period.

19. c) is the correct answer. Since the airline would have to bid more for a landing slot at a desirable time, it would experience an increase in costs, a portion of which would be passed on to consumers.

20. c) is the correct answer. Negative externalities, such as pollution, are examples of times when it is socially beneficial to place a limit on the exercise of property rights.

CHAPTER 14
THE THEORY OF RESOURCE MARKETS

OVERVIEW

In this chapter we develop the theory of resource markets. In particular, we examine how resource prices are determined. This analysis is particularly important in light of the fact that resource prices determine the share of income that accrues to each of the factors of production.

The first step in analyzing resource markets is to recognize that the demand for any resource is a derived demand. That is, the demand for a resource is derived from the demand for the good or service the resource is used to produce. Resource demand is determined by two factors--the productivity of the resource and the price of the output that it is produced. Marginal revenue product (MRP) is the dollar value of the additional output generated by hiring one more unit of a resource. It is calculated as the product of marginal physical product and marginal revenue, i..e, MRP = MPP x MR. From the employer's perspective it is profitable to hire additional units of a resource so long as the MRP from doing so is greater than the additional cost--marginal resource cost (MRC)--incurred.

In effect, the MRP curve for a resource is the firm's demand curve for the resource. A change in the price of a resource, e.g., the wage rate in the case of labor, cause a movement along the resource demand curve. A change in the marginal physical product of a resource or a change in product price will cause the MRP of each unit of a resource to change. This results in a shift of the entire MRP curve.

Just as we can measure the price elasticity of demand for goods and services, we can also measure the price elasticity of demand for resources. The coefficient of the price elasticity of demand for a resource is measured as the ratio of the percentage change in the quantity demanded of the resource to the percentage change in the price of the resource. In general, the price elasticity of demand for a resource increases 1) the slower the rate at which the marginal physical product of the resource declines, 2) the greater the price elasticity of demand for the firm's output, 3) the greater the share of total production costs accounted for by the resource, and 4) the greater the availability of substitutes for the resource. The elasticity of resource demand is greater in the long run than in the short run.

The supply curve for a resource is upward sloping, reflecting the fact that resource owners are willing to supply more units of a resource at higher prices. The short-run price elasticity of resource supply is determined by how broadly the resource market is defined and the degree to which resources are mobile. In general, the more broadly defined a resource market is, the less elastic is supply. In addition, the less mobile resources are, the less elastic resource supply will be. Time also affects the elasticity of resource supply. As the time horizon is allowed to expand, so does the elasticity of resource supply.

Equilibrium in resource markets is determined by the interaction of supply and demand. In competitive resource markets, the long-run equilibrium has several properties including 1) no shortage or surplus of the resource, 2) allocation of resources to their most highly valued uses, 3) equality of the value of the marginal unit of a resource used in production and its opportunity cost, and 4) equality of the price paid to the marginal unit of a resource and the value of its marginal product.

KEY GRAPHS AND TERMS

Graphs

One of the key models developed in this chapter is that of the demand for resources. Figure 1 illustrates the marginal physical product and marginal revenue product schedules for labor hired by a firm. Assuming that the firm competes in competitive output and resource markets, MRP = MPP x P. In addition, the firm takes the per unit price paid for the resource, the wage rate, as given. This wage rate, which represents the marginal resource cost of labor, is constant for the firm. The firm can hire as much or as little labor as wants at the going wage. To maximize profits, the firm will hire additional units of labor up to the point at which MRP = MRC.

Figure 2 illustrates the derivation of the market demand curve for a resource. Note that the market demand curve is steeper than the curve representing the sum of the individual firm's demand curves. This is the result of the fall in market price that follows from an increase in output in the product market. (Recall that the additional output is the result of hiring additional units of labor.)

Figure 7 illustrates the derivation of the long-run supply curve for a resource. In this particular example, the long-run supply curve is upward sloping, indicating an increase in the marginal cost of the resource. However, supply is nonetheless more elastic in the long-run than in the short run.

Terms
RESOURCE DEMAND SCHEDULE
DERIVED DEMAND
MARGINAL PHYSICAL PRODUCT
MARGINAL RESOURCE COST
PRICE ELASTICITY OF RESOURCE DEMAND
COEFFICIENT OF ELASTICITY
PRICE ELASTICITY OF SUPPLY
RESOURCE MOBILITY
HUMAN CAPITAL
LABOR FORCE PARTICIPATION RATE

EXERCISES

1. The demand for a resource is a ________________ demand, since it depends on the demand for the product it is used to produce.

2. Assume that when a firm increases its employment of labor from 12 units to 13 units, total output increases from 900 units to 937 units. In addition, the firm operates in a perfectly competitive market, and the current equilibrium price is $12 per unit. As such, the MRP of the 13th unit of labor is ___________.

3. How would your answer to #2 change if instead, the firm operated in an imperfectly competitive market?
____

4. The change in total cost resulting from the employment of an additional unit of a resource is called
________________ ________________ ________________.

5. Assume that we are looking at a perfectly competitive firm's demand curve for a particular resource (the firm is a perfect competitor in both the input and output markets). A change in the price of the resource will cause a ________________ ________________ the resource demand curve. On the other hand, a decrease in product price will cause the resource demand curve to ________________ ________________, while an increase in the productivity of the resource will cause the resource demand curve to ________________ ________________.

6. The market demand curve for a resource is (flatter, steeper) than the horizontal sum of the individual firms' demand curves due to the effect of a change in market output on ________________ ________________.

7. List the four factors that influence the short-run price elasticity of resource demand. ________________
____
____

8. Resource demand elasticity is ________________ in the long run than in the short run. This reflects the increased potential for ________________ among inputs to the production process.

9. ________________ ________________ refers to the ability of resources to move among alternative uses.

10. As the mobility of a resource increases, the elasticity of resource supply (increases, decreases). In addition, the elasticity of resource supply (increases, decreases) the longer the time period being considered.

11. ________________ ________________ refers to the productivity-determining skills and abilities embodied in labor.

12. According to the backward-bending supply curve for labor, at low wage rates, the value of income is (greater, less) than the value of leisure and the ________________ effect dominates. However, at higher wage rates, the value of income is (greater, less) than the value of leisure and the ________________ effect dominates.

13. List and describe the four major properties of long-run equilibrium in a competitive resource market that are discussed in the text. ____

____

____

____

14. Complete the following table which contains production data from Bonzo Kellerman's Fabulous Frozen Yogurt Shop.

Units of Labor	Total Product	Marginal Physical Product	Product Price	Marginal Revenue Product
0	0	---	--	---
1	22	___	$10	$___
2	38	___	10	___
3	50	___	10	___
4	58	___	10	___
5	62	___	10	___

15. Using the information from the table, plot Bonzo's labor demand curve in the graph and label it D1.

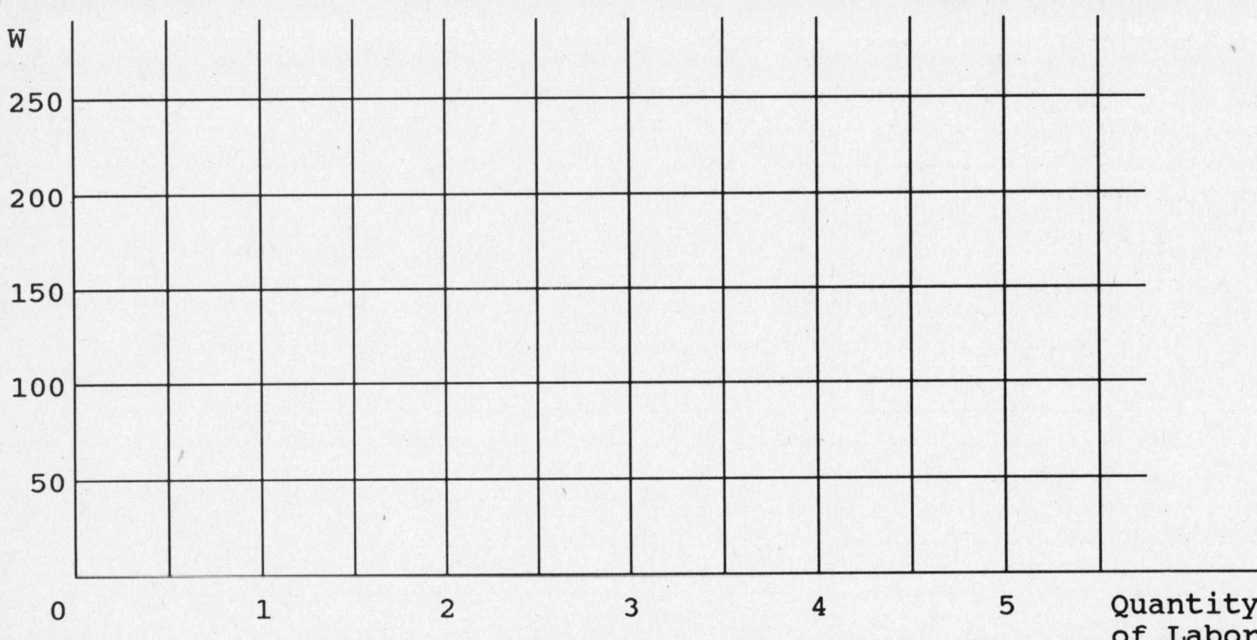

16. Assume that Bonzo competes with numerous other yogurt shops in the market for labor and that the current market wage is $85. How many workers should Bonzo employ? ____

17. Now assume that there is an increase in the price of the raw materials (milk, fruit flavors, etc.) used in the production of frozen yogurt. Show the effect of this change on Bonzo's demand for labor and label the effect in an appropriate manner.

18. List two factors that would INCREASE the elasticity of demand for labor employed in Bonzo's shop.

____

____

REVIEW QUESTIONS

1. In the resource market:

a) firms are suppliers.
b) households are demanders.
c) most individuals possess property rights mainly to their own labor.
d) Profits account for most of our national income, with wages a distant second.

2. Which of the following statements best illustrates the concept of derived demand?

a) When the price of gas rises, the demand for cars falls.
b) an increase in the demand for shoes will cause an increase in the demand for leather.
c) an increase in consumer incomes will cause an increase in the demand for most products.
d) an increase in the supply of cars will cause an increase in the quantity demanded.

3. In the short run, a decrease in product demand will:

a) cause the firm's demand curve for each resource to shift left.
b) cause the firm's demand curve for each resource to shift right.
c) leave the firm's demand curve for each resource unchanged.
d) cause the price of each resource to rise.

4. The firm adds to profits by employing more resources as long as:

a) the increase in revenues is less than the increase in costs.
b) the increase in revenues is greater than the increase in costs.
c) the firm is operating in a competitive labor market.
d) the marginal cost attributed to the last unit employed is greater than the marginal revenue attributed to the last unit employed.

Use the following table to answer questions 5 to 9.

Number of Workers	Total Physical Product	MPP	MRP
1	20	___	___
2	___	15	___

Assume that the price of output = $1.00 and the wage is $10/unit.

5. What is the marginal revenue product of the first unit of labor?

a) $1.00
b) $10.00
c) $15.00
d) $20.00

6. What is the total physical product when 2 units of labor are employed?

a) 10 units
b) 15 units
c) 20 units
d) 35 units

7. Which of the following statements is correct?

a) The firm will hire the second unit of labor, since MPP > wage.
b) The firm will not hire the second unit of labor, since MPP < wage.
c) The firm will hire the second unit of labor, since MRP > wage
d) The firm will not hire the second unit of labor, since MRP < wage.

8. Suppose the wage rises to $18. Which of the following will occur?

a) The firm will hire at least two units of labor.
b) The firm will hire exactly two units of labor.
c) The firm will hire one unit of labor.
d) The firm will hire no labor and shutdown.

9. In the above table, why does the marginal physical product of labor decline as more labor is employed?

a) Diminishing Marginal Utility
b) Marginal revenue is less than price.
c) Because marginal revenue product is rising.
d) Diminishing Returns

10. Marginal revenue product (MRP) measures the:

a) increase in total revenue that results from the production of one more unit of output.
b) increase in total cost that results from hiring one more unit of a resource.
c) decline in product price a firm must accept to sell the extra output of one more worker.
d) amount by which the additional output produced by one more unit of a resource increases a firm's total revenue.

11. The marginal revenue product of labor for the competitive firm is:

a) MPP x Price of output
b) MPP x Wage
c) MRC x Price of output
d) MRC x Wage

12. In a competitive labor market, the Marginal Resource Cost is equal to:

a) the price of labor.
b) he price of output.
c) MPP x the price of output.
d) MPP x the price of labor.

13. In a competitive labor market, the marginal revenue product of labor schedule:

a) is the firm's supply of labor.
b) is the firm's demand for labor.
c) is the workers' supply of labor.
d) is the workers' demand for labor.

14. As the wage falls:

a) the firm's employment falls and its output rises.
b) the firm's employment rises and its output falls.
c) the firm's employment and output rise.
d) the firm's employment and output fall.

15. Continuing the process started in the previous question, what else will occur?

a) The price of output will fall and the MRP curve will shift to the left.
b) the price of output will rise and the MRP curve will shift to the left.
c) the price of output will fall and the MRP curve will shift to the right.
d) the price of output will rise and the MRP curve will shift to the right.

16. Suppose that labor employment falls by 1% in the short-run when the wage rises by 4%. The elasticity coefficient in this case is:

a) 4.0
b) 2.0
c) 0.50
d) 0.25

17. Suppose that the demand for labor is elastic. If there is an increase in wages what will happen to the total income received by labor?

a) It will remain the same if labor markets are competitive.
b) It will increase, since quantity demanded is sensitive to changes in price.
c) It will decrease, since quantity demanded is sensitive to changes in price
d) It will increase, since quantity demanded is not sensitive to changes in price.

18. The following are determinants of the short-run resource demand elasticity except:

a) The rate at which marginal productivity declines.
b) The strength of the income effect relative to the substitution effect for workers.
c) The price elasticity of demand for the firm's output.
d) The availability of substitutes for the resource.

19. The demand for a productive input (resource) will be most elastic when product demand is:

a) inelastic.
b) elastic.
c) unit elastic.
d) quasi-inelastic.

20. Firm A operates in a monopolistically competitive industry which experiences a significant increase the number of different firms (and products) competing in the market. As a result of this change, the demand for labor by firm A will become:

a) more elastic.
b) less elastic.
c) unit elastic.
d) perfectly inelastic.

21. If wages are the main component of a firm's cost of production we would expect:

a) The demand for labor to be elastic.
b) The demand for labor to be inelastic.
c) Firms to be unresponsive to change in wages.
d) The labor demand function to be relatively steep.

22. Which of the following is the best example of substitution in production?

a) Auto manufacturers raising product prices as auto worker wages rise.
b) The university raising tuition as the cost of employing professors rises.
c) A firm employing more capital and less labor as wages in rise.
d) A firm holding smaller inventories when the interest rate rises.

23. In the short-run, resource supply is:

a) very elastic.
b) somewhat elastic.
c) very inelastic.
d) somewhat inelastic.

24. Surprisingly, land is sometimes considered to be a mobile resource in the long-run. This is because:

a) nations fight wars to take land from each other.
b) land has a number of alternative uses.
c) land is heavily taxed in most societies.
d) a) and c), but not b).

25. Which of the following resources is thought to be fairly mobile?

a) a general purpose resource.
b) highly-skilled labor.
c) labor that is very specialized in some particular skill.
d) medical equipment.

26. Which of the following is not true?

a) Education and training are examples of human capital.
b) In the long-run, the total supply of land is fixed.
c) The longer the period of time, the more elastic the resource supply curve will be.
d) The longer the period of time, the more elastic the resource demand curve will be.

27. The labor force participation rate:

a) has risen for married women over the last 40 years.
b) has fallen for older men over the last 40 years.
c) has fallen for the society as a whole over the last 40 years.
d) is the percent of the noninstitutionalized, nonmilitary population between the ages of 16 and 70 that are employed or seeking employment.

28. The backward-bending supply curve of labor:
a) occurs where the substitution effect outweighs the income effect.
b) occurs where the income effect outweighs the substitution effect.
c) occurs if the income effect just offsets the substitution effect.
d) occurs where wages and the quantity supplied of labor are very low.

29. Which of the following is not a condition for long-run equilibrium in a competitive resource market?

a) Resources are allocated to their most valuable uses.
b) The price of every resource is equal to its marginal revenue product.
c) There are no surpluses or shortages of any resources.
d) The price of every resource is equal to the marginal revenue of the good the resource is being used to produce.

30. Ceteris paribus, we would expect the labor demand curve of a perfectly competitive firm to be:

a) perfectly elastic.
b) less elastic than that of an imperfectly competitive firm.
c) more elastic than that of an imperfectly competitive firm.
d) unrelated to the market conditions in which the firm operates.

Chapter 14, The Theory of Resource Markets

ANSWER KEY

Exercises

1. derived
2. $444
3. The marginal revenue product of the 13th worker would be lower.
4. marginal resource cost
5. movement along, shift left, shift right
6. steeper, product price
7. 1) the rate at which the marginal physical product of the resource declines, 2) the price elasticity of demand for the firm's output, 3) the share of total production costs accounted for by the resource, and 4) the availability of substitutes for the resource.
8. greater, substitution
9. Resource mobility
10. increases, increases
11. Human capital
12. greater, substitution, less, income
13. 1) no shortage or surplus of the resource, 2) allocation of resources to their most highly valued uses, 3) equality of the value of the marginal unit of a resource used in production and its opportunity cost, and 4) equality of the price paid to the marginal unit of a resource and the value of its marginal product.
14.

Units of Labor	Total Product	Marginal Physical Product	Product Price	Marginal Revenue Product
0	0	---	--	---
1	22	22	$10	$220
2	38	16	10	160
3	50	12	10	120
4	58	8	10	80
5	62	4	10	40

16. 3
17. Note that these inputs, labor and raw materials, are complements. As such, the increase in the price of raw materials will cause the quantity demanded to decrease. Ceteris paribus, this will cause the demand for labor to decrease as well. The labor demand curve will shift left.
18. 1) an increase in the number of available substitutes for labor, 2) an increase in labor's share of total production costs, 3) a decrease in the rate at which the marginal physical product of labor declines, and 4) an increase in the price elasticity of demand for frozen yogurt.

Review Questions

1. c) is the correct answer. For most individuals, the only resource they possess in significant amounts is their own labor service.

2. b) is the correct answer. The demand for a resource is a derived demand because it depends on the demand for the final product. As the demand for the final product(shoes) rises, the firm needs to hire more of the resource(leather). Thus, the demand for leather is derived from the demand for shoes.

3. a) is the correct answer. As the demand for the firms product falls, the firm will produce less and therefore purchase less of each resource.

4. b) is the correct answer. As long as the increase in revenues is greater than the increase in costs, the firm will increase its total profits by employing more of the resource. This process will stop when the increase in revenue is exactly equal to the increase in costs.

5. d) is the correct answer. Marginal revenue product equals MPP x Price of output = 20 units x $1/unit = $20.

6. d) is the correct answer. Since the marginal physical product is 15 units, the change in total product due to the second is 15 units. 20 + 15 = 35 units.

7. c) is the correct answer. The marginal revenue product of the second unit of labor is 15 units x $1/unit = $15. If the wage is $10, then the firm will increase its profits by $5 if it employs the second unit.

8. c) is the correct answer. If the wage rises to $18, the firm will not hire the second unit of labor, since for that unit MRP($15) < wage($18). Therefore, the firm will hire only one unit of labor.

9. d) is the correct answer. Marginal Physical Product declines because the production function conforms to the Law of Diminishing Returns.

10. d) is the correct answer. The MRP is the change in total revenue due to employing one more unit of a resource.

11. a) is the correct answer. Since MRP = MPP x MR and under perfect competition MR = Price of output, MRP = MPP x Price of output.

12. a) is the correct answer. In a competitive resource market, the MRC = the price of the resource. This is because in a competitive resource market, the firm is too small to influence the resource price, so when it hires one more unit the price of the previous units hired remains the same.

13. b) is the correct answer. At any particular wage, the firm employs labor up to the point at which MRP is equal to that wage.

14. c) is the correct answer. As the wage falls, the firm is induced to hire more labor, expanding employment. This results in an increase in output.

15. a) is the correct answer. As the firms produce more due to the fall in the wage, the price of the output will fall. This will cause the MRP(= MPP x Price of output) to shift to the left as MRP falls at every unit of labor.

16. d) is the correct answer. The elasticity coefficient is the % change in the quantity of labor demanded(or employed) divided by the % change in price. In this case this is equal to 1%/4% = .25.

17. c) is the correct answer. The % change in quantity demanded will be larger than the % change in wages. Although the increase in wages will tend to increase the total income of labor, this will be more than offset by the fall in the employment of labor.

18. b is not a determinant of resource demand elasticity. The income and substitution effects are relevant to the labor supply function, not the labor demand function.

19. b is the correct answer. The greater the elasticity of demand for the firm's output, the more output will decline when there is an increase in wages that is partly passed on to consumers. Therefore, the more employment will fall for an increase in wages.

20. a) is the correct answer. As more firms enter a monopolistically competitive market, the demand for each of the firms differentiated product becomes more elastic. As demand for the firm's output becomes more elastic, the firm's demand for labor becomes more elastic.

21.a) is the correct answer. Labor cost is usually the main component of a firm's costs of production. Thus any change in wages will have a significant effect on the firm's total costs of production. Therefore, the firm will be quite sensitive to a change in wages and labor demand will be elastic.

22. c) is the correct answer. In this case, the firm is substituting capital for labor.

23. c) is the correct answer. The short-run resource supply is very inelastic for most resources. This is due mainly to resources being immobile in the short-run.

24. b) is the correct answer. Land is usually not mobile in a physical sense, but it can be moved into and out of industries. An example of this is the removal of land from agriculture to be used for residences or shopping malls.

25. a) is the correct answer. The more general the use of the resource, the greater its mobility. If a resource is very specialized in one industry, it is unlikely that it will be of use in another industry that might be expanding.

26. b) is not true. Even land is not fixed in the long-run. For example, if the price of land rises high enough, lakes can be drained or shorelines can be reclaimed.

27. c) is not true. The labor force participation has risen for the population as a whole over the last 40 years.

28. b) is the correct answer. The income effect refers to the tendency to demand more leisure when income rises. The substitution effect refers to the tendency to substitute work for leisure when the wage rises. When the supply of labor is backward-bending, the former outweighs the latter.

29. d) is not a condition for long-run equilibrium. The price of the resource must be equal to the MRP, but not to the MR of the good which is being produced. In fact, MRP = MPP x MR.

30. b) is the correct answer. As the wage falls, the firm hires more labor and increases output. The competitive firm can sell all the additional output at the market price. However, the imperfectly competitive firm must lower price to sell the additional output. Thus its marginal revenue will decline, so its MRP will decline more steeply than for the perfectly firm.

CHAPTER 15
THE MARKET FOR LABOR

OVERVIEW

The focus of this chapter is on the labor market. In particular, we consider how the wage and employment levels are determined for different types of labor. This issue is of particular importance since it has a significant influence on the personal distribution of income, i.e., the way in which income is distributed among households in the economy. We also consider why wages differ across jobs, and the effects of investment in human capital on earnings potential. The wage effects of the degree of competition in a labor market are also considered.

People possess a variety of labor skills, and the types of skills demanded vary within and across firms. As such, wages are determined in a set of labor markets rather than a single market. In addition, the wage rate paid to various types of labor varies widely. Observed wage differences can be categorized as being either equalizing or nonequalizing wage differences.

Equalizing wage differences compensate workers for variations in nonwage attributes of different jobs. For example, some jobs are more risky than others, which causes wages for such jobs to be relatively higher. In other cases, general working conditions are much better, which causes wages to be lower, ceteris paribus. Equalizing wage differences also compensate workers for costly training programs or educational requirements that must be met to enter a particular labor market. The size of equalizing wage differences is influenced by workers' preferences for various jobs with differing nonwage attributes. The effect of equalizing wage differences is to equalize the total benefits associated with employment in a given job.

Nonequalizing wage differences result in variations in the total benefits received from working in different jobs. The effect is to make some jobs more attractive than others. For a non-equalizing wage difference to persist over time, there must be some barrier to entry into the labor market in question. Examples of such barriers include special skills such as those possessed by certain athletes and specialized professionals, trade union restrictions that limit entry into certain occupations, and governmental restrictions such as occupational license requirements that also restrict entry into certain occupations.

Disequilibrium wage differences are the result of changes in market conditions that result in an imbalance between demand and supply in certain occupations. By their nature, such wage differences are transitory. Over the long run, responses to either a surplus or a shortage in the affected market will push the wage back to an equilibrium level.

From an economic perspective, education is an investment in human capital. The decision of whether to engage in such investment is influenced by the relative costs and benefits of doing so. Expected wage increases that result from an investment in education must exceed the costs of the education in order for such an investment to be profitable. The fact that college graduates are usually paid a higher wage than non-college graduates is another example of an equalizing wage difference.

In addition to equalizing and nonequalizing wage differences, labor market discrimination can also cause variations in wages received by different workers. The difference in this case is that the workers are engaged in the same line of employment and possess similar skills. Labor market discrimination occurs on the basis of race or sex. In trying to estimate the extent to which wage differences are the product of discrimination, it is necessary to consider other factors such as differences in skill and training levels and productivity differences.

When labor markets are perfectly competitive, the last worker hired is paid a wage equal to her marginal revenue product. In some cases, however, there is only one employer of labor. This situation is referred to as monopsony. In the case of the competitive employer, marginal resource cost is constant, and the firm's labor supply curve is perfectly elastic. The monopsonist, on the other hand, faces the entire market supply curve for labor, which is upward sloping. Thus, as the monopsonist increases employment, it moves up the market labor supply curve. Therefore, it must increase the wage its pays to each and every worker--both the new worker and existing workers. This causes marginal resource cost to increase as employment increases.

KEY GRAPHS AND TERMS

Graphs

This chapter uses the graphical analysis of supply and demand in the resource market developed in the previous chapter to analyze issues related to the labor market. As such, the majority of the graphs are not new. It is important to note, however, a subtle difference in Figure 3. In particular, the variable measured on the vertical axis is the wage difference between two jobs, as opposed to the actual wage rate. This is done to illustrate the effect of equalizing wage differences.

The new model in this chapter is that of the monopsonistic labor market. Figure 7 illustrates this type of situation. The labor demand curve is the firm's marginal revenue product curve for labor. Because the firm is the sole employer, it faces the market supply curve for labor. The firm's hiring decisions affect the wages of all new and existing workers, unlike the perfectly competitive employer, whose hiring decisions have no effect on the market wage. Consequently, the MRC curve differs from the supply curve. In particular, because an increase in employment means a higher wage for the new worker (as indicated by the supply curve) plus an increase in wages for existing workers, the MRC curve lies above the supply curve. Like any other firm, the monopsonist employees the number of workers at which MRP = MRC. However, the employer pays the lowest wage it can, which is found by reading off of the supply curve. Note that this amount is less than the marginal revenue product of the last worker hired.

Terms

FUNCTIONAL DISTRIBUTION OF INCOME
PERSONAL DISTRIBUTION OF INCOME
LABOR MARKET
EQUALIZING WAGE DIFFERENCES
NONEQUALIZING WAGE DIFFERENCES
RESERVATION WAGE
ECONOMIC RENT
DISEQUILIBRIUM WAGE DIFFERENCES
HUMAN CAPITAL
LABOR MARKET DISCRIMINATION
MONOPSONY

EXERCISES

1. The ________________ distribution of income describes the distribution of income among the factors of production, while the ________________ distribution of income describes the distribution of income among individuals and households in the economy.

2. List the three conditions that would have to be met in order for an economy to have an aggregate labor market with a single equilibrium wage. ____

____

3. ________________ wage differences are based on nonwage job characteristics and tend to ________________ the benefits offered by different jobs. As the nonwage attributes of a job become increasingly less appealing, the size of this wage difference tends to ________________.

4. ________________ wage differences cause the total benefits from working in different jobs to vary. In order for this type of wage difference to persist over time, there must be some type of ________________ ______ ________________ into the affected labor market.

5. The minimum amount of money that attracts an individual into a particular job is called their ________________ ________________, and any excess they receive over that amount is called ________________ ________________.

6. List three possible reasons for labor immobility. ____
____

7. Assume that the passage of new tax laws that greatly complicate the process of filing taxes creates a shortage of good tax accountants which drives up the going wage for tax accountants by 100 percent relative to the wages of accountants specializing in other areas. This type of wage difference is called a ________________ wage difference, which will be expected to ________________ over time.

8. In deciding whether to go to college first, or to work straight out of high school, so long as the present value of the ________________ earnings exceeds the present value of the ________________ plus ________________ costs, a rational individual will choose ________________.

9. The situation in which equally productive workers are paid less because of race or sex is called ________________ ________________ ________________.

10. A market in which there is a single buyer of a good or resource is called a ________________.

11. In the case of the perfectly competitive employer, the marginal resource cost of additional units of labor is ________________. In contrast, for the monopsonist the marginal resource cost of labor is an ________________ function of the number of units of labor hired.

12. Relative to the competitive employer, a monopsonist will pay a ________________ wage and hire ________________ workers.

13. List three reasons why workers and firms can benefit from long-term employment contracts.__________
____
____

Use the figure on the following page to answer questions 14 and 15.

14. Assume that the labor market is perfectly competitive. In this case, the equilibrium wage rate and level of employment will be __________ and __________. What is the individual employer's marginal resource cost of hiring one more unit of labor? __________

15. Assume, instead, that this labor market is monopsonistic. In this case, the equilibrium wage rate and level of employment will be __________ and __________. In addition, the marginal revenue product of the last unit of labor employed will be __________.

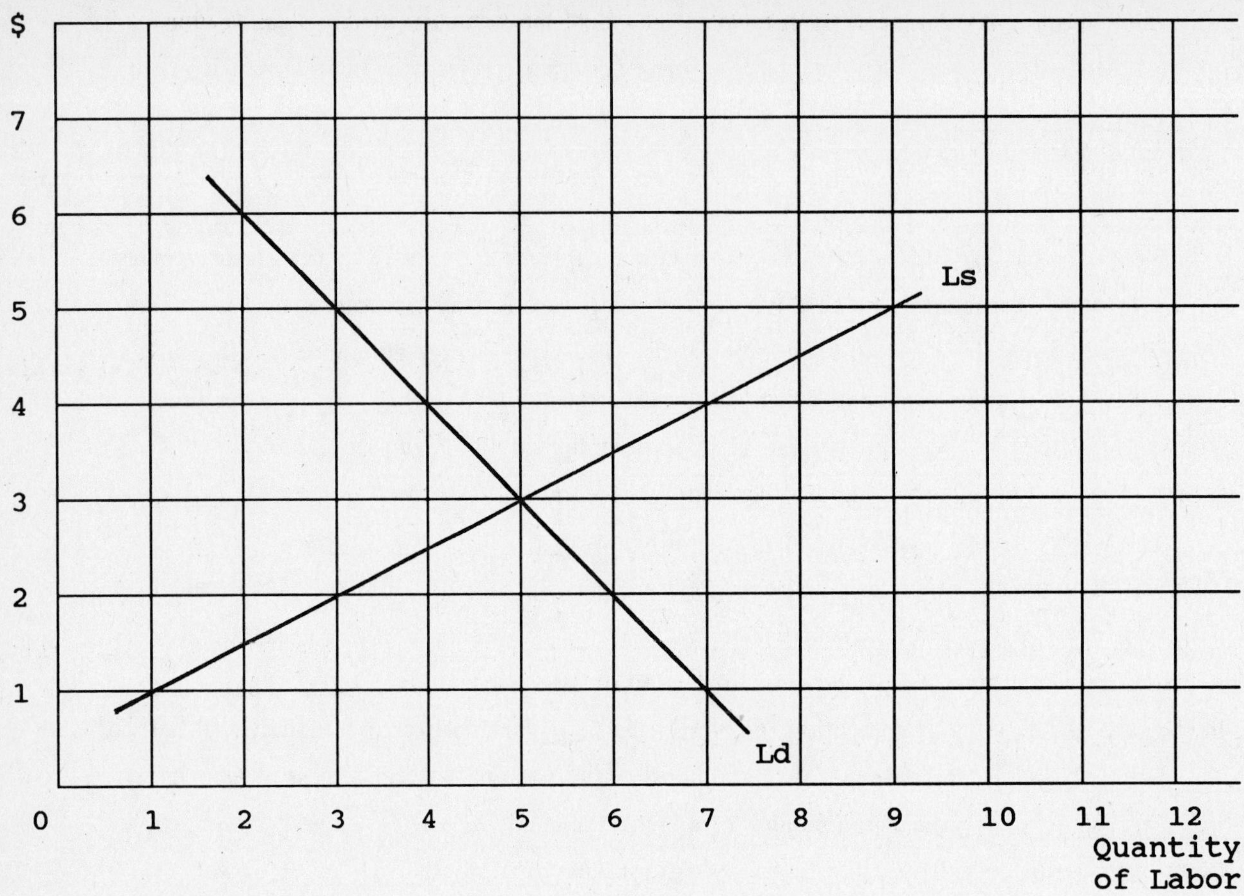

REVIEW QUESTIONS

1. Why is it significant that labor cannot be divorced from its owner?

a) The owner need not be present when labor is employed.
b) Nonwage factors are important in labor markets.
c) Because owners of labor do not have to worry about the wage under these circumstances.
d) Because economics teaches us that labor is a more important factor of production than is capital.

2. Which of the following is the best example of the functional distribution of income?

a) Labor receiving the largest share of national income.
b) Surgeons making a higher income than general practioners.
c) Major-league baseball players making a higher income than college professors.
d) More experienced workers receiving a higher salary than their less-experienced counterparts.

3. Each of the following is a reason wages might be different in different geographic areas except:

a) Imperfect information
b) Moving costs
c) Ease of entry into skilled labor markets.
d) Labor markets that are regionally-segmented.

4. Which of the following is <u>not</u> a desirable property of the labor market when it is in equilibrium?

a) Assuming there are no moving costs, the distribution of income will be equalized.
b) Unemployment = 0.
c) Wage = Marginal Revenue Product.
d) The marginal worker's productivity equals the opportunity cost of time.

5. Which of the following is <u>not true</u>?

a) Wage flexibility guarantees that there is no unemployment.
b) Unemployment occurs when there is disequilibrium in the labor market.
c) If people are unwilling to work at the prevailing market wage, but would be willing to work at a higher wage, they are considered to be unemployed.
d) The personal distribution of income refers to the distribution of income among individuals.

6. Those workers who are on the supply schedule above the equilibrium market wage:

a) Are unemployed due to the value they place on leisure time.
b) Are unemployed due to low marginal productivity.
c) Place a higher value on leisure time than the equilibrium wage.
d) Are actually considered to be employed, even though they are not working, because they would be willing to work if only there were jobs available at the equilibrium wage.

7. Which of the following occurs when labor productivity rises?

a) The equilibrium nominal wage falls.
b) The equilibrium quantity of labor falls.
c) Competitive firms will be induced to use more capital.
d) The labor demand function shifts to the right.

8. The difference in wages paid to two equally skilled people who are working different jobs is known as:

a) an equalizing difference.
b) a pecuniary difference.
c) a wage-skill difference.
d) a market imperfection.

9. In the analysis of differences among wages, the term "equalizing differences" refers to:

a) differences in labor skills that explain differences in wage rates paid to different workers.
b) differences in wage rates associated with union versus non-union labor.
c) differences in wage rates that reflect nonmonetary differences in various jobs.
d) differences in wage rates associated with fluctuations in the level of economic activity.

10. Nonequalizing wage differences:

a) Exist when there are not barriers to entry into the labor market.
b) Are not necessary to attract and retain workers.
c) Occur when no occupation is preferred to another.
d) Occur when there is completely free competition among workers for jobs.

11. Which of the following statements is correct?

a) Economic rent is the difference between the market wage and the reservation wage.
b) Economic rent is the amount one must pay to enter a desirable labor market.
c) The reservation wage is the maximum amount any firm will pay for a worker.
d) Most workers will work for less than their reservation wage.

12. Which of the following is not responsible for nonequalizing wage differences?

a) Restriction of entry into the labor market.
b) Trade unions.
c) The Davis-Bacon Act.
d) Higher wage levels attracting additional workers.

13. Suppose finance and accounting degrees require the same amount and difficulty of college course work and nonwage job conditions are similar. If the salary paid starting finance graduates is above the salary paid starting accountants, all of the following are true except:

a) The wage difference is transitional.
b) The wage difference will disappear in the long-run.
c) The labor market is at its long-run equilibrium.
d) Students will begin switching into finance.

14. When comparing the value of a college education to starting work right out of high school:

a) one must calculate the present value of the anticipated earnings from having a college degree.
b) the value of the benefits received in the future is greater than the value of those same benefits received today.
c) individuals will be more likely to choose not to attend college if the supply of those who work right out of high school is quite large.
d) attending college must be considered a consumption good, with immediate benefits, rather than an investment good.

15. In which of the following situations is labor market discrimination said to exist?

a) When one identifiable group is paid less on average than another identifiable group.
b) If equally productive workers are paid less because of race.
c) When women are paid less than men in the same labor market.
d) When one group is paid less than 90% of the wages paid to another group.

16. According to the text, what % of the difference between the wages paid to black workers and white workers is due to measurable differences in productivity, such as education and experience?

a) 100%
b) 90%
c) 50-80%
d) 10-20%

17. Compared to a perfectly competitive firm, a monopsonist will pay:

a) a higher wage to its workers.
b) lower wages but hire more workers than the perfectly competitive firm.
c) lower wages and hire the same number of workers as the perfectly competitive firm.
d) lower wages and hire less workers than the perfectly competitive firm.

18. Which of the following is <u>not</u> true?

a) About one-half of the differences in male-female earnings can be attributed to differences in training and experience.
b) Occupational segregation is a major reason for male-female earning differences.
c) Females have traditionally worked in jobs that are difficult to enter and exit.
d) Whether justified or not, firms reluctance to train women for fear that they will subsequently leave the labor force is one possible reason for the observed male-female wage differences.

19. Which of the following arguments are made by opponents of comparable worth legislation?

a) It is practically impossible to devise a system for measuring job characteristics and establish appropriate wage rates.
b) Secretarial work is low-paying because it is viewed as "women's work."
c) Differences in productivity characteristics explain a large part of the differences in the salaries between males and females.
d) Comparable worth legislation may create an excess supply of workers for jobs traditionally held by women, making employment in those jobs more difficult.

20. Which of the following statements is <u>NOT</u> correct?

a) In a perfectly competitive labor market, the labor supply curve for the individual firm is perfectly elastic.
b) Both the perfectly competitive firm and the monopsonist hire resources up to the level at which MRP = MRC.
c) The term "monopsonist" refers to a single buyer in a market.
d) For the monopsonist, W = MRC for the last unit of labor hired.

21. Which of the following statements about the labor market is correct?

a) We observe individuals over the age of 30 moving frequently to jobs that pay higher wages.
b) The labor market is much less sensitive to fluctuations in supply and demand than other markets.
c) Long-term relationships between employers and employees is not a characteristic of the U.S. economy.
d) Supply and demand conditions are more important in determining equilibrium in the labor market than in almost any other market.

22. Which of the following is <u>not</u> a reason workers and firms benefit from long-term contracts?

a) If firms train workers, they do not want to lose them.
b) Work incentives, such as bonuses, which make workers more productive.
c) Stable income and wages.
d) The ability to quickly take advantage of disequilibria in the labor market.

ANSWER KEY

Exercises

1. functional, personal
2. 1) Workers must be identical, 2) jobs must be identical, and 3) workers must be perfectly mobile
3. Equalizing, equalize, increase
4. Nonequalizing, barrier to entry
5. reservation wage, economic rent
6. 1) special skills, 2) trade union restrictions, and 3) government restrictions
7. disequilibrium, disappear
8. increased, explicit, implicit, college
9. labor market discrimination
10. monopsony
11. constant, increasing
12. lower, fewer
13. 1) Increased incentives for investment in productivity enhancing worker training, 2) increased incentive to avoid shirking and become more productive, 3) results in more stable wages and therefore more stable employment patterns
14. $3 and 5 units of labor, $3
15. $2.50, 4 units of labor, $4 (Hint: You need to calculate MRC and graph it.)

Review Questions

1. b) is the correct answer. It is significant that labor cannot be divorced from its owner because it makes such nonwage factors as working conditions important in labor markets.

2. a) is the correct answer. The functional distribution of income refers to the distribution of national income among the broad categories of factors of production, for example land, labor, and capital. Among these categories, about 70% of national income goes to labor.

3. c) is the correct answer. It may not be easy to enter some labor markets, even if the wages are enticing. This may be because the market is in an undesirable location or because of legal restrictions, such as licenses.

4. a) is not true of the labor market in long-run equilibrium. The differences is skills will cause wages to be different even if moving is costless and there is perfect information available.

5. c) is not true. If people are unwilling to work at the prevailing market wage, they are not in the labor market.

6. c) is the correct answer. Those workers who are on the labor supply function above the equilibrium wage place a higher value on their leisure time than the wage will pay them. Thus, it would take a higher wage to induce them to give up their leisure time.

7. d) is the correct answer. When there is an increase in labor productivity, firms will want to buy more labor at each nominal wage.

8. a) is the correct answer. Equalizing wage differences exist to compensate workers for nonwage job attributes, such as work-place conditions.

9. c) is the correct answer. Equalizing wage differences explain the differences in wages due to such nonmonetary attributes of a job as work conditions.

10. b) is the correct answer. Nonequalizing wage differences are not necessary to attract and retain workers. They must be due to some sort of barrier to entry into the labor market.

11. a) is the correct answer. The equilibrium wage is the difference between what one is paid(the market wage) and the minimum one will take to work(the reservation wage).

12. d) is the correct answer. For nonequalizing wage differences to occur, higher wages must not

be attracting workers into the market, due to some barrier to entry such as membership in a union.

13. c) is the exception. What has been described in the question is a disequilibrium wage difference. It will take some time for the market to eliminate the disequilibrium, which will require more students to major in finance and less students to major in accounting.

14. a) is the correct answer. An individual must calculate the present value of the anticipated earnings from having a college degree and compare that to the present value of the earnings from going to work right out of high school.

15. b) is the definition of labor market discrimination. We cannot simply attribute any wage difference among identifiable groups to labor market discrimination. We must look further to see if there are reasons why one group is less productive on average than other groups.

16. c) is the correct answer. According to the text, 50 - 80% of the differences in wages paid to black workers and white workers are due to measurable productivity differences. However, these observed productivity differences may be due to more complex forms of discrimination, such as limited access to education for minorities.

17. d) is the correct answer. MRC > wage for the monopsony since it must pay more in order to hire additional workers. Therefore, the monopsony's MRC = MRP profit-maximizing condition will occur at a lower quantity of labor than for a perfect competitor, who will hire up to the point at which MRP = wage.

18. c) is not true. Women have traditionally worked in jobs that are easy to enter and exit. In part this is because of the traditional role of women in child rearing.

19. b) is an argument made by advocates of comparable worth legislation. Opponents would argue that these jobs are low-paying because of low productivity.

20. d) is not correct. For the monopsonist, wage is not equal to MRC because the monopsonist must offer a higher wage in order to hire more of a resource.

21. b) is correct. The labor market is quite insensitive to changes in supply and demand conditions. Workers seem to prefer long-term employment and are not generally anxious to move to take advantage of some temporary disequilibrium in the labor market.

22. d is not true. Long-term contracts prevent workers from taking advantage of temporary disequilibria in the labor market.

CHAPTER 16
TRADE UNIONS AND COLLECTIVE BARGAINING

OVERVIEW

In this chapter we use the model of supply and demand to analyze the effect of labor unions on wages and employment levels. We begin by describing the different types of unions and how they work to increase the wages of their members. Next, we provide a brief history of the union movement in the United States. We then consider how unions achieve their primary goal of improved terms of employment for their members. We also examine how the effects of unions have been felt in the economy over time.

The two main types of unions are craft unions and industrial unions. A craft union represents a particular type of skilled worker and works to raise wages by restricting entry into the market. This has the effect of shifting the labor supply curve to the left. Hence, the equilibrium wage level increases, but at the expense of a reduced level of employment. An industrial union organizes all of the workers in a particular industry (regardless of their respective skills) and then works to negotiate, through a process known as collective bargaining, a higher wage for all of its members. This has the effect of altering the labor supply curve, as illustrated in Figure 2 of the text. Once again, wages are increased, but at the expense of a reduced level of employment.

Approximately 17 million workers--15 percent of the U.S. labor force--currently belong to a union. Of the approximately 200 national unions, about one-half are associated with the AFL-CIO. In addition, most of the 65,000 local unions are affiliated with a national union. Membership in unions peaked at about 25 percent in the mid-1950s. Since that time, this figure has steadily declined.

The general trend away from unionization has been credited to a number of different factors including unfavorable legislation, structural changes in the economy, the substitution of government services for services previously provided by unions, and more active management opposition to unions. The extent to which each of these factors is responsible for the decline in union membership is the subject of considerable debate.

The union's goal of improved terms of employment involves a trade-off between higher wages and increased employment. This trade-off is the result of the firm's downward-sloping demand curve for labor. In addition, unions work to achieve other objectives such as more time off, improved working conditions, and increased benefits and job security. The extent to which a union's efforts to raise wages results in unemployment depends in part, on the threat effect, i.e., the ability of nonunion workers to successfully demand an increase in wages in lieu of forming a union.

In an effort to minimize the adverse employment effects of an increase in wages, unions undertake a number of strategies to increase the demand for their members. Such strategies include support for trade barriers to reduce the number of available substitute products, encouraging consumers to buy only union-made goods and services, and efforts to reduce the number of labor substitutes such as unionizing other labor groups and support for increases in the minimum wage. Available evidence suggests that although unions appear to have increased the wages earned by their members, by and large, such increases have come at the expense of non-unionized workers.

In the case of a monopsony, it is possible for a union to raise both wages and the level of employment. This is possible because the union alters the labor supply curve faced by the monopsonist. In fact, because of the offsetting power of each side, the competitively-determined equilibrium is one possible solution.

KEY GRAPHS AND TERMS

Graphs

The key figures in this chapter are Figures 1, 2, and 7. In particular, Figures 1 and 2 illustrate how the two major types of unions effect the labor supply curve and therefore the equilibrium levels of wages and employment. Note that in the case of a craft union, the effect amounts to a shift of the labor supply curve. On the other hand, an industrial union alters the shape of the labor supply curve. In either case, the equilibrium wage is higher with the union than it is without the union. Figure 7 employs the model of the monopsonistic employer that was introduced in Chapter 15. As this figure demonstrates, when the monopsonist is confronted with a union, the equilibrium wage is indeterminate, and will depend on the relative bargaining strengths of the two sides. Figures 4, 5, and 6 are applications of the basic model of supply and demand. Be sure you understand how to construct each of these figures and can use them to illustrate the associated concepts.

Terms
LABOR UNION
CRAFT UNION
INDUSTRIAL UNION
STRIKE
COLLECTIVE BARGAINING
CLOSED SHOP
UNION SHOP
OPEN SHOP
DECERTIFICATION ELECTION
COST OF LIVING ADJUSTMENT
THREAT EFFECT

EXERCISES

1. A ________________ union is an organization that represents a particular type of skilled worker, while an ________________ union is an organization of workers in an entire industry.

2. The process in which a union represents a group of employees in wage negotiations with their employer is called ________________ ________________.

3. Approximately ________________ percent of the American workforce belongs to a labor union.

4. List four possible explanations for the decline in unions that has occurred over the last 35 years.

____

____

5. A negotiated automatic wage increase that is tied to increases in the rate of price inflation is called a ________________ ________ ________________ ________________.

6. The possibility that workers in a particular firm or industry will form a union if their wage demands are not met is called the ________________ ________________. The more effective the ________________ ________________ is, the ________________ difference in wages in the unionized and non-unionized sectors will be.

7. List three factors that improve the bargaining position of unions. ________________________

____

____

8. According to the available evidence, to the extent that unions have been successful at increasing the wages of their members, these increases have come at the expense of (employers' profits, other workers). In addition, to the extent that unions raise production costs, ________________ also pay for union gains.

Use the following figure to answer questions 9 - 12.

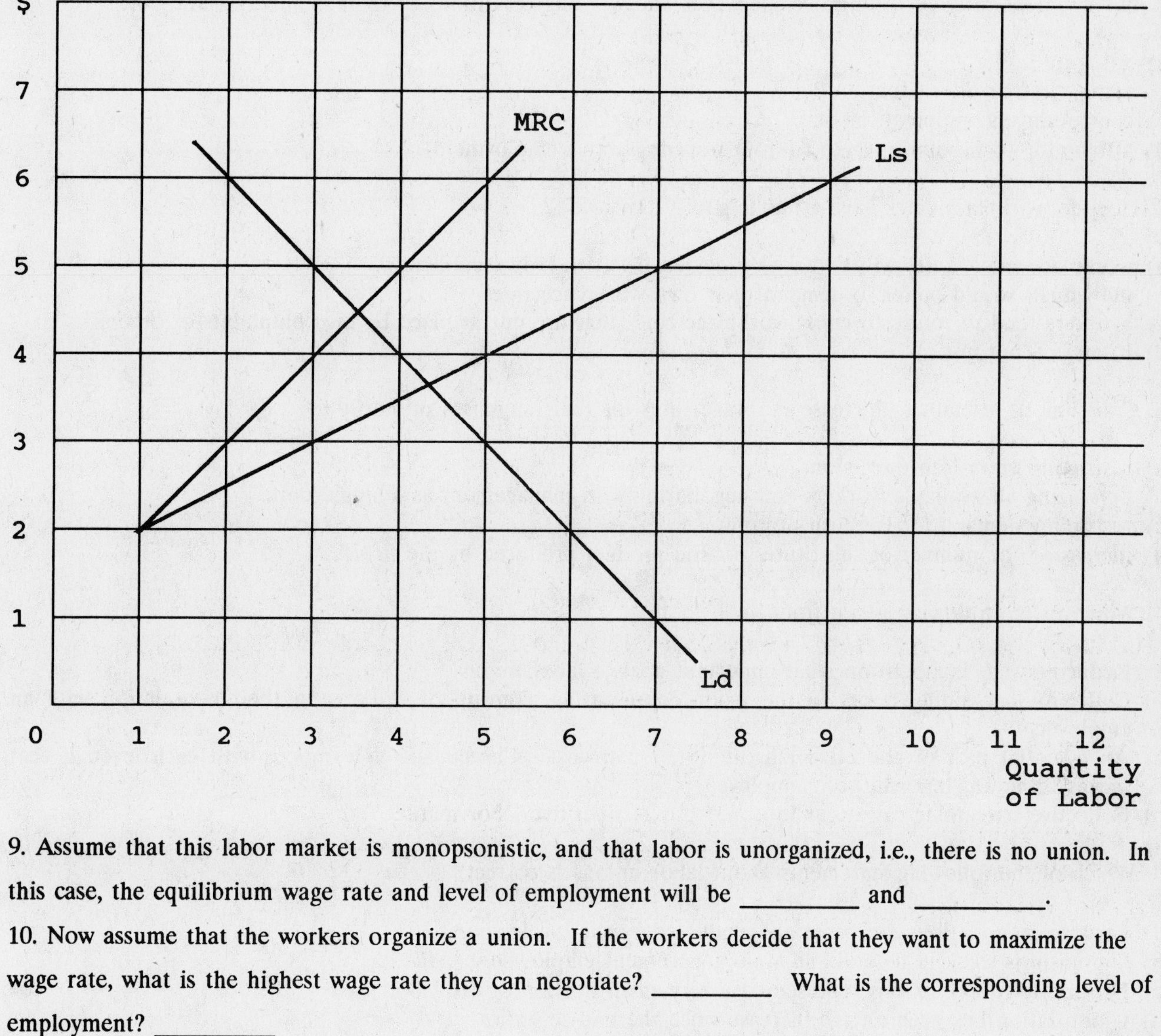

9. Assume that this labor market is monopsonistic, and that labor is unorganized, i.e., there is no union. In this case, the equilibrium wage rate and level of employment will be _________ and _________.

10. Now assume that the workers organize a union. If the workers decide that they want to maximize the wage rate, what is the highest wage rate they can negotiate? _________ What is the corresponding level of employment? _________

11. Assume instead that the workers decide to maximize the level of employment and that they are successful in their efforts. In this case, the equilibrium wage and employment level will be _________ and _________.

12. Draw the MRC curve that corresponds to the situation described in the previous question.

REVIEW QUESTIONS

1. Labor unions attempt to improve the wages and working conditions of their members mainly by:

a) going on strike.
b) using the free rider situation.
c) controlling the supply of labor.
d) attempting to maximize wages without worrying about employment.

2. How do workplace rules have a public goods dimension?

a) workplace safety rules will be under-provided if left to individual action.
b) individuals would prefer to demand their own workplace rules.
c) Workers tend to refuse to enjoy workplace rules that are put in place by the complaints of others.
d) b) and c), but not a)

3. Craft unions attempt to increase the wage rates for their members primarily by:

a) restricting entry into the union.
b) organizing all available workers and negotiating with management as a single unit.
c) restricting demand for the firm's output.
d) increasing the number of substitutes for the product produced by the firm.

4. Which of the following is not true:

a) Reducing wage competition is an important goal of labor unions.
b) Collective bargaining refers to the union representing a group of workers in their negotiation with an employer.
c) An essential part of collective bargaining is that workers agree not to compete with each, even if that means some of them will be unemployed.
d) Collective bargaining can occur in a perfectly competitive labor market.

5. Which of the following statements about labor unions is correct?

a) Contract negotiations are generally conducted by the local unions.
b) Unionism is weak in federal and state government employment.
c) Up through 1930, unions represented a very small portion of the labor force.
d) Unionization has been on the increase since the mid-seventies.

6. Which of the following statements is true?

a) Before the 1930's the legal system was generally supportive of labor unions.
b) In early court decisions, unions were considered criminal conspiracies, like cartels.
c) "Yellow Dog Contracts" make it mandatory that workers belong to the union.
d) In the 1950's, firms frequently refused to bargain with unions after they had been legally formed.

7. The Norris-La Guardia Act:

a) made unions criminal conspiracies.
b) said "Yellow Dog Contracts" were not enforceable in federal court.
c) encouraged states to enact "right to work" legislation.
d) made it easier to get court injunctions against striking unions.

8. The Wagner Act did all of the following except:

a) Outlawed unions in the government.
b) Established the National Labor Relations Board.
c) Said management had an obligation to bargain in good faith with an established union.
d) Established procedures for conducting union elections.

9. The Taft-Hartley Act:

a) has been viewed as favorable to labor unions.
b) said the states could pass "right to work" legislation.
c) made the "closed shop" legal.
d) attempted to increase the power of labor unions relative management.

10. Union membership has declined for all of the following except:

a) The Taft-Hartley Act
b) The increase in the size of the service sector relative to the manufacturing sector.
c) The expanding role of government in workplace safety.
d) The outlawing of yellow dog contracts.

11. All of the following are ways in which the government has substituted for unions except:

a) The Social Security System
b) Unemployment insurance
c) The government has organized most public sector occupations itself.
d) The Occupational Safety and Health Administration's rules for safety in the workplace.

12. As unions engage in policies that raise wages for its members:

a) it increases unemployment in the industry.
b) it shifts the demand for labor to the right.
c) it induces the industry to hire more labor.
d) it increases employment in the industry.

13. Unionization of an industry tends to have what effect on the other nonunion industries in the economy?

a) It tends to increase wages and employment.
b) It tends to increase wages, but reduce employment.
c) It tends to decrease wages and increase employment.
d) It tends to decrease wages and employment.

14. Under what circumstances will unions press most vigorously for an increase in wages?

a) When the economy is in recession.
b) When there are few substitutes for labor.
c) When the cost of labor as a percent of total costs is high.
d) When the demand for the output produced by the industry is elastic.

15. Under which of the following circumstances will a labor union be in a poor bargaining position in terms of raising the wage in an industry?

a) When the demand for the industry's product is inelastic.
b) When labor costs are a small portion of total costs.
c) When the economy is booming.
d) When the industry's output has many substitutes.

16. All of the following are methods unions use to prevent wages from falling in the long-run except:

a) The promotion of free international trade.
b) Featherbedding.
c) Preventing the firm from using substitutes for labor.
d) Advertising the union label.

17. Congress recently voted to increase the minimum wage to $4.25 per hour. Assuming that in the affected labor markets demand is elastic, the effect will be to:

a) increase the level of employment and the total income of affected wage earners.
b) increase the level of employment and decrease the total income of affected wage earners.
c) decrease the level of employment and increase the total income of affected wage earners.
d) decrease the level of employment and the total income of affected wage earners.

18. One reason unions support minimum wage legislation is:

a) it increases the price of substitutes to union labor.
b) it decreases the price of substitutes to union labor.
c) it increases total employment for all industries.
d) it increases the total income of the affected workers, if the demand for labor is elastic.

19. Which of the following is not an effect of unions?

a) In general, union workers earn more than their nonunion counterparts.
b) The union-nonunion wage gap rises during recessions.
c) There is evidence to suggest that the wages of nonunion workers can be reduced by the actions of unions.
d) Unions have reduced the prices of consumer products.

20. Unions can seek to raise the level of wages by doing all of the following EXCEPT:

a) increasing the demand for labor.
b) engaging in the collective bargaining process.
c) challenging the monopoly bargaining power of some employers.
d) increasing the available supply of labor.

21. Assume that initially a monopsonist is hiring the profit maximizing level of labor and paying a wage equal to that demanded by the marginal worker. Now assume that the labor force forms a union and forces the monopsonist to negotiate the wage rate. Assuming that both sides have some bargaining power, when negotiations are completed, the new wage rate:

a) will be higher and the level of employment will be lower.
b) will be lower and the level of employment will be higher.
c) and level of employment will both be higher.
d) and level of employment will both be lower.

ANSWER KEY

Exercises

1. craft, industrial
2. collective bargaining
3. fifteen
4. 1) The passage of unfavorable legislation such as the Taft-Hartley Act, 2) structural changes in the economy, 3) substitution of government for unions in terms of many the services unions have traditionally performed for their members, and 4) an increase in active management opposition to unions.
5. cost of living adjustment
6. threat effect, threat effect, smaller
7. 1) A decrease in the number of available substitutes for union labor, 2) A decrease in the elasticity of demand for the products produced by union labor, and 3) a decrease in the ratio of labor costs to total production costs
8. other workers, consumers
9. $3.25, 3.5 units of labor
10. $4.50, 3.5 units of labor
11. $3.75, approximately 4.33 units of labor
12. The MRC curve will be a horizontal line at $3.75 over the range between 0 units of labor and the point at which the labor demand curve and labor supply curve intersect. Beyond that point, the MRC curve will be linear and upward sloping passing through the point P = $5, Q = 5.

Review Questions

1. c) is the correct answer. The primary tool labor unions have available is the ability to control the supply of labor. Of course the strike is the most dramatic example of this, but unions use many other methods to control supply.

2. a) is the correct answer. Workers will not complain and risk losing their jobs if they can take a free ride on the complaints of a fellow worker. This an example of the free rider problem, which is frequently used to justify public goods provision by the government.

3. a) is the correct answer. Craft unions attempt to raise wages by restricting entry into the union and occupation, frequently by controlling access to training programs.

4. d) is not true. In the collective bargaining process, the union certainly can influence the market wage, so it is not consistent with a perfectly competitive labor market.

5. c) is the correct answer. Unions represented a small part of the labor force until the Great Depression and favorable legislation in the 1930's.

6. b) is the correct answer. Prior to the 1930's, the courts were generally hostile to unions. One of the reasons for this was the view that a union was a criminal conspiracy much like a cartel.

7. b) is the correct answer. The Norris-La Guardia Act declared yellow dog contracts to be

unenforceable in federal court and made it more difficult to get an injunction against a union.

8. a) is the exception. The Wagner Act did not outlaw unions in government. In fact unions are quite strong in the public sector.

9. b) is the correct answer. The most controversial part of the Taft-Hartley Act is that it allowed the states to pass "right to work" legislation which gives a worker the option of not joining a union, even if the workplace is organized.

10. d) is the exception. The yellow dog contract was one of the tools used by management to prevent the unions from organizing a workplace. They were made ineffectual by court decisions in the 1930's and are not important to the current decline of unions.

11. c) is the exception. Unionism is strong in the government, so the government has not organized its workforce itself.

12. a) is the correct answer. Unions face a trade-off. As they engage in policies to increase wages, unions must be prepared for a decline in employment as the firm moves along its negatively-sloped demand curve for labor.

13. c) is the correct answer. A union demands a wage that is above the equilibrium wage. This creates unemployment in the unionized industry. Workers from that industry seek work elsewhere. This increases the supply of labor in the nonunion industries, causing the wage to fall and the amount of labor employed to increase.

14. b) is the correct answer. When there are few substitutes for labor, the labor demand function will be relatively inelastic and an increase in wages will cause a relatively small decline in employment.

15. d) is the correct answer. If there are many substitutes for the industry's output, the demand for that output will be elastic. This means the union will have a hard time pressing for wage increases because they will be strongly resisted by the industry who will be able to pass forward only a small amount of the cost increase to consumers.

16 a) is the correct answer. Unions attempt to limit free trade, since it makes the demand curves for domestic industries more elastic and thus makes increasing wages more difficult.

17 d) is the correct answer. The increase in the minimum wage will reduce employment as firms move along the negatively-sloped demand function. If demand for labor is elastic, incomes of the affected workers will fall, since total revenue falls as price is increased when demand is elastic.

18. a) is the correct answer. Unskilled nonunionized labor is a substitute for unionized labor. To the extent that minimum wage legislation raises the price of this substitute, it is easier for unions to raise the wages of their members.

19. d) is not true. To the extent that unions raise costs of production, they also raise prices of final goods for consumers.

20. d) is the exception. Actually unions want to restrict the supply of labor in order to increase wages.

21. c) is the correct answer. The formation of a union removes the monopsonist's incentive to restrict hiring. The monopsonist can no longer reduce the wage by hiring fewer workers. In this case, the union can increase both wages and employment.

CHAPTER 17
THE CAPITAL MARKET

OVERVIEW

In this chapter we examine the market for capital and, in particular, the factors that determine how much capital investment takes place. The relationship between investment and savings, and the relationship between the interest rate and the rate of capital formation are also developed.

The simple model of the production possibilities frontier can be used to illustrate the importance of capital formation. To be specific, ceteris paribus, an increase in the economy's capital stock enables it to produce a greater level of total output. However, capital accumulation also involves a trade-off in the form of less consumer goods. Thus, it is necessary to balance the benefits and costs of capital accumulation.

Like any other resource, the demand for capital is a derived demand. However, unlike other resources, the decision to acquire additional capital is a long-run decision. A piece of capital generally yields a flow of benefits--revenues--over an extended period of time. In order to compare future benefits and current costs, it is necessary to calculate the present value of the stream of benefits that accrues over time. Present value is calculated by the process known as discounting. The basic idea behind discounting is that a future sum is worth less today since the lesser sum could be invested and earn interest over time. The initial amount invested plus the accumulated interest would then equal the future sum. Discounting is used to calculate the internal rate of return--the interest rate that makes the present values of the benefits and costs of an investment equal.

The demand curve for capital is constructed by ranking all investment projects from highest to lowest on the basis of their internal rates of returns. So long as the internal rate of return exceeds the market rate of interest, which is the opportunity cost of investment for the firm, an investment project is profitable. Thus, as the market interest rate falls, additional investment projects are undertaken.

Investment yields benefits not only to the individual firm, but to society as well. Such benefits include reduced production costs through economies of scale and technological innovation, the development of new products, and increases in productivity. Note that these benefits imply a greater selection of products for consumers and more efficient use of resources, which allows for an increase in the overall level of production.

The interest rate is determined by the interaction of the supply of and demand for investment funds. The demand for investment funds is downward sloping, reflecting the fact that additional investment projects become profitable as the market rate of interest falls. The supply of investment funds consists of savings, and is upward sloping on the assumption that the quantity of savings will increase as it becomes more profitable to save. This relationship between savings, investment and the interest rate suggests that policymakers could increase investment by stimulating savings and therefore reducing the interest rate.

KEY GRAPHS AND TERMS

Graphs

Two new concepts are introduced in this chapter: the investment demand curve and the model of the determination of the interest rate. Figure 2 illustrates the demand curve for capital. It is stair-step shaped rather than smooth to reflect the "lumpy" nature of investments for the individual firm. As the interest rate changes, we move along the investment demand curve. Changes in such factors as the price of the output the capital is used to produce and the marginal productivity of capital cause the investment demand curve to shift.

Determination of the equilibrium interest rate is illustrated in Figure 4. Once again, a change in the interest rate causes a movement along the respective curves. Changes n the other determinants of savings and investment cause the curves to shift.

Terms

RATE OF RETURN
TIME VALUE OF MONEY
PRESENT VALUE
FUTURE VALUE
DISCOUNTING

INTERNAL RATE OF RETURN
PRODUCTIVITYCAPACITY UTILIZATION RATE
FINANCIAL INTERMEDIARY

EXERCISES

1. As is illustrated by the production possibilities frontier, so long as an economy is producing efficiently, an increase in the production of capital goods requires society to incur an opportunity cost in the form of less

________________ ________________.

2. The decision of whether to invest in additional capital stock is a ________________ -____________ decision. In addition, the investment decision is based on ________________, as opposed to actual, costs and benefits.

3. The amount of capital a firm employs depends on the ________________ ________________ of capital, the ________________ of the firm's output, and the ________________ of capital.

4. Sheri is considering buying an exercise machine for her business (a work-out facility). The cost of the machine is $1,200, and it is expected to last 5 years. Assuming the interest rate is 11 percent, if Sheri can earn $250 a year in additional profits from the machine, should she buy it? ____________ What is the minimum annual amount of revenue Sheri could earn and still make a profit on the machine?

____

5. A change in the ________________ ________________ will cause a movement along the investment demand curve, while a change in the ________________ ________________ of capital, or the price of the firm's output will cause the investment demand curve to ________________.

6. List three possible social benefits from investment in capital stock. ____________________________

____

____

7. The equilibrium interest rate is determined by the interaction of the supply of ________________ and ________________ demand. Ceteris paribus, an increase in the productivity of capital will cause the interest rate to ________________ and the amount of investment to ________________. Alternatively, a decrease in the thriftiness of the economy will cause the interest rate to ________________ and the quantity of investment spending to ________________.

8. List four major reasons why interest rates differ. ____________________________________

____

____

Chapter 17, The Capital Market

REVIEW QUESTIONS

1. Investment:

a) should be undertaken up to the point at which its marginal benefits equal its marginal costs.
b) should be undertaken only if it does not reduce current consumption.
c) will not necessarily curtail consumption if it is undertaken in a perfectly competitive world.
d) is inversely-related to saving.

2. Investment:

a) is a short-run decision, since it is a variable cost.
b) benefits accrue immediately, but the cost of investment is spread over time.
c) decisions are made with an element of uncertainty.
d) is more stable than consumption.

3. Which of the following is a primary difference between labor and capital?

a) The demand for capital is derived, but the demand for labor is not.
b) Capital can be adjusted with relative ease, but labor cannot.
c) Labor can be adjusted with relative ease, but capital cannot.
d) Labor is not used up to the point at which marginal benefit = marginal cost.

4. Suppose a firm is considering purchasing a machine. Suppose the machine is expected to produce $1,000 worth of output per year and will last two years before it wears completely out. Assuming the interest rate is 10%, what is the present value of the machine?

a) $1,000/1.1
b) $1,000/(1.1)(1.1)
c) $1,000/(.10) + $1,000/(.10)(.10)
d) $1,000/(1.1) + $1,000/(1.1)(1.1)

5. Amounts to be received in the future will be discounted more:

a) the lower the interest rate.
b) the farther into the future they are discounted.
c) if there is a big increase in saving.
d) if the demand for investment funds is quite depressed.

6. How much would a firm be willing to pay for a machine with a life of two years that will produce $1,000 worth of benefits for each year? Assume the interest is 8%.

a) $1,000
b) $1,256
c) $1,598
d) $1,783

7. The internal rate of return:

a) must be less than the interest rate if the firm is to invest.
b) makes the present value of profits equal to the present value of costs.
c) falls as the annual yield of an investment rises.
d) is equal to the market interest rate for all of the firm's investments

8. As the number of investments made by a firm increases, its internal rate of return:

a) declines due to diminishing marginal productivity.
b) declines due to the Law of Diminishing Marginal Utility.
c) increases to compensate the firm for the current consumption foregone.
d) increases because the level of savings will fall.

9. Assuming there is one market interest rate, if a firm uses its own funds to finance an investment:

a) it will cost the firm more than it will cost the firm to borrow.
b) it will cost the firm less than it will cost the firm to borrow.
c) it will cost the firm the same as it would cost the firm to borrow.
d) the firm will not have to calculate the present value of the investment.

10. Advocates of the use of a "social discount rate":

a) argue that society is overly concerned about the welfare of future generations.
b) believe the private discount rate is too high for public projects.
c) believe the private discount rate is too low for public projects.
d) would be less likely to support government projects than those supporting the use of a private discount rate for government projects.

11. Additions to society's capital stock reduce costs for all of the following reasons except:

a) technological innovation
c) economies of scale
c) the minimum point on the LRAC function shifts down if there are economies of scale.
d) the interest rate will fall as the demand for investment increases.

12. One of the ways investment in research and development pays off is:

a) by a shift up in the LRAC function.
b) by being able to produce the same output with less inputs.
c) by being able to produce the same output with more inputs.
d) by a shift up in the SRAC function.

13. Why might the installation of robots in the auto industry not lead to unemployment?

a) The robots would not displace labor in the auto industry.
b) Older workers would be displaced in the auto industry.
c) Consumers would have more to spend on other goods.
d) Auto sales would fall.

14. All of the following cause increases in labor productivity except:

a) an increase in the size of the labor force.
b) additions to the capital stock.
c) improved technology.
d) greater utilization of existing plant and equipment.

15. Capacity Utilization:

a) is usually near 100%.
b) represents the percent of the labor force that is employed.
c) measures the proportion of the existing capital stock used for current production.
d) rises as the economy moves into a recession, since firms must replace unemployed workers with some other resource to maintain production.

16. Which of the following is not true? The real interest rate:

a) is determined by the interaction of savings and investment.
b) is the rate of exchange between current and future consumption.
c) includes an expected inflation component.
d) compensates individuals for saving and foregoing current consumption.

17. An increase in "thriftiness" in the U.S. economy will have which of the following results?

a) The interest rate will increase and the quantity of investment will fall.
b) The interest rate will decrease and the quantity of investment will rise.
c) Both the interest rate and the quantity of investment will fall.
d) Both the interest rate and the quantity of investment will rise.

18. As capital becomes more productive, which of the following will occur?

a) The saving function will shift to the left.
b) The saving function will shift to the right.
c) The investment function will shift to the left.
d) The investment function will shift to the right.

19. In an effort to stimulate investment during the 1980's, the government did all of the following except:

a) increase the top marginal income tax rate.
b) establish tax-deferred savings funds.
c) introduce IRA's.
d) accelerate the rate at which firms could depreciate their capital.

20. In the long-run, the marginal revenue product of capital equals:

a) the marginal productivity of labor.
b) the marginal revenue product of labor.
c) the market interest rate.
d) the price of the firm's output.

ANSWER KEY

Exercises

1. consumer goods
2. long-run, anticipated
3. physical productivity, price, cost
4. No (net present value of total revenue is only $741.29), $325 (approximate)
5. interest rate, physical productivity, price, shift

6. 1) A reduction in the average costs of production, and hence, more efficient use of resources, 2) the development of new and improved goods and services, and 3) productivity growth
7. savings, investment, increase, increase, increase, decrease
8. 1) Differences in the riskiness of loans, 2) differences in loan length, 3) differences in tax treatment, and 4) economies of scale in service loans

Review Questions

1. a) is the correct answer. Investment in capital goods is like the purchase of any other resource, it should be undertaken up to the point at which marginal benefits equal marginal costs.

2. c) is the correct answer. Investment decisions are always made with an element of uncertainty. This is because they are based on anticipated or expected costs and benefits, since they are long-run decisions.

3. c) is the correct answer. Capital cannot be adjusted very easily. For example, the firm can lay off workers fairly easily, but it cannot lay off its plant once it is built.

4. d) is the correct answer. The present value of what the machine will produce in the first year is $1,000/(1.1) and the present value of what the machine will produce in the second year is $1,000/(1.1)(1.1).

5. b) is the correct answer. The farther into the future an amount is to be received, the more it will be discounted to present value. $1,000 received next year has a greater present value than $1,000 received in twenty years.

6. d) is the correct answer. This is found by $1,000/1.08 + $1,000/(1.08)(1.08).

7. b) is the correct answer. The internal rate of return is the interest rate at which the present value of the stream of profits is equal to the present value of the stream of costs for an investment.

8. a) is the correct answer. Capital, like any other resource, is subject to diminishing marginal productivity. As the firm use more capital, the marginal product of capital falls.

9. c) is the correct answer. If there is only one interest rate, the cost to the firm will be the same whether the funds are borrowed or come from the firm itself. If the funds are borrowed, the firm will have to pay an explicit interest cost. If the funds are the firm's own, there is an implicit cost equal to the interest income the firm could have made by lending the funds. These two costs are the same if the interest rate is the same.

10 b) is the correct answer. Advocates of the use of a social discount rate argue that the private discount rate weights current consumption too heavily relative to future generations and that therefore it is too high.

11. d) is the correct answer. As the demand for investment grows, the interest rate will rise, ceteris paribus.

12. b) is the correct answer. R and D is aimed at producing technological innovation which will increase profits. One way the increase in profits is accomplished is by being able to increase the productivity of inputs so that more output can be produced with the same inputs.

13. c) is the correct answer. The increase in productivity in the auto industry would cause the prices of cars to decline. This would leave consumers with income left over to buy goods in other industries, which would therefore need to purchase more labor to expand output.

14. a) is the exception. An increase in the size of the labor force will cause a decline in labor productivity due to diminishing marginal productivity.

15. c) is the correct answer. Capacity Utilization measures the percent of the capital stock that is currently in use. If capacity utilization is 85%, that means that 15% of the existing capital stock is idle.

16. c) is the correct answer. The nominal interest rate includes an inflation component, but the real interest rate does not.

17. b) is the correct answer. An increase in "thriftiness" will increase the supply of saving. This will cause the interest rate to fall and will increase the quantity of investment.

18. d) is the correct answer. If the productivity of investment increases, the demand for investment will increase. This shifts the investment function to the right.

19. a) is the correct answer. The government did not raise the top marginal tax rate, it decreased it. This made it more attractive for high income taxpayers to save, since the tax they had to pay on their income from saving was lower.

20. c) is the correct answer. The firm will use capital up to the point at which the MRP of capital(expressed in percentage terms) equals the interest rate, just as the wage is equal to the MRP of labor.

CHAPTER 18
INCOME INEQUALITY AND POVERTY

OVERVIEW

In this chapter we examine the distribution of income in the United States. Our focus is on the issues of how to measure income distribution, and define poverty. In addition, we summarize the major characteristics of the poor in the United States.

The personal distribution of income refers to the percentage of income received by families at different income levels. In the United States the poorest fifth of families received less than 5 percent of total personal income, while the richest fifth received about 45 percent of total personal income in 1989. These figures are fairly representative of the distribution of income over the last 60 years, and suggest a substantial amount of income inequality. Adjusting these figures for taxes paid and nonmonetary transfers reduces the inequality of the distribution of income.

The unequal distribution of income is the result of a number of different factors including age, education, occupation, sex, race, differences in individual abilities and preferences, willingness to take risks in the effort to earn income, transfers of wealth (inheritance), and luck. To accurately assess the degree of income inequality, it is also important to consider the effects of income mobility. To be specific, many families and individuals move among income groups over time. Available data suggest that there is a fair degree of income mobility in the United States.

The unequal distribution of income can be justified, to some extent, on the basis of the incentives that it creates for people to work harder to try and get ahead. This tends to encourage a more efficient allocation of resources. However, the fairness of this outcome can also be questioned. As such, there is a trade-off between efficiency and equity that must be addressed by policymakers. One approach to this trade-off is to provide for equality of opportunity, as opposed to equality of income. This approach can be augmented by attempting to a provide a minimum standard of living for everyone.

Poverty refers to the condition that results when one's income is insufficient to maintain a minimum standard of living. In 1988 approximately 13 percent of U.S. families were at or below the poverty level. In 1989, a family of four was considered to be in poverty if its before-tax money income was below $12,676. Over the past thirty years the poverty rate has fluctuated between about 22.4 percent (1959) and 11.7 percent (1979). In the early 1980s the poverty rate was rising. However, it began to decline again between 1985 and 1988. Factors such the effects of non-cash benefits and the fact that most spells of poverty are of a relatively short duration suggest that the extent of poverty may be somewhat overstated by the figures just cited.

Poverty is caused by a number of factors including labor force nonparticipation, unemployment, and employment at low wages. Labor force nonparticipation is most often attributable to worker disabilities and child-care responsibilities that prevent an individual from being able to take a job. Most of the poor can be grouped into one of two categories, the working poor--those who are employed or who want to be employed but can't find a job--and the nonworking poor, e.g., the sick and disabled, and single parents.

A number of programs including the Comprehensive Employment and Training Act, Aid to Families with Dependent Children, and the Supplemental Security Income program have been implemented at the federal level to try to reduce the level of poverty. However, the effectiveness of such programs has been questioned by many critics. The available data does not allow one reach a definite conclusion on this issue.

KEY GRAPHS AND TERMS

Graphs

The Lorenz Curve is used in this chapter to illustrate the distribution of personal income across income groups. Refer to Figures 1 and 2 and be sure you understand how to read the Lorenz Curve.

Terms

PERSONAL DISTRIBUTION OF INCOME
LORENZ CURVE
INCOME MOBILITY
MEAN FAMILY INCOME
PER CAPITA INCOME
POVERTY

EXERCISES

1. The share of all personal income received by families at different income levels is called the

________ ________ ________ ________.

2. The ________ ________ is a functional relationship that indicates the percentage of the population that holds a given percentage of the total income in the economy.

3. ________ ________ refers to the tendency of individuals and families to move among income groups over time.

4. ________ ________ ________ is the average income for families in a particular category.

5. The average income for each individual in a particular category is called ________ ________ ________.

6. Government transfer payments and progressive taxation tend to ________ the actual inequality of the distribution of income.

7. List the major factors that appear to influence the distribution of income in the economy. ________

____

____

8. The debate over what constitutes an appropriate or acceptable distribution of income highlights the fact that there is a tradeoff between ________ and ________. As such, policy in the United States tends to stress equality of ________ as opposed to equality of ________. However, it is generally agreed that everyone should enjoy some minimum ________ ________ ________.

9. ________ is the result of a level of income that is insufficient to ensure some pre-determined minimum standard of living.

10. In 1989, the poverty level of income for a family of four was ________.

11. At a very basic level, poverty is caused by three factors: ________

____

REVIEW QUESTIONS

1. When the Census Bureau collects information on personal income, which of the following is not included?

a) Wages and salaries
b) Social Security payments
c) Interest payments
d) Food Stamps

2. In the U.S. distribution of income, the lowest one-fifth or quintile of the population would earn about what % of the income.

a) 1%
b) 5%
c) 8%
d) 10%

3. If the distribution of income is perfectly equal:

a) each quintile (20 %) would be earning 100% of national income.
b) the Lorenz Curve would be a backward L.
c) the Lorenz Curve would be a straight line.
d) the Lorenz Curve would be a half-circle.

4. Since 1950, the U.S. distribution of income:

a) has changed very little.
b) has become much more equal.
c) has become much more unequal.
d) could be represented by a Lorenz Curve that has become much closer in shape to a straight line.

5. Which of the following is <u>not true</u>?

a) The more equal the distribution of income, the more bowed the Lorenz Curve becomes.
b) The U.S. distribution of income became more equal between 1929 and 1950.
c) The top one-fifth of the population earns about 45% of national income in the U.S.
d) The Lorenz Curve shows the relationship between the percent of families who receive income and the cumulative share of total income received.

6. The U.S. distribution of income:

a) is one of the most unequal in the world.
b) is less unequal than that of most less-developed countries.
c) is less unequal than that of Denmark and Sweden.
d) is more unequal than Mexico's.

7. All of the following are reasons that the distribution of income <u>overstates</u> economic inequality in the U.S. <u>except</u>:

a) The income distribution is measured before the payment of taxes.
b) The U.S. tax system is progressive.
c) The income distribution includes nonmonetary government transfers.
d) The distribution of income omits goods and services produced by the households themselves.

8. Many economists suggest the "lifetime distribution of income" is important because:

a) Families frequently move among the quintiles of the income distribution with the passage of time.
b) Throughout their lives, most families have the same income relative to the rest of the population.
c) Retired persons are not included in the distribution of income measure.
d) Child rearing is irrelevant to the distribution of income.

9. Which of the following does <u>not</u> explain differences in incomes?

a) Income rises until about age 60 and then declines thereafter.
b) Service workers earn more than blue-collar workers.
c) Differences in education.
d) Work experience.

10. Income inequality may be due to risk-taking for which of the following reasons?

a) Risk-taking involves lower income groups only.
b) Risk-takers have high incomes.
c) Risk-takers have low incomes.
d) Risk-taking makes income more volatile.

11. Marginal Productivity Theory:

a) makes a case against income redistribution.
b) suggests that wages are determined mainly by monopsonies.
c) derives from the fact that resource markets are not competitive.
d) states what the income distribution should be rather than describes what it is.

12. Which of the following does not support the argument for redistributing income, according to the text?

a) The income distribution being determined by luck.
b) The income distribution being determined by inheritance.
c) Race and sex discrimination.
d) Individuals being paid their marginal revenue product.

13. If we are interested in preserving the incentives which lead to economic efficiency:

a) our policies should be oriented toward achieving equality of results rather than equality of opportunity.
b) our policies should be oriented toward achieving equality of opportunity rather than equality of results.
c) we should attempt to engage in policies that make the distribution of income as equal as possible.
d) we should place very high taxes on those in the higher income categories.

14. Which of the following statements is not correct?

a) A relative definition of poverty equates poverty with income inequality.
b) Under a relative definition of poverty, a rising real income of the poor would not necessarily eradicate poverty.
c) In theory, poverty could be eradicated under an absolute definition of poverty.
d) Under an absolute definition of poverty, poverty is strongly related to the distribution of income.

15. In the U.S., the official definition of poverty is based on:

a) a relative definition of poverty.
b) the lowest 20% of the population earning less than 5% of the income.
c) a minimum needs definition.
d) the lowest 20% of the income distribution, no matter what % of national income they earn.

16. All of the following are true about the poverty rate in the U.S. except:

a) It is over twice the national average for black families.
b) It is over twice the national average for female-headed families.
c) It is over one and a half times the national average for the elderly.
d) It is about 13%.

17. Which of the following statements is correct?

a) Poverty declined significantly for all groups during the 1960's.
b) Funding for all poverty programs declined during the years of the Reagan Administration.
c) Poverty has continued to rise for the elderly since the end of World War II.
d) Approximately 25% of U.S. citizens live in poverty, according to the governments's definition of poverty.

18. All of the following are reasons that poverty might be overstated except:

a) Only cash income is counted.
b) Food stamps and federal government-provided medical insurance do not count.
c) There is significant mobility across income categories.
d) The actual rise in the cost of living has been underestimated.

19. Which of the following statements is not true:

a) The most immediate cause of poverty in the U.S. is low wages.
b) The text's discussion of poverty suggests that we should be more concerned about lack of full-time employment than low wages.
c) The incidence of poverty is high for families whose head is young.
d) One of the reasons for people having part-time jobs is child rearing responsibilities.

20. Government policy decisions generally place more weight on:

a) marginal productivity theory.
b) economic efficiency arguments.
c) increased income equality.
d) incentives to engage in productive activities..

ANSWER KEY

Exercises
1. personal distribution of income
2. Lorenz curve
3. Income mobility
4. Mean family income
5. per capita income
6. reduce
7. The list of possible factors includes age, education, occupation, sex, race, differences in ability and preferences, willingness to assume risks, transfers of wealth, and luck.
8. equity, efficiency, opportunity, outcomes, standard of living
9. Poverty
10. $12,676
11. 1) Labor force nonparticipation, 2) unemployment, and 3) employment at low wages

Review Questions
1. d) is the correct answer. Income from capital gains and nonmonetary transfer payments, such as food stamps, are not included in the measure of personal income.

2. b) is the correct answer. The lowest one-fifth of the popualtion in the U.S. earns about 5% of national income.

3. c) is the correct answer. If the distribution of income is perfectly equal, the Lorenz Curve would be a straight line. This is because each quintile or 20% of the population would earn 20% of the national income.

4. a) is the correct answer. Since 1950, the U.S. distribution of income has changed very little(with income defined by Census Bureau standards). Since 1980, the share of income going to the top 20% has increased somewhat.

5. a) is not true. The more equal the distribution of income, the less bowed the Lorenz Curve becomes.

6. b) is the correct answer. The U.S. distribution of income is less unequal than that of most of the less-developed countries. It is more unequal than that of such countries as Denmark, Sweden, and Great Britain.

7. c) is not true. The distribution of income excludes nonmometary government transfers, such as food stamps and medical care. These transfers have a cash value to the recipients that is not included in the distribution of income.

8. a) is the correct answer. Families move frequently from one quintile of the income distribution to another. Families that are in the lower quintile because one of the parents is in school may quickly move into one of the higher quintiles when the parent graduates and takes a job.

9. b) is not a reason for income differences. While it is true that occupation is a reason for income differences, generally blue collar workers earn more income than service workers.

10 d) is the correct answer. If an individual assumes a risky financial transaction, the individual may gain a great of income or lose a great deal of income. Thus, if the risk is great enough, the individual could end up in the highest quintile or lowest quintile of the income distribution.

11. a) is the correct answer. Marginal Productivity Theory suggests that individuals are paid according to their marginal revenue product. To attempt to change the distribution of income results in economic inefficiency, according to this theory.

12. d) is the correct answer. Income is frequently redistributed away from those with high marginal revenue products to those with low marginal revenue products. This creates a disincentive to allocate resources to their most productive uses.

13. b) is the correct answer. Income distribution weakens the incentives which provide economic efficiency. Attempting to acheive equality of results implies an equal distrilbution of income, in which case there is very little incentive to obtain training or take the risks associated with investment in order to increase income.

14. d) is not correct. Under an absolute definition of poverty, raising the incomes of the poor could eliminate poverty, no matter what the distribution of income. Therefore, an absolute definition of poverty is not related to the distribution of income.

15. c) is the correct answer. The definition of poverty in the U.S. is an absolute definition of minimum needs.

16. c) is the exception. Actually, poverty rates for the elderly are below the national average.

17. a) is the correct answer. Poverty declined for all groups during the 1960's, stabilized during the 1970's, and rose somewhat during the first half of the 1980's.

18. d) is the exception. The Consumer Price Index is thought to have overestimated the increase in the cost of living, due to overemphasizing the cost of housing. Thus, real incomes of people are somewhat higher than estimated and therefore less people are living in poverty than was originally thought.

19. a) is not true. According to the text, the most immediate cause of poverty is lack of full-time employment, not low wages.

20. c is the correct answer. Government policy decisions have generally promoted increased income equality, at the expense of reliance on market forces to provide efficient outcomes.

CHAPTER 19
EXTERNALITIES, PUBLIC GOODS, AND COMMON PROPERTY RESOURCES: PROBLEMS FOR THE MARKET MECHANISM

OVERVIEW

In Chapter 5 we introduced the concepts of externalities and public goods as two examples of market failure. In this chapter we examine more closely these two concepts, along with the concept of common property resources. In addition, we consider a specific negative externality--environmental pollution. The focus of the analysis is on the conditions that give rise to each of these types of market failure, and the policies that can be used to address them.

The problems posed by externalities, public goods, and common property resources are, by and large, the result of poorly defined property rights. In such cases, it is not clear who has the right to a particular resource, such as the air water, or a fishery. Consequently, third parties can bear costs (or benefits) although they are not part of the original transaction. According to the Coase Theorem, so long as transactions costs are low, the affected parties can negotiate an efficient solution to the problem in question. However, as transactions costs increase, it may become necessary for an outside party such as the courts to impose a solution.

The general nature of external costs and benefits has already been discussed in detail in Chapter 5. It is sufficient to note here that in the absence of intervention in the market, a negative externality will result in an overallocation of resources to production. In the case of a positive externality, too few resources will be allocated to production.

Environmental pollution is a specific source of external costs. However, it is important to recognize that in most cases the efficient level of pollution is some positive amount, rather than zero. This is because pollution control involves both benefits and costs, and as we try to control additional units of pollution, the marginal opportunity costs of doing so increase; sometimes dramatically. Policies designed to control pollution can be grouped into two main categories: direct regulation, and incentives-based mechanisms. Direct regulation generally involves the imposition of a standard that limits the amount of pollution that firms can emit during a particular time period. Standards tend to be inefficient due to differences in pollution control costs across firms. Incentives-based mechanisms include the use of transferable discharge permits, taxes on pollution, offset programs, bubble policies, and emissions banking programs. Incentives-based mechanisms are more efficient than direct regulation since they allow for consideration of differences in pollution control costs across firms.

Public goods differ from private goods in that there is nonrivalry in the consumption of public goods (the amount of a public good consumed by one person does not affect the amount available for consumption by others), and nonexcludability, which means that the benefits of a public good are available to everyone regardless of who pays for the good. In general, the market will not provide public goods due to the problem of free riders. As such, it is often up to the government to provide such goods.

Common property resources include such things as the air, fisheries, and common grazing areas. In this situation, property rights to the resource are poorly defined, or do not exist at all. The end result is that common property resources tend to be overexploited. As such, it is once again necessary for the government to intervene and try to ensure a more efficient level of use of the resource.

In general, government intervention that is intended to address the types of market failure discussed in this chapter relies to some extent on the use of cost-benefit analysis. The purpose of this type of analysis is to generate an estimate of the benefits and costs of specific policy strategies, and help improve the efficiency of government actions. However, such analysis is usually complicated by such factors as equity considerations, and strategic political behavior.

KEY GRAPHS AND TERMS

Graphs

The various models that are employed in this chapter have been introduced previously. For example, the graphical analysis of externalities is addressed in Chapter 5. Two graphs that warrant further attention are Figure 4 and Figure 8. Figure 4 illustrates the determination of the efficient level of pollution. Note that, in effect, the MSC curve is the supply curve for pollution control, and that the MSB curve represents the demand for pollution control. Equilibrium occurs where the two curves intersect. Figure 8 illustrates the derivation of the demand curve for a public good. Note that this approach differs from that for deriving the demand curve for a private good. In particular, in the case of a private good, the quantities demanded at each price are added together to determine the total quantity that will be demanded at each price--individual demand curves are summed horizontally. In the case of public goods, however, the amount individuals are willing to pay for a given quantity are added together to determine the total price that will be paid for that quantity--individual demand curves are summed vertically.

Terms
PROPERTY RIGHTS
COASE THEOREM
EXTERNAL COST
EXTERNAL BENEFIT
SOCIAL COSTS
SOCIAL BENEFITS
ASSIMILATIVE CAPACITY
EMISSION STANDARD
TRANSFERABLE DISCHARGE PERMIT
OFFSET PROGRAM
BUBBLE POLICY
EMISSIONS BANKING
PUBLIC GOOD
FREE RIDER
COMMON-PROPERTY RESOURCE
COST-BENEFIT ANALYSIS

EXERCISES

1. The concept of ________________ ________________ refers to the legally sanctioned control that an individual exercises over a collection of goods, resources, and services.

2. According to the ________________ ________________, so long as all affected parties stand to gain from a transaction, and transactions costs are low, the transaction will take place.

3. A cost resulting from a production or consumption decision that is borne by a third party who is not part of the original transaction is called an ________________ cost, while a benefit resulting from a production or consumption decision that is borne by a third party who is not part of the original transaction is called an ________________ benefit.

4. In the case where production of a good results in external costs, the market-determined level of output is too ________________. As such, there is an ________________ of resources to the good in question. In the case where production of a good results in external benefits, the market-determined level of output is too ________________. As such, there is an ________________ of resources to the good in question.

5. One method that can be used to internalize an external cost is to impose a per unit ________________ on the producer that is equal to the marginal ________________ ________________. In the case of an external benefit, consumers or producers could be offered a ________________.

6. ________________ ________________ refers to the environment's natural ability to absorb, or assimilate, some pollutants.

7. The efficient level of a pollutant is the quantity at which ________________ ________________ ________________ equal ________________ ________________ ________________.

8. An ________________ ________________ is a legal limit on the amount of a pollutant an individual source is allowed to emit.

9. Direct regulation is generally an inefficient approach to pollution control since the marginal ________________ of control ________________ across firms.

10. Incentives-based approaches to pollution control include the use of ________________ ________________ ________________ which amount to property rights to discharge a specified quantity of a particular pollutant that can be traded among affected parties; an ________________ ________________, which allows a new pollution source in a particular geographic region to pay existing sources to reduce their emissions below that required by the existing standard, in lieu of installing control technology at the new plant; the ________________ ________________, which treats a group of closely-situated pollution sources as if they were encased in a giant bubble (the pollution standard then applies to emissions coming out of the bubble); and ________________ ________________ ________________, which grant a firm credit for reducing emissions below the existing standard that can be saved for later use or for sale to another firm.

11. A ________________ ________________ is a good whose use by one person does not reduce its availability for use by other people.

12. Assume that 100 individuals have indicated that they are each willing to pay $100 for 5 units of a particular public good. In this case, (assuming benefits exceed costs) the corresponding price and quantity on the demand curve will be ______________ and ______________.

13. An individual who receives benefits from a public good but does pay for those benefits is called a ________________ ________________.

14. A ________________ ________________ resource is a resource for which property rights are poorly defined or nonexistent and whose consumption results in a negative externality.

15. List the four basic steps in a cost-benefit analysis. ____

____

____

16. Assume that four different sizes for a reservoir are being considered by the Army Corps of Engineers (ACE) with benefits and costs indicated below.

Reservoir Size	Total Benefits	Total Costs
small	$ 5,000	$ 1,000
medium	$10,000	$ 4,000
large	$15,000	$ 8,000
huge	$20,000	$16,000

Which reservoir size should the ACE should select?

REVIEW QUESTIONS

1. When market outcomes may be inefficient if:

a) all costs are private.
b) all benefits are private.
c) all costs are "internalized" by the individual or firm.
d) some benefits are incurred by third parties.

2. Poorly-defined property rights:

a) are a main cause of pollution.
b) result in all costs being private.
c) cause common property resources to be used as if they were free.
d) a) and c), but not b).

3. For the Coase Theorem to be in effect, which of the following conditions does not have to exist?

a) a large number of people have to be affected to make it worthwhile for negotiation to take place.
b) transactions costs must be low.
c) there must a clear assignment of property rights.
d) the affected parties must be identifiable.

4. Suppose a firm is polluting a river. The courts determine that the small number of citizens in the community have property rights to the river and rule that the two parties will have to negotiate a settlement of the pollution problem. Which of the following will occur, according to the Coase Theorem?

a) the amount of pollution allowed by the community will be zero.
b) an inefficient level of output will be produced.
c) marginal private benefit = marginal external cost.
d) an inefficient level of pollution will be emitted by the firm.

5. Suppose in the previous example the courts had ruled that the firm had a property right to the river, so that its pollution was legal. According to the Coase Theorem, how much pollution would be emitted into the river?

a) the amount of pollution the firm was originally discharging.
b) the same amount of pollution as would be discharged if the community had been granted property rights.
c) more pollution than if the community had been granted property rights, but less than the firm was originally emitting.
d) zero pollution.

6. The economically efficient level of pollution:

a) is zero.
b) occurs where marginal private cost = marginal private benefit.
c) occurs where marginal private cost = price.
d) occurs where marginal external cost = marginal private benefit.

7. An example of a negative externality (spillover cost) is:

a) the cost a firm pays a garbage hauler to collect the firm's waste.
b) any overtime that a firm has to pay.
c) the noise created by a car with no muffler.
d) the effect of waste recycling on the amount of garbage that must be buried in landfills.

8. If a negative externality is associated with the production of a good in a competitive market:

a) Marginal private cost > marginal social cost
b) more than the optimal amount of the good is being produced.
c) price < marginal private cost.
d) price > marginal social cost.

9. When a homeowner improves the landscaping around his or her home, increasing the property values of nearby homeowners, it would suggest that there is:

a) an underallocation of resources to home landscaping.
b) an overallocation of resources to home landscaping.
c) a socially efficient allocation of resources to home landscaping.
d) none of the above.

10. Suppose there are positive externalities associated with the consumption of a good that is produced in a competitive market. Which of the following is not true?

a) Marginal private benefit = marginal private cost.
b) Marginal external cost > 0.
c) Marginal social benefit > marginal private benefit
d) Marginal social benefit > price.

11. Suppose a firm is polluting a river. All of the following statements are correct except:

a) An excise tax equal to the marginal external cost could be levied on the firm for the cost its pollution imposes on society.
b) An excise tax would cause the firm to internalize the external cost.
c) In practice, excise taxes imposed to reduce pollution are easy to administer.
d) An excise tax equal to the marginal external cost will cause the firm the reduce its output to the efficient level.

12. Which of the following statements is not true?

a) Pollution becomes a social problem when its discharge is so great that it exceeds the assimilative capacity of the environment.
b) Pollution should be reduced as long as the benefits of additional environmental quality exceed the additional costs.
c) Pollution should be reduced until all damage to vegetation and human health is eliminated.
d) The optimal amount of pollution control is where its marginal benefits equal its marginal costs.

13. Suppose pollution is reduced by direct regulation. Which of the following is correct?

a) If the standard for pollution is too restrictive, the demand curve will shift too far to the right.
b) If the standard for pollution is too restrictive, the supply curve will shift too far to the right.
c) The setting of standards which apply to all firms has the potential for creating inefficiency.
d) a) and b), but not c).

14. If a firm is creating a negative externality by emitting pollutants into the atmosphere in the process of producing its output, an emission charge:

a) should be set equal to the price of the good.
b) should be set equal to the firm's marginal private cost.
c) will result in the firm producing more output.
d) should be set equal to the marginal external cost.

15. Which of the following is a characteristic of a public good?

a) Its marginal social cost exceeds its marginal social benefit.
b) Its demand curves are summed horizontally rather than vertically.
c) It is provided by the private market in less than efficient amounts
d) Consumption by one individual reduces the amount available for others.

16. Which of the following properties of public goods is responsible for the "free-rider" problem?

a) non-rivalry in consumption.
b) non-excludability.
c) non-satiation in consumption.
d) non-determinacy of the equilibrium level of output.

17. The "Tragedy of the Commons" suggests that:

a) common property resources will be overutilzed to destruction.
b) common property resources will be underutilized due to lack of information.
c) people will be careful about their usage of public parks.
d) a laissez faire attitude toward fishing grounds will result in the efficient amount of fish being caught, if the industry is perfectly competitive.

18. Assume that the production of good X results in a large amount of water pollutants that are dumped into a nearby river. (Assume also that the demand for good X is perfectly inelastic) If the government fails to intervene in the market there will be:

a) a large misallocation of resources to the production of X.
b) a moderate misallocation of resources to the production of X.
c) a minimal misallocation of resources to the production of X.
d) no misallocation of resources to the production of X.

19. Suppose a college education is found to produce positive externalities. Which of the following is a method the government could use to get the market to provide the efficient amount of college education?

a) Impose an excise tax on colleges.
b) Subsidize college educations.
c) Shift the supply of colleges to the left.
d) Impose an excise tax on students.

20. In order to determine the quantity of a public good that the government should produce, which of the following rules should be followed?

a) Produce the quantity of the public good at which total benefits are at a maximum.
b) Produce the quantity of the public good at which total costs are at a minimum.
c) Produce the quantity of the public good at which marginal benefits equal marginal costs.
d) Produce the quantity of the public good at which marginal benefits are zero.

21. Assume that the production and consumption of a particular good entail both external costs <u>and</u> external benefits. In the absence of government intervention, the market-determined equilibrium will result in:

a) an underallocation of resources to the product.
b) an overallocation of resources to the product.
c) an optimal allocation of resources to the product.
d) an allocation of resources to the product that may or may not be optimal.

22. In a recent issue of the <u>Wall Street Journal</u>, it was reported that the Canadian government is trying to increase the demand for asbestos--a fire-resistant material that is also a suspected cause of cancer in humans--in third world countries. To the extent that the Canadian government is successful in its efforts, the result will be:

a) a level of output in excess of what is socially efficient.
b) an equilibrium price that is too high.
c) a more efficient allocation of resources.
d) a decrease in the profits of Canadian asbestos miners.

23. The conclusion that the Canadian government's efforts regarding the use of asbestos are wrong could potentially involve:

a) normative, but not positive, considerations.
b) neither positive nor normative considerations.
c) positive, but not normative, considerations.
d) both positive and normative considerations.

<u>ANSWER KEY</u>

<u>Exercises</u>
1. property rights
2. Coase Theorem
3. external, external
4. large, overallocation, small, underallocation
5. tax, external cost, subsidy
6. Assimilative capacity
7. marginal social benefits, marginal social costs
8. emission standard
9. costs, differ
10. transferable discharge permits, offset program, bubble policy, emissions banking programs
11. public good
12. $500 and 5 units
13. free rider

14. common-property
15. 1) Identify the effects of the project, 2) value the costs and benefits, 3) adjust the costs and benefits for equity considerations, and 4) evaluate the alternative projects
16. large

Review Questions

1. d) is the correct answer. If all costs or benefits are private or internalized to firms or individuals, then the market outcome is efficient. It is when some of either costs or benefits are not private(accrue to third parties) that the market outcome is inefficient.

2. d) is the correct answer. The lack of clear property rights is a reason firms use common property resources, such as rivers, as free resources in which wastes can be dumped. If it were clear who owned the river, the owner would never let the firm use it for free.

3. a) does not have to exist. In fact, the number of affected parties has to be small in order for negotiations to take place. It is difficult to get the parties to agree, the more individuals are involved.

4. c) is the correct answer. According to the Coase Theorem, if the community has a right to charge the firm for its pollution of the river, the firm will be willing to pay a fine up to the point at which its marginal private benefit equals the fine it has to pay. The community will levy a fine equal to the marginal external cost of the pollution. Thus, the efficient level of output will be produced and the efficient level of pollution will be emitted.

5. b) is the correct answer. According to the Coase Theorem, the amount of pollution at which MEC = MPB would be emitted no matter which way the courts decided the property rights.

6. d) is the correct answer. The economically efficient level of pollution occurs where MEC = MPB. If there is a negative externality, private costs and social costs deviate, so the MC = Price efficiency condition not longer holds.

7. c) is the correct answer. The noise from a car with no muffler imposes an external cost on a third party--anyone within earshot.

8. b) is the correct answer. More than the optimal amount of the good is being produced. This is because marginal private cost = price < marginal social cost.

9. a) is the correct answer. There is an underallocation of resources to home landscaping, because there are positive externalities associated with it.

10. b) is not true. Marginal external cost > 0 implies that there are negative externalities associated with the good, not positive externalities.

11. c) is the exception. An excise tax to reduce pollution is not easy to administer, mainly because it is difficult to measure the external cost accurately.

12. c) is not true. Pollution will undoubtedly do some damage to vegetation and to human health. The relevant question is whether additional cost of reducing pollution is greater than the additional benefits.

13. c) is the correct answer. Setting the same standard for all firms has the potential for creating economic inefficiency, since individual firms are not likely to face the same pollution control costs.

14. d) is the correct answer. If the emission charge is set equal to the marginal external cost, the MEC is internalized and the firm will produce the efficient amount of the good.

15. a) is the correct answer. A public good is provided by the private market in less than efficient amounts(if it is provided at all) because marginal social benefits > marginal private benefits.

16. b) is the correct answer. Nonexcludability means that once the good is provided, no consumer can be excluded from its benefits. This

creates an incentive for individuals to attempt to obtain the public good without paying for it.

17. a) is the correct answer. The "tragedy" to which Hardin refers is the overutilization of common grazing grounds.

18. d) is the correct answer. Actually, in this case there will be no misallocation of resources. This is because the quantity demanded does not respond to changes in price and internalizing the externality will result in an increase in price, but no change in quantity demanded or the amount of resources allocated to the industry.

19. c) is the correct answer. The optimal amount of the public good is where the benefit of an additional unit is equal to the cost of an additional unit. Total net benefits will be maximized at this quantity.

20. b) is the correct answer. One way to get the market to provide the efficient amount of a good which exhibits positive externalities is to shift the demand for the good to the right with a subsidy for consumption of the good.

21. d) is the correct answer. In this case, the social supply curve lies to the left of the private supply curve, while the social demand curve lies to the right of the private demand curve. In effect we are talking about a simultaneous increase in demand and decrease in supply. In this case, without further information of the relative magnitudes of the shifts of the two curves, the quantity effect is indeterminate.

22. a) is the correct answer. It is assumed that all of the external costs are not going to be taken into account. Hence total social costs will be understated.

23. d) is the correct answer. The efficiency aspects of the problem are an application of positive economic analysis--a statement of what is. To the extent what the government is doing is considered wrong, normative considerations come into play as well.

CHAPTER 20
PUBLIC CHOICE

OVERVIEW

In this chapter we examine the theory of public choice. In particular, we address the issue of how political decisions are made and the efficiency of the political process. We also consider the area of study known as constitutional economics, and how the approach known as federalism is used to limit the power of national government and the potential for abuse of that power.

Just as consumers and producers are assumed to maximize utility and profits, public officials are assumed to maximize their well-being. However, given the nature of their position, it is reasonable to assume that the first priority of most elected officials is to get reelected. Combined with the fact that most voters are poorly informed about most of the issues addressed by policymakers, it is reasonable to expect that inefficient political outcomes are a frequent result. Such factors as labels and endorsements can, to some extent, reduce this problem by providing voters with additional information at very low cost.

The efficiency of the political process is dependent on the extent to which voters are informed about the behavior of policymakers and the extent of freedom of entry into the political process. To the extent that these conditions are not met, the potential for efficiency is reduced. Special-interest groups can also reduce the efficiency of the political process. In many cases such groups are able to achieve goals that benefit a minority at the expense of the majority. This outcome often is the result of vote trading, or logrolling. There is evidence that the efforts of special-interest groups contribute to an inequitable distribution of income, as well as increased unemployment and slower economic growth.

Managers of private firms and public agencies are assumed to maximize their utility. However, the incentives that each type of individual faces differ. Managers of private firms can increase their utility by increasing profits or the perquisites associated with their job. Managers of government agencies, on the other hand, cannot gain from increased profits, and instead focus on increasing their perquisites or the size of their agency. As such, bureaucrats tend to be budget maximizers, rather than profit maximizers. There is considerable evidence to support the predictions that government agencies operate inefficiently relative to private firms, and that they tend to be too large relative to the efficient scale of operation.

We have already noted the importance of property rights in a market economy in earlier chapters. A system of well-defined property rights is required for a market economy to function smoothly. However, it is also necessary to develop laws that constrain the way in which property rights are exercised. In addition, it is necessary for government to provide public goods, since the market does not have an incentive to do so. The extent to which government should be able to constrain property rights and engage in the provision of goods and services is the subject of constitutional economics. The federalist approach to government is designed to limit the powers of government while giving it sufficient flexibility to fulfill its primary obligations.

KEY GRAPHS AND TERMS

Graphs

No "new" models or graphs are introduced in this chapter. However, it is important to understand how basic economic concepts, such as the principle of utility maximization, are used to analyze the political process and the behavior of politicians and bureaucrats.

Terms

SPECIAL-INTEREST GROUP
LOGROLLING
PERQUISITES
PROPERTY RIGHTS
CONSTITUTIONAL ECONOMICS
LEVIATHAN MODEL
FEDERAL REPUBLIC

EXERCISES

1. A group of people with an intense interest in a particular issue is called a ________________ ________________ ________________.

2. List two minimum conditions that must be met for a political outcome to be efficient.________________

____

____

3. Managers of government agencies can increase their utility by ________________________________

________________________________ or ________________

____.

4. ________________ ________________ is the study of the optimal rules with which to constrain the behavior of government.

5. To some extent the problem of uninformed voters is overcome through ________________ and ________________.

6. ________________ consist of nonincome job benefits such as expense accounts and company cars.

7. Bureaucrats tend to be ________________ ________________ rather than profit maximizers.

8. The system of representative government in which several coexisting levels of government handle different sets of issues is referred to as a ________________ ________________.

9. Explain why most voters do not have an incentive to gather more information on political candidates and specific issues. ________________________________

____

10. How do the incentives faced by managers of private firms differ from the incentives faced by managers of public agencies? How do these differences affect the relative efficiency of the outcome in each situation?

____

____

____

____

____

____

REVIEW QUESTIONS

1. According to the theory of public choice, the first priority of most elected officials is:

a) ensuring the efficient provision of public goods.
b) maximizing the amount of perks they receive.
c) getting reelected.
d) increasing their budget.

2. Which of the following is not true?

a) Maximizing the probability of reelection implies that a public official will vote in the manner preferred by the majority of his or her constituents on all issues.
b) If voters are ignorant of positions legislators take on most issues, legislators are free vote as they please.
c) U.S. voters are generally not well-informed about major policy issues.
d) Public choice theory views public officials as utility-maximizing suppliers of public services.

3. All of the following are reasons that it is rational for voters to be uninformed about political issues except:

a) Coalition-building is expensive.
b) Collecting information on policy issues is expensive.
c) Voters cannot tell how a candidate labeled as "liberal" or "conservative" will vote on a wide range of issues.
d) Voters can free-ride on the endorsements of editors of newspapers that they trust.

4. Which of the following helps to overcome the problem of voters being uninformed about political issues?

a) Voter "apathy."
b) Once a candidate adopts a label, the candidate has a strong incentive to vote as the label suggests.
c) Voters being unable to take a free ride on the knowledge of newspaper editors.
d) The fact that voters cannot tell what the stance of a candidate will be on a range of issues, if the candidate adopts a label.

5. Special interest groups:

a) would be even more powerful than they are if voters were better informed.
b) lobby well beyond the point at which the marginal benefit of political action outweighs the marginal cost.
c) have an impact on legislators out of proportion to the numbers they represent.
d) frequently harm each individual voter greatly on any particular issue.

6. All of the following are conditions for producing efficiency in political markets except:

a) Voters must monitor the behavior of their elected representatives.
b) Political information must be costly.
c) There must be no barriers to entry into campaigns.
d) Voters must be well informed.

7. According to some economists, special-interest groups tend to:

a) have a positive influence on long-run economic stability.
b) increase the unemployment rate and slow economic growth.
c) increase the efficiency of the political process.
d) ensure the efficient provision of public goods.

8. Which of the following statements is correct?

a) logrolling usually does not result in inefficient outcomes.
b) there are no barriers to entry into the political process in a democracy such as the United States.
c) special-interest groups do not influence the distribution of income.
d) endorsements can help overcome the problem of uninformed voters.

9. All of the following are reasons producers have an advantage over consumers in their ability to influence the political process except:

a) The ease of organizing producers.
b) The costs to consumers(as a whole) of special interest legislation favoring producers is low.
c) There are a large of number of consumers and it is therefore difficult to organize them for collective action.
d) It is not worth it to consumers to be well-informed on issues that are of special interest to producers.

10. Which of the following statements is correct?

a) government agencies tend to be larger than their private counterparts.
b) there is no difference in the costs of government agencies and comparable privately-run firms.
c) managers of government agencies enjoy far fewer perquisites than their counterparts in the private sector.
d) managers of government agencies have a strong incentive to minimize the size of their operating budget.

11. Managers of nonprofit organizations:

a) have the same incentives to minimize costs that profit-maximizing firms have.
b) are usually rewarded for achieving economic efficiency.
c) are much less concerned with perquisites than their profit-maximizing counterparts are.
d) frequently maximize utility by maximizing the budget of their organization.

12. Government agencies:

a) tend to operate efficiently(in an economic sense).
b) tend to minimize costs even though they are not profit-maximizers.
c) expand output beyond the profit-maximizing level.
d) restrict output in order to hold price above marginal cost.

13. Goods that are public in consumption, such are local fire protection:

a) will be provided in the efficient quantities by the market.
b) do not exhibit positive externalities.
c) are more expensive to produce privately than through the government.
d) need not be produced by the government.

14. Which of the following is not true:

a) Property rights are the most important set of rules determining behavior in a market economy.
b) Locke believed that society could operate in a well-behaved manner without a great deal of central government control.
c) Constitutional economics is designed to protect the government from the incursions of the market system.
d) The natural rights doctrine says that individuals have a right to life, liberty, and the pursuit of property.

15. The Leviathan Model:

a) suggests that firms will behave as profit-maximizers.
b) was bitterly criticized by Thomas Hobbes.
c) assumes that people will use government for their own ends.
d) suggests that the market system works most efficiently in a society of complete anarchy.

16. In which of the following cases would efficiency be best served by placing a limit on the exercise of property rights?

a) additional competition will drive economic profits to zero.
b) the developer of a new product has a monopoly on the production of the product.
c) the production of a good is generating substantial external costs.
d) a private firm offers to provide trash collection in a city where the service traditionally has been provided by the government.

17. In a federal republic:

a) goods and services are provided by multiple levels of government.
b) the federal government directs the decision-making of lower levels of government.
c) public goods are only provided by the federal government.
d) There is only one level of government.

18. With respect to efficient resource use, which of the following goods would economists argue should <u>not</u> be provided by government?

a) national defense.
b) parks.
c) roads.
d) trash collection.

19. Which of the following would be most likely to increase the efficiency of a government agency?

a) a limit on potential perquisites.
b) manager's salaries rising as their responsibility increased with rising agency budgets.
c) guaranteed job security.
d) an increase in the number of managers.

20. Which of the following is <u>not true</u>?

a) Voters cannot "unbundle" the set of public goods offered by a candidate, so they may vote for the provision of some goods for which they do not want to pay.
b) logrolling results in more special interest legislation.
c) economists argue that while special interest groups may result in policies which are not in the public interest, they make the economy more responsive to changes in economic conditions.
d) Firms that are part of special interest groups are at a disadvantage during times of change in the economy.

<u>ANSWER KEY</u>

<u>Exercises</u>

1. special-interest group.
2. Voters must be informed about the behavior of their elected representatives. There must be free entry into the political process.
3. increasing the number of perquisites they receive or increasing the size of their agencies.
4. constitutional economics
5. labels and endorsements
6. perquisites
7. budget maximizers
8. federal republic

9. In most cases the benefits of gathering additional information on candidates and issues is outweighed by the costs of doing so. This is due, in large part, to the minimal effect that most public policy decisions have on the individual.
10. In general, the benefits received by managers of private firms are directly related to the profitability of the firm. Since profits are increased when costs are minimized, there is a strong incentive for managers of private firms to hold down costs as much as possible. However, in the case of public agencies, benefits to managers are not determined by profits since public agencies are not operated to make a profit. Instead, managers of public firms increase their utility through increased perks and increased budgets. The result is that public agencies tend to have much higher cost structures than their private counterparts.

Review Questions

1. c) is the correct answer. Public choice theory views public officials as maximizing their utility subject to the constraints placed on them by the electorate. Public officials maximize utility by maximizing the probability of being reelected to office.

2. a) is not true. If a minority feels intensely about an issue that is of little interest to the majority, a public official may attempt to please the minority, even if the legislation is not in the interest of the majority.

3. c) is not true. Actually labels such as "liberal" or "conservative" help voters know how legislators will vote on a number of issues, without bearing the cost of collecting information on the candidates views on every individual issue.

4. b) is the correct answer. Once a candidate adopts a label, voters expect the candidate to vote a particular way on a whole range of issues. To get reelected, the legislator must fulfill the voters expectations. Thus, labels overcome some of the costs of obtaining information about candidates views on a number of issues.

5. c) is the correct answer. Special interests have an effect on legislators far out of proportion to their numbers if voters are ignorant of political issues. On any particular piece of legislation, the special interest may be intensely interested, but the majority of voters will be uninterested because the cost to any one member of the majority is very low.

6. b) is the exception. If political information is costly, then voters will not be well-informed and will not monitor their elected representatives.

7. b) is the correct answer. Special interest groups respond to disturbances in the economy much more slowly than competitive firms. Part of the reason for this is the time needed to build new coalitions to respond to whatever changes have occurred. This slow response is thought to be responsible for factor immobility which leads to unemployment and prolongs recessions.

8. d) is the correct answer. Political endorsements from newspapers, other politicians, trusted prominent figures, etc. give the voter some information on the stances of candidates on a number of issues.

9. b) is the exception. The costs to consumers as a whole may be quite high. For example, the costs to consumers as a whole of farm programs and tariffs and quotas on imports are very large, but the cost to each individual consumer is fairly low. Under these circumstances consumers are not likely to incur the costs necessary to take political action against legislation favoring producers.

10. a) is the correct answer. Government agencies tend to be larger than their private counterparts because they do not have an incentive to minimize costs since, they are not profit-maximizers.

11. d) is the correct answer. Nonprofit organizations do not have an incentive to minimize costs. Managers are not rewarded for profits and therefore attempt to maximize utility by maximizing their perquisites. Perquisites frequently increase with the size of the organization or its budget.

12. c) is the correct answer. Government agencies tend to expand output beyond its profit-

maximizing level. This is because they are not profit-maximizers and because the utility of the managers is frequently dependent on the size or budget of the agency. Restricting output to achieve a monopoly price and quantity is the behavior of a profit-maximizing imperfectly-competitive firm, not a government agency.

13. d) is the correct answer. Fire protection is a good example. While fire protection has positive externalities associated with it and therefore will not be provided in sufficient quantities by the market, it need not be provided by the government. That is, the government may find that it is less costly to contract with a private firm to provide fire protection.

14. c) is not true. Constitutional economics is the search for optimal rules to constrain governmental behavior in the economy.

15. c) is the correct answer. The Leviathan model of Thomas Hobbes assumes that if given the opportunity, people will use government to maximize their utility.

16. c) is the correct answer. If the production of a good is generating substantial external costs, the property rights of the firm should be limited to the extent that the external costs are made internal to the firm.

17. a) is the correct answer. The U.S. has a federal system of government in which public goods are provided by the federal, state, and local governments.

18. d) is the correct answer. Trash collection is public in consumption, but that does not mean it has to be directly provided by or produced by the government. As the text's example suggests, it appears that trash collection can be more efficiently provided by private trash-haulers with whom the government contracts.

19. a) is the correct answer. One of the inefficiencies associated with government agencies is their tendency to maximize perquisites for the managers, who are under no constraints to minimize costs.

20. c) is not true. Economists have argued that special interest groups make the economy less responsive to changes in economic conditions. This is due to the time it takes to build new coalitions when there has been a change in the economy that requires the interest group to respond in a different way than it has in the past.

CHAPTER 21
FROM INDIVIDUAL CHOICE TO MACROECONOMICS

OVERVIEW

In this chapter we begin the transition from the study of microeconomics, which focuses on the decision making of individuals, to macroeconomics, which focuses on the aggregate economy. We begin our analysis by examining the role of the budget constraint in the decision making process. After making the transition from decision making at the individual level to the economy-wide level, we discuss how aggregate prices and output levels are measured.

A budget constraint states that, in general, sources of funds spent must equal uses of funds. Sources of funds include income, sales of assets, borrowing, and the receipt of gifts. The uses of funds include purchases of new goods and services, purchases of financial assets or used real assets, repayment of debts and interest payments, and gifts. An important result of the budget constraint analysis is that total spending on newly produced goods and services in the economy and the total amount of income earned are equal. In addition, the sum of all quantities demanded in all markets must equal the sum of quantities supplied. This does not imply that all markets must be in equilibrium simultaneously. Rather, excess demands and excess supplies in individual markets cancel each other out.

The quantity of output purchased by an individual is determined by absolute prices and the budget constraint. What is purchased is determined by relative prices. As preferences in the economy change, so do the composition of output and relative prices. This is the result of the interrelatedness of the various markets in the economy.

In order to meaningfully measure the level of production in an economy, goods and services must be valued on a common basis. Gross National Product (GNP) is measured as the market value of all final goods and services produced in the economy in a given time period. Because total spending on new goods and services equals total income generated in production, GNP can be measured using either the expenditures approach or the income approach. The expenditures approach groups spending into four basic categories--consumption expenditures (C), investment spending (I), government purchases (G), and net exports (NX). GNP can be summarized by the equation GNP = C + I + G + NX. In the process of calculating GNP it is necessary to distinguish between final goods and intermediate goods. The latter are not included when calculating GNP since their value is reflected in the prices of the final goods.

The income approach to calculating GNP reflects the value added at each stage of production. Adding up value added yields the measure known as national income. National income differs from GNP by the amount of depreciation of capital stock--called the capital consumption allowance--that occurs during the course of production and the amount of indirect business taxes paid in the course of buying goods and services. As such, GNP minus depreciation minus indirect business taxes equals national income.

One of the many questions in macroeconomics concern what is happening to the level of production over time. Because GNP is calculated on the basis of market prices, adjustments for price changes must be made when comparing GNP for different years. Real GNP is GNP that has been adjusted for the effects of price changes by using a set of base year prices. A price index, which measures the change in the average level of prices over some time period, can be used to calculate Real GNP.

KEY GRAPHS AND TERMS

Graphs

Although they are not graphed, as such, the key concepts in this chapter include the budget constraint and the model of national income accounting, which enables us to measure the level of production in the economy and changes in production over time. Be sure you understand how the budget constraint yields the conclusion that total spending equals total income, and how to calculate GNP, Real GNP, and a simple price index.

<u>Terms</u>

TRANSFER PAYMENT
BUDGET CONSTRAINT
ABSOLUTE PRICE LEVEL
RELATIVE PRICES
GROSS NATIONAL PRODUCT
FACTOR INPUTS
INTERMEDIATE GOODS
CONSUMPTION EXPENDITURES
INVESTMENT SPENDING
GOVERNMENT PURCHASE
NET EXPORTS
EXPORTS
IMPORTS
INVENTORY CHANGES
VALUE ADDED
NATIONAL INCOME
BASE YEAR
REAL GNP
AVERAGE PRICE LEVEL

EXERCISES

1. List the four basic ways an individual can obtain spendable funds. Income, sales of assets, borrowing, receiving gifts

2. The single largest source of spendable funds is labor income.

3. The only source of income for an economy is PRODUCTION.

4. In the aggregate economy, total Spending on newly produced goods and services equals total income earned by members of the economy.

5. Given a budget constraint, absolute prices determine how much an individual can buy, while relative prices determine what the individual will buy.

6. According to the aggregate budget constraint, Sources of funds must equal uses of funds.

7. The total market value of all final goods and services produced in a given time period is called GROSS National Product.

8. Using the "expenditures approach," the four components of GNP are Consumption Expenditures, Investment SPENDING, GOVERNMENT Purchases, and Net Exports.

9. The difference between GNP and national income is equal to Capital Consumption allowance plus indirect business taxes.

10. The following data was collected for the country of Wannabegone for 1990. (The following data is in millions of dollars.)

Exports	$580	Purchases of Plant and Equipment	$300
Consumption	$500	Imports	$730
Transfer Payments	$150	Depreciation	$ 70
Government Purchases	$180	Indirect Business Taxes	$ 50

a. Using the data listed above, calculate the following: GNP = 830, National Income = 710.

b. Assuming that the Price Index is 123 (base year = 1985) calculate Real GNP for 1990. RGNP = 674.8.

11. Consider the following data on expenditures in Country X. (Figures are in millions of dollars.)

```
Consumption Expenditures........... $1,400
Government Purchases............... $  750
Investment Spending................ $  440
Net Exports........................ $  -80
```

Assuming that RGNP for 1990 = $1,970, the implicit price deflator = 127.4.

12. In 1982 Calvin bought 28 pizzas at $6.00 each and 20 six-packs at $2.50 each. In 1990 a pizza cost $8.25 and a six-pack cost $3.25. Using 1982 as the base year, calculate the price index for 1990. 138.5 135.8

REVIEW QUESTIONS

1. The largest component of spendable funds is

a) income.
b) assets sales.
c) borrowing.
d) gifts.

2. Which of the following contributes to national income?

a) The purchase of newly produced goods and services.
b) The purchase of financial assets, such as savings deposits in banks.
c) The purchase of used real assets, such as a building erected in 1987.
d) The use of funds to repay debts.

3. Which of the following statements is correct?

a) Total uses of funds equal total income.
b) Sources of funds plus savings equal uses of funds.
c) Total income and total sources of funds are the same.
d) Total spending on newly produced goods and services equals total income.

4. Which of the following statements is not true?

a) Sources of funds must equal uses of funds in the aggregate.
b) The aggregate budget constraint concept suggests that the sum of the quantities demanded equals the sum of the quantities supplied.
c) There can exist a budget for the economy as a whole.
d) Sources of funds includes only income earned from the sale of goods and services.

5. The notion of market interdependence suggests which of the following:

a) If there are three markets in an economy, it is possible for two of them to be in equilibrium and the third to be out of equilibrium.
b) If there are three markets in an economy, it is possible for two of them to be out of equilibrium and the third to be in equilibrium.
c) If the economy is in equilibrium and one of the markets moves into disequilibrium, no other market will necessarily change.
d) If an economy is in equilibrium and one market moves into disequilibrium, all other markets in the economy will move into disequilibrium.

6. Gross National Product (GNP) is defined as the market value of:

a) all goods and services sold during the year.
b) all final consumer goods produced during the year.
c) all intermediate goods produced during the year.
d) all final goods and services produced during the year.

7. The steel used to produce cars:

a) is an intermediate good.
b) should be counted in GNP along with the value of the cars it is used to produce.
c) is a final good.
d) can be a final or intermediate good, depending on when the car is purchased.

8. The four major categories of expenditures in the economy are:

a) consumption, gross investment, government purchases and exports.
b) consumption, net investment and net exports.
c) consumption, fixed investment, government purchases and net exports.
d) consumption, gross investment, government purchases and net exports.

9. In the equation GNP = C + I + G + (X-M), why are imports subtracted from the other types of expenditure?

a) Because imports reduce national welfare.
b) Because imports reduce GNP and national welfare.
c) Because the value of imports is included in the other components of spending.
d) Because the value of imports is difficult to determine due to the fact that they are frequently made in terms of foreign currency.

10. Which of the following statements is <u>not true</u>?

a) GNP includes an estimate of the services provided by owner-occupied housing to their owners.
b) GNP measures the value of production and sales.
c) The value of the food grown and consumed by farm families is included in GNP, even though it is not sold to anyone.
d) Any change in business inventories goes in the investment component of expenditure for GNP.

11. The difference between GNP and national income is:

a) equal to the difference between exports and imports.
b) equal to the difference between government purchases and investment.
c) the sum of depreciation and indirect business taxes.
d) the value of inventories accumulated during the year.

12. GNP is not a good measure of social welfare because:

a) the value of leisure time is not included in the calculation of GNP.
b) GNP ignores the effect of negative externalities.
c) GNP does reflect the effect of pollution..
d) all of the above.

13. Suppose 1991 Nominal GNP = $5200 billion. Suppose prices were 30% higher in 1991 than in 1982. What is 1991 Real GNP if 1982 is used as the base year?

a) $3600 billion
b) $4000 billion
c) $4400 billion
d) $ 4800 billion

14. Suppose 1980 Nominal GNP was $2400 billion. Suppose prices were 20% lower in 1980 than in 1982. What is 1980 Real GNP, using 1982 as the base year.

a) $2500 billion
b) $3000 billion
c) $3200 billion
d) $3500 billion

15. Suppose that in 1982, GNP was $2400 billion and in 1988 it was $4500 billion. Suppose the price index was 100 in 1982 and 125 in 1988. Based on this information we can conclude that between 1982 and 1988 real GNP, measured in 1982 dollars, rose by:

a) $1200 billion.
b) $1500 billion.
c) $1600 billion.
d) $2000 billion.

16. If the price of a new car rises from $5,000 to $10,000 while, on the average, other prices triple, then the relative price of a new car:

a) rises.
b) stays constant.
c) falls.
d) rises 30 percent.

17. Assume that C = $2,500, I = $650, G = $325, Exports = $300, Imports = $475, Depreciation = $175, and Indirect Business Taxes = $100. GNP equals:

a) $4,250
b) $3,575
c) $3,300
d) $3,125

18. Expenditures on residential homes are counted as part of:

a) consumption spending.
b) investment spending.
c) government spending.
d) none of the above.

19. Comparisons of per capita GNP among countries:

a) indicate differences in living standards fairly precisely.
b) underestimate the incomes of less developed countries due to people growing their food.
c) overestimate the incomes of less developed countries due to the fact that housing is not included in many of their GNP measures.
d) suggest that in reality U.S. per capita GNP is only slightly larger than India's.

20. Which of the following is not an example of investment?

a) Ford increasing its inventory of cars.
b) A firm purchasing an office building which was produced during the current year.
c) The purchase of corporate stock which was issued during the current year.
d) The purchase of a new house.

21. Which of the following would be included in 1992 GNP?

a) Money deposited in a savings account during 1992.
b) The purchase of a house built in 1980.
c) Social Security payments made to individuals during 1992.
d) The production of wheat during 1992 which is sold to China.

22. Suppose that 1982 GNP = $3000 billion. If 1992 Nominal GNP = $5000 billion and 1992 Real GNP = $4000 billion, with 1982 as the base year, what is the Implicit Price Deflator for 1992?

a) 1.25
b) 1.5
c) 2.0
d) 2.5

23. Suppose the cost of a loaf of bread to a grocery chain is $0.50 and the grocery's value-added through packaging and transporting the loaf is $0.75. Which of the following statements is true?

a) The price of the loaf will be $0.75.
b) The price of the loaf will be $1.25.
c) The price of the loaf will be $1.25 only if the grocery earns zero profits.
d) The price of the loaf will be $0.25.

24. Net National Product:

a) equals indirect business taxes + depreciation.
b) equals indirect business taxes - depreciation.
c) is always larger than GNP and is therefore the preferred measure for the incumbent political party.
d) is GNP - depreciation.

25. 1990 Nominal GNP is approximately equal to:

a) $360 billion.
b) $530 billion.
c) $5500 billion.
d) $7500 billion.

Chapter 21, From Individual Choice to Macroeconomics

ANSWER KEY

Exercises

1. Sources of funds include income, sales of assets, borrowing, and the receipt of gifts
2. labor income
3. production
4. spending, income
5. absolute, relative
6. sources of funds, uses of funds
7. gross national product
8. consumption expenditures, investment spending, government purchases, and net exports.
9. capital consumption allowance plus indirect business taxes

10.a. GNP = $830. NI = $710

b. Real GNP = $674.8

11.127.4

12.135.8

Review Questions

1. a) is the correct answer. By far the largest component of sources of funds is income from labor.

2. a) is the correct answer. Only the purchase of newly produced goods and services contributes to the economy's total income. The other answers refer to transfers of income within the economy. Only the production on new goods and services generates income.

3. d) is the correct answer. Total spending for newly produced goods and services equals total income.

4. d) is the correct answer. Sources of funds includes not only income from the sale of goods and services, but it also includes asset earnings, earnings from asset sales, money supplied, borrowing, and gifts received.

5. b) is the correct answer. If one market is out of equilibrium, then one or two of the other two markets will also be out of equilibrium. It is not possible in a three-market economy for one market only to be out of equilibrium.

6. d) is the correct answer. The value of all final goods and services produced during the year is the correct definition. It does include intermediate goods to avoid double-counting, and it includes other categories of spending besides consumption spending.

7. a) is the correct answer. The steel used to produce cars is considered an intermediate good because it is converted into something else--a final good. To count the steel itself and also the value of the car would result in double-counting of the value steel.

8. d) is the correct answer. The four major categories of expenditure for GNP are consumption, investment(gross), government purchases, and net exports(exports - imports).

9. c) is the correct answer. The other components of expenditure, C, I, and G, all include some expenditure for imported goods and services. For example, Consumption expenditure includes spending for consumption goods that are produced in the domestic economy as well as consumption goods are produced in foreign economies. These imports must be "netted out" at the end of the equation since they are not expenditures for goods and services produced domestically.

10. b) is the correct answer. GNP is the value of production, but not sales. If a good is produced during the current period, its value goes into GNP whether it is sold or not. Goods produced during the current period and not sold go into inventories and count as investment.

11. c) is the correct answer. National income refers to the total income earned by private economic units. Since depreciation is the value of

capital goods lost in the process of producing GNP and indirect business taxes go to the government before they are paid to private economic units, they must both be subtracted from GNP to arrive at national income.

12. d) is the correct answer. GNP does not measure leisure time. For example, if our society moved to a 12-hour workday, GNP would certainly increase, but it questionable whether our social welfare would. Increases in GNP may result in increases in pollution or negative externalities, which make the society worse off.

13. b) is the correct answer. Real GNP is found by dividing Nominal GNP by the price index with respect to the base year. In this case the calculation is: $5200 billion / 1.30 = $4000 billion.

14. b) is the correct answer. If prices were 20% lower in 1980 than in 1982, the 1980 price index is 80. In this case the calculation is
$2400 billion/0.8 = $3000 billion.

15. a) is the correct answer. 1988 Real GNP = $4500 billion divided by 1.25, which equals $3600 billion. $3600 billion - $2400 billion equals $1200 billion.

16. c) is the correct answer. Since other prices have tripled, while the price of cars has doubled, the relative price of cars has fallen.

17. c) is the correct answer. GNP = C + I + G + (X-M). Indirect business taxes are irrelevant in this calculation.

18. b) is the correct answer. Residential homes are counted as part of investment because, among other things, they provide services to their owners for a long period of time.

19. b) is the correct answer. Food production that does not go through markets does not count in GNP. If a significant portion of the population grows food for their own consumption, as is the case in some less developed countries, GNP underestimates the value of production per capita.

20. c) is the correct answer. The purchase of corporate stock represents a transfer of ownership and therefore does not add to production or national income.

21. d) is the correct answer. Exports count in GNP. The export of wheat which was produced during 1992 adds to the value of output and national income. All of the other responses represent transfers.

22. a) is the correct answer. The implicit price deflator is Nominal GNP / Real GNP. In this case, the calculation is equal to $5000 billion / $4000 billion = 1.25. The information about 1982 Real GNP is irrelevant.

23. b) is the correct answer. The value-added by the grocery chain is $0.75. Adding that to the cost of the loaf to the grocery gives us $1.25. Profits earned by the grocery are included in the grocery's value-added, so profits need not be zero.

24. d) is the correct answer. NNP is equal to GNP - depreciation. It measures the economy's output after depreciated capital goods have been replaced.

25. c) is the correct answer. 1990 Nominal GNP is roughly equal to $5500 billion. Since this is a nominal measure, it is in terms of "current" 1990 dollars.

CHAPTER 22
OVERVIEW OF MACROECONOMICS

OVERVIEW

In this chapter we identify the key macroeconomic variables we will be analyzing in subsequent chapters, and the markets in which these variables are determined. The chapter begins with a discussion of the circular flow model of the economy. The focus then moves to the recent performance of key variables, and a brief overview of the major aggregate markets in the economy.

The circular flow model illustrates how physical goods, services and productive inputs, and income and spending are related. As the model shows, the level of output and the level of spending in the economy are jointly determined. The circular flow model can be expanded to reflect many of the relationships that exist in a modern economy. In addition to the business and household sectors of the economy, activities in the financial sector, government sector, and foreign sector all influence the levels of output and income. In addition, activities in each of these sectors are highly interrelated, e.g., actions by the government can affect the foreign sector which can, in turn, influence decisions made in the business and household sectors.

Macroeconomic analysis focuses on a number of key variables including the output level, the price level, the unemployment rate, the federal budget deficit, and the international trade deficit. Over time the level of output varies, as illustrated by the business cycle, which is comprised of four phases--expansion, peak, recession, and trough. Although the price level also fluctuates over time, there is no distinct relationship between changes in the price level and the business cycle. The unemployment rate, which also fluctuates over time, exhibits a more distinct relationship to the business cycle, rising when the economy moves into recession and falling as the economy moves into an expansion.

During the 1980s, the twin deficits--the federal budget deficit and the U.S. international trade deficit--grew dramatically. Consequently, these variables have received an increasing amount of attention in recent years. Serious questions regarding the affects of the budget deficit on the level of economic activity and the international trade deficit are the subject of continuing debate.

Policymakers attempt to achieve a number of macroeconomic goals including rapid output growth, stable output growth, stable prices, and low unemployment. Although the available data would suggest that policymakers have been unsuccessful much of the time, it is important to note that there are often tradeoffs among these goals. As such, it is difficult, if not impossible, to achieve all of the goals simultaneously.

The macroeconomic model that will be used in the rest of the book focuses on four markets--the goods and services market, the labor market, the credit market, and the money market. The quantity of output produced in the economy is determined in the goods market by the interaction of aggregate supply and aggregate demand. The interaction of labor demand and labor supply determine the level of employment and wages, which in turn has a substantial effect on production costs, and therefore prices. The demand for and supply of credit determine the interest rate, which influences the level of spending in the economy and, in turn, the level of GNP. The interest rate is also determined in the money market.

KEY GRAPHS AND TERMS

Graphs

The key models in this chapter are the circular flow model and the model of the business cycle. The circular flow model is especially useful as a means of visualizing the flows of inputs, goods and services, and income and spending, and the interrelatedness of the various sectors in the economy. Pay particular attention to Figure 2, which depicts an expanded circular flow model. The model of the business cycle, which is illustrated in Figure 4, highlights the various phases of the business cycle and their relationship to the level of RGNP.

Terms

CIRCULAR FLOW MODEL
FINANCIAL SECTOR
GOVERNMENT SECTOR
BUDGET DEFICIT
BUDGET SURPLUS
FOREIGN SECTOR
CAPITAL FLOW
EXPANSION
RECESSION
BUSINESS CYCLE
TROUGH
PEAK
UNEMPLOYMENT RATE
BALANCE OF TRADE
AGGREGATE DEMAND
AGGREGATE SUPPLY
LABOR MARKET
CREDIT MARKET
INTEREST RATE
MONEY MARKET
MEDIUM OF EXCHANGE

EXERCISES

1. The simple two sector circular flow model illustrates the flow of resource inputs and consumer expenditures from __HousEholds__ to __Buisness__ and income payments and goods and services from __Buisness__ to __Households__.

2. The largest category of income in the U.S. is __WAGES__ __And__ __Salaries__.

3. The interaction of borrowers and lenders takes place in the __Financial__ sector.

4. The four phases of the business cycle include the __Trough__, __Expansion__, __PEAK__, and __Recession__.

5. The most important input in the production process is __LABOR__ __Services__.

6. The so-called twin deficits consist of the __GOVERNMENT__ __Budget__ __Deficit__, and the __Trade__ __Deficit__.

7. List the four major goals pursued by government policymakers. __rapid output growth, stable output growth, stable prices, and low unemployment__

8. The quantity of goods and services produced in the economy in a given time period is determined by the interaction of __AggregATE__ __Demand__ and __aggregate__ __Supply__.

9. The price of credit is the __interest__ __rate__.

10. The principal function of money is to serve as a __medium__ __of__ __exchange__.

REVIEW QUESTIONS

1. All of the following are studied predominantly in macroeconomics rather than microeconomics <u>except</u>:

(a) equilibrium in individual markets, in which interactions with other markets are ignored.
b) inflation.
c) aggregate markets.
d) the effect of changes in consumption expenditure on unemployment and national income.

2. Which of the following topics is a subject of macroeconomics?

a) the equilibrium price of steel.
b) the relationship between inflation and unemployment.
c) the determinants of wheat production.
d) the market for medical services.

3. In the circular flow model:

a) the business sector earns most of the income flow in the form of profit.
b) the business sector earns a small part of the income flow in the form of profit.
c) the household sector supplies resources to the business sector.
d) the business sector buys goods and services from the household sector.

4. Which of the following statements is <u>not true</u>?

a) In the circular flow model, the funds needed to finance investment spending come from the saving of the households.
b) In the circular flow model, GNP can be measured either by the income received or by the expenditures made.
c) Say's Law says: supply creates its own demand.
d) Say's Law predicted the Great Depression, in which there were surpluses of goods.

5. Which of the following is the <u>smallest</u> component of aggregate expenditures?

a) Consumption expenditures
b) Government purchases
c) Investment spending
d) Net exports

6. All of the following statements about the expanded circular flow model are true <u>except</u>:

a) Household savings flows through the financial sector to borrowers, including the government and foreign borrowers.
b) Income that the household sector uses to pay taxes does not return to the business sector as demands for goods and services.
c) The financial sector allows households' savings to be channeled into productive uses.
d) Household savings may take the form of savings accounts or the purchases of stocks and bonds issued by corporations.

7. Which of the following statements about the circular flow model is correct?

a) The financial sector connects savers with businesses that want to borrow.
b) The level of investment spending would be lower without the financial sector.
c) The level of income would be higher were it not for the drag of investment on the economy.
d) Government purchases, but not transfer payments, are expenditures for goods and services from the business sector.

8. The phase of the business cycle in which output is increasing is known as the:

a) peak.
b) recessionary phase.
c) trough.
d) expansionary phase.

9. Within the Circular Flow Model, which of the following is not represented as a flow of funds into firms?

a) Foreign purchases of goods and services.
b) Income payments.
c) Consumption spending.
d) Government Purchases.

10. Between 1970 and 1990, the number of people employed in the U.S. economy increased by approximately:

a) 10 percent.
b) 25 percent.
c) 50 percent.
d) 75 percent.

11. The unemployment rate is always positive for all of the following reasons except?

a) During recessions firms lay off workers rather than reduce their wages.
b) There are always workers who are unemployed due to changes in technology.
c) The U.S. economy has been in recession for the last twenty years.
d) Workers who lose their jobs frequently take several months to find new jobs.

12. The unemployment rate:

a) rises during expansionary periods.
b) falls during recessions.
c) equals the working age population that is not working divided by the total working age population.
d) equals the number of people searching for employment divided by the number of people searching for employment and the number of people working.

13. The unemployment rate:

a) was less than zero in the early 1970's.
b) rises during periods of recession.
c) has not changed in the U.S. since 1950.
d) was higher than it has ever been during 1981 and 1982.

14. Which of the following is not true?

a) The problem of the "Twin Deficits" refers to the federal budget deficit and the trade balance deficit.
b) The extent to which the trade deficit is a result of the budget deficit is controversial.
c) Government policymakers have pursued the goal of stable prices since the end of World War II.
d) Government policymakers have ignored the goal of rapid economic growth since 1945.

15. Examination of the business cycle and the data on output, prices, and unemployment suggests that which of the following would be the most compatible macroeconomic goals?

a) rapid output growth and low unemployment.
b) rapid output growth and stable prices.
c) low inflation and low unemployment.
d) low inflation and stable output growth.

16. Which of the following is not true? Aggregate Demand:

a) limits the quantity of goods and services all firms can profitably produce and sell.
b) relates the total quantity of output individuals and institutions want to buy to the price level.
c) depends on the availability of resources.
d) includes as its components consumption, investment, government purchases, and net exports.

17. Payments to workers for their labor services account for about:

a) one-third of GNP.
b) one-half of GNP.
c) two-thirds of GNP.
d) 90% of GNP.

18. Assume that in the market for credit the quantity of credit demanded exceeds the quantity supplied. This will cause the:

What is?

a) supply of credit to increase.
b) demand for credit to decrease.
c) interest rate to fall.
d) interest rate to rise.

19. All of the following are criticisms of macroeconomics except:

a) It is impossible to actually calculate aggregate variables such as GNP.
b) It is difficult to tell what aggregated variables mean.
c) Different sectors of the economy can grow at different rates, with the aggregate variables obscuring these changes.
d) The effect of macroeconomic policies differ across regions and industries.

20. Which of the following is not true:

a) The equilibrium interest rate can be determined in the money market.
b) A major component of money in the U.S. economy is checking accounts.
c) Reducing inflation and increasing output growth are compatible goals.
d) Over a short period of time, GNP cannot vary much unless the employment of labor changes.

ANSWER KEY

Exercises

1. households, businesses, businesses, households
2. wages and salaries
3. financial
4. expansion, peak, recession, and trough
5. labor services
6. government's budget deficit, trade deficit
7. rapid output growth stable output growth, stable prices, and low unemployment
8. aggregate demand and aggregate supply
9. interest rate
10. medium of exchange

Review Questions

1. a) is the correct answer. This is a topic that would be studied mainly in microeconomics, since it deals with an individual market and does not deal with interactions among markets.

2. b) is the correct answer. Inflation and unemployment are subjects mainly of macroeconomics, since they deal with aggregates or with the national economy as the main topic of analysis.

3. c) is the correct answer. The household sells resources or factors of production to the business sector. In return, the household sector is paid income. Thus, all income flows to the household sector.

4. d) is the correct answer. Say's Law certainly did not predict the Great Depression. In fact, some have used Say's Law to assert that general economic declines were impossible, since the very act of production creates the income and demand to purchase what has been produced.

5. d) is the correct answer. Net exports is the smallest component of aggregate expenditure. It has been roughly -$50 - -$100 billion in recent years. This is small compared to total expenditure of over $5000 billion.

6. b) is the correct answer. Income that is used by the household sector to pay taxes is revenue to the government which may be used to buy goods or services from the business sector.

7. c) is the correct answer. Were it not for investment, income would be lower. Investment is a demand on the business sector for a particular type of newly produced good. Without investment, the saving of households would not be spent on the goods produced by the business sector and income would be lower.

8. d) is the correct answer. The phase of the business cycle in which output is growing is known as the expansionary phase. The expansionary phase stops at the peak, which is the point at which income is at its highest level(for that particular cycle).

9. b) is the correct answer. Income payments are flows of funds into the household sector. Exports, consumption, and government purchases are all demands for goods and services produced by the business sector and are therefore represented by flows of funds into the business sector.

10. c) is the correct answer. Between 1970 and 1990 the number of people employed in the U.S. increased by 50%. This is because the working age population grew quite rapidly during this period of time.

11. c) is the correct answer. As you can see from the text's discussion of expansions and recessions, the U.S. has not been in recession for twenty years. During the past twenty years, there have been several expansionary periods in which unemployment fell, but it always remains above zero.

12. d) is the correct answer. To be considered unemployed, a person must be actively searching for work.

13. b) is the correct answer. The unemployment rate always rises during periods of recession. In part, this is because excess supply in the labor market is not reduced with falling wages.

14. d) is the correct answer. Government policymakers have pursued both the goals of rapid economic growth and stable prices since the end of World War II(1945).

15. a) is the correct answer. If output is growing rapidly, the demand for labor will be strong, allowing the economy to absorb increases in the labor force, so that unemployment is held low.

16. c) is the correct answer. Aggregate <u>supply</u> depends on the availability of resources.

17. c) is the correct answer. The payments to workers for labor services are by far the largest component of national income and account for about two-thirds of GNP.

18. d) is the correct answer. If the quantity supplied of credit exceeds the quantity demanded, the equilibrium price of credit(the interest rate) will be bid up as demanders of credit compete for the limited amount of credit available.

19. a) is the correct answer. Obviously, it is not impossible to calculate GNP, since it is done all the time. What is difficult and the source of much of the criticism of macroeconomics is the interpretation of what aggregated variables, such as GNP, mean.

20. c) is the correct answer. Policies that reduce inflation tend to reduce output growth(at least in the short-run). Thus, inflation and output growth are generally not considered to be compatible policy goals.

CHAPTER 23
AGGREGATE DEMAND FOR GOODS AND SERVICES

OVERVIEW

In this chapter we develop the theory of aggregate demand and derive the aggregate demand curve. The first part of the chapter is spent analyzing the determinants of the components of aggregate demand. The remainder of the chapter is devoted to the derivation of the aggregate demand curve and a discussion of the factors that cause shifts of the curve and movements along it.

Of the four major components of aggregate demand, consumption spending is the largest and the most stable. The consumption function, which relates consumption to disposable income, suggests that consumption is some fraction of disposable income. That portion of disposable income not used for consumption is saved. The modern theory of consumption maintains that consumption is a stable percentage of long-run average disposable income, implying that temporary changes in income will have a much smaller effect on consumption than will permanent income changes. This is because temporary changes have a much smaller effect on the long-run average level of income.

It is important to distinguish "consumption" from "consumption expenditures." Consumption refers to the actual use of goods and services. Nondurable consumption goods are goods that are consumed immediately. Durable goods, on the other hand, are goods that yield a stream of services over time. Expenditures on nondurables are fairly stable over time. In contrast, expenditures on durable goods fluctuate considerably depending on the state of the economy. Consequently, consumption expenditures are less stable than they would otherwise be.

Taxes and transfer payments influence the level of consumption spending as well. However, just as in the case of any other change in income, the magnitude of the effect of a change in disposable income caused by a change in taxes or transfer payments will depend on whether the change is considered to be permanent or temporary.

The second component of aggregate demand, and the most unstable, is investment spending, which consists of three components--purchases of capital stock, changes in inventories, and residential construction. Gross investment--total investment spending--differs from net investment by the amount of depreciation, i..e, wearing out of the existing capital stock. When net investment is positive there is a net addition to the economy's stock of productive resources, ceteris paribus.

The decision of whether to invest in capital stock is determined by the relationship between the real rate of return on the investment--measured as profit as a percentage of total cost--and the expected real rate of interest, which represents the opportunity cost of investment. So long as the real rate of return exceeds the expected real rate of interest, the investment is profitable and will be undertaken.

In addition to the expected real rate of interest, a number of factors including expectations, the level of income, the capacity utilization rate, and tax policy all influence the level of investment spending. For example, as expectations of the profitability of investment improve, the level of investment spending increases. In a similar manner, a decrease in taxes increases the profitability of investment and therefore the amount of investment by business.

Investment spending is extremely procyclical, meaning that it moves in the same direction as the business cycle--as real GNP increases or decreases, so does investment spending. This high degree of instability is attributable to a number of factors including the sensitivity of fixed investment to changes in real GNP, the sensitivity of fixed investment to changes in expectations, the sensitivity of residential construction to changes in the real interest rate, and the sensitivity of inventory investment to changes in the level of income.

Government purchases are the second largest component of aggregate demand. For the purposes of our analysis, government spending is treated as a policy variable, i.e., policymakers may vary the level of government spending to influence the level of aggregate demand.

Net exports are calculated as the difference between exports and imports. To the extent that exports exceed imports, net exports are positive and aggregate demand for U.S. goods and services increases. Imports are positively related to U.S. income, while exports are positively related to foreign income. Relative prices also influence imports and exports. As the price of U.S. goods rises relative to the price of foreign goods, U.S. goods become more expensive. This leads to an increase in imports and a decrease in exports--net exports decline. The exchange rate--the amount of foreign currency required to purchase a dollar--also influences net exports. As the exchange rate falls, foreigners can purchase more dollars and therefore more U.S. goods; exports increase. By the same reasoning imports decline. Hence there is an increase in net exports.

Aggregate demand is the sum of consumption spending, gross investment, government purchases, and net exports--GNP. The aggregate demand curve indicates the amount of real GNP that will be purchased at each price level (which is measured by a price index). The position of the aggregate demand curve is determined by autonomous variables--variables whose values are independent of the level of real GNP. Such variables include income and payroll taxes and transfer payments, the expected real interest rate, business taxes and investment tax credits, the level of government purchases, and factors affecting net exports such as relative prices between the United States and foreign countries, the exchange rate, and foreign real income.

The aggregate demand curve is downward sloping. The inverse relationship between the price level and Real GNP is attributable to three effects--the direct wealth effect, the indirect interest rate effect, and the international price ratio effect.

KEY GRAPHS AND TERMS

Graphs

The key models and associated graphs developed in this chapter include the consumption and savings functions, the model of investment demand and the investment demand curve, and the model of aggregate demand and the aggregate demand curve. The consumption function and savings function, illustrated in Figures 1 and 2, indicate how consumption and savings change as disposable income changes. The important point to remember in studying these graphs is that each of these uses of disposable income is a fraction of disposable income, and the two fractions add up to one.

The investment demand curve indicates the level of investment spending that will be undertaken at each level of the expected real interest rate. Referring to Figure 7, it is important to recognize that, in fact, two different percentages are measured on the vertical axis--the expected real interest rate and the rate of return on investment. The investment demand curve is generated by ranking all investments on the basis of rate of return, from highest to lowest. Thus, as we move down the investment demand curve, additional projects are less profitable as measured by their rate of return.

As with any demand curve, it is important to distinguish movements along the curve from shifts of the curve. A change in the expected real interest rate is the only factor that causes a movement along the investment demand curve. A change in any of the other determinants of investment spending, such as expectations, income, capacity utilization, and tax policy will cause the investment demand curve to shift.

The aggregate demand (AD) curve is a critical element of the macroeconomic model. The AD curve indicates the level of Real GNP that will be purchased at each price level. Thus, a change in the price level is the only factor that causes a movement along the AD curve. Factors that determine the level of spending at a given price level determine the position of the AD curve. As such, a change in taxes (income, payroll, business, etc.), a change in government spending (either purchases or transfer payments) a change in the level of the real interest rate, and changes in the ratio of U.S. prices to foreign prices or the exchange rate all cause the AD curve to shift. For example, a decrease in taxes, an increase in government spending, a decrease in the real interest rate, and a decrease in the exchange rate all cause the AD curve to shift to the right, i.e., there is an increase in aggregate demand.

Chapter 23, Aggregate Demand for Goods and Services

Terms
AGGREGATE DEMAND
CONSUMPTION FUNCTION
DISPOSABLE INCOME
AUTONOMOUS CONSUMPTION EXPENDITURES
MARGINAL PROPENSITY TO CONSUME
MARGINAL PROPENSITY TO SAVE
NONDURABLE CONSUMPTION GOODS
DURABLE CONSUMER GOODS
INVESTMENT
FINANCIAL INVESTMENT
GROSS INVESTMENT
DEPRECIATION
NET INVESTMENT
RATE OF RETURN ON INVESTMENT
REAL RATE OF RETURN
EXPECTED REAL INTEREST RATE
CAPACITY UTILIZATION RATE
INVESTMENT TAX CREDIT
INVENTORY
PROCYCLICAL
EXCHANGE RATE
AUTONOMOUS VARIABLE
AGGREGATE DEMAND CURVE

EXERCISES

1. Disposable income is calculated as GNP minus Taxes plus Transfer Payments.

2. The fraction of additional disposable income that is used for consumption is measured by the Marginal Propensity to Consume.

3. According to the modern theory of consumption, temporary changes in disposable income have a much smaller effect on consumption than permanent changes in income.

4. The most stable component of aggregate demand is Consumption expenditures. (Spending)

5. Consumption items such as cars, stereos, and ovens are referred to as Durable Consumer Goods.

6. The government can influence the level of disposable income and consumption spending by altering Taxe rates and transfer payments.

7. The three major categories of investment spending include FIXED Buisness investment, changes in the business INVENTORY LEVELS, and residential construction.

8. Net investment is calculated as gross investment minus depreciation.

9. The opportunity cost of investing funds in a business is the interest rate.

10. The level of production in an industry expressed as a percentage of the industry's maximum production level is referred to as the Capacity Utilization RATE.

11. An increase in the tax rate on business profits would cause the investment demand curve to shift Left.

12. Ceteris paribus, a decrease in the price of U.S. goods relative to the price of foreign goods would cause net exports to increase, and the AD curve to Shift right.

13. List four factors that would cause the AD curve to shift left. an increase in payroll taxes, a decrease in transfere payments, and an increase in the exchange rate. a decrease in gov purchase

14. a. Use the following data to graph the aggregate demand (AD) curve in the space provided, and label the curve AD1 (Real GNP is in trillions of 1988 $):

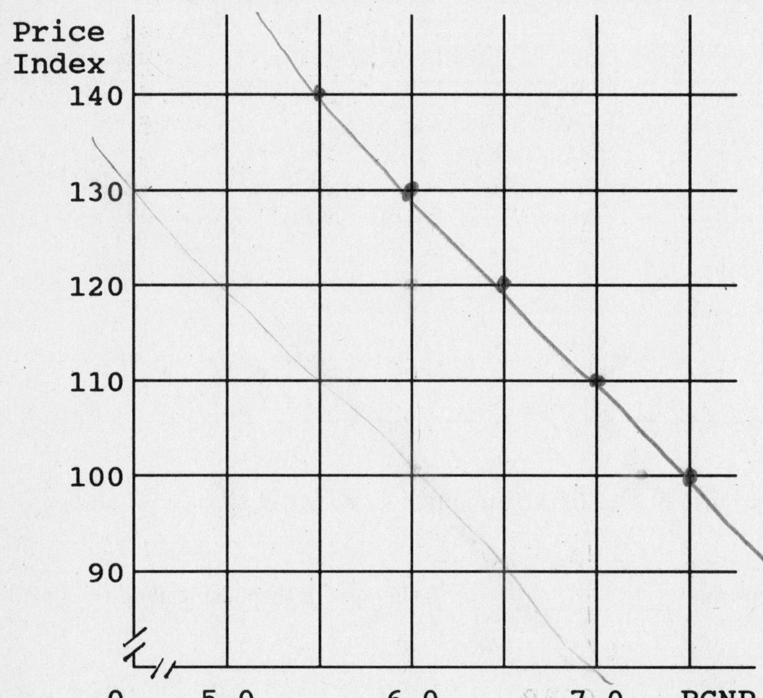

Price Index	Real GNP
100	$7.5
110	7.0
120	6.5
130	6.0
140	5.5

b. In the same figure, illustrate how each of the following will affect the AD curve you have constructed, and be able to explain why you illustrated the effect in the way you did.

-- a decrease in the price level from 130 to 100. *will increase the RGNP 7.5*

-- a decrease in the expected real interest rate. *curve will shift to the right*

15. a. Use the following data to graph the AD curve in the space provided and label the curve AD1 (Real GNP is in trillions of 1988 $):

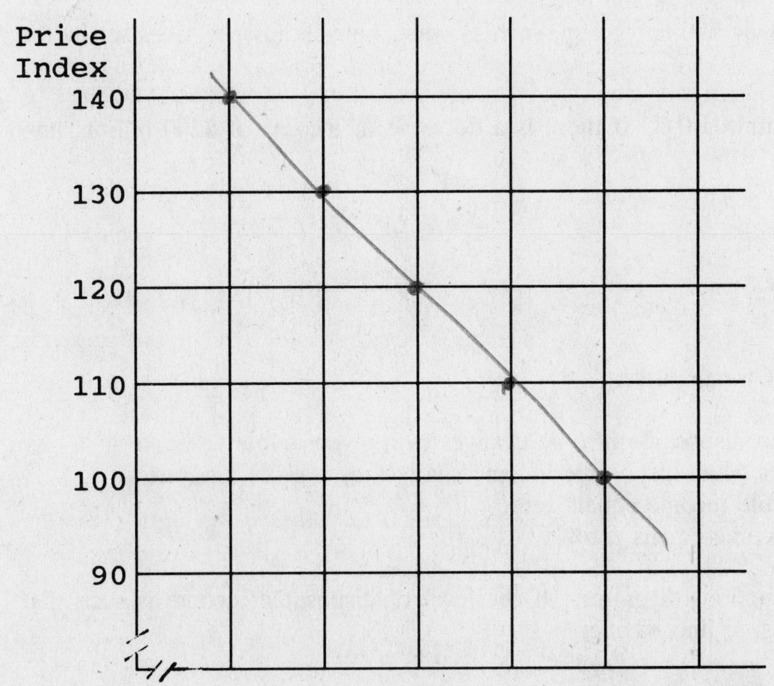

Price Index	Real GNP
100	$8.0
110	7.5
120	7.0
130	6.5
140	6.0

b. In the same figure, illustrate how each of the following will affect the AD curve you have constructed, and be able to explain why you illustrated the effect in the way you did.

-- an increase in government spending. shifts curve to right

-- an increase in the foreign exchange rate. shifts to left.

-- an adverse change in business expectations. shift to left.

REVIEW QUESTIONS

1. Which of the following is the largest component of aggregate demand?

a) Consumption
b) Investment
c) Government purchases
d) Net exports

2. Which of the following would cause aggregate consumption spending to increase?

a) An increase in the price level.
b) An increase in disposable income.
c) An increase in the interest rate.
d) A decrease in the expected level of future income.

3. The term "autonomous spending" refers to:

a) spending that does not vary with the level of income.
b) spending on such items as car payments that must be made every month.
c) speculative spending such as money spent on stocks and bonds.
d) spending by one group that is determined by another group, such as when households pay taxes set by the government.

4. Suppose the marginal propensity to consume is 0.8. If there is a decrease in income of $200 billion, how much will consumption change?

a) -$80 billion
b) -$100 billion
c) -$120 billion
d) -$160 billion

5. The marginal propensity to consume (MPC) measures:

a) the amount by which savings changes when disposable income changes by a given amount.
b) the amount by which consumption changes when disposable income changes by a given amount.
c) the amount of consumption when disposable income equals zero.
d) the amount of savings when disposable income equals zero.

6. Consider the consumption and savings functions diagrams. If the level of disposable income is such that the consumption function is above the 45-degree line, saving:

a) is equal to zero.
b) is positive.
c) is negative.
d) cannot be determined, since information about the marginal propensity to save is not provided.

7. Keynes:

a) theory of consumption says current consumption depends on long-run income.
b) theory of consumption says current consumption depends on current disposable income.
c) suggested that consumers take future income into account when making consumption decisions.
d) said people make consumption decisions on the basis of labor supply decisions.

8. How has actual consumption behavior differed from what Keynes predicted?

a) In the long-run, the ratio of consumption to disposable income has not fallen.
b) consumption spending has been stable in the short-run.
c) autonomous consumption has been quite large.
d) a) and b), but not c)

9. Statistical evidence about the marginal propensity to consume over the last 40 years shows that it is approximately equal to:

a) 0.75
b) 0.80
c) 0.90
d) 1.00

10. Suppose there is a fall in disposable income that is viewed as temporary. According to the long-run view of consumption, which of the following is most likely to occur?

a) Consumption will fall.
b) Consumption will rise.
c) Savings will fall.
d) Savings will rise.

11. The quarterly instability of MPC suggests:

a) consumption is stable with respect to short-run income changes.
b) consumption is unstable with respect to short-run income changes.
c) that current consumption is closely related to current disposable income.
d) that Keynes' views on consumption were accurate.

12. The modern theory of consumption is based on all of the following <u>except</u>:

a) Individuals attempt to maximize utility over long periods of time.
b) People don't plan for the future in making consumption decisions--they "live for today."
c) People prefer relatively stable patterns of consumption.
d) People attempt to maintain their levels of consumption when they experience temporary reductions in income.

13. The long-run consumption/income relationship is illustrated by college students who:

a) drop out of college to take jobs.
b) cut class because the professor is boring.
c) borrow so they can live relatively comfortably while they are in school.
d) work while attending college so that they will not have large debts when they graduate.

14. Suppose the consumption-disposable income relationship suggests that MPC = 0.9. Suppose there is an increase in disposable income of $10,000. Which of the following statements is correct?

a) If the change is viewed as permanent, the change in consumption will be $9,000.
b) If the change is viewed as permanent, the change in consumption will be $10,000.
c) If the change is viewed as temporary, the change in consumption will be $9,000.
d) If the change is viewed as temporary, the change in consumption will be $10,000.

15. In an effort to increase consumption spending in a recession, suppose the government announces that it is reducing taxes temporarily. If the long-run theory of consumption is correct, which of the following is likely to happen?

a) Consumption will rise by a relatively large amount.
b) Consumption will rise by a relatively small amount.
c) Consumption will fall.
d) Savings will fall by a relatively large amount.

16. If a consumer is <u>liquidity constrained</u>:

a) the consumer cannot borrow to support a desired level of income.
b) the long-run theory of consumption does not work.
c) the consumer has a simple Keynesian consumption function.
d) all of the above.

17. Which of the following is the best example of a consumer durable good?

a) Use of electrical energy.
b) Food purchases
c) A washing machine.
d) Gasoline for an automobile.

18. How is spending on durable goods like saving?

a) both provide for future consumption.
b) both increase when there are temporary increases in disposable income.
c) both increase when there are temporary decreases in disposable income.
d) a) and b), but not c).

19. Which of the following explains the difference between gross and net investment?

a) Net investment belongs in GNP, but gross investment does not.
b) Gross investment includes consumer durables, but net investment does not.
c) Gross investment includes spending on worn-out capital goods.
d) a) and b), but not c).

20. A firm can purchase a piece of capital for $5,000 that can be used to produce output worth $5,600. Assume the value of the capital depreciates to zero at the end of the first year. The current expected real interest rate is 11%. Based upon this information, the firm:

a) should buy the piece of capital.
b) should not buy the piece of capital.
c) is indifferent between buying and not buying the piece of capital.
d) cannot determine whether the piece of capital should be purchased.

21. Which of the following would cause a shift to the right in the investment function?

a) An increase in interest rates.
b) An increase in expected inflation.
c) An increase in taxes.
d) An increase in the capacity utilization rate above 85%.

22. All of the following are reasons investment spending is unstable <u>except</u>:

a) Residential construction does not change when the interest rate changes.
b) Investment is sensitive to changes in real GNP.
c) Investment is sensitive to changes in business optimism.
d) Inventories change a great deal with changes in real GNP.

23. As Japanese income rises, which of the following is most likely to happen as a result?

a) U.S. net exports will fall.
b) Japanese exports will increase.
c) U.S. exports will increase.
d) The U.S. will be made worse off.

24. Suppose the exchange rate changes from 125 Japanese Yen per dollar to 150 Japanese Yen per dollar. Which of the following will occur as a direct result?

a) U.S. exports will go up.
b) Japanese imports of U.S. goods will go down.
c) U.S. imports of Japanese goods will go down.
d) Japanese exports to the U.S. will go down.

25. According to the "international price ratio effect:"

a) a decrease in net exports causes aggregate supply to decrease.
b) a decrease in net exports causes aggregate supply to increase.
c) an increase in the price level causes net exports, and therefore the quantity of aggregate demand, to increase.
d) an increase in the price level causes net exports, and therefore the quantity of aggregate demand, to decrease.

26. Suppose estimated future incomes from capital goods increase. Which of the following will occur?

a) The investment demand curve will shift to the right.
b) The investment demand curve will shift to the left.
c) There will be a movement up and to the left along a single investment demand curve.
d) There will be a movement down and to the right along a single investment demand curve.

27. The aggregate demand function is negatively sloped for which of the following reasons?

a) As government purchases increase, aggregate demand increases.
b) As net exports increase, aggregate demand increases.
c) As the price level rises, household real wealth falls.
d) As the price level rises, real investment spending rises.

28. Which of the following would not cause the AD curve to shift?

a) a change in government spending.
b) a change in investment spending.
c) a change in tax rates.
d) a change in the price level.

29. In 1981, Congress lowered the effective tax rate on business profits and shortened the period of time over which a business could fully depreciate new capital stock. According to the theory of investment demand this should have caused the level of investment spending to:

a) increase.
b) decrease.
c) stay constant.
d) can't be determined.

30. Which of the following would cause U.S. exports to decrease?

a) A decrease in real GNP in the U.S.
b) An increase in the price of U.S. goods relative to the price of foreign goods.
c) An increase in the foreign exchange value of the dollar.
d) An increase in the level of Real GNP in the rest of the world.

ANSWER KEY

Exercises

1. GNP, taxes, transfer payments
2. marginal propensity to consume
3. temporary, permanent
4. consumption spending
5. durable consumer goods
6. tax rates, transfer payments
7. fixed business investment, changes in inventories, and residential construction.
8. gross investment, depreciation
9. interest rate
10. capacity utilization rate
11. shift left
12. increase, shift right
13. an increase in income taxes or payroll taxes, a decrease in transfer payments, a decrease in government purchases, an increase in the level of the expected real interest rate, an increase in business taxes, an increase in the ratio of domestic prices to foreign prices, an increase in the exchange rate (of foreign currency for a dollar), and a decline in foreign real income are all possible answers.
14. b. A decrease in the price level will cause a movement along the AD curve. Quantity of Real GNP demanded will increase from $6 trillion to $7.5 trillion. A decrease in the expected real interest rate will cause the AD curve to shift to the right. As the expected real interest rate falls, investment and consumption spending increase.
15. b. An increase in government spending shifts the AD curve to the right. An increase in the foreign exchange rate (i.e., an increase in the amount of foreign currency that can be purchased with a dollar) leads to an increase in imports and a decrease in exports--net exports decline--and the AD curve therefore shifts left. An adverse change in business expectations will lead to a reduction in autonomous investment, and the AD curve will shift left.

Review Questions

1. a) is the correct answer. Consumption is by far the largest component of expenditure for GNP.

2. b) is the correct answer. An increase in disposable income causes people to spend more on goods and services. It also causes people to save more.

3. a) is the correct answer. "Autonomous" in this case means independent of income. Autonomous spending is spending that depends on something other than income, such as the interest rate or expectations.

4. d) is the correct answer. The change in consumption is equal to the marginal propensity to consume multiplied times the change in income. In this case, the calculation is:
0.8 x -$200 billion = -$160 billion.

5. b) is the correct answer. The MPC is equal to the change in consumption divided by the change in disposable income. It measures the change in consumption spending when there is a $1.00 change in disposable income.

6. c) is the correct answer. If the consumption function is above the 45-degree line, then consumption is greater than disposable income. If this is the case, saving must be negative, that is, consumers are "dissaving."

7. b) is the correct answer. The simple Keynesian view is that current consumption depends on the current level of disposable income, no matter what the consumer expects of disposable income in the future. Empirical evidence suggests that consumers take a longer-run view when making consumption decisions and consider their expected future incomes.

8. d) is the correct answer. The ratio of consumption to disposable income has not fallen as disposable income has increased over time and

short-run consumption has been stable, especially when compared to short-run disposable income.

9. c) is the correct answer. Evidence shows that the MPC is approximately 0.9. That is, for every $1.00 change in disposable income there has been a $0.90 change in consumption.

10. c) is the correct answer. If there is a fall in disposable income that is perceived as temporary, the long-run view of consumption predicts that consumers will reduce their savings to protect their level of consumption. In other words, consumers will reduce their savings to maintain their current level of consumption.

11. a) is the correct answer. The short-run instability of MPC suggests that there is not a strong relation between consumption and disposable income in the short-run. This tends to support the long-run view of consumption.

12. b) is the correct answer. Modern consumption suggests that people <u>do</u> plan for the future and base their current consumption decisions on future income.

13. c) is the correct answer. Students who borrow while they are in college are expecting their incomes to be higher when they graduate. Thus, they are taking a long-run view of consumption by borrowing from their future earnings.

14. a) is the correct answer. If the change is viewed as permanent, consumers will increase their consumption by the long-run MPC multiplied times the change in disposable income. In this case, 0.9 x $10,000 = $9,000. If the change is viewed as temporary, much of the change in disposable income will flow into savings and the change in consumption will be <u>less</u> than $9,000.

15. b) is the correct answer. Since the government has announced that the tax reduction is temporary, the effect on consumption will be small. Most of the increase in disposable income will flow into savings. In other words, the government policy will fail to achieve its goal, if the long-run theory of consumption is valid.

16. d) is the correct answer. If a consumer is liquidity constrained that means the consumer cannot borrow to finance current consumption at a desired level. This tends to refute the long-run theory of consumption.

17. c) is the correct answer. A durable good is one that provides services to the consumer over a long-period of time. The consumer certainly hopes that the washing machine will provide services for several years. The other answers refer to nondurables that will be consumed shortly.

18. d) is the correct answer. Disposable income is saved in order to consume in the future. Similarly, a durable good provides services into the future. When there are increases in disposable income that are perceived as temporary both saving and expenditure on durable goods increase, while consumption of nondurables remains constant.

19. c) is the correct answer. Gross investment - depreciation = net investment. Therefore, gross investment includes depreciation, while net investment does not. Depreciation refers to the value of capital that needs to be replaced.

20. a) is the correct answer. The firm should buy the piece of capital since its percent return(= $600 / $5000 = 12%) is greater than the expected interest rate.

21. d) is the correct answer. When the capacity utilization rate increases to above 85% there is usually an increase in investment. This is because firms are using a large part of their capital stock and need to expand.

22. a) is the correct answer. In fact, residential construction of houses and apartments is quite sensitive to changes in the interest rate and is partly responsible for the instability of investment.

23. c) is the correct answer. As Japanese income rises, the Japanese will spend more on domestic goods as well as foreign goods. Some of the increase in Japanese spending will be for U.S. goods. Therefore, U.S. exports will increase.

24. b) is the correct answer. If the amount of yen the Japanese have to trade for a dollar goes up,

U.S. goods become more expensive in Japan, so Japanese imports of U.S. goods will fall. Japanese goods become less expensive in the U.S., so U.S. imports of Japanese goods will rise.

25. d) is the correct answer. An increase in the U.S. price level means that the prices of U.S. goods on domestic and foreign markets are rising. This causes an increase in imports as U.S. residents substitute foreign goods for domestic goods. It also causes a decrease in exports as foreigners buy less U.S. goods. Both of these effects decrease net exports and the demand for U.S. goods. Thus, aggregate demand falls.

26. a) is the correct answer. An increase in the estimated future incomes from investment will increase the demand for investment. That is, at each real interest rate, the quantity demanded for investment will be larger.

27. c) is the correct answer. As the price level rises, real wealth falls and consumers buy less goods and services. Thus, the aggregate quantity demanded falls.

28. d) is the correct answer. A change in the price level moves the economy along a single aggregate demand curve.

29. a) is the correct answer. The change in taxes made expected investment income increase and therefore increased the demand for investment.

30. c) is the correct answer. An increase in the exchange value of the dollar means that foreigners have to trade more foreign currency for a dollar in order to buy U.S. goods. Thus, the amount of U.S. goods foreigners want to buy(U.S. exports) will fall.

CHAPTER 24
AGGREGATE SUPPLY OF GOODS AND SERVICES

OVERVIEW

In this chapter we derive the short-run and long-run aggregate supply curves. We begin the chapter by developing the model of the aggregate labor market. We then consider how changes in the level of price expectations affect employment levels and output. Other real factors that influence the economy's ability to produce output are considered as well.

The economy's ability to produce output is determined by a number of factors including the stock of available resources, the size of the capital stock, the level of technology, the economy's market organization, and the level of employment. Of these factors, the level of employment is most susceptible to short-run changes. The other factors are considerably more stable in the short run, tending to change over longer periods of time.

The equilibrium level of employment of labor is determined by the interaction of aggregate labor supply and aggregate labor demand. Aggregate labor supply is influenced by a number of factors including the expected real wage rate--the ratio of the nominal wage rate to the expected price level--and the labor force participation rate. Aggregate labor demand is determined by the productivity of labor, the price level, and the wage rate.

The short-run equilibrium wage rate and employment level occur at the intersection of the labor demand and labor supply curves. However, it is important to note that this is not necessarily a long-run equilibrium position. So long as the actual price level and the expected price level differ, there will be pressure on the labor supply curve to shift as workers attempt to alter their real wage. When expectations are fulfilled--the actual and expected price levels are the same--long-run equilibrium is achieved. The corresponding level of employment is called the natural level of employment. The only factors that cause the natural level of employment to change are real factors, such as those that affect labor productivity or the labor force participation rate. Changes in the price level do not affect the natural level of employment.

The natural level of output is determined by the natural level of employment, available resources, the amount of capital stock, technology, and market organization. A change in any one of these factors will cause the natural level of output to change.

The aggregate supply curve shows the amount of output firms are willing and able to produce at different price levels. When considering aggregate supply, it is necessary to take account of the time dimension. The short-run aggregate supply (SRAS) curve is upward sloping to reflect the fact that wages are slow to adjust to price level changes. Hence, the short run is the period of time during which markets are adjusting to a shock. Because wages adjust more slowly than prices, output can deviate from the natural level in the short run. For example, an increase in aggregate demand will cause an increase in prices. Because wages, and therefore costs, adjust more slowly, firms' profits increase. So long as the expected price level exceeds the actual price level, firms respond to the higher prices by producing more output.

In the long-run, markets are able to fully adjust to shocks to the economy. An implication of this property is that in the long run, the expected price and the actual price level are equal. The long-run aggregate supply (LRAS) curve is vertical at the natural level of output, indicating that over time, the economy will tend toward that output level. It is also apparent that the price level is not a determinant of the natural level of output. Finally, the price level at which the SRAS curve and the LRAS curve intersect is the expected price level.

The position of both the LRAS curve and the SRAS curve are determined by the same factors that determine the natural level of output. In addition, the position of the SRAS curve is influenced by the expected price level.

KEY GRAPHS AND TERMS

Graphs

The key models introduced in this chapter are the models of the aggregate labor market and the model of aggregate supply. The aggregate labor market, which is illustrated in Figures 1-7, is especially important since the short-run equilibrium level of employment can vary significantly.

Changes in the level of employment are caused by shifts in the labor supply curve and labor demand curve. In the case of the labor supply curve, a change in the expected price level or the labor force participation rate will cause the curve to shift. The expected price level will change in response to a deviation of the actual price level from the prevailing expected price level. The position of the labor demand curve will change if there is a change in labor productivity or the actual price level.

The models of short-run aggregate supply and long-run aggregate supply are derived graphically in Figures 8 and 12. Because wages are assumed to adjust slowly to changes in the level of output and prices, the SRAS curve is upward sloping. In the short run, firms are able to vary the levels of employment and output in response to changes in the price level, and in so doing increase profits or reduce losses. Changes in the price level cause a movement along the SRAS curve. A change in any of the real factors of production, as well as the expected price level, causes the SRAS curve to shift.

The position of the LRAS curve is determined by real factors including the natural level of employment, resources, capital, and technology. An increase in any one of these factors will cause the LRAS curve to shift right, ceteris paribus, implying an increase in the natural level of output as well.

As is illustrated in Figure 8, the SRAS curve and the LRAS curve intersect at the expected price level which, in this case, is PI_0. Recalling that the SRAS curve is constructed holding the expected price level constant, since the long-run is defined as the period time sufficient for all expectations to be met, PL_0 must be the expected price level by definition.

Terms
NOMINAL WAGE RATE
EXPECTED PRICE LEVEL
EXPECTED REAL WAGE RATE
AGGREGATE LABOR SUPPLY CURVE
LABOR FORCE PARTICIPATION RATE
AGGREGATE LABOR DEMAND CURVE
MARGINAL PRODUCTIVITY OF LABOR
SHORT-RUN LABOR MARKET EQUILIBRIUM
LONG-RUN LABOR MARKET EQUILIBRIUM
NATURAL LEVEL OF EMPLOYMENT
NATURAL OUTPUT LEVEL
INFRASTRUCTURE
AGGREGATE SUPPLY CURVE
EXPLICIT LABOR CONTRACT
IMPLICIT LABOR CONTRACT
SHORT-RUN AGGREGATE SUPPLY CURVE
CYCLICAL UNEMPLOYMENT
LONG-RUN AGGREGATE SUPPLY CURVE

EXERCISES

1. The expected real wage rate is calculated by dividing the Nominal wage rate by the Expected price level.

2. The position of the aggregate labor demand curve depends on the price Level and the productivity of Labor.

3. The level of employment associated with long-run equilibrium in the labor market is called the Natural Level of employment, which is, in turn, a major determinant of the natural output Level.

4. List the five primary determinants of the position of the LRAS curve. Natural Level of employment, quantity of available resources, capital stock, Level of technology, and market organization.

5. The support system of public capital that produces transportation and utility services is called an economy's infrastructure

6. Because wages are sticky, the labor market tends to adjust slowly to a particular shock.

7. An Explicit Labor Contract is a signed legal agreement setting wages and working conditions.

8. The labor market achieves long-run equilibrium when the Expected price level equals the actual price level.

9. Cyclical unemployment refers to unemployment caused by a fall in aggregate demand.

10. Each SRAS curve is constructed for a given value of the Expected price level. In addition, at the intersection of the SRAS curve and the LRAS curve, the Expected price level and the actual price level are equal.

11. An increase in the expected price level will cause the SRAS curve to shift Left.

12. Distinguish between the short run and the long run in macroeconomics. The short-run is the time during which the market is still adjusting to macro shock, the long-run is the time that the wages and price adjust to shock.

13. Define the aggregate labor supply curve and the aggregate labor demand curve. the aggregate labor supply curve shows the quantity of labor workers are willing to supply at various wages. The ALD shows the quantity of labor firms want to employ at various wage rates.

14. Define the short-run aggregate supply curve. the short-run aggregate supply curve shows the aggregate quantity of output firms are willing and able to produce at each price level.

15. Define the long-run aggregate supply curve. The long-run aggregate supply curve is vertical at the natural level of output. It indicates the level of output the economy will produce over the long-run with a given amount of factors of production.

16. a. Use the following data to graph the short-run aggregate supply (SRAS) curve in the space provided and label the curve SRAS1 (Real GNP is in trillions of 1988 $).

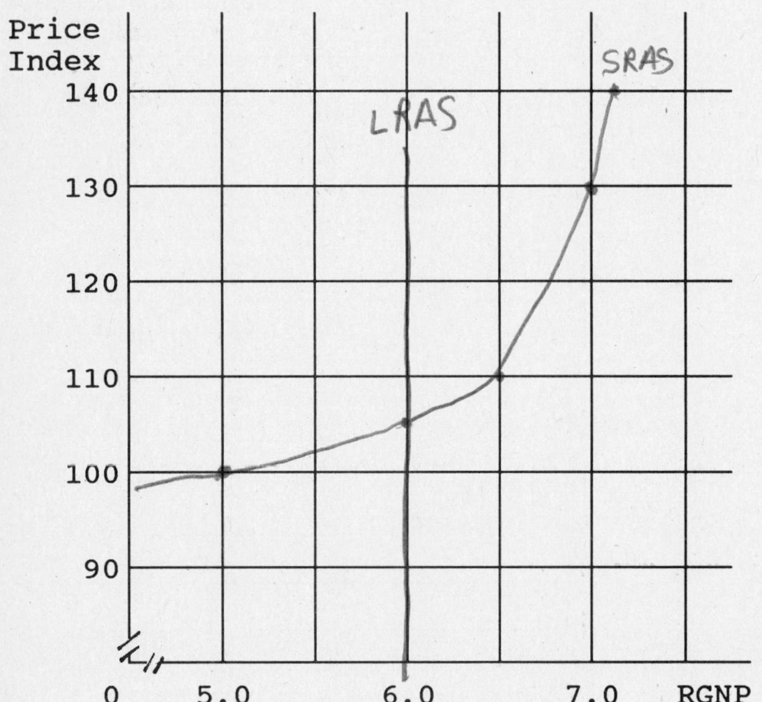

Price Index	Real GNP
100	$5.0
105	6.0
110	6.5
130	7.0
140	7.25

b. In the same figure, illustrate how each of the following will affect the SRAS curve you have constructed, and be able to explain why you illustrated the effect in the way you did.

-- an increase in the price level from 105 to 120 (holding input prices constant). movement up along the curve GNP supplied will increase from $5 → $6.75

-- a decrease in the price of raw materials. lower the production costs and shift SRAS to the right.

c. Assume the natural level of output is $6 trillion of RGNP. Construct the corresponding LRAS curve. According to the figure, what is the expected price level associated with SRAS1? 105

17 a. Use the following data to graph the SRAS curve in the space provided and label the curve SRAS1 (Real GNP is in trillions of 1988 $).

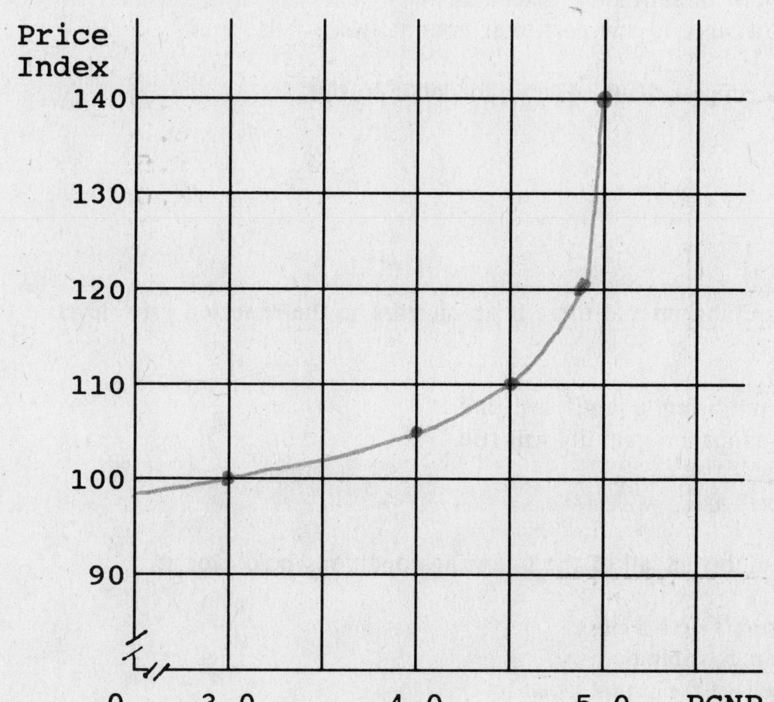

Price Index	Real GNP
100	$3.0
105	4.0
110	4.5
120	4.75
140	5.0

b. In the same figure, illustrate how each of the following will affect the SRAS curve you have constructed, and be able to explain why you illustrated the effect in the way you did.

-- a decrease in the average level of wages. lower production cost. Shift to the right

-- a decrease in the average level of taxes. increase incentive to invest. Shift to right

-- an increase in the expected price level. workers demand higher wage rates, higher production costs, shift to left.

REVIEW QUESTIONS

1. Labor supply depends on:

a) the nominal wage.
b) the expected real wage.
c) the expected price level.
d) the current real wage.

2. Which of the following causes a movement along the labor supply function, rather than a shift in the labor supply function?

a) a change in the nominal wage.
b) an increase in the expected price level.
c) an increase in the working age population.
d) an increase in labor force participation.

3. Why is the labor demand function negatively sloped?

a) as employment expands, the expected price falls.
b) as employment expands, the expected price rises.
c) as employment expands, the marginal benefit of another worker falls.
d) as the firm hires more capital, the value of labor at any particular nominal wage falls.

4. Which of the following would cause the aggregate demand curve for labor to shift left?

a) an increase in the nominal wage rate.
b) an increase in labor productivity.
c) a decrease in the actual price level.
d) an increase in the expected price level.

5. Suppose the labor market is initially in equilibrium and there is an increase in the expected price level. Which of the following will occur?

a) The equilibrium wage will rise and the equilibrium quantity will fall.
b) The equilibrium wage will fall and the equilibrium quantity will rise.
c) Both the equilibrium wage and quantity will rise.
d) Both the equilibrium wage and quantity will fall.

6. When the labor market is in long run equilibrium, all of the following conditions hold <u>except</u>:

a) Workers' expected price equals the economy's actual price.
b) The unemployment rate is as low as it can possibly be.
c) Both firms and workers have fully adjusted to the actual price level.
d) The equilibrium quantity is the natural level of employment.

7. Suppose there is an unexpected increase in the price level. Which of the following is true of the adjustment of the labor market in the short run?

a) Firms reduce their quantity demanded for labor.
b) The nominal wage falls.
c) Labor supply shifts to the right.
d) Employment increases.

8. Which of the following will cause a change in the natural level of employment?

a) An increase in the real wage.
b) An increase in the nominal wage.
c) An improvement in technology.
d) A decrease in the expected price level.

9. Which of the following is a reason immigration could be considered good for the U.S.?

a) Social costs
b) The effect on low-skill U.S. labor
c) The effect on the size of the market for U.S. goods.
d) The fact that the skills of new immigrants are much higher than the skills of past immigrants into the U.S.

10. The natural level of output:

a) is the maximum the economy can produce.
b) is associated with rising wages.
c) can occur independently of equilibrium in the labor market.
d) is the highest level of output associated with stable prices.

11. Which of the following is <u>not true</u>?

a) The Soviet Union is considered to have a relatively high national income because of its vast natural resources.
b) Japan and Taiwan have relatively few natural resources.
c) The word "infrastructure" refers to the support system of public capital.
d) An improvement in technology can reduce the amount of time it takes to produce a unit of output.

12. Predictions of natural resource depletion:

a) have been fairly accurate over the years.
b) have been made on the basis of prices of natural resources rising, with the resulting economizing on their use.
c) have failed to take into account the effect of price on the search for substitutes.
d) have been based mainly on economic analysis.

13. The short run is defined in macroeconomics as:

a) a period in which all inputs are fixed.
b) a period insufficiently long for all inputs to be varied, but long enough for some inputs to be varied.
c) a period of time short enough so that wages are not "sticky."
d) a period of time over which markets are adjusting to a change in equilibrium.

14. Which of the following is <u>not true</u> in long run macroeconomic equilibrium?

a) all inputs are variable.
b) prices have fully adjusted.
c) wages have fully adjusted.
d) the labor market is in equilibrium.

15. The labor market:

a) is an auction market.
b) moves rapidly to equate quantity supplied and quantity demanded.
c) is characterized by flexible wages, particularly in a downward direction.
d) is in equilibrium when the expected price and the actual price are equal.

16. Suppose the long-run equilibrium of the economy is disturbed by an increase in aggregate demand. Which of the following will occur?

a) The price level will rise and most workers will experience a decline in real wages in the short run.
b) The price level will rise and most workers will experience an increase in real wages in the short run.
c) The actual price will be less than the expected price.
d) Income will temporarily be lower than its natural level.

17. The SRAS curve tells us how much output is produced:

a) as the labor force changes.
b) at each price level.
c) as wages vary.
d) in the long run.

18. If the actual price level is not equal to the expected price level:

a) The aggregate quantities demanded and supplied may be equal, but the labor market is not in equilibrium.
b) The labor market may be in equilibrium, but aggregate quantities demanded and supplied are not equal.
c) Aggregate quantity demanded does not equal aggregate quantity supplied nor is the labor market in equilibrium.
d) The wage rate will adjust in the short run to prevent changes in the level of employment.

19. Unemployment that is caused by a decline in aggregate demand is called:

a) structural unemployment.
b) cyclical unemployment.
c) frictional unemployment.
d) variable unemployment.

20. An increase in nominal wages causes:

a) the SRAS function to shift to the left.
b) the SRAS function to shift to the right.
c) the LRAS function to shift to the right.
d) an increase in the natural level of output.

21. All of the following will cause the SRAS curve to shift <u>except</u>:

a) a change in price expectations.
b) a change in the capital stock.
c) a change in technology.
d) a change in the actual price level.

22. Assume that there is an increase in the marginal productivity of labor. This will have the effect of:

a) shifting the LRAS curve to the left.
b) increasing the natural level of output.
c) shifting the SRAS curve to the left.
d) all of the above.

23. If nominal wages do not fall in response to a decline in labor demand, what restores equilibrium in the labor market?

a) An increase in the price level.
b) A decrease in the price level.
c) An increase in structural unemployment.
d) Labor market equilibrium is not necessarily restored in the long run, making unemployment possible.

24. Since wages do not respond immediately to changes in the price level:

a) the economy tends to stay at the natural level of employment.
b) the natural level of employment varies with the price level.
c) the level of employment varies with the level of output.
d) unemployment is more stable than otherwise would be.

25. The long run aggregate supply function:

a) is upward sloping.
b) is horizontal at the natural price level.
c) illustrates the strong relationship between the price level and the level of output in the long run.
d) illustrates points at which wages and prices have fully adjusted to changes in aggregate demand.

26. The shape of the LRAS curve suggests that, in the long run:

a) the level of output is independent of the level of aggregate demand.
b) the level of output is completely determined by the level of aggregate demand.
c) the price level cannot vary.
d) inflation is zero.

27. Which of the following is not held constant when constructing the Long-Run Aggregate Supply (LRAS) Curve?

a) Technology.
b) The amount of capital.
c) Labor productivity.
d) The price level.

28. If the SRAS curve is not stable:

a) output will not deviate from its natural level for a long period of time.
b) output will be able to deviate from its natural level for a long period of time.
c) nominal wages adjust slowly to changes in the economy.
d) b) and c), but not a).

29. If price expectations and wages adjust sluggishly:

a) the SRAS curve is considered to be unstable.
b) increases in aggregate demand will not be able to influence output for very long.
c) the aggregate demand curve will not be able to shift very far when there is an increase in spending.
d) output can deviate from its natural level for a long time.

30. Which of the following statements is correct?

a) Wages are assumed to be completely flexible in both the short run and the long run.
b) The natural level of output is produced when the unemployment rate is equal to zero.
c) Ceteris paribus, an increase in the amount of capital in the economy would cause the LRAS curve to shift to the right.
d) A change in the expected price level causes a movement along the SRAS curve.

REVIEW QUESTIONS: APPENDIX

31. The aggregate labor supply curve:

a) is drawn assuming the expected price level is held constant.
b) is drawn so that the expected real wage rises as the nominal wage rises.
c) is the horizontal sum of the individual labor supply curves.
d) all of the above.

ANSWER KEY

Exercises

1. nominal, expected
2. price level, productivity of labor
3. natural level of employment, natural output level
4. natural level of employment, quantity of available resources, capital stock, level of technology, and market organization
5. infrastructure
6. sticky
7. explicit contract
8. expected, actual
9. Cyclical, fall
10. expected, expected, actual
11. shift left
12. The short run is the period of time during which markets are still adjusting to a macroeconomic shock, while the long run is a period of time long enough for all wages and prices to adjust to a shock.
13. The aggregate labor supply curve shows the quantity of labor workers are willing to supply at various levels of the real wage rate. The aggregate labor demand curve shows the quantity of labor firms want to employ at various wage rates.
14. The short-run aggregate supply curve shows the aggregate quantity of output firms are willing and able to produce at each price level.
15. The long-run aggregate supply curve is vertical at the natural level of output. It indicates the level of output the economy will produce over the long run with a given amount of the factors of production.
16. b. An increase in the price level will cause a movement up the SRAS curve in the short run. Quantity of real GNP supplied will increase from \$5 trillion to \$6.75 trillion. A decrease in the price of raw materials will result in lower production costs and the SRAS curve will shift to the right.
    c. The LRAS curve is a vertical line at RGNP = \$6 trillion. 105.
17. b. A decrease in the average level of wages will result in lower production costs, and the SRAS curve will shift to the right. A decrease in the average level of taxes will increase the incentives to invest, causing the SRAS curve to shift right. An increase in the expected price level causes workers to demand higher wages which in turn results in higher production costs, causing the SRAS curve to shift left.

Review Questions

1. d) is the correct answer. Labor depends on the nominal wage, the expected price level, and the expected real wage(the nominal wage divided by the expected price level).

2. a) is the correct answer. A change in the nominal wage moves us along a single labor supply function. All of the other answers cause shifts in the labor supply function.

3. c) is the correct answer. As the firm hires more workers, with the amount capital fixed, the marginal productivity of labor falls, so that an additional worker is worth less and less to the firm. Therefore along the labor demand function,

in order for the firm to hire more units of labor, the wage must fall.

4. b) is the correct answer. An increase in labor productivity means that, at a given nominal wage, an extra unit of labor will be worth more to the firm, so the firm will want to hire more labor at that wage.

5. a) is the correct answer. A rise in the expected price level causes the labor supply function to shift to the left. At any nominal wage workers are willing to offer less labor, since they anticipate that their real wage will be lower. This causes an increase in the equilibrium wage and a fall in the equilibrium quantity.

6. b) is the correct answer. When the labor market is in long run equilibrium, unemployment is at its natural level, but it is not as low as it can possibly be. In the short run, it is possible for income to increase beyond its natural level and therefore unemployment can be below its natural level.

7. d) is the correct answer. The increase in the price level causes the current real wage to fall so that firms demand more labor. This causes a temporary increase in employment or the equilibrium quantity of labor.

8. c) is the correct answer. An improvement in technology means that the labor force can produce more with a given capital stock. It is possible to sustain a higher level of output without experiencing inflation.

9. c) is the correct answer. The new immigrants increase the size of the U.S. goods' market, enabling U.S. firms to produce and sell more.

10. d) is the correct answer. The natural level of output is the maximum level of output that can be sustained over an extended period without causing inflation. It is possible for output to be greater than the natural level, but inflation will occur.

11. a) is the correct answer. The Soviet Union is considered to be a relatively <u>low</u> income country, <u>despite</u> its vast natural resources.

12. c) is the correct answer. Many of the predictions of natural resource depletion have been based on technological rather economic grounds. As the supply of a resource begins to get tight, its price rises. This creates an incentive for people to economize on the use of the resource and it also causes it to be worthwhile to search for substitutes.

13. d) is the correct answer. The short run in macroeconomics is the time over which markets are adjusting to "shocks" or disturbances to macroeconomic equilibrium.

14. a) is the correct answer. Whether inputs are fixed or variable is a subject of <u>micro</u>economics, not macroeconomics. In long run macroeconomic equilibrium, all prices and wages have fully adjusted.

15. d) is the correct answer. The labor market is in equilibrium when the expected price equals the actual price, because under these circumstances labor is receiving exactly the wage it expects and has no desire to adjust further.

16. a) is the correct answer. The increase in aggregate demand will cause an increase in the price level above what workers had expected. Since most workers are supplying their labor under contracts of at least a year, they will not be able to increase their wages in the short run, so they will experience a decline in their real wages.

17. b) is the correct answer. The SRAS curve relates the level of output to the price level in the short run. Each SRAS curve is drawn for a particular level of price expectations.

18. c) is the correct answer. If actual and expected prices are not equal, both the aggregate demand-aggregate supply and labor markets are out of <u>long run</u> equilibrium. If the labor market is out of equilibrium, then the aggregate demand-aggregate supply market is also out of <u>long run</u> equilibrium.

19. b) is the correct answer. During a period of recession, there is an increase in cyclical unemployment. However, not all unemployment is cyclical, and this is why unemployment persists even when the economy is not in recession.

20. a) is the correct answer. An increase in nominal wages causes an increase in costs to firms at each price level, so they offer less at each price level.

21. d) is the correct answer. A change in the price level causes a movement along the SRAS curve, not a shift in it.

22. b) is the correct answer. An increase in the marginal productivity of labor results in each unit of labor being able to produce more, so the natural level of output increases at the natural level of employment.

23. a) is the correct answer. An increase in the price level can restore equilibrium, by causing the real wage to fall. However, this will change the position of both the labor demand and labor supply functions.

24. c) is the correct answer. If wages adjusted immediately to changes in the price level, wages would move in the same proportion as the change in prices and the level of employment would stay at its natural level. Since wages are sticky and do not move in this manner, the employment of labor adjusts. So if the price level falls, causing the real wage to rise, the quantity demanded for labor falls and employment falls.

25. d) is the correct answer. The LRAS function illustrates the relationship between output and the price level for which all wages and prices have adjusted to any change in aggregate demand.

26. a) is the correct answer. The vertical LRAS suggests that in the long run, output is independent of the level of aggregate demand. This is because at every point on the LRAS all adjustments to aggregate demand disturbances have occurred and the economy has adjusted to the natural levels of output and employment.

27. d) is the correct answer. The price level can vary along the LRAS function, but it has no effect on output.

28. a) is the correct answer. If the SRAS is not stable, then the nominal wage can change rapidly in response to changes in the economy. In this case, adjustment to long run equilibrium will take place quickly and output will not deviate from its natural level for very long.

29. d) is the correct answer. If adjustment is sluggish, the SRAS function will not shift very far or very quickly, so it is possible for income to be above or below its natural level for extended periods of time.

30. c) is the correct answer. An increase in the amount of capital makes a given amount of labor more productive. This increases the natural level of output and LRAS shifts to the right.

31. d) is the correct answer. See the discussion in the appendix.

CHAPTER 25
THE LONG-RUN MODEL: THE ECONOMY WITH FLEXIBLE PRICES

OVERVIEW

In this chapter we combine the theories of aggregate demand and aggregate supply to develop the long-run model of the macroeconomy. In the first part of the chapter we examine the characteristics of long-run equilibrium and the factors that determine the natural level of output and the price level in the long run. The analysis then turns to the question of what determines the growth of output in the economy. The chapter concludes by considering the relationship between changes in the money supply, aggregate demand, and the price level.

Because the long-run aggregate supply (LRAS) curve is vertical (see the previous chapter), the long-run equilibrium level of output is independent of the level of aggregate demand. By the same token, for a given LRAS curve, the price level is determined solely by aggregate demand. The long-run supply curve only affects the price level when there is a change in the economy's productive capacity, i.e., the LRAS curve shifts. Available data support the model's predictions in this regard. In particular, there appears to be no relationship between changes in nominal GNP (a proxy for aggregate demand) and real GNP. However, there is a distinct positive relationship between nominal GNP and the price level.

We have noted previously that the position of the LRAS curve is determined by the amount of available resources, capital stock, the level of technology, the size of the labor force, and market organization. Ceteris paribus, a change in any one of these factors causes the LRAS curve to shift. Throughout the twentieth century, the LRAS curve has shifted to the right, i.e., the economy has experienced economic growth. However, as the data in the text indicate, the rate of growth has varied considerably over time.

Factors contributing to economic growth are generally grouped into three categories: growth in capital stock, growth in labor supply, and growth in factor productivity. Of these three factors, a decline in the growth of productivity has been identified as the prime cause of the decline in output growth that occurred in the 1970s. The decline in productivity growth has in turn been attributed to, among other things, a decline in spending on research and development, low capacity utilization rates, large energy price increases, a decline in government investment in core infrastructure, and a shift in the composition of U.S. output away from manufacturing and towards services.

With regard to government policies designed to encourage economic growth, the greatest potential for success lies with investment in infrastructure and developing policies that encourage savings and investment. The latter is the result of the fact that, ultimately, investment is constrained by the level of savings in the economy. As such, policies that increase the after-tax return on investment will encourage growth of the capital stock. In addition, policies that stimulate savings should ultimately lead to increased investment. One of the tradeoffs incurred when the economy grows is that there is usually a change in the composition of output. As such, some workers are displaced and different geographical regions can experience growth and decline simultaneously.

With respect to changes in the price level, the growth rate of the price level depends on the growth of aggregate demand relative to the growth of output. The growth of output is limited since it depends on real factors and how rapidly they can change. The growth of spending, on the other hand, depends not only on the growth of the different components of spending (consumption, investment, government purchases, and net exports) but on the growth of the money supply as well. Given the type of money used in the United States there is no real limit on the potential growth of the money supply.

According to the Quantity Theory of Money, over the long run, changes in the price level are positively related to changes in the money supply. Available data indicate that, in fact, that the growth rate of the price level is significantly related to the growth rate of the money supply.

KEY GRAPHS AND TERMS

Graphs

The key model in this chapter is the long-run model of the macroeconomy, which focuses on the interaction between the aggregate demand curve and the LRAS curve (see Figure 1). Recall that the LRAS curve intersects the horizontal axis at the natural level of output, which is determined by the current levels of resources, capital, and technology; the natural level of employment; and market organization. Ceteris paribus, a change in any one of these factors causes the natural level of output to change and the LRAS curve to shift.

We have already noted that the natural level of output is independent of the level of aggregate demand. Over the long run, changes in aggregate demand only affect the price level. This fact is easily seen in Figure 1. This assumes, however, that the determinants of the natural level of output are held constant. As Figure 3 illustrates, if one of these factors should change, and the position of the aggregate demand is held constant, the price level will change. It is important to keep this distinction in mind as you study the long-run model. Finally, as Figure 7 illustrates, simultaneous increases in long-run aggregate supply and aggregate demand, i.e, a rightward shift of each curve, will have an indeterminate effect on the price level if the relative magnitude of the shifts is unknown.

Terms

FACTORS CONTRIBUTING TO GROWTH
FACTOR PRODUCTIVITY
GROWTH RATE
CORE INFRASTRUCTURE
QUANTITY THEORY OF MONEY
GNP DEFLATOR

EXERCISES

1. The long-run equilibrium output level is determined solely by the level of aggregate supply while the price level is determined by aggregate demand.

2. List the three categories of factors that contribute to economic growth. growth in capital stock, growth in the labor supply, and growth in factor productivity

3. Of the three categories you listed in question 2, a decline in which one is considered to be the main cause of the decline in growth that occurred in the 1973-1981 time period? growth in factor productivity

4. List three factors that are believed to have contributed to the decline in factor productivity growth experienced in the 1970s. decline in spending on research and development, volume changes, large energy price increases, a decline in investment in core infrastructure, and a shift the composition of U.S. production

5. In the aggregate, all investment spending must be financed by savings.

6. Total savings in the economy is calculated as domestic savings plus the government budget surplus minus net exports.

7. In order for the price level to rise over a long period of time, it must be the case that aggregate demand is growing faster than aggregate supply.

8. The one determinant of aggregate demand that can grow without limit is the money supply.

9. According to the quantity Theory of Money, over significant periods of time the inflation rate is closely related to the growth rate of the money supply.

10. According to the available data, short-run changes in the money supply and the price level are largely unrelated while long-run money supply growth and inflation are highly positively related.

11. Assume that disposable income = \$1.2 billion, consumption spending = \$1 billion, government purchases = \$0.2 billion, government transfers = \$0.1 billion, taxes = \$0.25 billion, imports = \$0.25 billion, and exports = \$0.2 billion. Based on this information, calculate gross investment. \$ 0.1.

12. The aggregate labor market and the long-run model of the macroeconomy are illustrated in the figures below. As the figures indicate, the economy is currently in long-run equilibrium at output level RGNPn and price level PL1. The labor market is in equilibrium at employment level Ln and wage level W1. Assume that there is an autonomous decrease in net exports. In the figures, illustrate the long-run effects of this change on the short-run and long-run equilibrium levels of the wage rate, employment level, output, and the price level. What will happen to the equilibrium level of the real wage?

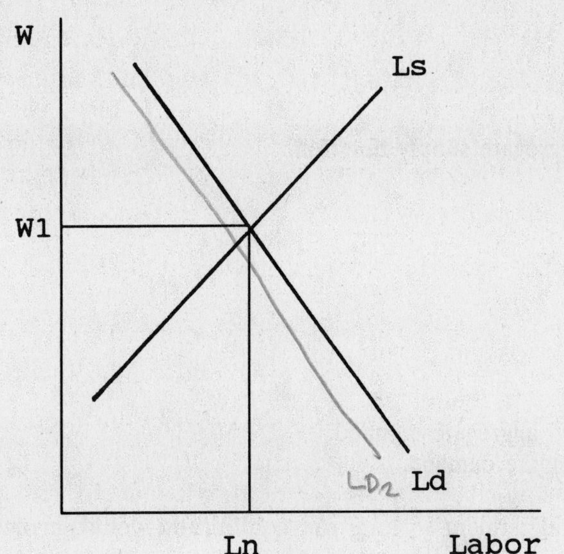

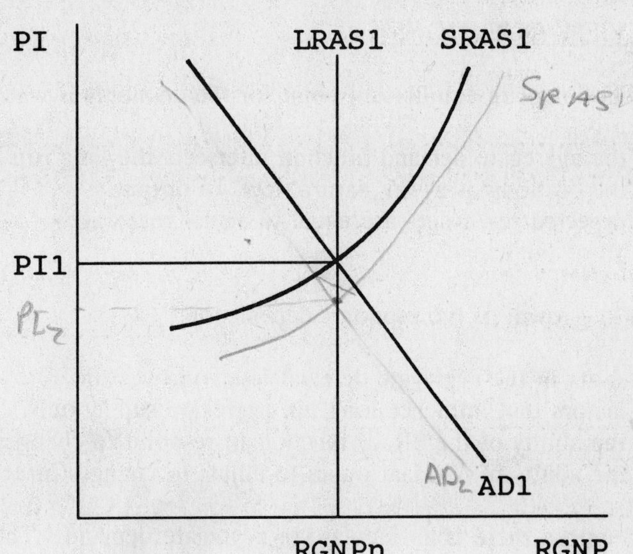

13. In the figure below, illustrate the effect of a simultaneous increase in the capital stock and government spending. What will happen to the long-run equilibrium level of output and the price level?

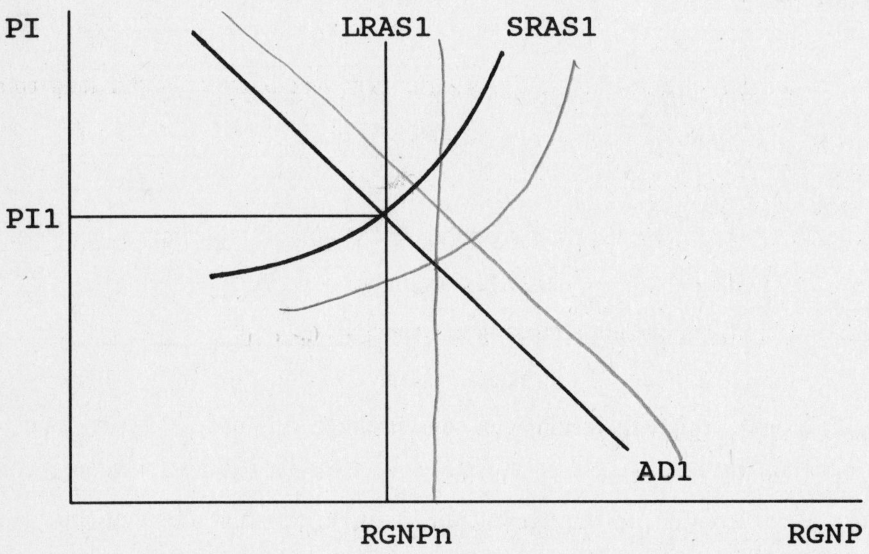

REVIEW QUESTIONS

1. The long run equilibrium point for the economy is where:

a) the aggregate demand function intersects the long run aggregate supply function.
b) the economy is at the natural level of output.
c) expected real wages are equal to actual real wages.
d) all of the above.

2. The growth of the economy depends on:

a) shifts in the aggregate demand function over time.
b) factors that influence long run aggregate supply only.
c) the ability of the SRAS function to respond to changes in aggregate demand.
d) the ability of nominal wages to adjust to changes in aggregate demand.

3. Suppose there is an increase in aggregate demand. The adjustment to long run equilibrium would involve which of the following:

a) an immediate increase in expected prices.
b) a shift to the left in the SRAS function as workers change their price expectations.
c) a change in the natural level of output.
d) a decrease in the actual price level as workers change their price expectations.

4. Referring to the previous question, what will be the long run effects of the increase in aggregate demand?

a) a rise in output and a rise in the price level.
b) a rise in output and a fall in the price level.
c) an increase in the natural level of output.
d) an increase in the price level only.

5. Suppose technology improves. If aggregate demand remains constant, what will happen to the long run equilibrium price level and output.

a) The price level will fall, and the level of output will rise.
b) The price level will rise, and the level of output will rise.
c) The price level will fall, and the level of output will fall.
d) The price level will rise, and the level of output will fall.

6. Assume that there is a decrease in the amount of capital. This will have the effect of:

a) shifting the LRAS curve to the left.
b) increasing the level of full employment output.
c) shifting the PPF out.
d) all of the above.

7. The shape of the LRAS curve suggests that, in the long run:

a) prices cannot vary.
b) inflation is zero.
c) the equilibrium level of Real GNP is not affected by the level of aggregate demand.
d) the price level is determined only by the level of aggregate demand.

8. Over this century, real GNP:

a) has shown a general downward trend.
b) has shown a strong upward trend.
c) has risen and fallen, but stayed fairly stable around a single natural level of output.
d) has grown more rapidly than nominal GNP.

9. All of the following are factors generally thought to contribute to economic growth <u>except</u>:

a) Growth in aggregate demand
b) Growth in the capital stock
c) Growth in the labor supply
d) Increases in factor productivity

10. U.S. economic growth slowed during the 1970s. A major factor causing this decline was:

a) a slowing in the growth of aggregate demand.
b) falling factor productivity.
c) the instability of aggregate demand.
d) the growth of trade with Japan.

11. Why did productivity growth decline in the 1970s?

a) A decline in spending on research and development.
b) A reduction in efficiencies from large scale production.
c) The rising trade balance deficit.
d) a) and b), but not c).

12. How did the rise in the price of oil during the 1970s contribute to the decline in productivity?

a) By causing the U.S. to become more dependent on foreign oil.
b) By reducing the incentive to engage in technological innovation.
c) Because costs of production fell, delaying the search for substitutes.
d) a) and c), but not b).

13. Which of the following is not true?

a) The term "core infrastructure" refers to government capital.
b) Government expenditure to improve the transportation system increases productivity.
c) The U.S. spends about the same percent of its GNP on nondefense research and development as Japan and West Germany.
d) Productivity growth was somewhat higher in the 1980s than in the 1970s.

14. Double taxation:

a) increases the incentive to invest in capital equipment.
b) refers to individuals who make a certain level of income paying both federal and state income taxes.
c) refers to individuals paying both state and local sales taxes.
d) refers to corporate profits being taxed by both corporate and personal income taxes.

15. In the equation, $I = S + (T - G) - NX$:

a) NX = exports - imports
b) NX represents the amount of foreign savings flowing into the U.S.
c) $(T - G)$ equals the government deficit.
d) all of the above.

16. The equation $I = S + (T - G) - NX$ suggests that if there is an increase in the budget deficit with the level of saving assumed constant:

a) there must be an increase in foreign savings flowing into the U.S. in order to maintain the level of investment.
b) the level of investment must increase in order to pay for the increase in the deficit.
c) the level of exports must rise and the level of imports must fall in order to maintain the level of investment.
d) b) and c), but not a).

17. People are concerned about the low savings rate in the U.S. because:

a) savings prevents consumption from creating inflation.
b) savings is morally preferable to consumption because it represents a sacrifice.
c) investment must be financed by savings.
d) overconsumption has caused the aggregate demand function to shift to the left.

18. The difference between the U.S. and Japanese savings rates:

a) is due in large part to differences in accounting methods.
b) is due in part to the way in which depreciation is handled in the two national accounts.
c) is even larger than the popular press has suggested.
d) a) and b), but not c).

19. If LRAS and aggregate demand shift to the right by the same amount over time:

a) natural output will increase, but the price level will remain constant.
b) both the price level and the level of output will increase.
c) neither the price level nor the level of output will change.
d) both the price level and the level of output will decrease.

20. Suppose over time aggregate demand grows more rapidly than aggregate supply. Which of the following will occur?

a) natural output will increase, but the price level will remain constant.
b) both the price level and the natural level of output will increase.
c) neither the price level nor the natural level of output will change.
d) both the price level and the natural level of output will decrease.

21. Suppose over time aggregate demand grows less rapidly than aggregate supply. Which of the following will occur?

a) natural output will increase, and the price level will fall.
b) both the price level and the natural level of output will increase.
c) neither the price level nor the natural level of output will change.
d) both the price level and the level of output will decrease.

22. During most of this century:

a) the natural level of output has exhibited a downward trend.
b) the price level has exhibited an upward trend.
c) the price level has exhibited a downward trend.
d) the natural level of output has exhibited no trend at all, but the price level has been falling.

23. Which of the following determinants of aggregate demand can grow without limits?

a) consumption
b) investment
c) exports
d) the money supply

24. The quantity theory of money suggests:

a) there is a weak relationship between money supply growth and the price level.
b) increases in government purchases drive the money supply up.
c) money supply growth is the cause of sustained inflation.
d) the quantity of money depends on the rate at which aggregate demand is growing relative to the rate at which aggregate supply is growing

25. Short-run changes in the price level:

a) are generally unrelated to changes in the money supply.
b) are usually due to increases in the natural level of output.
c) are frequently due to decreases in aggregate demand.
d) are unrelated to changes in the SRAS function.

26. Which of the following is not true:

a) The U.S. aggregate supply curve has shifted to the right almost continuously during this century.
b) Today most economists are skeptical that the government can contribute to the growth of real GNP, outside of its contribution to the infrastructure.
c) Reducing crowding in airports is an example of infrastructure improvement that could contribute to economic growth.
d) As the level of income falls, investment spending generally rises.

27. Suppose 1984 real GNP = $3500 billion and 1989 real GNP = $4160 billion. What is the approximate growth rate over that five year period?

a) 3%
b) 3.5%
c) 4%
d) 4.5%

28. Suppose 1985 real GNP = $3000 billion. Suppose the rate of growth for the five years between 1985 and 1990 was 25%. What is 1990 real GNP?

a) $3750 billion
b) $4000 billion
c) $4250 billion
d) $4500 billion

29. Assume that the aggregate demand (AD) curve and short-run aggregate supply (SRAS) curve intersect such that Real GNP is greater than the natural level of Real GNP. Over the long run:

a) wages and the price level will decrease.
b) aggregate expenditures will increase due to a decrease in the price level.
c) the expected price level will be adjusted upward and real GNP will decrease.
d) the LRAS curve will shift right to reestablish long-run equilibrium.

30. Which of the following is not true?

a) Higher income countries usually have more suicides than lower income countries.
b) In an efficient, growing economy the breakdown of human relationships due to changes may make people unhappy.
c) Under our present monetary system, there is a limit imposed on the money supply by the gold held by the U.S. government.
d) The taxes paid on investment in the U.S. are among the highest in the world.

Chapter 25, The Long-Run Model: The Economy with Flexible Prices

ANSWER KEY

Exercises

1. aggregate supply, aggregate demand
2. 1) growth in the capital stock, 2) growth in the labor supply, and 3) growth in factor productivity
3. A decline in factor productivity growth
4. Possible answers include a decline in spending on research and development, volume changes, large energy price increases, a decline in investment in core infrastructure, and a shift the composition of U.S. production from manufacturing to services.
5. savings
6. domestic savings, government's budget surplus, net exports
7. aggregate demand, aggregate supply
8. money supply
9. quantity theory of money, money supply
10. unrelated, positively related
11. $0.1 billion
12. In the short run, the decline in net exports will cause the AD curve to shift to the left, putting downward pressure on the price level and level of output. This will cause the labor demand curve to shift left and the nominal wage rate and employment level will fall. The resulting unemployment in the labor market will put downward pressure on the nominal wage. Over the long run, as a result of the lower price level, workers will be willing to accept a lower nominal wage--the labor supply curve will shift right. This will cause the SRAS curve to shift right. Since none of the real factors affecting aggregate supply have changed, the LRAS curve will remain at LRAS1. After all long-run adjustments have occurred, the price level and nominal wage will be lower, but the level of employment, output level, and the real wage will return to their former levels.
13. The increase in the capital stock will cause the AD, SRAS, and LRAS curves to shift right. The increase in government spending will cause the AD curve to shift right as well. As such, the long-run equilibrium output level will increase. However, the equilibrium price level will increase, decrease, or stay the same depending on the relative magnitudes of the shifts in aggregate demand and aggregate supply.

Review Questions

1. d) is the correct answer. Long run equilibrium for the economy occurs where the aggregate demand function intersects the long run aggregate supply function. At this point, expected real wages equal actual real wages, since expected prices equal actual prices. This can occur only at the natural level of output.

2. b) is the correct answer. Growth occurs in the long run. In the long run, the location of the LRAS function determines the natural level of output, where the economy will be in long run equilibrium. The location of the aggregate demand function along the LRAS has no effect on the level of income in the long run. Therefore, only factors that influence LRAS influence growth.

3. b) is the correct answer. An increase in aggregate demand causes the level of income to rise above the natural level and prices to rise above their expected level. When workers have a chance to adjust their contracts, they will demand a higher nominal wage. This increases costs of production for firms and shifts the SRAS function to the right.

4. d) is the correct answer. A change in the aggregate demand function has no long run effects on <u>real</u> variables. The level of output and the real wage stay the same. The only long run change is a higher price level.

5. a) is the correct answer. An improvement in technology will cause the LRAS function to shift to the right. If aggregate demand remains the same, the economy will move along this single aggregate demand function. Therefore, output will rise and the price level will fall.

6. a) is the correct answer. A decrease in the amount of capital available to the economy will reduce the natural level of output, since each unit of labor now has less capital with which to work and is therefore less productive. This will decrease the natural level of output and shift the production possibilities frontier in toward the origin.

7. c) is the correct answer. The vertical LRAS function suggests that in the long run the economy will be at the natural level of output, no matter where the aggregate demand function is located.

8. b) is the correct answer. From 1900 to 1989, GNP has shown a strong upward trend. This does not mean that it has been continually growing. There have been periods of negative and low growth, but today real GNP is much larger than it was at the beginning of this century.

9. a) is the correct answer. Changes in aggregate demand have no effect on the natural level of output in the long run.

10. b) is the correct answer. Most economists agree that declining factor productivity was the main cause of the fall in economic growth during the 1970s.

11. d) is the correct answer. It is argued that there was a decline in research and development spending which caused the "advance of knowledge" to slow down. There were also "volume" changes, which means that the economy was operating below the natural level of income and was not able to take advantage of some efficiencies of large scale production.

12. b) is the correct answer. Many times firms must use more energy to employ new technology. If the price of energy rises, the incentive to seek new technology falls.

13. c) is the correct answer. The U.S. spends about 1.9% of GNP, while West Germany spends about 2.6% and Japan spends about 2.7%.

14. d) is the correct answer. Corporate profits are taxed once by the corporate income tax and then again, when they are distributed as dividends, by the personal income tax.

15. d) is the correct answer. NX represents the difference between exports and imports and it is also equal to the foreign savings flowing into our economy in the form of purchases of government and corporate bonds, bank deposits, etc. (T - G) represents the government deficit.

16. a) is the correct answer. In order to maintain the level of investment, there must be an increase in the level of foreign savings flowing into the U.S. This is the same thing as saying that the trade balance must become more negative.

17. c) is the correct answer. Saving is important to economic growth because it is used, along with foreign saving, to finance investment.

18. d) is the correct answer. Much of the apparent difference in the savings rates of the two countries is due to different accounting methods used with respect to depreciation and government capital formation. Nevertheless, the Japanese savings rate is higher than the U.S. savings rate.

19. a) is the correct answer. This example is shown in Figure 6 in the text. Output will increase, but the price level will stay constant.

20. b) is the correct answer. This example is shown in Figure 7(a) in the text.

21. a) is the correct answer. This example is shown in Figure 7(b) in the text.

22. b) is the correct answer. This suggests that aggregate demand has been growing faster than aggregate supply.

23. d) is the correct answer. In our monetary system, the money supply is not tied to any physical standard, so in theory it could grow without limit. This is not to suggest that we move to a gold standard, but to point out that long run inflation is frequently due to excess growth of the money supply.

24. c) is the correct answer. Since all of the determinants of aggregate demand except the money supply are limited in some way, if there is

inflation over a long period of time, it is usually caused by excessive money growth.

25. a) is the correct answer. Changes in the price level are usually unrelated to changes in the money supply in the short run. But there is a strong relationship in the long run.

26. d) is the correct answer. As the level of income rises, capacity utilization increases, increasing the incentive for firms to undertake investment projects.

27. b) is the correct answer. The calculation is found by: (4160 / 3500) taken to the 0.2 power.

28. a) is the correct answer. If the growth rate over the five years was 25%, 1990 real GNP is found by: 1.25 x $3000 billion = $3750 billion.

29. c) is the correct answer. When workers get a chance to adjust, they will demand higher wages. This shifts the SRAS function back to the left, causing an increase in the price level and a decrease in output. This process continues until the economy returns to the natural level of income.

30. c) is the correct answer. There is no such limit on the money supply in the U.S. The Federal Reserve could, in theory, increase the money supply to infinity.

CHAPTER 26
THE SHORT-RUN MODEL: THE ECONOMY WITH WAGE AND PRICE RIGIDITIES

OVERVIEW

In this chapter we consider the short-run model of the macroeconomy. In particular, we examine the factors that can cause the level of output to deviate from its natural level. In addition, we address the question of what influences the length of time it takes the economy to re-adjust to long-run equilibrium. The potential for effective stabilization policy is also briefly considered.

In the short-run, an increase (decrease) in aggregate demand will cause the price level and the level of aggregate output to increase (decrease). However, as we saw in the previous chapter, the long-run effects of changes in aggregate demand are confined to changes in the price level. Over time, the economy adjusts to changes in aggregate demand through changes in price expectations and corresponding shifts of the SRAS curve. An important question that arises, however, is how much time such adjustment processes require. The answer to this question depends, in large part, on how peoples' price expectations are formed.

According to the theory of adaptive expectations, price expectations are backward looking, i.e., they are formed on the basis of past movements in the price level. There are, however, problems with this view. First, if people behave in this manner, they will tend to make errors in the same direction, e.g., underestimate price increases, for long periods of time. Second, this theory suggests that people do not behave rationally with respect to the acquisition and use of information since they do not use any information on current changes that may affect the price level in the future.

The theory of rational expectations has been proposed as an alternative to the theory of adaptive expectations. For expectations to be formed rationally, individuals must make efficient use of available information, they must use a reasonable model to process the information, and forecast errors must be random. Note that rational expectations theory does not imply that individuals' expectations will always be correct. Rather, the result is that expectations are adjusted more quickly to new information. As such, the adjustment process is shorter with the assumption of rational expectations than with the assumption of adaptive expectations.

The available evidence is mixed with regard to which theory of expectations formation is more accurate. Although prices appear to adjust fairly rapidly over time, output adjustments generally occur more slowly. There are a number of possible explanations for the latter observation including the possibility that expectations are not formed rationally, firms make capital-investment mistakes that prolong output effects, and prices and wages change only slowly after expectations have adjusted. The existence of explicit and implicit contracts that set wages at fixed levels for periods generally ranging from one to three years suggests that wage stickiness is the most likely cause of slow output adjustments.

Shifts of both the AD curve and the SRAS curve will cause the equilibrium price level and output level to change in the short run. In the case of aggregate demand, a number of factors can cause the AD curve to shift (see Chapter 23). The extent to which the AD curve actually shifts depends on the size of the change in the autonomous variable causing the shift and whether the change is considered to be temporary or permanent. Large permanent changes have a larger effect on aggregate demand, ceteris paribus.

The position of the SRAS curve depends on production costs, and in particular, labor and energy costs. As we have previously noted, a change in price expectations will cause wages, and therefore the SRAS curve to shift. In a similar manner, a change in energy prices, e.g., the price of oil, increases or decreases production costs and causes a shift of the SRAS curve. In the case where the change in the price of energy is permanent, the position of the LRAS curve will be altered as well.

Data from the period 1961-1989 indicate that aggregate demand fluctuated over the period, increasing rapidly in the 1960s, and then rising and falling in the 1970s and 1980s. In addition, the SRAS curve remained fairly stable during the 1960s, due in large part to stable price expectations. However, the oil price and food price shocks in the 1970s caused the SRAS curve to shift left. This was especially true with respect to the oil price shocks in 1974 and 1979. The instability of the SRAS curve in the 1970s led to the development of supply-side policies that are designed to alter the position of both the short-run and long-run aggregate supply curves. In the early 1980s, efforts by the Federal Reserve to reduce the inflation rate, combined with a net reduction in energy prices, led to increased stability of the SRAS curve and the economy enjoyed its longest post war period of expansion.

The fact that changes in aggregate demand and short-run aggregate supply cause the level of output to deviate from its natural level has raised the question of whether government can implement policies that will stabilize the economy and offset shocks to the economy. Stabilization policies are grouped into two categories--fiscal policy, which uses changes in government spending and taxes to alter aggregate demand, and monetary policy, which affects aggregate demand through changes in the money supply and interest rates. It would seem that so long as short-run aggregate supply is relatively stable, policymakers should be able to manipulate aggregate demand in such a way as to maintain the natural level of output. However, as we shall see in subsequent chapters, there are a number of reasons why this may not be the case.

KEY GRAPHS AND TERMS

Graphs

The key model in this chapter is the short-run macroeconomic model, which combines the SRAS curve, LRAS curve, and the AD curve to analyze short-run deviations from the natural level of output. A number of points are worth noting regarding this model. First, referring to Figure 1 in the text, note that the economy is in long-run equilibrium at point A, i.e., where AD0, SRAS0 and LRAS intersect (the LRAS curve is the vertical line at RGNPn). Because, in the long-run, all expectations are fulfilled, price level PI0 is also the expected price level.

When long-run equilibrium is disturbed by a change in either aggregate demand or short-run aggregate supply, the level of output increases or decreases and the price level deviates from its expected level. So long as price expectations remain constant, the economy will not return to long-run equilibrium. However, as price expectations are revised--upward when the actual price level rises and downward when the actual price level falls--labor supply, wage rates, and short-run aggregate supply will change as well. Unless the initial change affects long-run aggregate supply--as is the case with a permanent change in energy prices, the economy will eventually return to the natural levels of output and employment.

Terms

ADAPTIVE EXPECTATIONS
RATIONAL EXPECTATIONS
RESTRICTIVE MONETARY POLICY
OUTPUT PERSISTENCE
REAL GNP
MULTIPLIER EFFECT
SUPPLY-SIDE POLICIES
THRESHOLD EFFECT
SUPPLY SHOCK
ECONOMIC INSTABILITY

EXERCISES

1. The basic feature of adaptive expectations is that they are Backward looking.

2. List the three criteria that must be met for expectations to be formed rationally. Forcasters must make efficient use of available information, use a reasonable model to process information, and forecast errors must be random, i.e. they are not systematically pos or neg.

3. The adjustment to long-run equilibrium is shorter with the assumption of rational expectations than with the assumption of adaptive expectations.

4. Prolonged periods of output above or below the natural level of output are referred to as Output Persistence.

5. Many economists believe that __Wage__ __stickyness__ is the major factor generating output persistence.

6. According to the __Multiplier__ __effect__, a change in autonomous spending causes subsequent changes in consumption spending, resulting in a larger overall change in aggregate demand.

7. A permanent decrease in energy prices will cause the SRAS and LRAS curves to __Shift__ __right__.

8. Regarding stabilization policy, __fiscal__ policy consists of the use of changes in government spending and taxes to alter __aggregate__ __demand__, while __monetary__ policy consists of changes in the money supply to alter __aggregate__ __demand__.

9. a. Using the data from the table, and assuming that RGNPn = \$5.5 trillion, plot the corresponding AD, SRAS, and LRAS curves in the figure below.

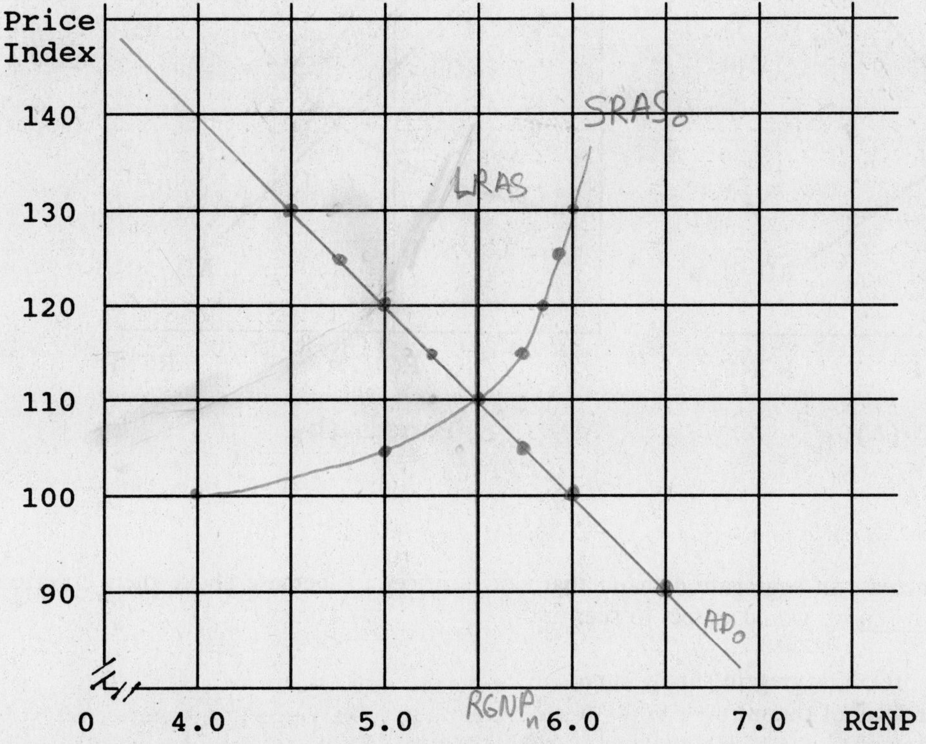

PI	AD	SRAS
90	\$6.5	---
100	6.0	\$4.0
105	5.75	5.0
110	5.5	5.5
115	5.25	5.7
120	5.0	5.8
125	4.75	5.9
130	4.5	6.0

b. Is the economy currently in long-run equilibrium? __Yes__

c. What is the long-equilibrium level of output? __5.5__

d. What is the long-run equilibrium price level? __\$110__

e. What is the current expected price level? __\$110__

f. Assume that in an effort to balance the budget, the federal government reduces government spending while leaving taxes unchanged. Illustrate the effect of this action in the figure. What happens to the equilibrium level of RGNP in the short run? Shift left ____________ What happens to the actual price level in the short run? Decrease ____________

g. Explain how the economy will adjust to the change in government policy over the long run if there are no further changes in aggregate demand. price expectations will fall, and the SRAS curve will shift right until long-run equilibrium is re-established at RGNPn

10. In the following two figures, determine the short-run equilibrium and label it RGNPsr. Is the economy in long-run macroeconomic equilibrium? NO ________ In each case, if your answer is no, describe the economy's short-run situation, and explain how the economy will re-adjust to long-run equilibrium.

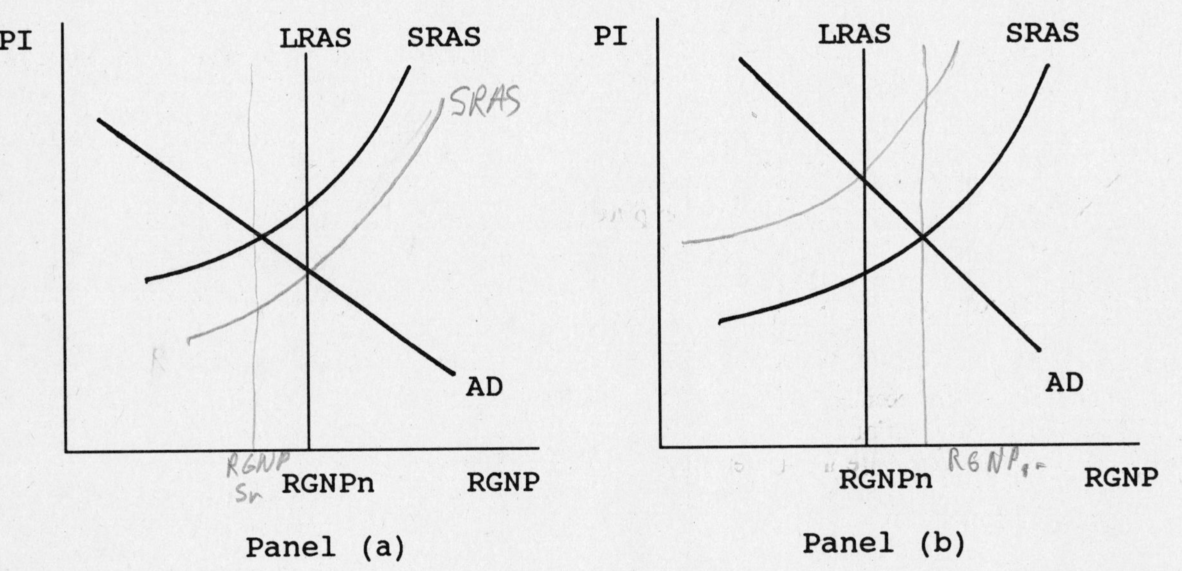

REVIEW QUESTIONS

1. Assume that there is an increase in aggregate demand that causes prices to increase above their expected level. As a result, in the short-run we would expect to see:

a) a shift to the left of the short-run aggregate supply curve.
b) a continued increase in the level of output.
c) a reduction in the rate of interest.
d) a reduction in government purchases to restore equilibrium.

2. Referring to the previous question, why is the intersection of the new aggregate demand and the original short run aggregate supply function not a long run equilibrium point.

a) The labor market is not in equilibrium.
b) Actual and expected prices are not equal.
c) Output is greater than its natural level.
d) all of the above.

3. Referring to the adjustment process discussed in the previous two questions, why does the SRAS function shift from the initial short run equilibrium point?

a) Because firms change their price expectations.
b) Because firms restrict supply in an effort to take advantage of the situation and charge a monopoly price.
c) Because firms' costs of production rise when wages rise.
d) all of the above.

4. As workers adjust to a situation in which the economy is above the natural level of output, why is there an increase in the price level?

a) Simply due to the upward trend in long run prices in the U.S.
b) Firms raise their prices to cover higher costs of production.
c) Prices always must rise to move the economy from a short run equilibrium to a long run equilibrium.
d) Because aggregate demand falls as the economy adjusts to the change in price expectations.

5. Suppose the economy is well below the natural level of output and there is an increase in aggregate demand. Which of the following will occur?

a) Prices will rise quickly.
b) Price expectations will be adjusted quickly upward.
c) There will be relatively little upward pressure on prices.
d) a) and b), but not c).

6. Adaptive expectations:

a) are "forward looking."
b) use information from the recent past.
c) use all the available information.
d) neither consistently overestimate nor underestimate price level changes.

7. Adaptive expectations:

a) are always behind changes in the actual value of the variable being predicted.
b) consistently underestimate inflation when the inflation rate is rising.
c) consistently overestimate inflation when the inflation rate is falling.
d) all of the above.

8. Suppose the economy is in long run equilibrium and there is an increase in aggregate demand. If expectations are formed adaptively:

a) the expected price level will adjust quickly.
b) wages will adjust rapidly to move the economy to its long run equilibrium.
c) it is possible for actual output to deviate from the natural level of output for a long time.
d) a) and b), but not c).

9. All of the following are criteria for rational expectations <u>except</u>:

a) There are no errors in the forecast.
b) Information is collected until marginal benefit equals marginal cost.
c) A reasonable economic model is used to process the information.
d) Errors in the forecast are not systematic.

10. Why do many economists find rational expectations appealing?

a) Because it is human nature to make mistakes.
b) Because people apply the Fundamental Principle of Economics to expectations.
c) Because it is irrational to attempt to use information from the future, since the future is unknown.
d) Because people can form expectations without relying on economic models, which the average person does not understand.

11. Which of the following is an implication of rational expectations?

a) Changes in government purchases to increase output above its natural level will be quite effective.
b) Changes in the money supply to increase output above its natural level will be quite effective as long as the public expects the change.
c) Only unanticipated changes in aggregate demand will affect output.
d) a) and b), but not c).

12. The answer to the above question suggest that if prices and wages are flexible and expectations are formed rationally:

a) government policies aimed at influencing income will be very effective in the short run.
b) the LRAS function will be horizontal.
c) the SRAS function will be vertical
d) increases in aggregate demand will influence output, but not prices.

13. Output persistence refers to:

a) prolonged periods of output above or below the natural output level.
b) persistent errors made in the formation of rational expectations.
c) the tendency of output to continually rise over time.
d) the tendency of output to remain the same over time.

14. How do long term contracts account for output persistence?

a) Workers are usually contracted to produce a certain, fixed amount of output in their fixed contracts.
b) Long term contracts make the SRAS very responsive to changes in price expectations.
c) Long term contracts prevent the aggregate demand function from shifting.
d) Wages adjust according to the contract rather than to market conditions.

15. Which of the following does not shift the aggregate demand function?

a) An increase in consumption spending.
b) An increase in price expectations.
c) An increase in the money supply.
d) A decrease in investment.

16. Suppose investment spending rises by $100 billion. Assume the marginal propensity to consume is 0.8. What will the change in spending be in the second round of the multiplier process?

a) $180 billion
b) $156 billion
c) $80 billion
d) $64 billion

17. In the previous example what will the change in income be when the multiplier process continues to its ultimate effect?

a) $164 billion
b) $288 billion
c) $400 billion
d) $500 billion

18. Suppose the economy experiences a "supply shock" due to a rise in oil prices. In the short run the price level will ______________ and the level of output will ______________.

a) increase; increase
b) increase; decrease
c) decrease; increase
d) decrease; decrease

19. Why was the short run aggregate supply function stable during the sixties?

a) Inflationary expectations were not changing.
b) Spending for the Great Society programs.
c) Because the economy was in a recession for most of the decade.
d) All of the above.

20. The basic notion of stabilization policy is to:

a) shift the SRAS function in response to supply shocks.
b) shift the SRAS function when output deviates from its natural level.
c) shift the aggregate demand function when output deviates from its natural level.
d) stabilize the output level, but allow inflation to occur.

21. All of the following are ways the government can alter aggregate demand <u>except</u>:

a) By purchasing more goods and services.
b) By increasing taxes.
c) By increasing price expectations.
d) By decreasing the money supply.

22. Suppose the economy is operating well below the natural level of output. What should the government do in terms of its stabilization policy tools?

a) reduce the money supply.
b) reduce taxes.
c) reduce transfer payments.
d) reduce the level of government purchases.

23. If the stabilization policy from the previous question works as expected, which of the following will occur?

a) Output will increase a little and prices will increase substantially.
b) Output will increase substantially and prices will increase a little.
c) Output will increase substantially and prices will decrease.
d) Output will decrease a little and prices will decrease substantially.

24. Suppose the economy is operating above the natural level of output. In terms of its stabilization policy tools, what should the government do?

a) Increase the money supply.
b) Reduce taxes.
c) Increase government transfer payments.
d) Reduce government purchases.

25. In the previous question what will happen in the aggregate demand-aggregate supply diagram?

a) AD will shift to the left.
b) AD will shift to the right.
c) LRAS will shift to the right.
d) LRAS will shift to the left.

26. The oil price shocks of the 1970s:

a) caused an increase in aggregate demand.
b) resulted in output being pushed above its natural level.
c) caused a fall in the natural level of output.
d) resulted in falling agricultural prices.

27. The oil price shocks of the 1970s confronted U.S. policymakers with a dilemma because:

a) policies to raise output would result in further rises in the price level.
b) policies to raise output would result in deflation.
c) policies to lower inflation would result in a further fall in output.
d) a) and c), but not b).

28. Which of following is not true:

a) The shape of the SRAS depends primarily on the amount that marginal costs rise as output is increased.
b) The SRAS curve becomes quite steep to the right of the natural level of output.
c) The rationally expected price level is the price level the model predicts.
d) The LRAS function shifts to the left as price expectations rise.

29. Which of the following is not true:

a) Ronald Reagan advocated supply-side policies during his 1980 campaign.
b) Most economists now believe that supply-side policies will alter the SRAS function over a short period of time.
c) The "threshold" is the level of inflation at which it becomes too costly to ignore.
d) The stability of the SRAS function in the 1960s led some economists to think that the economy could be controlled indefinitely by regulating aggregate demand.

REVIEW QUESTIONS: APPENDIX

30. Which of the following is a reason for price inflexibility?

a) Long-term customer relationships
b) The costliness of obtaining price information
c) The cost of changing prices
d) All of the above

31. Which of the following is not true?

a) Most customer market prices behave as if the market supply curve were relatively steep.
b) Firms tend to respond to demand changes slowly.
c) Firms tend to respond quickly and strongly to cost changes.
d) Firms do not respond strongly to demand changes unless they are expected to be long lasting.

32. It is difficult to distinguish between demand-pull and cost-push inflation because:

a) an increase in aggregate demand eventually causes the SRAS curve to shift left.
b) increasing real GNP leads to increasing production costs.
c) workers demand higher wages when output is above the natural level of output.
d) all of the above.

ANSWER KEY

Exercises

1. backward looking
2. 1) forecasters must make efficient use of available information, 2) forecasters must use a reasonable model to process the information, and 3) forecast errors must be random, i.e., they are not systematically positive or negative
3. shorter
4. output persistence
5. wage stickiness
6. multiplier effect
7. shift right
8. fiscal, aggregate demand, monetary, aggregate demand
9. b. Yes.
   c. $5.5 trillion.
   d. 110.
   e. 110.
   f. If the federal government reduces government spending while leaving taxes unchanged, the AD curve will shift to the left of its current position, causing RGNP to fall below RGNPn in the short run. The actual price level will fall as well (PI < PIe).
   g. Over time, price expectations will fall, wages will fall, and the SRAS curve will shift right until long-run equilibrium is re-established at RGNPn.
10. In panel (a) the economy is not in long-run equilibrium since RGNPsr is less than RGNPn. The actual price level is lower than the expected price level (which corresponds to the intersect of the LRAS and SRAS curves). Over time, price expectations will be lowered, wages will fall, and the SRAS curve will shift right until long-run equilibrium is re-established. In panel (b) the economy is not in long-run equilibrium since RGNPsr is greater than RGNPn. The actual price level is higher than the expected price level. Over time, price expectations will rise, wages will rise, and the SRAS curve will shift left until long-run equilibrium is re-established.

Review Questions

1. a) is the correct answer. An increase in aggregate demand that results is a short run equilibrium above the natural level of output causes prices to rise above their expected level. This will result in workers demanding higher wages when they are able to adjust to the change in expected prices. The higher wages shifts the SRAS to the left.

2. d) is the correct answer. For all of the reasons listed in a) through c), the economy has not yet adjusted to the change in aggregate demand.

Therefore, the intersection of the aggregate demand function and the original SRAS function is not a long run equilibrium point.

3. c) is the correct answer. When the economy is above the natural level of output, prices are greater than expected by workers. When workers adjust their expectations, they demand a higher wage. The higher wage increases the firms' costs of production and this is reflected in a shift to the left in the SRAS function.

4. b) is the correct answer. When output is above its natural level, prices are greater than workers expected. When workers demand higher wages it causes an increase in costs for firms, who raise their prices to cover the higher costs.

5. c) is the correct answer. Since the economy is below the natural level of output, there is excess capacity. Thus, output can be expanded without creating much upward pressure on resource prices, including wages. Labor is not in a good bargaining position to ask for higher wages, because unemployment exists.

6. b) is the correct answer. Adaptive expectations use information from the recent past to predict the future. All available information is not used. It is possible when expectations are formed in this way for people to make systematic errors and consistently overestimate or underestimate price level changes.

7. d) is the correct answer. Many economists are skeptical of adaptive expectations because it results in the systematic errors described in answers a), b), and c). If an individual is forming expectations adaptively, it is possible to underestimate or overestimate inflation for years without ever catching on to the systematic nature of the errors being made.

8. c) is the correct answer. If expectations adjust adaptively, then the SRAS function will shift upward relatively slowly, since expectations lag behind reality. Thus, it may take output a long period of time to move back its natural level.

9. a) is the correct answer. It is certainly possible for expectations formed rationally to be wrong, so errors are possible. But errors are not systematically wrong. That is, the expectations which are formed do not consistently overestimate or underestimate variables.

10. b) is the correct answer. Rational expectations are appealing to economists because people use all the available information up to the point where the cost of obtaining additional information is equal to the benefit of obtaining information. This is the Fundamental Premise of Economics.

11. c) is the correct answer. If the change in aggregate demand is fully anticipated, workers will demand an increase in wages before the actual shift in AD occurs. Thus, price and real wage expectations increase immediately with the shift in the AD function and there is no change in output from its natural level.

12. c) is the correct answer. If prices and wages are flexible and expectations are formed rationally, then any anticipated shift in the AD function will result in an immediate adjustment in expected prices and wages upward by the vertical shift in the AD function. Under these circumstances, the SRAS is vertical.

13. a) is the correct answer. Output is measured by the percentage deviation of actual output from its natural level.

14. d) is the correct answer. If wages cannot adjust, even when price expectations change due to long term contracts, the SRAS function will shift very slowly and output can deviate from its natural level for long periods of time.

15. b) is the correct answer. An increase in price expectations shifts the SRAS function, not the aggregate demand function.

16. d) is the correct answer. The increase in investment spending causes $100 billion x 0.8 = $80 billion of spending in the first round of the multiplier process. In the second round the change in spending is $80 billion x 0.8 = $64 billion.

17. d) is the correct answer. In this case we apply the multiplier formula to the initial change in expenditure to get:

\$100 billion x 1 / (1 - .8) = \$100 billion x 5 = \$500 billion.

18. b) is the correct answer. A supply shock will cause a shift to the left in the SRAS function(and the LRAS function as well if the change is not temporary). This causes the price level to rise and the level of output to fall.

19. a) is the correct answer. The position of the SRAS function depends on expectations about prices and real wages. Since inflation had been quite low for a number of years, people were not concerned about it and did not adjust their expectations very rapidly to changes in the economy.

20. c) is the correct answer. The stabilization policy tools currently available all influence the aggregate demand function directly.

21. c) is the correct answer. Changes in price expectations influence the short run aggregate supply function, not the aggregate demand function. The government also does not directly control price expectations, which may change as a result of something the government does.

22. b) is the correct answer. The government should reduce taxes. This has the effect of increasing disposable income and consumption.

23. b) is the correct answer. If the economy is operating well below the natural level of output, the SRAS curve is relatively flat. This is due to the excess capacity in the economy. An increase in aggregate demand along a relatively flat SRAS curve will cause output to increase a relatively large amount and prices to increase a relatively small amount.

24. d) is the correct answer. A reduction in government purchases reduces aggregate demand and lowers output toward its natural level.

25. a) is the correct answer. A decrease in government purchases reduces aggregate demand.

26. c) is the correct answer. The U.S. natural level of output fell because part of the U.S. capital stock could no longer be used profitably.

27. d) is the correct answer. If the level of output is increased by increasing aggregate demand, then prices would rise even more. If aggregate demand is reduced to lower the level of prices, output would suffer further declines.

28. d) is the correct answer. The SRAS function shifts to the left(or up) as price expectations increase.

29. b) is the correct answer. Most economists believe that supply side policies will take several years to influence the aggregate supply functions.

30. d) is the correct answer. It is costly to change price due to the information requirements, just as it is costly for the consumer to search for the lowest price. These effects tend to make prices stay the same. Long-term customer relationships exist to reduce the informational costs of price changing and searching.

31. a) is the correct answer. b), c), and d) are all correct statements. The fact that b) is correct makes a) incorrect. See the discussion in the appendix.

32. d) is the correct answer. See the discussion in the appendix.

CHAPTER 27
MONEY: WHAT IT IS AND WHY PEOPLE HOLD IT

OVERVIEW

In this chapter we begin to explore the role of money in the macroeconomy. In the first part of the chapter we define money, and identify the various functions it serves. We then develop the theory of money demand, and analyze the sources and effects of changes in the demand for money. In particular, we focus on the relationship between changes in money demand and the level of aggregate demand.

Without money, the exchange of goods and services could only be completed through the process of barter, i.e., direct trade. A barter economy has several drawbacks--it necessitates double coincidence of wants, there can be no large scale production, and it is necessary to establish exchange rates for every pair of goods and services traded. Money overcomes these problems by serving as a medium of exchange that allows for indirect trade. Various commodities have for a very long time served as media of exchange in different economies.

In addition to serving as a medium of exchange, money also serves as a standard of value that is used to measure the value of the economy's different outputs. Hence, it is unnecessary to establish exchange rates between each pair of tradable items. Finally, money serves as a store of value, i.e., it can be held as an asset over time.

There are four different measures of the money supply in the U.S. economy. These measures--M1, M2, M3, and L--differ according to the degree of liquidity associated with the assets in each measure, with M1 being most liquid and L being least liquid. For example, M2 includes all of the components of M1 (currency, checkable deposits, and traveler's checks) plus savings deposits, small time deposits, money market deposit accounts, and money market mutual funds. The definitions of the money supply evolve over time as a result of the effects of financial innovation.

According to the transactions theory of money demand, the amount of money people want to hold depends primarily on the amount of transactions they wish to engage in. The level of transactions in turn depends primarily on the level of nominal income. An increase in either the price level or real income will cause money demand to increase. In the case of an increase in the price level, it takes more money to finance the same level of real purchases. In the case of an increase in real income, people simply want to buy more goods and services. The quantity of money demanded is also influenced by the rate of return--the interest rate--on financial assets. The interest rate on financial assets is the opportunity cost of holding money. Finally, money demand is influenced by the rate of return on real assets, which is measured by the expected inflation rate.

Changes in money demand affect aggregate demand through a budget constraint effect and an interest rate effect. (The budget constraint states that the sum of the supplies of goods and services, financial assets, and money must equal the sum of the demands for those variables). For example, as a result of the budget constraint, to the extent that people decide to hold more money, they must reduce their demand for goods and services and financial assets. Thus, an increase in money demand causes a decrease in aggregate demand, ceteris paribus. In addition, an increase in money demand (money supply held constant) causes the interest rate to rise in order to restore equilibrium in the money market. The increase in the interest rate causes investment spending to decline, causing aggregate demand to fall further. As this example suggests, increases in money demand that are not matched by an increase in the money supply could have serious negative effects on the macroeconomy.

The fact that financial innovation can have a significant effect on the magnitude of different measures of the money supply poses special problems for policymakers. In particular, care must be taken to accurately measure the money supply and money demand so that policymakers are able to correctly interpret changes in these variables.

KEY GRAPHS AND TERMS

Graphs

The key graph introduced in this chapter is the model of the money market. The money demand curve is constructed to illustrate the relationship between the quantity of money demanded and the nominal interest rate (see Figure 3 in the text). The money demand curve is downward sloping, reflecting the fact that as the interest rate falls, so does the opportunity cost of holding money. Changes in the other factors that influence money demand--the price level, RGNP, and the expected inflation rate (which measures the rate of return on real assets)--cause the money demand curve to shift.

The money market is linked to the output market through the effects of changes in money demand on the level of aggregate demand, as well as changes in RGNP on the level of money demand. Note that the direction of causality--from the money market to the output market or vice versa--depends on which variable changes first. For example an autonomous change in money demand will result in shifts of the aggregate demand curve. However, a change in aggregate demand that causes RGNP to change will result in a shift of the money demand curve.

Terms

BARTER ECONOMY
MEDIUM OF EXCHANGE
DOUBLE COINCIDENCE OF WANTS
COMMODITY MONEY
BULLION
STANDARD OF VALUE
STORE OF VALUE
LIQUIDITY
M1
DEMAND DEPOSITS
M2
MONEY MARKET DEPOSIT ACCOUNT
MONEY MARKET MUTUAL FUND
M3
L
MONETARY AGGREGATE
FINANCIAL INNOVATION
TRANSACTIONS THEORY OF MONEY DEMAND
REAL MONEY BALANCES
CAPITAL GAIN
CAPITAL LOSS
BUDGET-CONSTRAINT EFFECT
INTEREST-RATE EFFECT
MUTUAL FUND

EXERCISES

1. One of the problems with barter is that both parties to a trade have to want what the other has to trade. This problem is called the Double Coincidence of wants.

2. Goods that are desired both for consumption and as a medium of exchange are referred to as Commodity money.

3. The three primary functions served by money are Standard of Value, Store of value, and medium of exchange.

4. liquidity refers to the ease with which an asset can be converted into a medium of exchange.

5. The primary components of the M1 measure of the money supply include currency, checkable deposits, and Traveler's checks.

6. Demand deposits, NOW accounts, and credit union share draft accounts are all examples of Checkable deposits.

7. The development of NOW accounts and money market mutual funds are examples of Financial innovation.

8. A change in the nominal interest rate causes a movement along the money demand curve, while a change in RGNP, the price level, or the expected inflation rate causes the money demand curve to shift.

9. Ceteris paribus, a decrease in the availability of credit cards would cause the money demand curve to shift right.

10. In general, financial asset prices and interest rates are inversely related.

11. A decrease in money demand will cause the interest rate to decrease, aggregate demand to increase, and the price of financial assets to increase.

Use the figure below to answer questions 12 - 15.

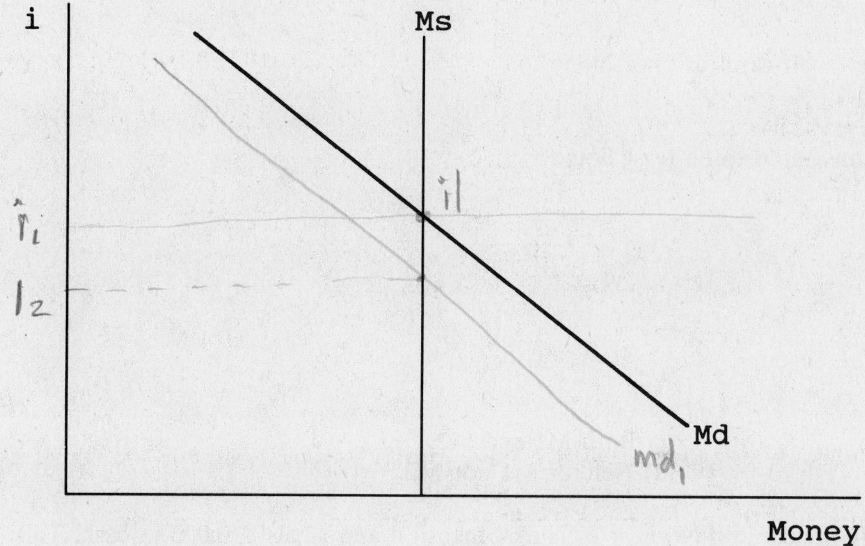

12. Locate the current equilibrium interest rate and label it i1.

13. Assume an autonomous decrease in money demand. Show the effect of this change in the figure.

14. As a result of the change described in question 13, what has happened to the equilibrium interest rate? It has decreased. Label the new equilibrium interest rate i2.

15. Assuming that the economy was initially in long-run equilibrium, explain how the changes in the money market identified in questions 13 and 14 will affect the short-run model of aggregate demand and aggregate supply. In particular, describe any shifts that will occur, and the short-run effects on the price level and the level of real GNP. The decline in the equilibrium interest rate will cause the aggregate demand curve to shift to the right, which will in turn cause the short-run values of the price level and RGNP to increase.

REVIEW QUESTIONS

1. All of the following are considered to be functions of money except:

a) store of value.
b) standard of value.
c) medium of exchange.
d) measure of power.

2. Which of the following is not a determinant of the demand for money?

a) the price level
b) real GNP
c) money supply
d) the nominal interest rate

3. Ceteris paribus, a significant increase in the availability of credit cards would be expected to cause:

a) money demand to decrease.
b) money demand to increase.
c) no effect on money demand since credit cards are not money.
d) none of the above.

4. Which of the following assets is considered to be least liquid?

a) demand deposits
b) small denomination time deposits
c) money market deposit accounts
d) Treasury Bills

5. Demand deposits are included in:

a) M1.
b) M2.
c) Both M1 and M2.
d) Neither M1 nor M2.

6. Assume that Machine Gun Freddy breaks into Norbert Nobanks' mansion and steals $10,000 in cash. This would cause a change in:

a) M1.
b) M2.
c) both M1 and M2.
d) neither M1 nor M2.

7. If banks were to develop a new type of checkable deposit account that replaced highly illiquid long-term certificates of deposit, this would have an effect on:

a) M1.
b) M2.
c) both M1 and M2.
d) neither M1 nor M2.

Check

8. Ceteris paribus, an increase in the demand for bonds causes the:

a) price of bonds to increase and the interest rate earned on bonds to decrease.
b) price of bonds to decrease and the interest rate earned on bonds to increase.
c) price of bonds and the interest rate earned on bonds to decrease.
d) price of bonds and the interest rate earned on bonds to increase.

9. Which of the following statements is correct?

a) financial innovation tends to reduce the demand for money as it is conventionally measured.
b) As a result of financial innovation, money demand grew substantially in the 1970s.
c) financial innovation usually makes it more difficult for people to switch between more liquid and less liquid forms of money.
d) The different measures of the money supply are unaffected by financial innovation.

10. If the Federal Reserve doubled the amount of currency in circulation, this would affect:

a) M1.
b) M2.
c) both M1 and M2.
d) neither M1 nor M2.

11. The transactions demand for money depends primarily upon:

a) the interest rate.
b) income and the price level.
c) the interest rate and the price level.
d) the supply of money.

12. Which of the following causes the money demand curve to shift left?

a) An increase in the nominal interest rate.
b) A decline in the expected inflation rate.
c) A decrease in the price level.
d) An increase in real GNP.

13. Assuming that the money market is initially in equilibrium, an increase in the supply of money will cause:

a) real GNP to decline.
b) money demand to decrease.
c) the price level to decrease.
d) the interest rate to decrease.

14. Which of the following statements is correct?

a) The M2 measure of the money supply is smaller than M1.
b) Credit cards are the largest component of M1.
c) Liquidity refers to the ease with which an asset can be converted into a medium of exchange.
d) The most liquid measure of the money supply is M3.

15. Ceteris paribus, in the short run, a decrease in aggregate demand will cause the interest rate to:

a) increase.
b) stay the same.
c) decrease.
d) cannot be determined.

16. Ceteris paribus, an increase in real GNP will cause money demand to:

a) increase and the interest rate to rise.
b) increase and the interest rate to fall.
c) decrease and the interest rate to rise.
d) decrease and the interest rate to fall.

17. Assuming that the money market is initially in equilibrium, a simultaneous increase in the demand for money and the money supply will cause the interest rate to:

a) increase.
b) decrease.
c) stay the same.
d) cannot be determined.

18. Money that is made of something of value, such as gold or silver, is referred to as:

a) fiat money.
b) bank money.
c) commodity money.
d) paper money.

19. In the short run, an increase in aggregate demand will cause:
a) money demand to increase.
b) unemployment to increase.
c) the real money supply to increase.
d) the interest rate to fall.

20. Which of the following functions does money serve when it used to measure the prices of different goods and services?

a) store of value.
b) standard of value.
c) medium of exchange.
d) measure of power.

21. Which of the following statements regarding a barter economy is not correct?

a) A barter economy faced with the double coincidence of wants problem.
b) A barter economy is unable to support large scale production.
c) A barter economy entails substantial information requirements.
d) A barter economy is more efficient than an economy that utilizes a medium of exchange.

22. According to the aggregate budget constraint, an increase in the demand for goods and services will cause:

a) an increase in the demand for money.
b) a decrease in the demand for financial assets.
c) a decrease in the supply of goods and services.
d) an increase in the interest rate.

23. Ceteris paribus, an autonomous decrease in the demand for money will cause the level of real GNP:

a) and the price level to increase.
b) and the price level to decrease.
c) to increase and the price level to decrease.
d) to decrease and the price level to increase.

24. All of the following are considered to be important (necessary) physical characteristics of a medium exchange except:

a) there must be an unlimited supply of the medium of exchange so that it doesn't run out.
b) the medium of exchange must be durable.
c) the medium of exchange must be portable.
d) the medium of exchange must have an easily ascertained value.

25. Which of the following statements is not correct?

a) The price of a financial asset and the interest rate are inversely related.
b) The interest rate is the opportunity cost of holding money.
c) Ceteris paribus, a change in autonomous money demand causes real GNP to change in the same direction.
d) Ceteris paribus, in the short run a change in the money supply causes the interest rate to change in the opposite direction.

26. The largest component of the M1 measure of the money supply is:

a) currency held by the public.
b) travelers checks.
c) checkable deposits.
d) savings accounts.

27. Ceteris paribus, as the interest rate sensitivity of money demand gets ______________, a change in the money supply will cause the interest rate to change by a ______________ amount.

a) smaller; smaller
b) larger; larger
c) smaller; larger
d) none of the above

ANSWER KEY

Exercises

1. double coincidence of wants
2. commodity money
3. medium of exchange, standard of value, store of value
4. Liquidity
5. currency (held by households and businesses), checkable deposits, traveler's checks
6. checkable deposits
7. financial innovation
8. movement along, shift
9. shift right
10. inversely
11. decrease, increase, increase
12. the equilibrium interest rate is found by drawing a horizontal line through the point at which the money demand and money supply curve intersect and reading the corresponding value of the vertical axis.
13. The money demand curve will shift left.
14. The decrease in money demand, money supply held constant, will cause the interest rate to fall. The new interest rate is found in the manner described in the answer for question 12.
15. The decline in the equilibrium interest rate will cause the aggregate demand curve to shift to the right, which will in turn cause the short-run values of the price level and RGNP to increase.

Review Questions

1. d) is the correct answer. a), b) and c) are the three generally agreed upon functions of money in an economic sense.

2. c) is the correct answer. As in all other cases involving supply and demand, supply does not determine demand, but interacts with demand to determine the equilibrium price and quantity.

3. a) is the correct answer. Credit cars serve as a substitute for money in making transactions. As such, an increase in the availability of this substitute will decrease the demand for money.

4. d) is the correct answer. a), b) and c) are components of either M1 or M2. Treasury Bills are a component of M3, which is less liquid than M1 or M2.

5. c) is the correct answer. Since demand deposits are part of M1 and M1 is part of M2, demand deposits are included in both M1 and M2.

6. d) is the correct answer. Freddy's actions simply amount to a reallocation of currency with out any change in the amount of currency held by the public. Hence, M1, and therefore M2, has not changed.

7. c) is the correct answer. Highly illiquid long-term CDs are part of M3. As such, replacing them with a checkable deposit would increase M1 and therefore M2. (What was formerly in M3 would now be in M1.)

8. b) is the correct answer. The price of bonds and the interest rate are inversely related. Moreover, a decrease in demand causes the price of a good to fall. As such, the price of bonds will fall when demand falls, implying an increase in the interest rate.

9. a) is the correct answer. According to the empirical evidence, money demand declined substantially in the late 1970s and 1980s; a period of time during which substantial financial innovation occurred.

10. c) is the correct answer. Currency is part of M1 and therefore part of M2 as well.

11. b) is the correct answer. Transactions demand refers to the amount of money required to facilitate transactions of goods and services over a period of tie. Transactions are, in turn, a function of the level of income and the prices of goods being purchased.

12. c) is the correct answer. A decrease in the price level reduces the amount of money needed to purchase a fixed quantity of goods and services, i.e., transactions demand is lower. A change in the nominal interest rate causes a movement along the money demand curve. b) and d) cause the money demand curve to shift right.

13. d) is the correct answer. When the supply of money increases, it creates an excess supply of money at the prevailing equilibrium interest rate, which in turn puts downward pressure on the interest rate to re-equilibrate the money market.

14. c) is the correct answer. This is the definition of liquidity. By the definitions of M1, M2, M3, and money, all of the other statements are incorrect.

15. c) is the correct answer. A decrease in aggregate demand will cause real GNP and the price level to both decrease in the short rn. This will cause money demand to decrease, and the interest rate will then fall to re-equilibrate the money market.

16. a) is the correct answer. This is just the reverse of question 15.

17. d) is the correct answer. An increase in money demand and money supply means that both curves are shifting right. By itself, an increase in money demand would cause the interest rate to fall, while an increase in money supply causes the interest rate to rise. Without knowing the relative magnitudes of the two shifts, we can't say anything about the overall effect on the interest rate.

18. c) is the correct answer. This is the definition of commodity money.

19. a) is the correct answer. The increase in aggregate demand causes an increase in real GNP

and the price level, which causes the transactions demand for money to increase.

20. b) is the correct answer. This is the definition of the standard of value.

21. d) is not a correct statement for the reasons listed in a), b), and c) (which are correct statements).

22. b) is the correct answer. If an individual wants to purchase more goods and services with a fixed amount of assets (the budget constraint) they must forego some amount of money (which puts downward pressure on interest rates) and/or financial assets.

23. a) is the correct answer. According to the budget constraint, a decrease in money demand implies an increase in the demand for financial assets and goods and services. As such, aggregate demand increases, causing real GNP and the price level to increase.

24. a) is the correct answer. For a medium of exchange to maintain its value there must be a limited supply. This is just a simple application of supply and demand analysis.

25. c) is not a correct statement. Because of the budget constraint, a change in money demand causes aggregate demand, and therefore real GNP, to change in the opposite direction.

26. c is the correct answer. See Figure 2 in the text which illustrates the breakdown of M1 into its various components.

27. c is the correct answer. Note that as the interest sensitivity of money demand becomes smaller, the money demand curve becomes steeper. As such, for a given change in the money supply, the interest rate must change by a greater amount to re-equilibrate the money market.

CHAPTER 28
THE BANKING SYSTEM, THE FEDERAL RESERVE, AND MONETARY POLICY

OVERVIEW

In this chapter we examine the banking system in the United States and, in particular, the process of money creation. The functions of the Federal Reserve System are considered, and the tools the Fed can use to alter the money supply are discussed at some length. We also consider how monetary policy can be used to influence the level of macroeconomic activity.

Banks are one example of what are referred to as financial intermediaries--firms that bring savers and borrowers together. Other examples of financial intermediaries include savings and loan associations, mutual funds, and insurance companies. By accepting deposits from savers and making loans to borrowers, financial intermediaries perform a number of valuable services for the economy. The benefits of financial intermediation include the encouragement of increased savings, reduced risks associated with lending (and hence an increase in the amount of lending that occurs), and a reduction in the costs of borrowing and lending.

The Federal Reserve System (Fed) oversees the operation of the nation's banking system, and is responsible for controlling the money supply. The primary policy tools used by the Fed to control the money supply include the required reserve ratio, the discount rate and open market operations.

Understanding how the Fed controls the money supply requires an understanding of how money is created. In this regard, it is important to recall the basic components of the money supply, in particular, currency and demand deposits. When a bank accepts a deposit, say in a checking account, it keeps part of the deposit in the form of reserves to cover withdrawals. The remainder of the deposit can be used to engage in profit-oriented activities such as making loans. When a bank makes a loan, to the extent that the proceeds of the loan find their way into another demand deposit account, money is created. Banks create money by making loans. Note that as a result of the loan, demand deposits can increase, thus increasing the money supply.

Because of fractional reserve banking, an initial increase in bank reserves can lead to a multiple expansion of the money supply. The maximum change possible is calculated as the product of the initial change in reserves and the inverse of the reserve ratio. However, the money supply may not (and usually does not) expand by this full amount as a result of currency holdings (part of a loan does not make its way into a demand deposit), the existence of nonmoney deposits, and the maintenance of reserves in excess of the required amount.

The Fed influences the lending practices of banks, and therefore the money supply, by manipulating the size of the monetary base, which consists of currency held by the public and bank reserves. The money supply is equal to the monetary base times the money multiplier. As such, actions that change the size of either the monetary base or the money multiplier will result in a change in the money supply.

The primary tool used by the Fed to alter the monetary base is open market operations (OMOs). OMOs consist of the buying and selling of bonds by the Fed to alter the amount of currency in the banking system. When the Fed buys bonds, the result is an increase in the monetary base, and hence an increase in the money supply (via the creation of new loans and the multiplier process). When the Fed sells bonds, the opposite effect occurs. The discount rate--the interest rate the Fed charges commercial banks for loans--is also used to alter the monetary base by influencing the amount of borrowing of excess reserves that banks engage in. For example, when the Fed increases the discount rate, banks reduce their borrowing of reserves from the fed and hence the money supply is reduced. The Fed can also change the required reserve ratio, and in so doing, alter the size of the money multiplier. Increases in the required reserve ratio cause the money supply to decrease while decreases in the ratio have the opposite effect.

The overall goals of monetary policy are to maintain a full employment, non-inflationary level of output and steady economic growth. However, the policies that are used to achieve these goals depend in large part on the degree of stability inherent in the economy, and views on the relative costs of inflation and unemployment. The model developed in the text, combined with the empirical evidence, suggest that the long-term goal of monetary policy should be price stability. However, this does not rule out the possibility of using monetary policy to achieve other short-term goals.

Changes in the money supply can affect output and the price level through a number of channels. In general, the effects of monetary policy work through changes in interest rates, or directly, to influence the level of aggregate demand. Expansive monetary policies--those that lead to an increase in the money supply--result in a lower interest rate which, in turn, encourages increased consumption and investment spending. Hence the aggregate demand curve shifts right. Monetary policies that lead to a decrease in the money supply have the opposite effect on aggregate demand.

KEY GRAPHS AND TERMS

Graphs

The key graph in this chapter is once again the graph of aggregate demand and aggregate supply. As illustrated in Figure 7 in the text, changes in the money supply cause the aggregate demand curve to shift. Assuming the economy is initially in long-run equilibrium, the shift in aggregate demand and the resulting change in the actual price level and real GNP set in motion the series of adjustments in price expectations and wage demands that eventually move the economy back to long-run equilibrium.

Although it is not graphed as such, another key concept developed in this chapter is the process of money creation. Be sure you understand how to work through the process illustrated in Figures 4 and 5, and that you understand the logic of the money multiplier process.

Terms

FINANCIAL INTERMEDIARY
INTERMEDIATION
BANK RUN
ELASTIC CURRENCY
BOARD OF GOVERNORS
RESERVE REQUIREMENT RATIO
RESERVES
DISCOUNT RATE
FEDERAL OPEN MARKET COMMITTEE
OPEN MARKET OPERATIONS
FRACTIONAL RESERVE BANKING
EXCESS RESERVES
MONETARY BASE
FEDERAL RESERVE NOTES
BOND DEALERS
FEDERAL FUNDS
FEDERAL FUNDS RATE
MONETARY POLICY TARGET

EXERCISES

1. Firms that collect funds by issuing claims against themselves and use the funds to purchase financial assets or make loans are called Financial Intermediary.

2. List the three benefits of financial intermediation that are discussed in the text. encourage increase savings, reduces the risk associated with lending, and reduces the cost of borrowing and lending

3. A widespread demand for the conversion of deposits into currency is called a Bank Run.

4. The minimum legal amount of deposits that a bank must hold in the form of reserves is determined by the Reserve requirement ratio.

5. The most important and frequently used tool of monetary policy is OPEN Market Operations

6. The practice of holding less than one dollar in reserves for every dollar of deposits is called FRACTIONAL Reserve Banking.

7. List three factors that reduce the amount by which the money expands when reserves are increased. currency holdings, the existence of nonmoney deposits, and the maintenance of Reserves in excess of required amount

8. The sum of currency in circulation and bank reserves is called the monetary Base.

9. The three major monetary policy tools available to the Fed include OPEN Market OPERATIONS, the Discount rate, and the Reserve requirement ratio.

10. If the Fed wants to increase the money supply using open market operations, it must go out and Buy bonds.

11. The interest rate charged on a loan made by one bank to another bank is called the Federal Fund rates.

12. A change in the reserve requirement ratio changes the money supply by affecting the size of the money multiplier.

13. In your own words, summarize the major goals of monetary policy discussed in the book. The goals are high employment, economic growth high enough to maintain high employment, stable price level, and stability of the Real GNP around trend growth.

14. The complete strategy of monetary policy consists of using policy tools to alter specific targets, in the effort to achieve specific policy goals.

15. An increase in the money supply causes the AD curve to shift right, while a decrease in the money supply causes the AD curve to shift Left.

16. Assume that Joey deposits $10,000 in cash in the Freemont State Bank in the form of a checking account.

a. In the spaces provided, indicate the amount of the change in the bank's total demand deposits and total reserves resulting from Joey's deposit. Change in demand deposits = 10,000. Change in total reserves = 10,000.

b. Assuming the reserve requirement ratio is 15 percent (0.15), by what amount could the Freemont State Bank increase its loans? 8,500.

c. Assuming that the bank loans out the full amount you calculated in part b, what is the resulting maximum possible increase in the money supply? 56,666 (Aprox).

$\frac{1}{.15}$

17. Assume that the Fed engages in open market operations that consist of selling $100 million of government bonds. Assume also that the reserve requirement ratio is 20 percent (0.20). As a result of this policy action what will happen to the monetary base? will decline by 100 million. What is the maximum possible change in the money supply attributable to this policy action? reduced by 500 mil.

18. Referring to the previous question, assume that Chris writes a check for $100,000 worth of the bonds being sold. As a result, what will happen to the total amount of reserves held by Chris' bank? Total reserve will fall by $100,000. By what amount will required reserves change? – $10,000

19. Use the following figure to illustrate the short-run and long-run effects of a decrease in the money supply on RGNP and the price level. Which curve is shifting at each stage in the adjustment process and why?

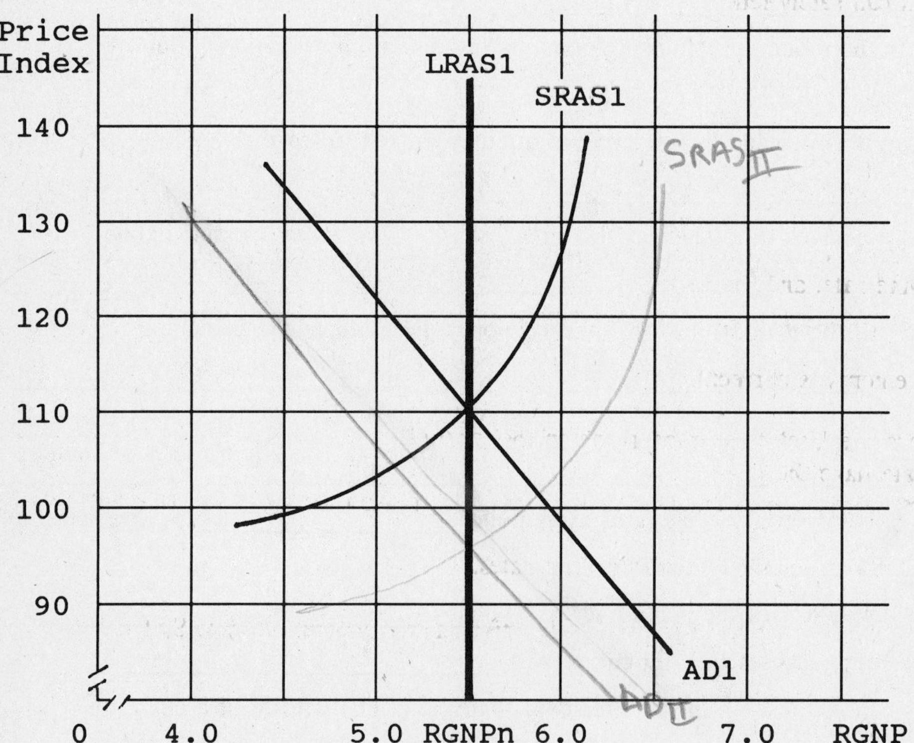

REVIEW QUESTIONS

1. Which of the following is not considered to be a beneficial service performed by financial intermediaries?

a) The costs of matching borrowers and lenders are reduced.
b) The risks of lending are reduced.
c) The possibility of loan defaults is eliminated.
d) Financial intermediaries encourage increased savings.

2. Since 1982, the primary target of the Fed's monetary policy has been:

a) the M3 measure of the money supply.
b) the inflation rate.
c) the general level of interest rates.
d) the unemployment rate.

3. Assume that a bank has $80,000 in demand deposits, total reserves of $60,000, and a reserve requirement ratio of .20 (20%),. This bank can safely lend:

a) $16,000.
b) $44,000.
c) $60,000.
d) $80,000.

4. The primary policy tools used by the Fed include the:

a) reserve requirement ratio, moral suasion, and the discount rate.
b) reserve requirement ratio, the discount rate, and the prime rate.
c) federal funds ratio, the prime rate, and the discount rate.
d) reserve requirement ratio, the discount rate, and open market operations.

5. Which of the following statements is correct?

a) Open market operations are the least often used monetary policy tool.
b) Changes in the discount rate have the most drastic effect on the money supply.
c) Monetary policy influences the money supply primarily by altering the amount of excess reserves held by banks.
d) Monetary policy affects the money supply, but not interest rates.

6. Which of the following is considered the most important function of the Federal Reserve System?

a) supervising member banks.
b) supplying the economy with paper currency.
c) controlling the money supply through monetary policy.
d) providing for the collection of checks.

7. If the economy is stuck in a recession, an appropriate policy for the Federal Reserve might be to:

a) increase the reserve requirement ratio.
b) reduce the amount of currency in circulation.
c) reduce excess reserves.
d) buy bonds.

8. The amount of reserves that a commercial bank is required to maintain is equal to:

a) the amount of its demand deposits.
b) the sum of its demand deposits and savings deposits.
c) its demand deposits multiplied by the reserve requirement ratio.
d) its reserves multiplied by the reserve requirement ratio.

9. If the Federal Reserve wants to decrease the money supply, which of the following is considered to be the least effective approach?

a) buy bonds.
b) raise the discount rate.
c) increase the reserve requirement ratio.
d) none of the above.

10. The Monetary Base consists of:

a) bank reserves and currency in circulation.
b) the Fed's gold reserves.
c) government bonds and Federal Reserve Notes outstanding.
d) M1 plus savings deposits.

11. A bank has $80,000 in demand deposits and total reserves of $60,000. Assuming the reserve requirement ratio (rr) is .10 (10%), if this bank lends out all of its excess reserves the money supply could expand by as much as:

a) $ 52,000.
b) $520,000.
c) $600,000.
d) $800,000.

12. All of the following are examples of financial intermediaries except:

a) a bank.
b) a credit union.
c) an insurance company.
d) a currency exchange.

13. Which of the following statements is not correct?

a) The Federal Reserve System was created in 1913 and began operations in 1914.
b) The Federal Reserve issues the paper currency used in the United States.
c) The Federal reserve system consists of a single bank located in New York city.
d) The Federal Reserve system is managed by a Board of Governors composed of seven individuals who are appointed by the president of the United States.

14. If the deposit multiplier is equal to 4, this means that the reserve requirement ratio is:

a) 10 percent.
b) 20 percent.
c) 25 percent.
d) 40 percent.

15. Assume that the Bozo State bank has $500,000 in demand deposits, total reserves of $150,000, and the reserve requirement ratio is 10 percent (.10). Assuming that some loans take the form of cash, if Bozo loans out all of its excess reserves, the money supply will expand by:

a) less than $1,000,000.
b) more than $1,000,000 but less than $1,500,000.
c) at least $1,500,000.
d) at least $4,500,000.

16. When the Fed pursues open market operations that consist of buying bonds, this has the effect of

a) increasing the money supply, increasing interest rates, and reducing the level of aggregate demand.
b) increasing the money supply, decreasing interest rates, and reducing the level of aggregate demand.
c) increasing the money supply, increasing interest rates, and increasing the level of aggregate demand.
d) increasing the money supply, decreasing interest rates, and increasing the level of aggregate demand.

17. Assuming that banks are currently holding excess reserves, the money supply might not expand by the maximum amount possible because:

a) banks may be unwilling to lend out all of their excess reserves.
b) some loans may be deposited in nonmoney accounts (savings and time deposits).
c) some loans may take the form of cash rather than new demand deposits.
d) all of the above.

18. When the Fed engages in Open Market Operations (OMOs) that involve the selling of government bonds, this has the effect of:

a) reducing the monetary base.
b) increasing the money supply.
c) decreasing the interest rate.
d) increasing money demand.

19. Assume that a bank has demand deposits of $300,000, total reserves of $75,000 and a reserve requirement ratio (rr) of .15 (15%). This bank can safely lend:

a) $30,000.
b) $45,000.
c) $55,000.
d) $200,000.

20. The interest rate that is charged on loans made between commercial banks is called the:

a) discount rate.
b) prime rate.
c) federal funds rate.
d) commercial bank rate.

21. An increase in the discount rate:

a) encourages more aggressive lending by banks and therefore increases the money supply.
b) reduces the amount of borrowing from the Fed by commercial banks and therefore reduces the money supply.
c) reduces the amount of loans between commercial banks, which enables them to lend more to their customers.
d) makes borrowing from the Fed less expensive (there's a bigger discount) and thus increases the money supply.

22. If the Federal Reserve wants to increase the money supply, which of the following is considered to be the most effective approach?

a) buy bonds.
b) lower the discount rate.
c) increase the reserve requirement ratio.
d) use moral suasion.

23. Which of the following is not a generally agreed upon goal of monetary policy?

a) economic growth sufficient to maintain high employment.
b) stability of the price level.
c) stability of real GNP around trend growth.
d) zero unemployment.

24. The macroeconomic model suggests that, over the long run, attempts to increase the level of real GNP beyond the natural level by continually increasing the money supply will:

a) cause the level of real GNP and the price level to increase.
b) have no effect on the natural level of real GNP, but will increase the price level.
c) have no effect on the level of real GNP or the price level.
d) cause the level of real GNP and the price level to both fall.

25. Assume that the level of real GNP has increased above the natural rate as a result of an autonomous increase in aggregate demand. In this case, to restore real GNP to its natural level, it might be appropriate for the Fed to:

a) sell bonds.
b) lower the discount rate.
c) lower the reserve requirement ratio.
d) lower the federal funds rate.

26. A bank has $50,000 in demand deposits and total reserves of $30,000. Assuming the reserve requirement ratio is .20 (20%), if this bank lends out all of its excess reserves the money supply could expand by as much as:

a) $ 50,000.
b) $100,000.
c) $150,000.
d) $250,000.

27. Which of the following statements is correct?

a) The Fed's policy actions are controlled directly by the Congress.
b) The Fed's policy actions are controlled directly by the President.
c) To a large extent, the Fed is independent of control by elected officials.
d) The Fed's policy decisions are totally unaffected by political considerations.

28. The reserve requirement ratio enables the Federal Reserve to:

a) alter the amount of revenue it collects from member banks.
b) prevent commercial banks from earning excess profits.
c) influence the lending ability of commercial banks.
d) prevent banks from hoarding too much vault cash.

29. When the Fed engages in Open Market Operations (OMOs) that involve the buying of government bonds, this has the effect of:

a) reducing the monetary base.
b) increasing the money supply.
c) increasing the interest rate.
d) none of the above.

REVIEW QUESTIONS: APPENDIX

30. Which of the following was not a principal cause of the savings and loan crisis?

a) A simultaneous reduction in restrictive regulations and oversight of the activities of the savings and loan industry.
b) The high inflation rates in the 1960s and 1970s and their effects on nominal interest rates and asset values.
c) A decrease in competition from other types of financial intermediaries.
d) A large increase in risky investment activities by managers of savings and loan institutions in the 1980s.

31. Which of the following steps is considered necessary for the savings and loan industry to be able to overcome its problems?

a) An increase in the types of loans they can make.
b) Lower insurance rates for all members of the FDIC.
c) Reinstatement of all of the regulations that were removed in the 1970s and 1980s.
d) An increase in the limit on the amount of a person's deposits that are federally insured.

ANSWER KEY

Exercises
1. financial intermediaries
2. Financial intermediaries 1) encourage increased savings, 2) reduce the risks associated with lending, and 3) reduce the costs of borrowing and lending.
3. bank run
4. reserve requirement ratio
5. open market operations
6. fractional reserve banking
7. 1) currency holdings (part of a loan that does not make its way into a demand deposit), 2) the existence of nonmoney deposits, and 3) the maintenance of reserves in excess of the required amount.
8. monetary base
9. open market operations, discount rate, reserve requirement ratio
10. buy
11. federal funds rate
12. money multiplier
13. The standard goals are high employment, economic growth sufficient to maintain high employment, stability of the price level, and stability of real GNP around trend growth.
14. tools, targets, goals
15. shift right, shift left
16. a. $10,000, $10,000 b. $8,500 c. $56,667 (approximate)

17. The monetary base will decline by $100 million. The money supply will be reduced by a maximum of $500 million.
18. Total reserves will fall by $100,000. -$10,000.
19. In the short run, a decrease in the money supply will cause the AD curve to shift left. This will cause equilibrium RGNP and the price level to fall. Over the long run, the decrease in the price level will cause individuals to lower their price expectations, and consequently their nominal wage demands, which will in turn cause the SRAS curve to shift right until long-run equilibrium is once again re-established at RGNPn and a lower price level.

Review Questions

1. c) is the correct answer. Loan defaults are still a possibility. Financial intermediaries are simply able to spread the risk of defaults more and thus lower the costs of defaults.

2. c) is the correct answer. During the period 1979 - 1982 the Fed targeted the money supply. However, beginning in 1982 it once again targeted interest rates, while keeping an eye on the money supply as well.

3. b) is the correct answer. The bank's required reserves are .2($80,000) = $16,000. The difference between total reserves and required reserves, $60,000 - $16,000 = $44,000, is its excess reserves, which is the total amount the bank can lend.

4. d) is the correct answer. These are the three primary policy tools discussed in the chapter, and constitute the primary methods used by the Fed to control the money supply.

5. c) is the correct answer. By altering the amount of excess reserves held by banks, the Fed influences the ability of the banking system to increase the money supply through the process of loans and deposit expansion. The other three statements are all incorrect.

6. c) is the correct answer. As our analysis of the macroeconomy is beginning to make clear, changes in the money supply have significant effects on the level of real GNP and the price level.

7. d) is the correct answer. By buying bonds the Fed increases banks' excess reserves which in turn leads to an increase in the money supply and consequently lower interest rates. This has an expansionary effect on the level of aggregate demand and therefore real GNP.

8. c) is the correct answer. This is the definition of required reserves.

9. a) is the correct answer. Increasing the reserve requirement ratio and the discount rate would both decrease the money supply. However, buying bonds would increase the money supply. Hence, it is the least effective approach of the three.

10. a) is the correct answer. This is the definition of the monetary base.

11. b) is the correct answer. Using the approach discussed in question 3, the bank has excess reserves of $52,000. When the reserve requirement ratio is 10 percent, the deposit multiplier is 1/.1 = 10. Hence the money supply could expand by a maximum of 10 x $52,000 = $520,000.

12. d) is the correct answer. By definition, financial intermediaries accept deposits and make loans. A currency exchange simply swaps one currency for another, there is no deposit or lending activity.

13. c) is not a correct statement. The Federal Reserve System is decentralized, consisting of twelve regional banks. (See Figure 1 in the text.) All of the other statements are correct.

14. c) is the correct answer. The formula for the deposit multiplier is 1/rr. Letting 1/rr = 4 and solving for rr yields 1/4 = .25.

15. a) is the correct answer. Using the approach outlined in questions 3 and 11, Bozo has excess reserves of $100,000 and a deposit multiplier of 10. Bozo could therefore lend a maximum of $1,000,000. However, since some loans are in the form of cash, the total amount of new money will be something less than $1,000,000.

16. d) is the correct answer. When the Fed buys bonds this increases banks' excess reserves, which in turn leads to an increase in the money supply. This causes interest rates to fall and investment spending and consumption spending increase, implying an increase in aggregate demand.

17. d) is the correct answer. As is discussed in the text, a), b), and c) are all factors that limit the expansion of the money supply.

18. a) is the correct answer. When the Fed sells bonds, this reduces the amount of bank reserves and currency in circulation, which just happen to be the two components of the monetary base, i.e., the monetary base is reduced.

19. a) is the correct answer. See question 3.

20. c) is the correct answer. This is the definition of the federal funds rate.

21. b) is the correct answer. The discount rate is the interest rate charged on loans made by the Fed to member banks. An increase in the cost of borrowing leads banks to borrow less and to lend less so that they can avoid having to borrow from the Fed to cover their reserve requirements in the event of an unexpected shortfall. Hence, the money supply grows more slowly (decreases).

22. a) is the correct answer. Buying bonds is an example of open market operations, which are the Fed's most effective policy tool. Buying bonds increases banks' reserves and therefore the money supply through the process of loans and deposit expansion.

23. d) is the correct answer. As we will see in later chapters, zero unemployment is essentially impossible to achieve, let alone maintain for any period of time. The other three goals are discussed in the text.

24. b) is the correct answer. As is discussed in the text, an increase in the money supply can increase real GNP in the short run. However, after all adjustments take place, the economy will return to the natural level of output, which is in turn determined by real, as opposed to monetary, factors. In addition, the price level will be higher due to increases in wages caused by the increase in demand and real GNP in the short run.

25. a) is the correct answer. Selling bonds causes the money supply to decrease, which causes interest rates to rise and aggregate demand to decrease. This will tend to drive the level of real GNP back toward its natural level. Note that policies b) and c) would cause the money supply to increase, which is the opposite of what is needed. The Fed does not have direct control over the federal funds rate.

26. b) is the correct answer. See question 11.

27. c) is the correct answer. Neither the Congress nor the president have any direct control over the Fed's actions. Nonetheless, the Fed does respond to political pressures on occasion.

28. c) is the correct answer. By altering the reserve requirement ratio, the Fed can alter the amount of excess reserves in the banking system and consequently its lending potential.

29. b) is the correct answer. When the Fed buys bonds this increases bank reserves and therefore the lending potential of banks. It also results in an increase in the monetary base and puts downward pressure on interest rates.

30. c) is the correct answer. Just the opposite occurred, .i.e., S&Ls faced increasing competition which further eroded their profits.

31. a) is the correct answer. By increasing the types of loans they can make, S&Ls would be able to compete more effectively with other financial intermediaries. b), c) and d) are all sources of the problems S&Ls currently face.

CHAPTER 29
THE CREDIT MARKET

OVERVIEW

In this chapter we develop the theory of the credit market and examine how the interest rate is determined. You will recall that we analyzed interest rate determination in the context of the money market as well. The advantage of the credit market approach is that it is a direct approach to the determination of the equilibrium rate of interest. We also explain why there is actually a set of interest rates in the economy rather than a single rate.

An important distinction between money and credit involves their respective prices. In short, the price of credit is the interest rate, while the price of money is the inverse of the price level. Credit and money are related to the extent that obtaining credit amounts to renting money for a specified period of time. The demand for credit represents a desire to use money, while the demand for money represents the desire to hold money.

Credit can assume a number of different forms. For example, a loan from a bank or a saving and loan association is a form of credit. In a similar manner, the purchase of a bond amounts to the extension of credit. The buyer is loaning money to the issuer of the bond for a specified period of time at a fixed rate of interest. Bonds are often traded before they mature. To sell a bond, however, it may be necessary to lower its price in order for the buyer to be able to earn the rate of interest being offered on new issues. The result is that the price of bonds and the interest rate are inversely related. As the interest rate rises, the price of bonds falls, and vice versa.

The fact there are a number of different interest rates rather a single interest rate reflects the effects of a number of factors in addition to the pure rental price of money. Many interest rates reflect varying degrees of risk associated with different loans. In addition, part of the interest rate may reflect different lengths to maturity of the loan and the resulting effects of expected inflation. The interest rate on short-term U.S. Treasury bonds is generally used as a measure of the pure rate of interest.

The credit market is simply another application of the model of supply and demand. The demand for credit can be broken down according to the sectors of the economy demanding credit, i.e., households, businesses, the government, and the foreign sector.

Demand for credit by households is derived primarily from the demand for consumer durables and houses. The primary factors influencing households' demand for credit include the level of national income, and the level of existing borrowing in the household sector.

Businesses demand credit to finance inventory changes and purchases of capital stock. The major factors affecting businesses' demand for credit at a given nominal interest rate include the expected real interest rate, the levels of national income and capacity utilization, and tax policy.

Demand for credit in the government sector is positively related to the size of the government deficit, and is largely unaffected by the interest rate.

Foreign sector demand for credit depends on the demand for U.S. dollars and the level of the U.S. real interest rate relative to the foreign real interest rate.

The supply of credit is determined by the level of savings in the economy. Although the business sector is the largest saver overall, the household sector is the only net saver. It is generally assumed that although the relationship is weak, the quantity of credit supplied is positively related to the interest rate. The level of savings at a given interest rate is determined by the level of income, inflationary expectations, and foreign real interest rates.

The equilibrium rate of interest rate is determined by the intersection of the credit supply and credit demand curves. A change in either the credit supply curve or the credit demand curve will cause the interest rate to change. However, in the case of national income, the direction of the change is ambiguous. Because the level of national income affects both the supply of and demand for credit, a change in national income causes both curves to shift. However, both curves shift in the same direction as the change in income. Without knowing the relative magnitudes of the shifts in the two curves it is not possible to say whether the equilibrium interest rate will increase, decrease, or stay the same. Empirical evidence does suggest a direct relationship between interest rates and the level of national income.

The credit market and the money market are linked through the market for financial assets. For example, a decrease in the demand for money implies an increase in the demand for financial assets (as well as goods and services) and this amounts to an increase in the supply of credit. Changes in the supply of money also amount to changes in the supply of credit. In either case, the resulting change in the interest rate in one market corresponds to the change in the interest rate in the other market. The question of which model to use to analyze the interest rate effects of a particular change in the economy depends on the nature of the problem in question (see Table 3 in the text).

KEY GRAPHS AND TERMS

Graphs

The model of the credit market is illustrated graphically in Figure 5. The graph depicting the credit market is manipulated in the same way as any other model that uses the basic principles of supply and demand. In particular, it is necessary to distinguish among factors that cause movements along the demand and supply curves and factors that cause the curves to shift. The only factor that causes a movement along the credit demand or credit supply curve is a change in the nominal interest rate. Changes in any of the other factors that influence the demand for and supply of credit, such as the level of national income, the level of outstanding consumer debt, the level of capacity utilization, the size of the government deficit, tax policy, the expected real interest rate, and foreign real interest rates, cause one or both of the curves to shift. It is important that you understand the effect of specific changes in these variables on the position of each curve in order to be able to analyze the effects of specific changes on the level of the interest rate.

Terms

STOCK
FLOW
DEFAULT RISK
COUPON BONDS
FACE VALUE
SECONDARY MARKET
COUPON RATE
PURE INTEREST RATE
RISK PREMIUM
TERM TO MATURITY
TERM STRUCTURE
TIME PREFERENCE
INTERNATIONAL
RESERVE CURRENCY
RETAINED EARNINGS

EXERCISES

1. The _interest_ _rate_ is the price of credit, while the price of money is the inverse of the aggregate _Price_ _level_.

2. The possibility that a borrower will fail to meet the principal or interest payment on a loan on schedule is called _default_ _risk_.

3. Ceteris paribus, a decrease in the demand for bonds will cause the price of bonds to _decrease_, and the interest rate to _increase_.

4. List two factors that can cause the actual interest rate and the pure interest rate to differ. _the inclusion of a risk premium, and the effects of an expected rate of inflation_

5. The primary factors that influence the demand for credit by households are the levels of _national_ _income_ and _existing_ _debt_.

6. Ceteris paribus, a reduction in the expected real interest rate or taxes on corporate profits would cause businesses' demand for credit to __increase__.

7. Ceteris paribus, a decrease in U.S. real interest rates relative to foreign real interest rates will cause the demand for credit to __increase__.

8. The only net saving sector in the economy is __household__.

9. A change in the nominal interest rate causes a __movement__ __along__ the credit supply curve, while a change in the expected inflation rate causes the credit supply curve to __shift__.

10. Businesses' savings are called __retained__ __earnings__.

11. A decrease in foreign real interest rates relative to U.S. real interest rates will cause the credit demand curve to __shift__ __left__ and the credit supply curve to __shift__ __right__, which will in turn cause the equilibrium interest rate to __decrease__.

12. A decrease in the demand for money causes the supply of credit to __increase__, which causes the interest rate to __decrease__.

Use the following figures to answer questions 13 - 15.

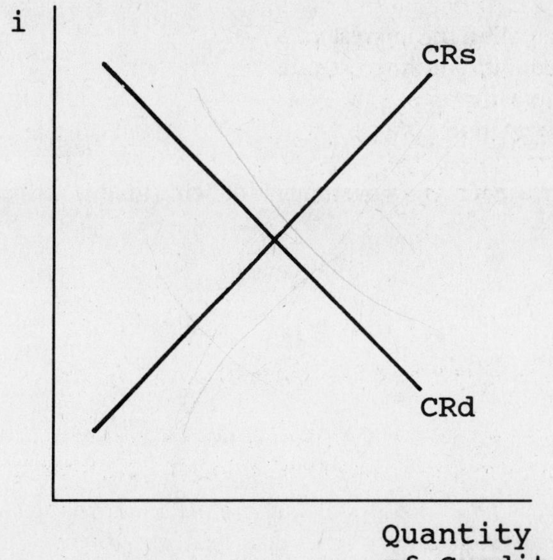

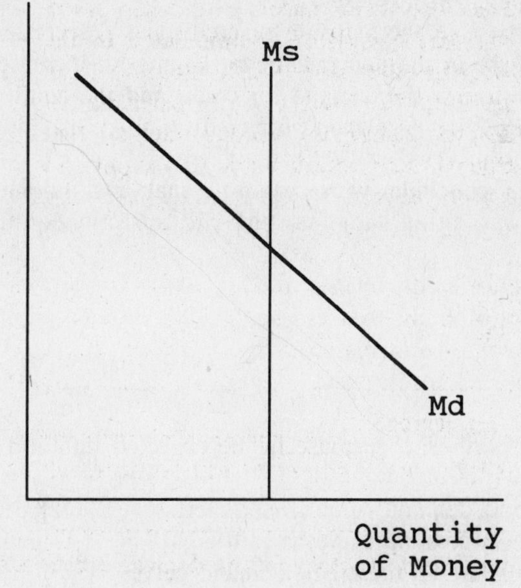

13. In each of the figures determine the equilibrium interest rate, and the equilibrium quantity of credit and money, respectively, and label them using appropriate subscripts.

14. Assume that there is an increase in the government deficit as a result of an increase in government spending (taxes are assumed to be held constant). Illustrate the effect of this change in the credit market. What has happened to the equilibrium interest rate and quantity of credit.

15. Now consider the effect of the increase in the deficit on the money market. Considering the source of the deficit and the implications for aggregate demand and consequently real GNP, how would this change show up in the money market? Is the resulting effect on the interest rate consistent with the conclusion you reached in your credit market analysis?

REVIEW QUESTIONS

1. Which of the following statements is correct?

a) Money and credit are both flow variables.
b) The price of money is the inverse of the price level, while the price of credit is the interest rate.
c) The demand for credit and the demand for money are, in fact, the same thing.
d) As the price level increases, so does the value of money.

2. Assume that when the inflation rate is 3 percent, the nominal interest rate is 9 percent. If the inflation rate rises to 9 percent, what will the nominal interest rate be?

a) 9 percent.
b) 12 percent.
c) 15 percent.
d) 18 percent.

3. Assume that business expectations change such that the expected real rate of return on all investment projects increases. In the credit market we would expect this to cause:

a) an increase in the demand for credit and a decrease in the equilibrium interest rate.
b) a decrease in the demand for credit and an increase in the equilibrium interest rate.
c) an increase in the demand for credit and the equilibrium interest rate.
d) a decrease in the demand for credit and the equilibrium interest rate.

4. We can conclude, with certainty, that a simultaneous increase in the government deficit (that is debt financed) and autonomous savings will cause the equilibrium:

a) quantity of credit to increase.
b) quantity of credit to decrease.
c) interest rate to increase.
d) interest rate to decrease.

5. Ceteris paribus, a decrease in the expected inflation rate will cause:

a) the credit demand curve to shift left.
b) the credit demand curve to shift right.
c) a movement up the credit demand curve.
d) a movement down the credit demand curve.

6. Ceteris paribus, a decrease in the expected inflation rate in foreign countries will cause:

a) foreign real interest rates to increase and the U.S. nominal interest rate to decrease.
b) foreign real interest rates and the U.S. nominal interest rate to increase.
c) foreign real interest rates to decrease and the U.S. nominal interest rate to increase.
d) foreign real interest rates and the U.S. nominal interest rate to decrease.

7. Which of the following sources of credit demand is <u>least</u> susceptible to changes in the nominal interest rate?

a) The household sector.
b) The business sector.
c) The government sector.
d) The foreign sector.

8. The only net saving sector in the economy is the ________________ sector.

a) household
b) business
c) government
d) foreign

9. The expected real interest rate is equal to the:

a) total interest expense over the life of a loan.
b) nominal interest rate minus the expected inflation rate.
c) nominal interest rate divided by the expected inflation rate.
d) expected inflation rate minus the nominal interest rate.

10. Ceteris paribus, an increase in expected inflation will cause:

a) a movement up the credit supply curve.
b) a movement down the credit supply curve.
c) the credit supply curve to shift right.
d) the credit supply curve to shift left.

11. On the basis of economic theory alone, we can say, with certainty, that a decrease in the level of income will:

a) create a shortage in the credit market at the initial interest rate.
b) create a surplus in the credit market at the initial interest rate.
c) cause the equilibrium quantity of credit to decrease.
d) cause the equilibrium quantity of credit to increase.

12. In the short run, a decrease in the demand for money causes the supply of credit to ________________, while a decrease in the money supply causes the supply of credit to ________________.

a) increase; increase
b) decrease; decrease
c) increase; decrease
d) decrease; increase

13. Assume that a coupon bond has a face value of $1,000 and a coupon paying $110, and has one year left to maturity. The current interest rate is 9 percent. The price of this bond is:

a) $900.90
b) $917.43
c) $1,000.00
d) $1,018.35

14. Ceteris paribus, a change in the quantity of credit demanded is caused by a change in:

a) the number of households demanding credit.
b) the size of the government's budget deficit.
c) the nominal interest rate.
d) the amount of existing consumer debt.

15. The money demand-money supply model is preferred to the credit market model for analyzing the interest rate effects of a change in:

a) inflationary expectations.
b) the government deficit.
c) the foreign real interest rate.
d) the money supply.

16. Which of the following statements is not correct?

a) The interest rate is the rental price of money.
b) There is a strong negative relationship between the money supply and the quantity of credit extended in the economy.
c) The demand for credit and the demand for money are not the same thing.
d) The demand for money refers to the desire to hold money balances.

17. Ceteris paribus, an increase in the supply of credit will cause the:

a) interest rate and the price of bonds to increase.
b) interest rate and the price of bonds to decrease.
c) interest rate to increase and the price of bonds to decrease.
d) interest rate to decrease and the price of bonds to increase.

18. Assume an individual takes out a one year loan at 12 percent interest. The nominal interest rate reflects a 3 percent risk premium and an expected inflation rate of 5 percent. Based on this information, the pure interest rate is:

a) 3 percent.
b) 4 percent.
c) 7 percent.
d) 9 percent.

19. An increase in the capacity utilization rate will cause the equilibrium:

a) interest rate and quantity of credit to decrease.
b) interest rate and quantity of credit to increase.
c) interest rate to increase and quantity of credit to decrease.
d) interest rate to decrease and quantity of credit to increase.

20. All of the following will result in a change in demand for credit except:

a) an increase in income.
b) a change in price expectations.
c) a decrease in the nominal interest rate (inflationary expectations held constant).
d) an increase in the number of borrowers.

Chapter 29, The Credit Market

ANSWER KEY

Exercises

1. interest rate, price level
2. default risk
3. decrease, increase
4. the inclusion of a risk premium, and the effects of the expected rate of inflation on term structure.
5. national income, existing debt
6. increase
7. increase
8. households
9. movement along, shift
10. retained earnings
11. shift left, shift right, decrease
12. increase, decrease
13. See pages 754 and 761 of the text. (If you are using the macro split of the text, the correct page numbers are 386 and 393.)
14. the increase in the government deficit will cause the credit demand curve to shift right, resulting in an increase in the equilibrium interest rate and quantity of credit.
15. The increase in government spending will cause the level of real GNP to increase, resulting in an increase in money demand--the money demand curve will shift right. This will in turn cause the equilibrium interest rate to rise. The results are the same as those in the credit market.

Review Questions

1. b) is the correct answer. Money is a stock variable, not a flow variable. In addition, the demand for credit represents the desire to use money, while the demand for money represents the desire to hold money. Finally the price level and the value of money are inversely related.

2. c) is the correct answer. The nominal interest rate is equal to the sum of the expected inflation rate and the expected real rate of interest. Hence, in this case the expected real interest rate is 9% - 3% = 6%. If the expected inflation rate rises to 9 percent, the nominal interest rate will be 9% + 6% = 15%.

3. c) is the correct answer. An increase in the expected rate of return causes investment demand and therefore credit demand to increase. Ceteris paribus, this will cause the equilibrium interest rate to increase as well.

4. a) is the correct answer. This situation amounts to a simultaneous increase in the supply of and demand for credit. As such, without knowing the relative shifts in the two curves, we can only say that the equilibrium quantity will increase. The effect on the interest rate is uncertain without more information.

5. a) is the correct answer. A decrease in the expected inflation rate means an increase in the expected real interest rate. Hence the demand for credit will decrease--the credit demand curve will shift left.

6. b) is the correct answer. The decline in the foreign expected inflation rate causes the expected foreign real interest rate to increase. Hence, foreign demand for credit in the domestic credit market increases, driving up the interest rate.

7. c) is the correct answer. The extent to which governments, especially the federal government, run deficits depends on other considerations.

8. a) is the correct answer. This is an empirical fact.

9. b) is the correct answer. Since the nominal interest rate is equal to the sum of the expected inflation rate and the expected real interest rate, it follows that this is the expression for the expected real interest rate.

10. d) is the correct answer. An increase in the expected inflation rate implies a decrease in the expected real interest rate, and therefore a

reduction in the incentive to save at each nominal interest rate--the credit supply curve shifts left.

11. c) is the correct answer. A decrease in income will cause both the demand for credit and the supply of credit to decrease--both curves shift left. Without knowing the relative magnitudes of the two shifts, the effect on the interest rate is uncertain, but the quantity of credit will decline.

12. c) is the correct answer. A decrease in the demand for money implies an increase in the demand for financial assets, i.e., the supply of credit. In a similar manner, a decrease in the supply of money means banks will be able to lend less, i.e., supply less credit.

13. d) is the correct answer. The price of a bond is equal to the value of the bond x 1/(1+i), or in this case, \$1110 x 1/1.09 = \$1018.35.

14. c) is the correct answer. A change in quantity demanded implies a movement along the demand curve and is caused by a change in the variable on the vertical axis, in this case, the interest rate.

15. d) is the correct answer. The money demand-money supply model is obviously the most direct means of assessing the interest rate effects of a change in the money supply.

16. b) is not a correct statement. In fact, as the money supply increases, so does the ability of banks to make loans, i.e., extend credit. See question 1 as well.

17. d) is the correct answer. An increase in the supply of credit means the credit supply curve has shifted left. As such, the interest rate will fall to re-equilibrate the credit market. As the interest rate falls, existing bonds with higher interest rates become more valuable. Hence the price of bonds increases.

18. b) is the correct answer. The pure interest rate is equal to the nominal rate less any premiums for risk, expected inflation, and so forth. In this case we have 12% - 3% - 5% = 4%.

19. b) is the correct answer. An increase in the capacity utilization rate will cause investment demand to increase, causing an increase in credit demand. This will cause the interest rate and quantity of credit to increase as well (a movement up the credit supply curve).

20. c) is the correct answer. See question 14. In addition, changes in all of the other factors cause the credit demand curve to shift, i.e., they cause a change in demand.

CHAPTER 30
GOVERNMENT FINANCE AND FISCAL POLICY

OVERVIEW

In this chapter we take a closer look at the role of government in the economy. We begin the chapter with an overview of the recent trends in the levels of government spending and taxes, and then go on to consider how changes in these variables affect aggregate demand and aggregate supply. We then consider the effect of deficits on the level of economic activity. The possible burdens of the public debt are also considered.

Measured as a percentage of GNP, government expenditures have risen significantly over the past 40 years. However, most of the increase in spending is the result of increases in transfer payments. Government revenues, which consist of taxes, earnings from government enterprises, licence fees, user charges, and earned interest have also increased steadily over the same time period. However, since 1960, spending has tended to grow more rapidly than revenues at the federal level.

Fiscal policy consists of the use of government spending and taxes to influence the level of economic activity through their effects on aggregate demand and aggregate supply. The effects of government spending on aggregate demand and aggregate supply depend on the type of spending in question, i.e., purchases of goods and services versus transfer payments. A further distinction can be made regarding whether purchases are for consumption items or on public investment in infrastructure and so forth. Government purchases have a direct effect on aggregate demand while transfer payments affect aggregate demand indirectly through their effect on consumption spending. In either event, an increase in spending causes an increase in aggregate demand.

Government spending has a positive effect on aggregate supply to the extent that government investment in infrastructure increases the economy's long-run ability to produce output. On the other hand, there is also evidence that transfer payments may reduce incentives to save, causing the supply of credit to decline. This may in turn cause interest rates to rise and private investment to fall.

Taxes affect aggregate demand through their effects on consumption and investment spending. Individual income taxes influence the level of disposable income--an increase in taxes causes disposable income, and therefore consumption spending, to decline. As such, aggregate demand falls as well. Corporate taxes affect investment by altering the real rate of return on investment projects. An increase in the corporate income tax reduces profits and therefore the real rate of return and the level of investment spending. In contrast, policies such as an investment tax credit reduce the actual cost of investment, and thus have a positive effect on the real rate of return and the level of investment spending.

Taxes affect aggregate supply primarily through their effect on the level of investment spending. Over the long run, a reduction in corporate taxes may have a positive effect on the level of investment spending, resulting in a significant increase in aggregate supply. Tax policy can also affect aggregate supply through its effects on the incentive to work. In particular, higher marginal tax rates may reduce the incentive to work, causing a reduction in labor supply. Since an increase in taxes may lead people to work more to maintain the same level of disposable income, the overall effect is not clear. Finally, taxes may affect the supply of and demand for credit, causing the interest rate and therefore investment to change.

Like any other economic unit, government faces a budget constraint. As such, spending in excess of revenues must be financed either through borrowing or an increase in the monetary base. The government finances the bulk of its deficit by borrowing from the public. Although spending and tax policies are the primary determinants of the size of the deficit, automatic stabilizers, such as transfer payments and the graduated-rate income tax, also tend to force the budget into deficit during recessions. In order to accurately determine the extent to which fiscal policy is, in fact, expansionary or contractionary it necessary to calculate the high employment budget deficit--the deficit that would result with current spending and tax policies if the economy were operating at the natural level of employment, i.e., on the LRAS curve.

Deficits affect the economy through their effects on the credit market, aggregate demand,

and aggregate supply. In the case of the credit market, a deficit results in an increase in credit demand and, consequently, the interest rate. The increase in the interest rate can in turn result in a reduction in investment spending, or "crowding out." However, to the extent that the deficit has an expansionary effect on aggregate demand and real GNP, and investment is positively related to real GNP, investment spending may be "crowded in." The effect of a deficit on aggregate supply depends on whether crowding out or crowding in occurs. If crowding out occurs, aggregate supply increases more slowly. If crowding in occurs, we get the opposite result. There is strong evidence that, to the extent that deficit spending is for public investment, there are both direct and indirect positive effects on aggregate supply.

The question of what to do about the trend toward increasing deficits is difficult to answer. Although there are strong theoretical arguments for the use of countercyclical fiscal policy, which calls for deficit spending in recessions, there is an inherent tendency toward deficits in all cases since increases in taxes and spending cuts are politically unattractive. Some observers have suggested a constitutional amendment requiring a balanced budget. However, there a substantial problems with such an approach.

The government debt is the sum of all deficits and surpluses generated by the federal government and represents current debt outstanding. Although the total debt has grown dramatically in recent years, measured as a percentage of GNP it was the same in 1990 as it was in 1960. In general, because the large majority of the debt is held by U.S. citizens, it would not appear to be a significant burden to future generations. However, it is likely that the debt results in a redistribution of income. In addition, financing the debt may inhibit capital accumulation through its effects of interest rates. Finally, to the extent that the Federal Reserve monetizes the debt, there may long-run increases in the rate of inflation and interest rates.

KEY GRAPHS AND TERMS

Graphs

All of the graphs used in this chapter have been introduced previously. As such, you should use this opportunity to test your understanding of how to use these models, e.g., the credit market and the model of aggregate demand and aggregate supply, to analyze the effects of changes in specific variables.

Terms

GOVERNMENT BUDGET DEFICIT
FISCAL POLICY
PAYROLL TAX
GRADUATED-RATE INCOME TAX
TAX DEDUCTION
PERSONAL EXEMPTION
MARGINAL TAX RATE
AVERAGE TAX RATE
STANDARD DEDUCTION
INVESTMENT TAX CREDIT
AUTOMATIC STABILIZER
HIGH EMPLOYMENT
BUDGET DEFICIT
STRUCTURAL DEFICIT
CROWDING OUT
CROWDING IN
FEDERAL DEBT
COUNTERCYCLICAL FISCAL POLICY
OFF-BUDGET ITEMS
HYPERINFLATION

EXERCISES

1. The amount by which government spending exceeds government revenues is called the government budget deficit__________.

2. The use of government spending and tax policies to influence aggregate demand and aggregate supply is called Fiscal________ Policy________.

3. In the short run, an increase in government spending on infrastructure will cause the aggregate demand curve to ___shift___ ___right___, and the level of real GNP to ___increase___. In addition, over the long run, this increase in spending will cause aggregate supply to ___increase___.

4. In the United States, the personal income tax is a ___graduated___ - ___rate___ income tax, meaning that the marginal tax rate ___increases___ as an individual moves into higher income brackets.

5. Assume that the annual income of the Smith family (consisting of Mr. and Ms. Smith and their two children) is $48,000. Assume also that the standard tax deduction is $5,100, the personal exemption is $2,100, and the tax rate structure is set up such that the marginal tax rate on the first $20,000 of taxable income is 15 percent, and the marginal tax rate on taxable income in excess of $20,000 is 28 percent. What is the Smith's total tax bill? ___7,060___

6. Referring to the previous question, what is the Smith's average tax rate? ___14.7 percent___

7. A decrease in the personal income tax will cause the level of disposable income, and therefore consumption and the level of aggregate demand to ___increases___.

8. A decrease in the corporate profits tax will cause aggregate demand to ___increases___ in the short run, and aggregate supply to ___increases___ over the long run. As such, the equilibrium level of real GNP will ___increases___. However, the effect on the price level will be ___uncertain___.

9. Assume that the government passes new tax legislation that reduces the tax rate on savings and also reduces the amount of interest payments that can be deducted from one's taxes. Together these changes will have the effect of causing the equilibrium interest rate to ___decrease___.

10. According to the federal government's budget constraint, the three sources of funds to finance expenditures are ___tax___ ___revenue___, changes in the ___monetary___ ___base___ and ___borrowing___.

11. The ___high___ ___employment___ ___budget___ ___deficit___ refers to the budget deficit that would occur if the economy were operating at the natural level of output.

12. Assume that the economy is in a recession and the government is running a budget deficit. If the level of real GNP begins to increase, ceteris paribus, automatic stabilizers will cause the budget deficit to (increase, decrease, stay the same). (circle the correct answer)

13. An increase in the government deficit that is financed by increased borrowing in the credit market may cause the interest rate to ___increase___, which may in turn result in ___crowding___ - ___out___ of investment spending.

14. ___Crowding___ ___in___ refers to the possible increase in investment spending resulting from an increase in deficit spending and a corresponding increase in real GNP.

15. List three problems associated with implementing a constitutional amendment that requires the government budget to be balanced each year. determining how to define the budget deficit, determining how to treat cap expenditures, creation of incentives, and determining how to cope with cyclical budget deficits

16. Two of the possible costs of the national debt include a redistribution of income, and a reduction in the growth rate of the capital stock.

Use the figures below to answer questions 17 - 21.

PI

LRAS1 SRAS1

P_{e2}

P_{e1}

P_e

NE

E

AD2

AD1

RGNPn RGNP

Panel (a)

i

CRs

I_1

I_0

E

K

CR_{d1}

CR_{d2}

CRd

C_r^0

Credit

Panel (b)

17. Referring to panel (a), locate the equilibrium level of output and price level and label them using appropriate subscripts. Is the economy in long-run equilibrium? No Is the actual price level equal to, greater than, or less than the expected price level? less than

18. Assume that, in response to the situation you have described in your answer to the previous question, the federal government, which is already running a deficit, decides to increase purchases of goods and services while holding taxes constant. Illustrate the short-run effect of this decision graphically in panel (a).

19. Referring to panel (b), which illustrates the credit market, locate the initial equilibrium interest rate and quantity of credit and label them appropriately. Assume that the government finances the increase in the deficit by borrowing from the public. Show the effect of this action in panel (b). What has happened to the interest rate? ~~it is grow~~

20. What effect would the change in the interest rate you described in your answer to the previous question have on the level of investment spending? Show the demand-side effects of this change in panel (a). What term is used to describe the effect you have just illustrated? (In formulating your answer, assume that changes in Real GNP do not affect the level of investment spending.) crowded out

21. Without illustrating it graphically, describe the possible supply-side effects of the changes described in the previous questions. At a minimum, the effect of crowding out would be to slow the rate of capital accumulation and therefore the rate of economic growth.

REVIEW QUESTIONS

1. The single largest category of real government spending is:

a) federal transfers.
b) federal purchases.
c) state and local transfers.
d) state and local purchases.

2. Assume that the government decides to spend an additional $10 billion dollars on infrastructure--roads, buildings, and so forth--over the next five years. The result of this policy will be:

a) an increase in aggregate demand in the short run, but only a higher price level over the long run.
b) an increase in aggregate demand in the short run, and an increase in long-run aggregate supply over the long run.
c) no long-run effects on real GNP or the price level.
d) crowding-out of private investment spending.

3. According to the text and the lectures, which of the following is considered to be a <u>real</u> burden of the public debt?

a) the interest paid on debt held by U.S. citizens.
b) the burden placed on future generations.
c) the potential reduction in capital accumulation.
d) all of the above.

4. Countercyclical fiscal policy consists of:

a) increasing spending and taxes in recessions, and decreasing spending and taxes in expansions.
b) decreasing spending and taxes in recessions, and increasing spending and taxes in expansions.
c) decreasing spending and increasing taxes in recessions, and increasing spending and decreasing taxes in expansions.
d) increasing spending and decreasing taxes in recessions, and decreasing spending and increasing taxes in expansions.

5. The situation in which the total amount of government spending exceeds total revenues is called a:

a) balanced budget.
b) budget surplus.
c) budget deficit.
d) fiscal surplus.

6. According to the "multiplier effect:"

a) consumption is typically several times as large as investment.
b) a small change in autonomous spending can cause income to change by a larger amount.
c) a small decline in the MPC can cause income to increase by several times that amount.
d) a small change in consumption can cause a much larger change in government spending.

7. Assume that the Congress is considering revising the tax laws such that the following marginal tax rates would apply: 10% on the first $10,000 earned, 20% on the second $10,000 earned, and 25% on all earned income greater than $20,000. If an individual earns $42,000 per year they would prefer a proportional tax--a tax which is a flat percentage of a person's income--so long as it did not exceed (indicate the highest acceptable rate):

a) 10%.
b) 15%.
c) 20%.
d) 25%.

8. Assume that a permanent change in personal income taxes is used in an attempt to pull the economy out of a recession. Which of the following does current theory suggest as the most likely long-run result?

a) an increase in the level of real GNP and the price level.
b) a decrease in the level of real GNP and the price level.
c) an increase in the level of real GNP and uncertain effect on the price level.
d) an uncertain effect on the level of real GNP and the price level.

9. "Crowding-out" refers to the possibility that:

a) Investment spending may decline as a result of increases in the interest rate caused by an expansionary fiscal policy.
b) devaluation of the dollar may "crowd-out" exports.
c) increases in marginal tax rates may cause consumption to decline by an accelerating amount as income increases.
d) increases in government purchases of goods may result in a decrease in the purchase of similar goods by households.

10. In order to correctly determine whether current fiscal policy is, in fact, expansive or restrictive, we need to estimate:

a) the high employment budget deficit.
b) the current surplus or deficit.
c) the current level of unemployment.
d) the natural rate on output.

11. Which of the following is not an example of an automatic stabilizer?

a) Unemployment insurance benefits.
b) Social security payments.
c) Income taxes.
d) Welfare payments.

12. Assume that the government finances it's deficit (the result of increased spending) through the sale of bonds to the public i.e., the debt is sold in the credit market. (For simplicity, assume the economy is operating close to the natural level of real GNP.) A likely result in the short run will be:

a) a decrease in the price level.
b) an increase in interest rates.
c) an increase in investment spending.
d) all of the above.

13. Assume the economy is in a deep recession and investment spending is relatively unresponsive to changes in the interest rate. In this case, an increase in government deficit spending is most likely to:

a) increase aggregate demand directly, but at the expense of lower investment spending.
b) decrease aggregate demand directly, but stimulate investment spending.
c) increase aggregate demand directly, and stimulate investment spending.
d) decrease aggregate demand directly, as well as investment spending.

14. Measured as a percentage of GNP, over the past 40 years, government expenditures have:

a) fallen by approximately 25 percent.
b) stayed relatively constant.
c) increased by approximately 13 percent.
d) increased by more that 50 percent.

15. A decrease in government expenditures on national defense will cause:

a) the aggregate demand curve to shift right, and the long-run aggregate supply curve to shift left.
b) the aggregate demand curve to shift left, and the long-run aggregate supply curve to shift right.
c) the aggregate demand curve to shift left, and have no effect on the long-run aggregate supply curve.
d) the aggregate demand curve to shift right, and have no effect on the long-run aggregate supply curve.

16. Government purchases affect aggregate demand ________________. Government transfer payments affect aggregate demand ________________ through their effect on consumption spending.

a) directly; directly
b) indirectly; indirectly
c) directly; indirectly
d) indirectly, directly

17. The use of government spending and taxes to affect aggregate demand and aggregate supply is called:

a) monetary policy.
b) expenditures policy.
c) fiscal policy.
d) functional finance.

18. Which of the following situations would be most likely to result in significant "crowding out" of investment spending?

a) Increase in government purchases, and investment spending unresponsive to changes in the interest rate.
b) Increase in government purchases, and investment spending responsive to changes in the interest rate.
c) Decrease in government purchases, and investment spending unresponsive to changes in the interest rate.
d) Decrease in government purchases, and investment spending responsive to changes in the interest rate.

19. Assume the government engages in deficit spending and finances the spending by selling bonds to the Fed, i.e., by monetizing the debt. In the short run, this will cause:

a) real GNP and the price level to increase, and the interest rate to decrease.
b) real GNP and the price level to decrease, and the interest rate to increase.
c) real GNP, the price level, and the interest rate to decrease.
d) real GNP, the price level, and the interest rate to increase.

20. The recent demand by many politicians that the federal budget be balanced could result in:

a) a significant cut in government spending.
b) a reduction in the level of output.
c) an increase in the level of unemployment.
d) all of the above.

21. Which of the following statements is correct?

a) The multiplier effect of a change in government purchases is greater than the multiplier effect of a change in government transfers.
b) The multiplier effect of a change in government purchases is equal to the multiplier effect of a change in government transfers.
c) The multiplier effect of a change in government purchases is smaller than the multiplier effect of a change in government transfers.
d) The relationship between the multiplier effects of a change in government purchases and government transfers is indeterminate.

22. Assume that the economy is currently operating well below the natural rate of output. In which of the following cases would an increase in government spending be most effective as a means of increasing real GNP?

a) Investment demand is totally sensitive to changes in the interest rate, and insensitive to changes in real GNP.
b) Investment demand is very sensitive to changes in the interest rate, and somewhat insensitive to changes in real GNP.
c) Investment demand is slightly sensitive to changes in the interest rate, and somewhat insensitive to changes in real GNP.
d) Investment demand is totally insensitive to changes in the interest rate, and sensitive to changes in real GNP.

23. Which of the following is not a source of government revenues?

a) Taxes.
b) License fees.
c) Interest on government-owned bonds.
d) Borrowing through the credit market.

24. For the purposes of economic analysis, government spending can be broken down into two broad categories:

a) defense spending and transfer payments.
b) government purchases and transfer payments.
c) defense spending and civilian spending.
d) government expenditures and tax revenues.

25. Which of the following would be most likely to have an expansionary effect on aggregate demand?

a) a temporary decrease in taxes.
b) a temporary increase in transfer payments.
c) a permanent reduction in government purchases.
d) a permanent reduction in taxes.

26. Assume that, without changing the total amount of money spent, the government decides to reallocate its expenditures in such a way that less money is spent on such programs as welfare and unemployment compensation, and more money is spent on the construction of roads and sewage treatment plants. Such a reallocation of government expenditures would:

a) cause the aggregate demand curve to shift right.
b) cause the aggregate demand curve to shift left.
c) have no effect on the aggregate demand curve.
d) have an indeterminate effect on the position of the aggregate demand curve.

27. Assume that Bonzo Kellerman's annual income is $52,000, the standard tax deduction is $5,100, the personal exemption is $2,100, and the graduated-rate tax structure is as follows: 15 percent on the first $18,000 of taxable income, and 28 percent on taxable income in excess of $18,000. What is Bonzo's total tax bill?

a) $10,204
b) $11,140.
c) $12,220.
d) $12,544.

28. Investment tax credits have the effect of ________________ the rate of return on investment projects. This causes the demand for investment goods to ________________ and the aggregate demand curve ________________.

a) decreasing; decrease; shifts left
b) decreasing; decrease; shifts right
c) increasing; increase; shifts left
d) increasing; increase; shifts right

29. If the government decides to reduce the tax rate on interest income from saving, and offset this with a reduction in the amount of interest payments on loans that are tax deductible, this will:

a) cause the equilibrium interest rate to increase.
b) cause the equilibrium interest rate to decrease.
c) have no effect on the equilibrium interest rate.
d) have an indeterminate effect on the equilibrium interest rate.

30. Which of the following statements is correct?

a) Government budget deficits are always expansionary and government budget surpluses are always contractionary.
b) The size of the federal deficit is completely under government control.
c) Automatic stabilizers have the effect of offsetting fluctuations in the levels of output and income.
d) The high employment budget deficit is the size of the deficit needed to achieve the natural level of employment.

31. Deficit spending by the government is best described as:

a) expansionary fiscal policy.
b) contractionary fiscal policy.
c) expansionary monetary policy.
d) contractionary monetary policy.

ANSWER KEY

Exercises

1. deficit
2. fiscal policy
3. shift right, increase, increase
4. graduated-rate, increases
5. $7,060
6. 14.7 percent
7. increase
8. increase, increase, increase, uncertain
9. decrease
10. tax revenue, monetary base, borrowing
11. high employment budget deficit
12. decrease
13. increase, crowding out
14. Crowding in
15. Possible answers include determining how to define the budget deficit, determining how to treat capital expenditures, the possible creation of incentives to shift spending programs to state and local governments, and determining how to cope with cyclical budget deficits.
16. income, reduction
17. Equilibrium output and the price level occur at the intersection of the AD curve and the SRAS curve. Because equilibrium is less than RGNPn, the economy is not in long-run equilibrium. In addition, expected price level is the value of the price level at the intersection of the SRAS curve and LRAS curve. As such, the actual price level is less than the expected price level.
18. The aggregate demand curve will shift right, causing real GNP and the price level to increase.
19. The equilibrium interest rate and quantity of credit occur at the intersection of the credit demand and credit supply curves. The increase in borrowing by the federal government causes the credit demand curve to shift right, resulting in an increase in the interest rate.
20. The level of investment spending will decrease. This is shown by a leftward shift of the new AD curve to position somewhere between AD1 and AD2 (the AD curve associated with the increase in government purchases). This effect is called "crowding out."
21. At a minimum, the effect of the crowding out will be to slow the rate of capital accumulation and therefore the rate of economic growth.

Review Questions

1. d) is the correct answer. This is an empirical fact. See Figure 2 in the text.

2. b) is the correct answer. Government investment in infrastructure increases aggregate demand and the productivity of the factors of production, and encourages additional investment in the private sector. Thus, there is an increase in the capital stock which, ceteris paribus, increases the economy's productive capacity.

3. c) is the correct answer. To the extent that additional debt requires the government to borrow more and this forces up interest rates, investment spending will decline, reducing the rate of capital accumulation. So long as interest is owed to ourselves, no money leaves the country. The level of debt as a percentage of real GNP is not much greater now than it has been in the past.

4. d) is the correct answer. Countercyclical policy is intended to offset the business cycle. As such, policy should be designed to increase aggregate demand in a recession (increase G and decrease T) and decrease aggregate demand in an inflation (decrease G and increase T).

5. c) is the correct answer. This is the definition of a budget deficit.

6. b) is the correct answer. When spending increases this has the effect of increasing

disposable income which in turn causes consumption spending to increase. This leads to further increases in disposable income and additional consumption spending. The resulting change in income is a multiple of the original change in autonomous spending.

7. c) is the correct answer. With the marginal tax rate the individual's total tax bill will be .1($10,000) + .2($10,000) + .25($22,000) = $8,500. In addition, $8,500/$42,000 = 20.24 percent. The person will be better off so long as the proportional tax does not exceed this amount.

8. d) is the correct answer. If the economy is in a recession and taxes are going to be used to expand the economy, the appropriate policy is a tax cut. This will increase aggregate demand. However, according to economic theory, it is not clear whether the tax cut will increase or decrease aggregate supply. Hence, the overall effect is uncertain.

9. a) is the correct answer. This is the definition of crowding out.

10. a) is the correct answer. The high employment budget indicates whether the budget would be in deficit or surplus with current tax and spending policies and income equal to the natural level. If the economy is in a recession and the budget is currently in deficit, fiscal policy would appear to be expansionary. However, this could simply be the result of the recession. At the natural level of output, the same policies could generate a surplus, which is, in fact, contractionary.

11. b) is the correct answer. Automatic stabilizers are taxes and spending that change automatically with changes in the level of real GNP. Social security payments are not tied to the level of real GNP. Hence, they are not automatic stabilizers.

12. b) is the correct answer. When the government sells bonds it is increasing the demand for credit--the credit demand curve shifts right. Ceteris paribus, this results in a higher interest rate.

13. c) is the correct answer. An increase in government spending increases aggregate demand and real GNP. To the extent that investment is positively related to the level of real GNP, as government spending increases aggregate demand and the level of real GNP (as the AD curve shifts right) this will cause investment spending to increase as well.

14. c) is the correct answer. In 1950, government spending was 22 percent of GNP. In 1990 this figure rose to almost 35 percent. Hence, we have 35% - 22% = 13%.

15. c) is the correct answer. The decline in expenditures will cause aggregate demand to decline. However, spending on national defense does not affect the quantity of the factors of production. Hence the long-run aggregate supply curve does not shift.

16. c) is the correct answer. Government purchases are a component of aggregate spending and, as such, have a direct affect on spending. Transfers affect aggregate demand through their effect on disposable income and, therefore, consumption.

17. c) is the correct answer. This is the definition of fiscal policy.

18. b) is the correct answer. The increase in government spending causes aggregate demand, real GNP, money demand, and therefore the interest rate, to increase. The more sensitive investment spending is to the interest rate, the greater the change in investment spending will be. As the interest rate increases, the quantity of investment spending declines, i.e., it is crowded out by the increase in government spending.

19. a) is the correct answer. In the short run, the increase in deficit spending shifts the aggregate demand curve to the right and causes real GNP and the price level to increase. Monetizing the debt amounts to an increase in the money supply, which puts downward pressure on interest rates.

20. d) is the correct answer. Eliminating the deficit will require a cut in spending, an increase in revenues, (e.g., taxes) or both. These are both contractionary policies--they cause output and employment to decrease.

21. a) is the correct answer. See question 16. Since purchases have a direct effect on aggregate demand, an increase in purchases results in a greater initial increase in spending than does the same size increase in transfers which work through their effect on disposable income and consumption. To the extent that any portion of the transfers is saved, the initial increase in spending is reduced. Hence, the multiplier effect will be smaller.

22. d) is the correct answer. In this case, crowding out is not a problem. (See question 18.) On the other hand, the increase in government spending will cause real GNP to increase. If investment is sensitive to a change in real GNP, investment spending will be crowded in, causing a further increase in aggregate demand and output.

23. d) is the correct answer. Revenues are funds that do not have to be repaid. Borrowing has to be repaid.

24. b) is the correct answer. This is the convention used in economic analysis in general, and this book in particular.

25. d) is the correct answer. An increase in government spending and a decrease in taxes are both expansionary. Moreover, a permanent change in either of these variables has a larger effect than a temporary change. Hence, of the choices offered, the permanent reduction in taxes will be most expansionary.

26. a) is the correct answer. See questions 16 and 21. The reallocation results in more money being injected directly into the economy as opposed to indirectly through transfers and therefore consumption spending. In addition, the increase in infrastructure will eventually stimulate additional investment spending.

27. a) is the correct answer. Taxable income is \$52,000 - \$5,100 - \$2,100 = \$44,800. Applying the marginal tax rates we then have .15(\$18,000) + .28(26,800) = \$10,204.

28. d) is the correct answer. An investment tax credit reduces the effective cost of investment, thus increasing profits and the real rate of return on investment. This causes investment demand to increase--the investment demand curve shifts right. As such, the quantity of investment spending and aggregate demand increase.

29. b) is the correct answer. The decrease in the tax rate on interest income from savings will cause the supply of credit (savings) to increase--the credit supply curve shifts right. The decrease in the tax deduction for interest paid on loans will make credit more expensive, thus causing credit demand to decrease--the credit demand curve shifts left. The result is a decrease in the interest rate and uncertain effect on the quantity of credit.

30. c) is the correct answer. Automatic stabilizers slow the rate at which income declines in a recession and grows in an expansion, thus offsetting contractions and expansions to some extent. The other three statements are all incorrect.

31. a) is the correct answer. Deficit spending implies government spending is greater than tax revenues. Since spending increases aggregate demand while taxes reduce aggregate demand, the overall effect is expansionary. See question 17 as well.

CHAPTER 31
LABOR MARKET RIGIDITIES AND UNEMPLOYMENT

OVERVIEW

In this chapter we take a closer look at the labor market, focussing on the types and causes of unemployment. Because the simple model of the aggregate labor market does not adequately explain the existence and persistence on unemployment, we consider two additional theories of unemployment. The chapter concludes with a brief discussion of policies that can be used to reduce unemployment.

In the simple model of the labor market, labor demand and labor supply determine the equilibrium levels of employment and wages. However, this model does no allow for the existence of unemployment in the economy, although the unemployment rate is always positive. The unemployment rate, which is calculated as the number of unemployed divided by the number of people in the labor force (employed plus unemployed) varies over time, but rarely falls below about 5 percent.

The flow model of unemployment groups noninstitutionalized people over age 16 into one of three groups (or pools): 1) employed, 2) unemployed, and 3) not in the labor force. Over time individuals move, or flow, between these three pools. Depending on the flow rates into and out of specific pools, the unemployment rate may increase, decrease, or stay the same. The rates of flow into and out of the unemployment pool are determined by the frequency of unemployment and the duration of unemployment. An increase in either of these factors causes the unemployment rate to increase.

Unemployment is commonly broken down into three categories--frictional, structural, or cyclical. Frictional unemployment, which is attributable primarily to imperfect information and mobility, consists of workers who are voluntarily between jobs and new entrants into the labor market seeking their first job. Structural unemployment is the result of a mismatch between the requirements of available jobs and the skills possessed by workers seeking employment. Cyclical unemployment is the result of decreases in aggregate demand and rigid wages that do not adjust to allow labor markets to clear.

The natural rate of unemployment is equal to the sum of frictional plus structural unemployment, i.e., it is the rate of unemployment when frictional unemployment is zero. The natural rate of unemployment is determined by such factors as demographic characteristics; technology, resource availability, and the capital stock; government income maintenance programs; and government tax and regulatory policies.

In order for the result of the simple labor market model to hold, i.e, unemployment is zero at equilibrium, at least four conditions must hold: 1) workers must be homogeneous, 2) workers must be perfectly mobile, 3) workers and employers must have perfect information, and 4) the labor market must be highly competitive. In fact, none of these conditions are met in the real world. As such, two complementary theories have been developed to explain unemployment and its behavior over time--search theory and contract theory.

According to the search theory of unemployment, workers and employers do not have perfect information on wages and workers' skills. As such, workers gather information on going wage rates and then determine the minimum wage for which they are willing to work--their reservation wage. Firms, on the other hand, adjust wage rates to alter hiring rates and quit rates to achieve the desired level of employees in their firm. Firms adjust the wage rate they offer in order to alter hiring and quit rates and, consequently, the level of employment. In addition, reservation wages are assumed to adjust slowly over time. In general, search theory does a good job of explaining frictional unemployment and cyclical variations in unemployment. However, the theory does not allow for the existence of layoffs and only partially explains wage rigidities.

Contract theory complements search theory by providing a more complete explanation of observed wage rigidities. The model assumes that because worker training costs are substantial, cost-minimizing firms have an incentive to develop wage plans that induce workers to stay with the firm for an extended period of time. To this end, firms often use explicit or implicit wage contracts, which assure workers of future wage increases. In order to accommodate explicit contracts and maintain credibility in the case of implicit contracts, it is often necessary to lay off workers rather than lower wages in the face of declining demand for the firm's output. From the firm's perspective, layoffs are preferable to wage cuts to the extent that the firm is able to retain at least some of its skilled workers and create incentives for worker loyalty among senior workers. The contract theory of unemployment does a good job of explaining observed fluctuations in the number of worker layoffs and provides a sound rationale for observed wage rigidities.

With respect to policy options, the potential for reducing unemployment depends on the type of unemployment in question. For example, at least theoretically, it may be possible to offset cyclical unemployment through the use of aggregate demand management policies. However, reducing frictional unemployment requires a reduction in the length of the search process. Structural unemployment is the most difficult to address. To date, no good solutions for the problem of structural unemployment have been identified.

KEY GRAPHS AND TERMS

Graphs

This chapter uses the simple model of the aggregate labor market to set the stage for the discussion of alternative theories of unemployment. Two new graphs, which depict the hiring rate and quit rate curves for a firm, are illustrated in Figure 7 in the text. Note that a change in the wage rate causes a movement along each of the curves. A change in searcher and worker reservation wages causes each curve to shift.

It is also important to note the shape of the labor supply curves in Figure 11. These curves illustrate the existence of wage rigidities. They are horizontal at the prevailing wage rate up to the corresponding equilibrium level of employment to illustrate the fact that there is not a reduction in the wage rate if the level of employment falls below the equilibrium level.

Terms

UNEMPLOYED
UNEMPLOYMENT RATE
LABOR FORCE
FLOW MODEL OF UNEMPLOYMENT
FREQUENCY OF UNEMPLOYMENT
DURATION OF UNEMPLOYMENT
FRICTIONAL UNEMPLOYMENT
STRUCTURAL UNEMPLOYMENT
CYCLICAL UNEMPLOYMENT
NATURAL RATE OF UNEMPLOYMENT
SEARCH
SEARCH THEORY
CONTRACT THEORY
RESERVATION WAGE
HIRING RATE
RETENTION RATE
QUIT RATE
SCREENING
IMPLICIT CONTRACT

EXERCISES

1. The number of people employed plus the number of people unemployed equals the Labor Force.

2. Assuming that there 5 million unemployed workers and 87 million workers currently employed in the economy of country A, the unemployment rate is 5.4% percent.

3. People who decide to leave the labor force as result of unsuccessful job search efforts are referred to as discouraged workers.

4. The rates of flow into and out of the pool of unemployed workers are determined by the frequency and duration of unemployment.

5. Frictional unemployment includes people who are voluntarily between jobs, while Cyclical unemployment arises when aggregate demand falls and wages do fall enough to clear the labor market.

6. Of the three types of unemployment, Structural unemployment is the most serious and the most difficult to reduce.

7. The natural rate of unemployment is equal to Frictional plus Structural unemployment. When the economy is at the natural rate of unemployment, the Cyclical rate is equal to zero.

8. List four factors that affect the natural rate of unemployment. (1) demographic characteristics, (2) technology, resource availibility, capital stock, (3) government income maintenace programs, and (4) government tax and regulatory policies.

9. According to the Search theory of unemployment, most unemployment is due to the time required to gather information about job characteristics and alternatives.

10. The minimum wage that will induce a job searcher to accept a job is called the reservation wage.

11. The retention rate refers to the percentage of a firm's employees who choose to remain in their jobs during a period of time.

12. According to the search theory of unemployment, the quit rate will decrease during economic expansions and increase during recessions. According to the evidence on quit rates this prediction is (correct, incorrect). (Circle one)

13. Firms can enter into contracts that are either Implicit or Explicit. In either case, a major effect of contracts is to increase the rigidity of wages.

14. According to the contract theory of unemployment, firms respond to a reduction in the demand for their products first by increasing inventories. The next step is to cease hiring new workers. Finally, if the demand reduction persists, firms begin to lay off workers.

15. In the effort to reduce the level of unemployment in the economy, it might be possible to use monetary and fiscal policies to reduce or limit the extent of cyclical unemployment.

16. Examine the following list of possible changes in factors that influence the labor market and indicate, in the space provided, whether the change in question would cause the natural level of unemployment to increase, decrease, stay the same, or have an uncertain effect.

An increase in the average age of workers: decrease

An increase in resource availability: decrease

An increase in unemployment benefits: increase

A decrease in the corporate profits tax: decrease

A decrease in the price level: stay the same

Use the following figure, which depicts the hiring rate curve and quit rate curve for a hypothetical firm, to answer questions 17 - 19.

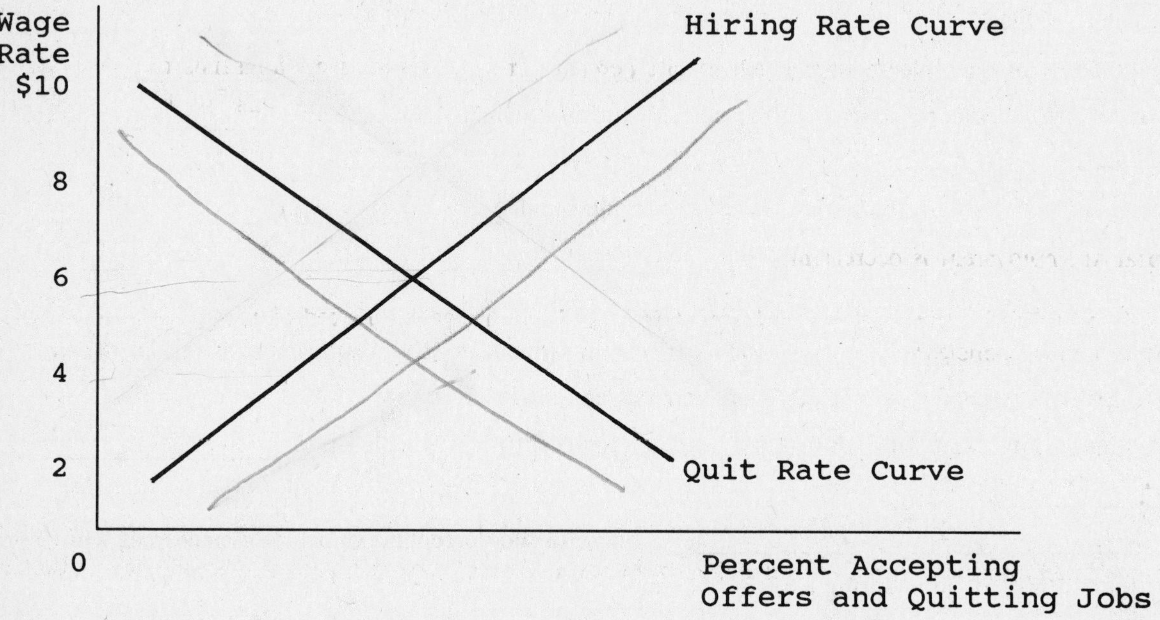

17. At what wage rate will the firm's number of employees stay constant? $6

18. Assume that the firm reduces its wage offer to a wage rate of $4. What will happen to the number of workers employed by the firm? # of employed worker fall Why? because the quite rate exceeds the hiring rate at $4.

19. Assume that as a result of a severe downturn in the level of economic activity, the reservation wage of job searchers and workers in revised downward. Show the effect of this change in the figure. What has happened to the wage rate at which the level of employment in the firm stays constant? The wage rate at which employment is stays constant will decline.

REVIEW QUESTIONS

1. The labor force consists of:

a) all people over the age of 16.
b) all people between the ages of 16 and 65.
c) all people who are officially employed.
d) all people who are officially employed or unemployed.

2. Assume that at a firm's current wage rate, the hiring rate and the quit rate are equal. If the firm decides to increase the wage rate it is offering, this will:

a) cause the total number of the firm's employees to increase.
b) cause the total number of the firm's employees to decrease.
c) leave the firm's total number of employees unchanged.
d) have an indeterminate effect on the total number of the firm's employees.

3. Assume that the current unemployment rate is 6.2 percent. In addition, tens of thousands of people have been laid off from their jobs in recent months as a result of a recession. These fact suggest that:

a) the economy is currently at full employment.
b) the natural rate of unemployment is less than 6.2%.
c) the frictional rate of unemployment is greater than 6.2%.
d) structural unemployment is decreasing.

4. Which of the following types of unemployment is most likely to be influenced significantly by aggregate demand management policies?

a) frictional unemployment.
b) structural unemployment.
c) cyclical unemployment.
d) all of the above.

5. The type of unemployment that includes people who are voluntarily between jobs and looking for a better job is referred to as:

a) structural unemployment.
b) cyclical unemployment.
c) frictional unemployment.
d) regional unemployment.

6. Of the following statements, which one is correct in all cases?

a) a simultaneous increase in the duration and frequency of unemployment will cause the unemployment rate to increase.
b) a simultaneous decrease in the duration and frequency of unemployment will cause the unemployment rate to increase.
c) a simultaneous increase in the duration of unemployment and decrease in the frequency of unemployment will cause the unemployment rate to increase.
d) a simultaneous decrease in the duration of unemployment and increase in the frequency of unemployment will cause the unemployment rate to increase.

7. Suppose it has been estimated that the frictional rate of unemployment is 3 percent, the structural rate of unemployment is 2.5 percent, and the cyclical rate of unemployment is 1.5 percent. Based on these data, the natural rate of unemployment is:

a) 4 percent.
b) 4.5 percent.
c) 5.5 percent.
d) 7 percent.

8. Which of the following would be expected to increase the natural rate of unemployment?

a) A reduction in the number of new entrants into the labor force.
b) An increase in the growth rate of the capital stock.
c) A reduction in the corporate profits tax.
d) An increase in the level of unemployment compensation paid to unemployed workers.

9. Which of the following conditions is not necessary for the unemployment rate to be zero when the economy is operating at the natural level of output?

a) All workers must be perfectly homogeneous.
b) All workers must be perfectly mobile.
c) All workers must have perfectly monopoly on the their job skills.
d) All workers and employers must have perfect information.

10. An increase in reservation wages will cause:

a) a movement up the quit rate curve.
b) a movement down the quit rate curve.
c) the quit rate curve to shift left.
d) the quit rate curve to shift right.

11. The type of unemployment that is characterized by a mismatch between the skills possessed by people looking for work and currently available jobs is referred to as:

a) structural unemployment.
b) cyclical unemployment.
c) frictional unemployment.
d) regional unemployment.

12. A decrease in reservation wages will cause the wage rate required to maintain a constant number of employees to:

a) increase.
b) stay the same.
c) decrease.
d) cannot be determined.

13. Which of the following statements is not correct?

a) The economy is considered to be at the natural rate of unemployment when the unemployment rate is greater than 0, (approximately 6%).
b) To be considered unemployed, an individual must not have a job and must be looking for work, or they must be on temporary layoff.
c) The unemployment rate is equal to the number of people who are unemployed divided by the number of people in the labor force.
d) The Natural Rate of Unemployment is equal to frictional plus structural plus cyclical unemployment.

14. According to the search theory of unemployment, a decrease in aggregate demand should result in:

a) an increase in unemployment and a decrease in the quit rate.
b) an increase in unemployment and an increase in the quit rate.
c) a decrease in unemployment and an increase in the quit rate.
d) a decrease in unemployment and a decrease in the quit rate.

15. All of the following factors can affect the natural rate of unemployment except:

a) a change in the age-sex composition of the labor force.
b) a change in the aggregate price level.
c) a change in the capital stock.
d) a change in government tax policies.

16. Which of the following statements is not correct?

a) From the firm's perspective, the most important cost of an explicit contract is the reduced flexibility on the part of the firm.
b) The use of contracts enables firms to reduce the costs associated with hiring and training new employees.
c) Firm's prefer implicit contracts relative to explicit contracts since implicit contracts are much less costly to break.
d) In general, many firms find it less costly to lay off workers than to cut wages and maintain the same size work force.

17. The primary contribution of the contract theory of the labor market is its ability to explain:

a) why quit rates rise in expansions and fall in recessions.
b) why wages are downward rigid, and hence, the occurrence of cyclical unemployment.
c) how firms can avoid layoffs in recessions.
d) why layoffs are less costly to the firm than wage cuts.

18. Of the different types of unemployment, which one can actually benefit the economy?

a) frictional unemployment.
b) structural unemployment.
c) cyclical unemployment.
d) none of the above.

19. The most difficult type of unemployment to attempt to deal with is:

a) frictional unemployment.
b) structural unemployment.
c) cyclical unemployment.
d) all of the above.

20. According to the aggregate labor demand-labor supply model, when the economy is operating at the natural level of output:

a) the unemployment rate is equal to the sum of the frictional and structural unemployment rates.
b) the unemployment rate is equal to the sum of the frictional and cyclical unemployment rates.
c) the unemployment rate is equal to the sum of the cyclical and structural unemployment rates.
d) the unemployment rate is equal to zero.

21. Country A has a population of 500 million people. 330 million people are employed and 39 million people are unemployed. What is the unemployment rate (approximate)?

a) 6%.
b) 7.5%.
c) 8.3%.
d) 9.1%.

22. Of the following predictions of the search theory of unemployment, which one is contradicted by the empirical evidence?

a) The employment rate increases in expansions.
b) The average duration of unemployment increases in recessions.
c) The unemployment rate decreases in expansions.
d) The quit rate increases in recessions.

23. Assume that as a result of an improvement in technology, the work done by Smith (who works on an assembly line) can be done more efficiently by a machine. According to the definitions of unemployment, Smith would be considered to be:

a) cyclically unemployed.
b) frictionally unemployed.
c) structurally unemployed.
d) terminally unemployed.

ANSWER KEY

Exercises

1. labor force
2. 5.4
3. discouraged workers
4. frequency, duration
5. Frictional, cyclical
6. structural
7. frictional, structural, cyclical
8. 1) demographic characteristics; 2) technology, resource availability, and the capital stock; 3) government income maintenance programs; and 4) government tax and regulatory policies.
9. search
10. reservation wage
11. retention rate
12. decrease, increase, incorrect
13. explicit, implicit, rigidity
14. increasing, cease hiring, lay off
15. cyclical
16. decrease, decrease, increase, decrease, no effect
17. $6
18. the number of employed workers will fall. The quit rate exceeds the hiring rate at a wage rate of $4.
19. When the reservation is revised downward, the hiring rate curve will shift right and the quit rate curve will shift left. As such the wage rate at which employment is stays constant will decline.

Review Questions

1. d) is the correct answer. This is the definition of the labor force.

2. a) is the correct answer. An increase in the wage will cause a movement up the hiring rate curve and the quit rate curve. As such the quit rate will decline and the hiring rate will increase, causing the number of employees to increase.

3. b) is the correct answer. The natural rate of unemployment is equal to the sum of structural and frictional unemployment. When the economy is at the natural rate of unemployment, the cyclical unemployment rate is zero. The fact that people have been laid off means the cyclical unemployment rate is positive, which in turn implies that 6.2% is greater than the natural rate.

4. c) is the correct answer. Cyclical unemployment is the result of fluctuations in the level of output which are often caused by changes in the level of aggregate demand. To the extent that demand management policies dampen the business cycle, cyclical unemployment will be reduced. The other two types of unemployment--frictional and structural--are caused by other factors.

5. c) is the correct answer. This is the definition of frictional unemployment.

6. a) is the correct answer. Ceteris paribus, an increase in the duration of unemployment or the frequency of unemployment causes the unemployment rate to increase. Thus, a) is the only situation in which unemployment will definitely increase.

7. c) is the correct answer. The natural rate of unemployment is equal to the sum of structural and frictional unemployment. In this case we have 2.5% + 3% = 5%.

8. d) is the correct answer. Increased unemployment compensation reduces the costs of being unemployed. a) results in lower frictional unemployment and hence lower unemployment overall. b) and c) both increase labor productivity, thus increasing the demand for labor and the number of people employed at any given time.

9. c) is the correct answer. A monopoly implies the presence of market power, i.e. a lack of competition, which will lead to unemployment. See the discussion in the text.

10. d) is the correct answer. The reservation wage determines the position of the quit rate curve. An increase in the reservation wage implies that people earning a particular wage are more likely to quit and go in search of a higher wage elsewhere. The quit rate curve shifts right indicating more quits at each wage rate.

11. a) is the correct answer. This is the definition of structural unemployment.

12. c) is the correct answer. A decrease in the reservation wage causes the quit rate curve to shift to the left and the hiring rate curve to shift to the right. As such, the two curves intersect at a lower wage rate, and at each wage there is now a greater number of hires and lower number of quits.

13. d) is the correct answer. See question 7. b) and c) are the definitions of unemployment and the unemployment rate, respectively.

14. b) is the correct answer. A decrease in aggregate demand causes real GNP to decrease, implying that the unemployment rate is increasing. In addition, as real GNP falls, wages tend to fall, which causes a movement down the quit rate curve--the quit rate increases.

15. b) is the correct answer. a) can permanently alter the position of the labor supply curve relative to the position of the labor demand curve. c) and d) can permanently alter the position of the labor demand curve relative to the position of the labor supply curve. a) can cause both curves to shift, but their relative positions, and therefore the equilibrium levels of employment and unemployment, remain the same.

16. c) is the correct answer. a), b) and d) are all correct; see the text. However, c) is an incorrect statement. When a firm starts to break its implicit contracts, workers are less likely to agree to their use, thus eliminating the benefits from contracts.

17. b) is the correct answer. As is discussed in the text, because contract theory is able to explain wage rigidity, it is able to explain the occurrence of cyclical unemployment, a feature not found in other theories of unemployment.

18. a) is the correct answer. Frictional unemployment consists of people looking for their first job and people voluntarily between jobs. Assuming that people are looking for the best paying jobs, this implies that resources are going to their most highly-valued uses, which is one of the conditions for economic efficiency.

19. b) is the correct answer. Structural unemployment is due to changes in the economy and socio-demographic characteristics that are very

difficult to change. See the discussion at the end of the chapter.

20. d) is the correct answer. According to the aggregate model, when the aggregate labor market is in equilibrium, all people who are willing and abe to work at the going wage have a job--involuntary unemployment is zero. This is why this model is not useful for explaining unemployment in the economy.

21. c) is the correct answer. The unemployment rate is equal to the number of unemployed divided by the number in the labor force (the number of employed plus unemployed). In this case we have 30m/(330m + 30m) = 30m/360m = .083, or 8.3%.

22. d) is the correct answer. The empirical evidence on this issue indicates that the opposite is true. See the discussion in the text.

23. c) is the correct answer. This is consistent with the definition of structural unemployment.

CHAPTER 32
CYCLICAL BEHAVIOR: THEORY AND EVIDENCE

OVERVIEW

In this chapter we examine the nature of the business cycle. In particular, we consider alternative theories that have been developed to explain the existence of the business cycle. After the different theories have been explained, we examine empirical evidence to determine the extent to which theories explain actual fluctuations in the level of economic activity. We conclude the chapter with a brief discussion of the Great Depression and the potential for effective stabilization policy.

Theories of the business cycle can be categorized as being either endogenous or exogenous. The original Keynesian theory of the business cycle was an exogenous theory since it assumed that unstable investment spending is the primary cause of business cycles, but did not explain why investment spending is unstable--instability was treated as a given, i.e., determined outside the model. In a similar manner, the monetarist theory of the business cycle is exogenous, since it attributes fluctuations in the level of economic activity to instability in the money supply, which in turn is assumed to be determined outside the economic system.

According to the Keynesian theory, a change in the level of investment spending leads to a larger change in consumption spending (the multiplier effect) and hence a substantial change in the levels of output and employment. However, empirical evidence suggests that the multiplier effect is, in fact, very small, contradicting the theory. The Keynesian theory was augmented with the accelerator principal, which makes investment a function of output growth. As such the theory was transformed to an endogenous theory since output, and therefore investment, are determined within the model. In addition, the model was modified to account for the effects of the real interest rate and changes in the money supply.

According to the monetarist model, business cycles are primarily the result of shocks to the economic system. The monetarist model is grounded in the equation of exchange, which suggests that, over the long run, changes in the price level are directly related to changes in the money supply. Assuming that prices are not completely flexible in the short run, however, changes in the money supply will cause the level of output to change. Furthermore, lags in the effects of changes in the money supply may cause the level of economic activity to fluctuate considerably. This is especially true if policymakers attempt to use changes in the money supply to alter the level of output, but the effects only begin to occur after the level of output has begun to adjust due to changes in other factors. In such a case, changes in the money supply would be destabilizing.

Recent modifications to the two aforementioned theories involve the application of rational expectations theory. The New Classical economists modified the monetarist theory by assuming people behave according to the theory of rational expectations (as opposed to the assumption of adaptive expectations in the monetarist model). The effect of this modification is that only unanticipated changes in the money supply (or, more generally, aggregate demand) will alter the level of output; anticipated changes will have no effect. The New Keynesian Economics provided additional insights into the sources and nature of wage and price rigidities. The implication of at least partially rigid wages--the new Keynesian view--is that even with the assumption of rational expectations, anticipated changes in aggregate demand will cause the level of output to change, although by a smaller amount than would an unanticipated change of the same amount.

Examination of the empirical evidence suggests that inventory investment is the most unstable component of aggregate demand and that the accelerator model does a reasonably good job of explaining the business cycle. As such, there is some support for the Keynesian model. However, the Keynesian view that consumption spending fluctuates considerably is not supported by the evidence.

The data also suggest that the economy appears to fairly stable, which is consistent with the monetarist view. Moreover, there is evidence to support the monetarist assertions that changes in the money supply and the level of nominal GNP are positively correlated, changes in the money supply will cause the level of real GNP to change in the short run, and over the long run changes in the money supply only affect the price level, not real GNP.

With regard to New Classical and New Keynesian theories, the evidence suggests that anticipated changes in aggregate demand do have real output effects in the short run. However, the magnitude of the change in real GNP does not appear to depend on whether the change is anticipated or unanticipated.

An examination of the events and policies surrounding the Great Depression suggests that its major cause was a failure of monetary policy. Although such factors as the Smoot-Hawley Tariff Act and fiscal policy blunders also contributed to the decline in real GNP, the Federal Reserve's failure to pursue an expansionary policy in the face of a declining money supply was disastrous for the economy.

It is reasonable to conclude that it is not possible to develop economic policies that would eliminate all fluctuations in the level of economic activity. However, it may nonetheless be possible to create a more stable environment within which the economy can operate. For example, monetary policy designed to maintain long-term price level stability and fiscal policies such as the use of transfer payments to offset fluctuations in the level of income are likely to be beneficial.

KEY GRAPHS AND TERMS

Graphs

Many of the figures in this chapter provide excellent visual illustrations of the relationships among key variables such as changes in the money supply and real GNP, and so forth. In addition, Figures 4, 5, 6, 8, and 14 employ previously developed models, e.g., the money market and the AD-AS model, to illustrate specific points. Be sure you understand the issue each figure is used to illustrate and that you can reproduce such graphical analyses on your own.

Terms

TURNING POINTS
AMPLITUDE
ENDOGENOUS CYCLE THEORIES
EXOGENOUS CYCLE THEORIES
KEYNESIAN CYCLE THEORY
MONETARIST CYCLE THEORY
EXOGENOUS
ACCELERATOR PRINCIPLE
EQUATION OF EXCHANGE
VELOCITY
QUANTITY THEORY OF MONEY
POLICY LAGS
NEW KEYNESIAN ECONOMICS
BANK RUN

EXERCISES

1. Since WWII, the ________________ of business cycle has been smaller than it was prior to the war.

2. ________________ business cycle theories link cycles to processes normally occurring within the economy, while ________________ theories link business cycles to factors outside of the economy.

3. According to the original Keynesian theory of the business cycle, fluctuations in the level of economic activity are the result of changes in ________________ spending, which Keynes considered to be highly ________________, and highly dependent on investors' ________________.

4. In the Keynesian model, assuming that the expected inflation rate is zero, a decline in the expected rate of return on investment will cause the investment demand curve to ________________ ________________ and the level of investment spending to ________________. This will in turn cause real GNP and therefore ________________ spending to fall.

5. According to the ________________ ________________, which states that net investment spending depends on the growth of real GNP, if the growth in real GNP increases, the level of investment spending will ________________, causing a multiple increase in the level of ________________ ___________.

6. According to the monetarist theory of the business cycle, which is an ________________ theory, the economy is inherently (stable, unstable). As such, cycles are primarily the result of (internal, external) shocks to the economic system.

7. The average number of times a unit of money is spent during a time period is called the ________________ of money. According to the equation of exchange, the ________________ ________________ multiplied by ________________ equals ________________ ________________ or, in equation form, ____ x ____ = ____ x ____.

8. According to the equation of exchange, if we assume that ________________ and ________________ are constant (fixed), in the long run, an increase in the ________________ ________________ will cause the ________________ ________________ to increase by the same proportion.

9. According to the New Classical economics, an ________________ change in the money supply will have no effect on output. This outcome is the result of the assumption of ________________ ________________.

10. According to New Keynesian theory, a decrease in aggregate demand that is anticipated will cause the level of output to ________________ by a ________________ amount than a similar-sized decrease in aggregate demand that is unanticipated.

11. According to the empirical evidence, ________________ investment, as opposed to nonresidential investment, is the most unstable component of aggregate demand.

12. List the four monetarist propositions regarding the relationship between the money supply and the price level and level of output that are discussed in the text. ________________________________

____

____

____

____

13. Of the four propositions you listed in the previous question, which follows direct from the monetarists' interpretation of the equation of exchange? ________________________________

14. An examination of the events surrounding the Great Depression suggests that, in fact, it was the result of a failure of ________________ policy.

Use the figure on the following page to answer questions 15 - 17.

15. Assume that the economy depicted in the figure experiences an anticipated decrease in aggregate demand. Illustrate the effect of the decrease in demand.

16. Assuming that the economy behaves according to the New Classical theory, illustrate any additional shifts that would occur and locate the new equilibrium price level and level of output, and label them PI_1 and $RGNP_1$.

17. Assuming instead that the economy behaves according to the New Keynesian theory regarding wage rigidities, how would your answer to the previous question change, i.e., are the new equilibrium price level and level of output the same, and do the same shifts occur? Why or why not?

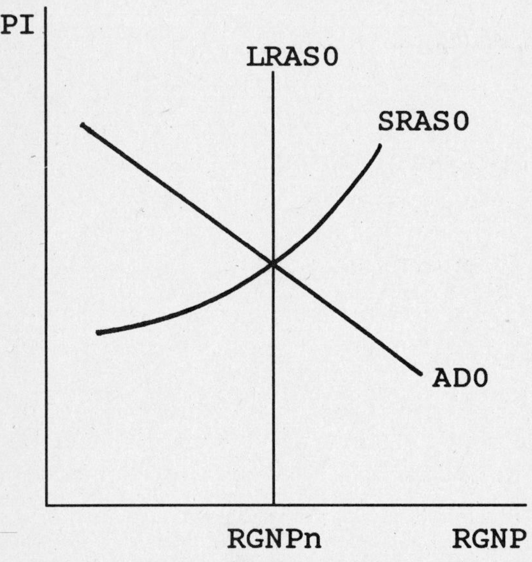

REVIEW QUESTIONS

1. The phase of the business cycle in which output and the level of employment are both falling is called the:

a) recessionary phase.
b) trough.
c) peak.
d) expansionary phase.

2. According to the Keynesian view of the business cycle, an appropriate response to recession would be:

a) a decrease in the money supply.
b) an increase in taxes.
c) an increase in government purchases.
d) a decrease in transfer payments.

3. Which of the following statements is not correct?

a) In order to carry out successful countercyclical monetary policy, the Fed must able to predict changes in the level of economic activity before they occur.
b) There is considerable evidence that the use of countercyclical monetary policy contributed greatly to inflation in the 1960s and 1970s.
c) There are variable time lags between the point at which a monetary policy is initiated and when it has an effect on the economy.
d) A monetary policy geared toward long-term price stability does not require any sacrifice of short-term gains in output and employment.

4. According to the accelerator principle, if the accelerator coefficient is 2, there is a $0.2 trillion increase in RGNP, and depreciation is $0.5 trillion, gross investment will equal:

a) $0.05 trillion.
b) $0.25 trillion.
c) $0.35 trillion.
d) $0.45 trillion.

5. Empirical evidence indicates that the primary cause of the Great Depression was:

a) the stock market crash of 1929.
b) a severe decrease in government purchases and transfers.
c) a sharp decline in foreign trade and an overly restrictive monetary policy.
d) an overly expansive monetary policy.

6. According to the monetarist view of the business cycle, cycles are primarily the result of:

a) insufficient spending by the household sector.
b) external shocks to the system, such as large changes in the money supply.
c) an overly passive fiscal policy.
d) unstable investment demand.

7. Which of the following is the correct expression for the equation of exchange?

a) GNP = C + I + G + NX
b) M x V = PI x RGNP
c) S = I
d) I = j(RGNP)

8. Which of the following would the new classical economists recommend as the best approach to addressing the business cycle?

a) Use active changes in fiscal policy to offset fluctuations in the level of aggregate demand.
b) develop, and stick to, a consistent predictable monetary policy.
c) use frequent changes in the money supply to "fine tune" the economy.
d) Do not announce any monetary policies in advance of their implementation in order to avoid the effects of rational expectations.

9. According to the accelerator-multiplier theory of the business cycle, if there is a decrease in real GNP, this will cause:

a) investment to fall, but total output will fall by a smaller amount due to the multiplier effect on consumption.
b) gross investment to fall by a multiple of the decline in net investment.
c) depreciation to increase by a multiple of gross investment.
d) investment to fall, which will cause a further reduction in real GNP through the multiplier effect on consumption.

10. Assume there is an anticipated decline in aggregate demand that is caused by a decrease in the money supply. In this situation the new classical economists would argue that:

a) the price level will decline, but there will be no output effect in the short run or the long run.
b) the price level will decline, and output will decline in the short run but not in the long run.
c) the price level and the output level will decline over the long run.
d) there will be no price level or output effects in the short run or the long run.

11. Referring to the previous question, the New Keynesian view is consistent with answer:

a) a.
b) b.
c) c.
d) d.

12. Which of the following is not a generally agreed upon monetarist proposition?

a) The money supply is the primary determinant of the long-run level of real GNP.
b) Inflation is highly correlated with the long-run growth rate of the money supply.
c) A change in the money supply will cause real GNP to change in the short run.
d) changes in the money supply are a primary cause of fluctuations in the level of real GNP.

13. With regard to the views of the new classical economists and the New Keynesian theory on the effects of unanticipated changes in aggregate demand, the empirical evidence supports:

a) the new classical theory.
b) the New Keynesian theory.
c) both the new classical and the New Keynesians.
d) neither the new classical nor the New Keynesians.

14. According to the empirical evidence on business cycles, it appears that the economy:

a) is relative unstable, and fluctuations in investment and the money supply contribute to business cycles.
b) is relative unstable, and fluctuations in investment, but not the money supply, contribute to business cycles.
c) is relative stable, and fluctuations in investment and the money supply contribute to business cycles.
d) is relative stable, and fluctuations in the money supply, but not investment, contribute to business cycles.

15. The original Keynesian theory of the business cycle focused on the behavior of:

a) consumption spending.
b) investment spending.
c) government spending.
d) net exports.

16. Which of the following is not cited as a factor that has contributed to a moderation in the size of business cycles since World War II?

a) The increase in government spending as a share of GNP.
b) The elimination of most automatic stabilizers.
c) The use of a more active monetary policy.
d) Growth in the size of the service sector of the economy.

17. Based on the available evidence, which of the following types of stabilization policy would appear to hold the greatest promise of success?

a) The active use of fiscal policy to offset changes in the level of economic activity and the avoidance of any type of monetary policy.
b) Exclusive reliance on changes in the money supply to offset cyclical fluctuations in the economy.
c) A steady increase in the money supply and avoidance of any sudden changes in fiscal policy.
d) The active use of fiscal and monetary policy to offset cyclical fluctuations in the level of economic activity.

18. The argument that a decrease in autonomous expenditures will lead to a decrease in investment spending and consequently a sharp downturn in the level of economic activity is most consistent with the _____________ view of the business cycle.

a) monetarist
b) neo-monetarist
c) new classical
d) Keynesian

19. If monetary policy is to be used to offset an inflationary upsurge in the business cycle in which real GNP is greater than the natural level of output, an appropriate action would be for the Fed to:

a) lower the discount rate.
b) sell bonds.
c) lower the reserve requirement ratio.
d) reduce the federal funds rate.

20. According to the equation of exchange, if M = \$1.25 trillion, V = 4, and PI = 1.1 (110 percent), then real GNP is approximately:

a) \$1.14 trillion.
b) \$3.64 trillion.
c) \$4.15 trillion.
d) \$4.55 trillion.

21. Based on the monetarists' views of the business cycle and its causes, of the following policies, which one would a monetarist consider to be the most appropriate?

a) increase the money supply by a constant rate each year.
b) attempt to "fine-tune" the economy by constantly manipulating the money supply.
c) hold the money supply constant over time.
d) use discretionary fiscal policy.

22. Based on the empirical evidence, with respect to spending, the major contributors to post-war recessions have been declines in spending on:

a) inventory investment and non-residential fixed investment.
b) consumer durables and non-durables.
c) non-residential investment and net exports.
c) inventory investment and government purchases.

23. The primary difference between the new classical economic theory and the New Keynesian view concerns:

a) the assumption of rational expectations.
b) the effects of unanticipated changes in aggregate demand.
c) the degree to which prices and wages are flexible in the short run.
d) the effects of an unanticipated supply shock on the level of real GNP.

24. Assuming that individuals behave according to the theory of rational expectations, a large increase in the money supply that is anticipated will:

a) cause output to increase in the short-run but not in the long run.
b) cause output to increase in the long run but not in the short run.
c) cause output to increase in both the short-run and the long-run.
d) not have any meaningful effect on output in the short or long run.

25. Which of the following statements is correct?

a) The length of a business cycle is fairly stable, averaging approximately 5 years in duration.
b) An exogenous business cycle theory stresses the internal characteristics of the economy that cause business cycles.
c) There is new evidence which, although subject to considerable criticism, suggests that there is no real difference in the amplitude of business cycles prior to and after World War II.
d) A theory that emphasizes the role of supply side shocks as the major cause of business cycles is an example of an endogenous theory.

26. According to the monetarists' view of the equation of exchange, if the economy is currently operating at the natural level of output and the money supply is reduced, the result will be:

a) an increase in real output.
b) an increase in inflation.
c) a decrease in nominal output.
d) a decrease in velocity.

27. In the spring of 1991, an article in the Wall Street Journal reported that although thousands of workers in the auto industry had been laid off in recent months, many of them would continue to receive approximately 85% of their base pay as a result of provisions in the contracts between auto makers and the workers' union. In terms of the business cycle, the effect of this provision might be to:

a) reduce the contractionary phase of the business cycle.
b) deepen the trough of the business cycle.
c) reduce the peak of the business cycle.
d) increase the length of time before we reach the next expansion phase of the business cycle.

ANSWER KEY

Exercises

1. amplitude
2. Endogenous, exogenous
3. investment, unstable, expectations
4. shift left, decline, consumption
5. accelerator principle, increase, real GNP
6. exogenous, stable, external
7. velocity, money supply, velocity, nominal GNP, M, V, PI, RGNP
8. velocity, real GNP (or output), money supply, price level
9. anticipated, rational expectations
10. decrease, smaller
11. inventory
12. 1) changes in the money supply and the level of nominal GNP are positively correlated, 2) changes in the money supply are the exogenous variable causing changes in GNP (not vice versa), 3) changes in the money supply will cause the level of real GNP to change in the short run, and 4) over the long run, changes in the money supply only affect the price level, not real GNP.
13. Over the long run changes in the money supply only affect the price level, not real GNP.
14. monetary
15. The AD curve will shift to the left.
16. Because the decrease in aggregate demand is anticipated, according to the New Classical theory, which assumes individuals use rational expectations, the aggregate supply curve will shift right on the

expectation of lower prices. The new AD curve and the new SRAS curve will intersect at RGNPn and a lower price level.

17. In contrast to the New Classicals, the New Keynesian theory suggests that, due to wage rigidities, the SRAS curve will shift right, but will only partially offset the decrease in aggregate demand. As a result, the SRAS curve will end up somewhere in between the initial SRAS curve and the new SRAS curve in the New Classical case. Output and the price level will both fall in the short run.

Review Questions

1. a) is the correct answer. This is the definition of the recessionary phase of the business cycle.

2. c) is the correct answer. The Keynesians feel that the economy will take too long to pull itself out of a recession and that active policy should be used to restore the natural level of output. An increase in government purchases increases aggregate demand, causing real GNP to increase.

3. d) is the correct answer. Theory and the available evidence suggest that long-term price stability requires a stable growth rate for the money supply. As such, short-run changes in the money supply cannot be used to alter the level of output without sacrificing some amount of long-term price stability.

4. d) is the correct answer. According to the accelerator principle, net investment equals the product of the accelerator coefficient and the change in real GNP. In addition, gross investment is equal to the sum of net investment and depreciation. Thus we have gross investment = 2($0.2 trillion) + $0.5 trillion = $.45 trillion.

5. c) is the correct answer. See the discussion in the text (near the end of the chapter).

6. b) is the correct answer. This is the monetarists' exogenous theory of the business cycle. See the discussion in the text.

7. b) is the correct answer. This is the formal statement of the equation of exchange.

8. b) is the correct answer. According to the new classicals, certainty of outcomes and the effects of rational expectations are two of the principal determinants of the behavior of economic agents. A stable consistent policy increases the certainty of outcomes and enables people to form more accurate expectations about the future.

9. d) is the correct answer. See question 4. When RGNP falls, the change in RGNP is negative. Hence, investment falls. The multiplier effect results in a further decrease in consumption and output continues to fall further.

10. a) is the correct answer. The new classical economists argue that people behave according to the assumption of rational expectations. As such, if a decline in aggregate demand is anticipated, people will adjust their expectations accordingly and revise their wage demands downward (wages are assumed to be flexible in the short run) in anticipation of a lower price level as a result of the decrease in aggregate demand. Consequently, as the AD curve shifts left, the SRAS curve shifts right. Hence, there is no change in output; only the price level, which falls.

11. b) is the correct answer. The New Keynesians argue that wage rigidities prevent wages and prices from falling by the full amount in the short run. Thus, the decrease in demand is greater than the increase in supply, and output and prices fall in the short run.

12. a) is the correct answer. The monetarists contend that real GNP is determined by real, not monetary, factors. As such, they argue that in the long run there is no correlation between changes in the money supply and changes in the level of real output. The other choices are all propositions that are discussed in the text.

13. b) is the correct answer. This is an empirical observation. See the discussion in the text.

14. c) is the correct answer. Once again, this conclusion is based on analysis of empirical evidence. See the discussion in the text.

15. b) is the correct answer. Keynes considered investment spending to be the most unstable component of aggregate demand and therefore the

primary source of fluctuations in the level of economic activity.

16. b) is the correct answer. Just the opposite is true. Automatic stabilizers offset cyclical fluctuations in the economy and have steadily increased as a component of fiscal policy. See the discussion in the Does it Make Economic Sense? box.

17. c) is the correct answer. Since the economy appears to be inherently stable, it would appear that enhancing the stability of the system is the best approach. In fact, many efforts involving the use of active countercyclical policy appear to have been destabilizing.

18. d) is the correct answer. This is a simplified description of the accelerator-multiplier theory developed by the Keynesians.

19. b) is the correct answer. A contractionary policy is called for. Selling bonds reduces the money supply and drives up interest rates, which in turn puts downward pressure on aggregate demand and the level of real GNP.

20. d) is the correct answer. The equation of exchange is M x V = PI x RGNP. Substituting for M, V, and PI yields ($1.25 trillion)4 = 1.1(RGNP). solving for RGNP we get $5 trillion/1.1 = $4.55 trillion.

21. a) is the correct answer. The monetarists consider b) and d) to be destabilizing. c) would not accommodate any growth in the level of real GNP. a) enhances the inherent stability in the economy.

22. a) is the correct answer. This is an empirical observation. See the discussion in the text.

23. c) is the correct answer. See the answers to questions 10 and 11.

24. d) is the correct answer. See the answers to questions 8 and 10.

25. c) is the correct answer. This is the conclusion reached by Professor Romer; see the discussion in the text. With regard to the other responses, the length of the business cycle is highly variable, b) is the definition of an endogenous business cycle, and a supply-side shock is an example of an exogenous change.

26. c) is the correct answer. The monetarists assume that velocity is constant, or at least relative stable. Hence, a decrease in M will cause PI x RGNP to fall. PI x RGNP is nominal output. Monetarists also contend that a decrease in the money supply causes both PI and RGNP to fall in the short run.

27. a) is the correct answer. The effect of this contract provision is to limit the loss in disposable income and hence the decrease in consumption spending attributable to the recession. The clause acts much like an automatic stabilizer in the short run.

CHAPTER 33
MONETARY POLICY: A FURTHER TREATMENT

OVERVIEW

In this chapter we take a much more detailed look at monetary policy. We begin the chapter with a review of the means by which changes in the money supply affect the level of aggregate demand, output, and the price level. We then consider alternative views of what constitutes appropriate monetary policy. After examining the record on monetary policy, we consider the strengths and weaknesses of each approach and offer some general conclusions.

Views of how changes in the money supply affect aggregate demand, output, and the price level have varied over time. According to the Keynesian view, a change in the money supply affects aggregate demand primarily through its effect on the interest rate. In the monetarist view, a change in the money supply works not only through the interest rate, but also through its effects on the prices of equities and real assets. As such, there are wealth effects and direct effects on the level of real GNP as well. Today, most economists generally accept the monetarist view of the transmission mechanism.

Determining the best type of monetary policy depends not only on the money supply transmission mechanism, but on views about the stability of the economy and the degree of wage and price rigidity as well. Because Keynesians consider investment spending to be relatively unstable, and wages and prices to be downward rigid, they tend to argue for the active use of monetary policy to offset declines in the level of aggregate demand. Monetarists, on the other hand, perceive the economy as being inherently stable. In addition, although they agree that wages and prices are somewhat rigid in the short run, they consider them to be much more flexible than do the Keynesians. As such, monetarists argue for some form of monetary policy rule--either passive or active--be followed over time. This has the effect of reducing the level of uncertainty associated with changes in the money supply, and thus facilitates planning by economic decision makers.

An examination of the empirical evidence from the postwar time period suggests that contractionary monetary policy was responsible for four of the seven recessions experienced during the period. The contractionary policies were, in turn, responses to excessively expansionary policies pursued by the Fed. This suggests that monetary policy has tended to be destabilizing.

There are a number of possible reasons why countercyclical monetary policy has not been more effective in the past. First, it is possible that the Fed has pursued unrealistic goals. For example, there is evidence that the Fed has, on occasion, underestimated the natural level of unemployment and has thus tried to hold the unemployment rate at a level that is unrealistically low. Second, political pressures have on occasion led the Fed to pursue excessively expansionary or contractionary policies. Third, it is extremely difficult to forecast turning points in the business cycle in advance of their occurrence. In addition, a change in monetary policy only effects the economy after a period of time, i.e., with a lag. These facts have led monetary policy to be procyclical on many occasions. Fourth, monetary policy has traditionally targeted interest rates, rather than the growth rate of the supply.

Until 1979, the Fed tried to control the expected real rate of interest as a means of influencing spending. However, efforts to reduce interest rates through an increase in the growth rate of the money supply are doomed to failure in the long-run as a result of the income effect and the Fisher effect. To be specific, efforts to reduce the interest rate in the short run through increases in the money supply cause the interest rate to rise over the long run. In addition, so long as inflationary expectations are positively related to the growth rate of the money supply, it will be impossible to alter the real interest rate. This problem is compounded by the Fed's inability to know the actual values of the expected inflation rate and the expected real rate of interest.

The case for active monetary policy would appear to be fairly weak. However, there are also strong arguments against relying on strict money supply targeting. First, reliance on a strict money supply rule requires policymakers to ignore valuable information that might be used to fine tune the economy through adjustments in the money supply. Second, the stability of velocity, on which the monetarist argument for stable money growth rests, has come into question in the past decade. The effects of financial innovations in the 1980s have been to substantially reduce the velocity of the M1 measure of the money supply. To the extent that velocity is not stable, or does not change in a stable manner, the effectiveness of a money growth rule is weakened. Third, supply shocks may require offsetting changes in the money supply if serious losses of output are to be avoided. Note that in all of these cases, however, active rules could be developed that may be relatively effective.

KEY GRAPHS AND TERMS

Graphs

The analyses in this chapter employ previously developed graphical models, such as the money market, the credit market, and the AD-AS model. By now you should be quite familiar with these graphs and how to manipulate them. Note that much of the discussion in this chapter concerns relative rates of change in the positions of the curves in the graphs. This is the case, for example, in the discussion of the Keynesians versus the monetarists and the speed with which the economy adjusts to a decline in aggregate demand. Figure 6 warrants further attention. The issue illustrated here is the effect of an incorrect estimate of the natural level of output. To the extent that this estimate is incorrect, the economy may be perceived to be above or below the natural level when, in fact, the opposite is true.

Terms

COUNTERCYCLICAL MONETARY POLICY
LAG IN THE EFFECT OF MONETARY POLICY
POLICY RULE
ACTIVE RULE
PASSIVE RULE
TIME-INCONSISTENCY PROBLEM
CREDIBILITY THESIS
FOREIGN EXCHANGE MARKET
DATA LAG
RECOGNITION LAG
MONETARY POLICY TARGET
FEDERAL FUNDS RATE
LIQUIDITY EFFECT
INCOME EFFECT
INFLATIONARY EXPECTATIONS (FISHER) EFFECT

EXERCISES

1. According to the monetary transmission mechanism developed by Keynes, a change in the money supply affects the level of economic activity through its effect on the ________________ ________________ and therefore ________________ spending.

2. According to the monetarist transmission mechanism, an increase in the money supply causes real GNP to ________________ through its effects on the ________________ ______________, a direct effect on the purchase of ______________ assets, and a wealth affect associated with an ________________ in the price of financial assets.

3. Keynesians argue that because the private sector of the economy is relatively (stable, unstable), and there is a high degree of ________________ wage and price ________________, the Fed should pursue an active ________________ monetary policy to offset fluctuations in the level of real GNP.

4. Monetarists argue that best monetary policy is to establish a policy ______________ that is either ________________ or ________________. This position is based on the belief that the economy is inherently (stable, unstable), and that such a policy will serve to reduce uncertainty on the part of decisionmakers.

5. The fact that optimal long-run policy differs from optimal short-run policy, and therefore gives policymakers an incentive to cheat on long-run policy rules is called the ________________-________________ ________________.

6. According to the credibility thesis, the output and employment effects of credible policy will be ________________ than the effects generated by noncredible policy. However, this thesis only makes sense if future ________________ are important in setting wages and prices.

7. Examination of postwar monetary policy strongly suggests that monetary policy has been, by and large, (stabilizing, destabilizing).

8. List four possible reasons why countercyclical monetary policy has not worked as well as policymakers would like. ____

____

____

9. The time it takes to interpret data correctly and determine which phase of the business cycle the economy is currently in is called the ________________ ________________.

10. List the three factors it is most important to forecast accurately for countercyclical monetary policy to be effective. ____

____

____

11. According to the ________________ effect, a decrease in the money supply will cause interest rates to ________________ initially. However, the initial ________________ in the interest rate will cause spending to ________________, and this will lead to an ________________ effect that causes money demand and the interest rate to begin to ________________. If the decrease in the money supply causes a decrease in inflationary expectations, the ________________ ________________ effect will push the nominal interest rate ________________ its initial level.

12. Assume that the expected inflation rate and the money supply growth rate are both 6%, and the nominal interest rate is 10%. What is the expected real interest rate? ________ Assuming expectations adjust rapidly and the Fed reduces the growth rate of the money supply to 3%, what will happen to the nominal interest rate? ________________________________ What will happen to the expected real interest rate? ________________________________

13. Assume that real GNP is growing at an annual rate of 3% per year and velocity is stable. In this case, if the Fed wants to hold the price level constant, it should let the money supply grow at a rate of ________ percent per year.

14. List three reasons why many economists oppose the adoption of strict money supply targeting. ________

____

____

REVIEW QUESTIONS

1. The velocity of money measures:

a) the amount of spending in the economy.
b) the average number of times a dollar is spent on new goods and services in a year.
c) the relationship between the value of money and the price level.
d) the relationship between the money supply and interest rates.

2. In which of the following cases would advocates of a money growth rule be most willing to consider the use of active countercyclical monetary policy?

a) a large decline in investment spending.
b) a large increase in imports.
c) a large supply-side shock.
d) a large increase in government spending.

3. According to the empirical evidence:

a) M1 velocity was relatively stable until about 1980, and then became unstable after that point.
b) M1 velocity has been consistently more stable than the velocity of M2.
c) There is no difference in the velocity of M1 and M2.
d) The velocity of M2 increased dramatically in the 1980s.

4. Which of the following best characterizes the Keynesian view of how monetary policy works?

a) an increase in the money supply leads to an increase in the interest rate which leads to a decrease in investment which leads to a decrease in aggregate demand.
b) an increase in the money supply leads to a decrease in the interest rate which leads to a decrease in investment which leads to a decrease in aggregate demand.
c) an increase in the money supply leads to a decrease in the interest rate which leads to an increase in investment which leads to a decrease in aggregate demand.
d) an increase in the money supply leads to a decrease in the interest rate which leads to an increase in investment which leads to an increase in aggregate demand.

5. According to the evidence from the past forty years, the use of countercyclical monetary policy has tended to be:

a) stabilizing, which in turn supports the Keynesian view.
b) stabilizing, which in turn supports the monetarist view.
c) destabilizing, which in turn supports the Keynesian view.
d) destabilizing, which in turn supports the monetarist view.

6. Assume that the Fed mistakenly estimates the natural level of output to be greater than it actually is. If the Fed uses monetary policy to achieve and maintain the estimated level of real GNP, the long-run result will be:

a) an increase in real GNP, and no effect on the price level.
b) an increase in the price level, and no effect on real GNP.
c) an increase in both real GNP and the price level.
d) no effect on real GNP or the price level.

7. In the context of the Keynesian view of how monetary policy works, in which of the following cases would monetary policy have the greatest effect on the equilibrium level of output?

a) Money demand is responsive to a change in the interest rate, but investment demand is unresponsive to a change in the interest rate.
b) Money demand and investment demand are both responsive to a change in the interest rate.
c) Money demand is unresponsive to a change in the interest rate, but investment demand is responsive to a change in the interest rate.
d) Money demand and investment demand are both unresponsive to a change in the interest rate.

8. Assume that the economy experiences a severe supply-side shock in the form of higher oil prices. In the short run, the use of active monetary policy to offset the output effect of the supply-side shock would cause:

a) output to increase, and the price level to decrease.
b) output to decrease, and the price level to increase.
c) output and the price level to both increase.
d) output and the price level to both decrease.

9. Assume the economy is experiencing a high rate of inflation as a result of excess aggregate demand. Which of the following would be considered an appropriate countercyclical monetary policy?

a) a decrease in the reserve requirement ratio.
b) an increase in the discount rate.
c) purchases of government bonds by the Fed.
d) a decrease in government transfers of cash to the poor.

10. Keynesian base their view of appropriate monetary policy on all of the following arguments except:

a) the private sector is inherently unstable.
b) wage and price rigidities prevent the economy from adjusting quickly back to long-run equilibrium.
c) the costs incurred in allowing the economy to bring itself back to long-run equilibrium are too high and unnecessary.
d) monetary policy affects the economy without any meaningful lag, and is therefore highly effective.

11. According to the monetarists, in the short-run, an unanticipated increase in the money supply will:

a) raise interest rates and lower investment.
b) lower the price level and raise unemployment.
c) have no significant effects.
d) none of the above.

12. Assume that the Fed has decided to use active countercyclical monetary policy. If the Fed overestimates the public's expected inflation rate, and in so doing concludes that the expected real interest rate is too low, it will end up pursuing:

a) an overly expansionary monetary policy.
b) an overly contractionary monetary policy.
c) a policy that may or may not be overly expansionary.
d) a policy that may or may not be overly contractionary.

13. Viewed from the perspective of monetarist theory and its assumptions, the equation of exchange suggests that:

a) in the short run, an increase in the money supply causes a decrease in velocity.
b) ceteris paribus, the long-run effect of a decrease in the money supply will be a decrease in the price level.
c) an increase in the quantity of money will cause the quantity of real GNP to increase over the long run.
d) real GNP is determined solely by the quantity of money in the economy.

14. Which of the following is an example of an active policy rule?

a) Increase government purchases at a rate of 3 percent per year.
b) Increase the money supply at a rate of 5 percent per year.
c) Hold the money supply constant over time.
d) Increase government purchases by 3 percent when real GNP declines below the natural rate and decrease government purchases by 3 percent when real GNP increases above the natural rate.

15. According to the "credibility thesis:"

a) the output and price effects of a credible policy are larger than the output and price effects of a noncredible policy.
b) the output and price effects of a credible policy are smaller than the output and price effects of a noncredible policy.
c) a credible monetary policy is capable of influencing the level of real GNP, but not the price level.
d) a credible monetary policy is capable of influencing the price level, but not the level of real GNP.

16. Which of the following statements is <u>not</u> correct?

a) The decline in inflation that occurred during the Reagan Administration's term was due primarily to restrictive monetary policy and a fall in oil prices.
b) During the Carter Administration's term, expansionary monetary policy was used to reduce unemployment, but at the expense of higher inflation.
c) During the Nixon Administration's term, wage and price controls were combined with a contractionary monetary policy to effectively reduce the long-term inflation rate.
d) During the Kennedy and Johnson Administrations' terms an easy money policy was used primarily to hold down interest rates and tended to be inflationary.

17. According to the monetarist transmission mechanism, changes in the money supply affect real GNP:

a) directly, not through interest rates.
b) only through a wealth effect and the interest rate effect.
c) only through an interest rate effect.
d) through a wealth effect, a direct effect, and the interest rate effect.

18. From the Keynesian viewpoint, in which of the following cases will monetary policy be <u>least</u> effective if it is used to alter the equilibrium level of output?

a) Money demand is responsive to changes in the interest rate, but investment demand is unresponsive to changes in the interest rate.
b) Money demand is unresponsive to changes in the interest rate, but investment demand is responsive to changes in the interest rate.
c) Money demand and investment demand are both responsive to changes in the interest rate.
d) Money demand and investment demand are both unresponsive to changes in the interest rate.

19. Which of the following statements is correct?

a) A procyclical policy works to offset (dampen) the business cycle.
b) Many economists have argued that the Fed's use of an interest rate target prior to 1979 was procyclical.
c) It is possible to simultaneously control the money supply and the interest rate.
d) Since 1982 the Fed has targeted money supply growth rates rather than interest rates.

20. Careful analysis of the relationship between the money supply, inflation, and interest rates suggests that it may be necessary for the Fed to:

a) lower reserve requirements to reduce inflation.
b) increase inflation now to lower interest rates later.
c) lower interest rates in the short run in order to lower them over the long run.
d) raise interest rates in the short run in order to lower them over the long run.

21. Assume that the Fed has been pursuing a consistent monetary policy rule for an extended period of time and that it then unexpectedly reduces the money supply by a large amount. In this case, monetarists and new classicals would predict that in the short run:

a) output will fall by a large amount but there will be very little affect on the price level.
b) the price level will fall by a large amount but there will be very little affect on the level of output.
c) output and the price level will both fall by a large amount.
d) output and the price level will both fall by a very small amount.

22. When the money supply is decreased:

a) the liquidity effect causes the interest rate to increase initially, while the income effect and the Fisher effect cause the interest rate to increase overall.
b) the liquidity effect causes the interest rate to increase initially, while the income effect and the Fisher effect cause the interest rate to decrease overall.
c) the liquidity effect, the income effect, and the Fisher effect all cause the interest rate to increase.
d) the liquidity effect, the income effect, and the Fisher effect all cause the interest rate to decrease.

23. Monetarists take the position that:

a) active fiscal policy is relatively destabilizing.
b) the private sector of the economy is relatively stable.
c) changes in the money supply are the single most important determinant of output, employment, and prices.
d) all of the above.

24. Assume that the Fed embarks on a contractionary monetary policy and sticks to it for an extended period of time. According to the Fisher effect, over time, inflationary expectations will:

a) decrease, causing the credit demand curve to left and the credit supply curve to shift right, and the interest rate to decrease.
b) decrease, causing the credit demand curve to right and the credit supply curve to shift left, and the interest rate to increase.
c) increase, causing the credit demand curve to left and the credit supply curve to shift right, and the interest rate to decrease.
d) increase, causing the credit demand curve to right and the credit supply curve to shift left, and the interest rate to increase.

25. According to the equation of exchange, so long as velocity is stable, any instability in aggregate demand must be due to instability in:

a) the price level.
b) real GNP.
c) the money supply.
d) consumption spending.

26. In the context of monetary policy, the recognition lag refers to the period of time it takes to:

a) assemble the data needed to recognize a particular type of problem.
b) interpret economic data correctly.
c) observe the effects of a particular economic policy.
d) implement a specific monetary policy.

27. Assume that policymakers have decided to adopt a modified policy growth rule that adjusts for changes in the growth rate of velocity. If the growth rate of velocity falls by 3 percent and real GNP is increasing by 4 percent, then the price level would theoretically be held constant by setting the growth rate of the money supply equal to:

a) 1 percent.
b) 3 percent.
c) 4 percent.
d) 7 percent.

28. Assume that you are the President's chief economic adviser and a Monetarist. It has been determined that the economy may be headed into an inflationary situation. Which of the following policies would you recommend?

a) decrease the money supply.
b) pursue a contractionary fiscal policy.
c) keep the money supply growing at a stable rate and avoid active countercyclical fiscal policy.
d) use a combination of accommodating countercyclical fiscal and monetary policies.

29. Assume that as a result of a large increase in autonomous aggregate demand the current level of real GNP is in excess of the natural level of output. According to Keynesian theory, the most appropriate monetary policy would be for the Fed to:

a) decrease the required reserve ratio.
b) sell government bonds.
c) decrease the discount rate.
d) none of the above.

30. Which of the following factors argues most strongly against the use of countercyclical monetary policy?

a) Empirical evidence indicates that changes in the money supply do not affect the level of real GNP in the short run or the long run.
b) There is a variable lag in the effect of monetary policy which can cause it to be procyclical.
c) The Fed does not have enough tools to adequately control the money supply.
d) Monetary policy can only be used to decrease the money supply, not increase it.

Chapter 33, Monetary Policy: A Further Treatment

ANSWER KEY

Exercises

1. interest rate, investment
2. increase, interest rate, real, increase
3. unstable, downward, rigidity, countercyclical
4. rule, active, passive, stable
5. time-inconsistency problem
6. smaller, expectations
7. destabilizing
8. 1) Policymakers may have pursued unrealistic goals, 2) political pressures may have led to overly expansive or overly restrictive monetary policy, 3) lags and forecasting errors make policy difficult to develop and administer, and 4) until 1979, the Fed targeted interest rates, which in turn created inflationary pressures.
9. recognition lag
10. 1) The timing of business cycle turning points, 2) the growth of real GNP, and 3) the growth of the price level.
11. liquidity, increase, increase, decrease, income, fall, inflationary expectations (or Fisher), below
12. 4%. It will fall to 7%. Assuming the credit market was initially in equilibrium, the expected real interest rate will remain at 4%.
13. 3%
14. 1) Strict money targeting leads policymakers to ignore valuable information, 2) velocity is too unstable for a money growth rule to work, and 3) the adverse effects of supply-side shocks require that monetary policy be flexible.

Review Questions

1. b) is the correct answer. This is the definition of the velocity of money.

2. c) is the correct answer. In this case, it may be more difficult for the economy to adjust back to long-run equilibrium and hence, active monetary policy might be used to accelerate the adjustment process. a) and b) are endogenous changes the economy can adjust to on its own. In the case of d) the argument would be to simply cut government spending if it proves to be inflationary.

3. a) is the correct answer. This is an empirical fact. See the discussion in the text.

4. d) is the correct answer. The Keynesians argue that monetary policy influences the level of economic activity through its effect on the interest rate, An increase in the money supply causes the interest rate to decline. Investment is inversely related to the interest rate. Hence, when the interest rate declines, investment spending increases, which in turn results in an increase in aggregate demand.

5. d) is the correct answer. This is the conclusion that is reached by observing the relationship between the type of monetary policy pursued during various presidential administrations and the resulting performance of the macroeconomy. See the discussion in the text.

6. b) is the correct answer. Real GNP is determined by real factors, as opposed to monetary factors. In this case, the Fed is trying to push real GNP above the natural level by expanding aggregate demand. However, over the long run the SRAS curve will shift left due to higher prices, and output will fall back to the natural level.

7. c) is the correct answer. When money demand is unresponsive to changes in the interest rate a small change in the money supply causes the interest rate to change by a relatively large amount to re-equilibrate the money market. Combined with investment demand that is sensitive to changes in the interest rate, this results in a relatively large change in investment

demand and therefore a large change in aggregate demand and real GNP.

8. c) is the correct answer. The supply-side shock will cause the SRAS curve to shift left, resulting in a higher price level and a lower level of real GNP. To offset the output effect, the money supply must be increased to shift the AD curve to the right. This will cause output to increase, but at the expense of even higher prices.

9. b) is the correct answer. The objective of monetary policy will be to reduce aggregate demand. Hence, it is necessary to reduce the money supply. a) and b) will cause the money supply to increase. d) is fiscal policy, not monetary policy. An increase in the discount rate causes the money supply to decrease.

10. d) is the correct answer. With respect to answers a), b), and c) see the discussion in the first part of the chapter. Keynesians do not argue that there is no lag associated with the effects of monetary policy, but rather that the potential benefits of using active monetary policy outweigh the potential costs.

11. d) is the correct answer. If the change in the money supply is unanticipated it will cause interest rates to fall. As such, investment spending, aggregate demand, real GNP, and the price level will all increase in the short run. Recall that the monetarists assume that wages are somewhat rigid in the short run.

12. b) is the correct answer. The Fed will try to increase the expected real interest rate by reducing the money supply and driving up the nominal interest rate. However, the actual expected real interest rate is higher than the Fed's estimate. Hence the Fed will be overly contractionary.

13. b) is the correct answer. The monetarists assume that velocity is stable. Hence, changes in the money supply cause nominal GNP--PI x real GNP--to change in the short run. In the long run, however, real GNP is determined by real, not monetary, factors. Hence, over the long run changes in the money supply only affect the price level.

14. d) is the correct answer. a), b), and c) are all passive rules since they do not change in the face of changing economic conditions. Note that d) responds systematically to changes in the level of economic activity; the definition of an active policy rule.

15. b) is the correct answer. This is the formal statement of the credibility thesis. See the discussion in the text.

16. c) is the correct answer. These statements are all a matter of the historical record. Refer back to the corresponding discussion in the text to confirm each of the responses. Nixon's wage and price controls were a general failure.

17. d) is the correct answer. This is a statement of fact. See the discission in the text.

18. a) is the correct answer. This is the direct opposite of question 7. See the answer to question 7.

19. b) is the correct answer. A procyclical policy amplifies the business cycle. If the Fed selects a target interest rate and the interest rate changes, the Fed must alter the money supply to it restore it to its desired level. Alternatively, if the Fed decides to control the money supply it must leave the interest rate alone since altering the interest rate requires changes in the money supply. Since 1982 the Fed has focused more on interest rates and less on the money supply as its primary target. b) is a statement of fact. See the discussion in the text.

20. d) is the correct answer. a) is an expansionary policy that puts upward pressure on the price level. Increasing inflation causes interest rates to rise. Regarding c) and d), the income effect and the Fisher effect combine to increase interest rates over the long run when the money supply is increased (and interest rates initially fall). On the other hand, these same effect cause interest rates to fall over the long run when contractionary monetary policy is pursued (which increases interest rates in the short run).

21. a) is the correct answer. In this case, the decrease in the money supply will cause a substantial decrease in aggregate demand.

However, since the policy is such a surprise, wages and prices will be slow to adjust--there is little change in expectations in the short run. Hence, most of the effect is an output effect rather than a price effect.

22. b) is the correct answer. When the money supply is initially decreased, there is less liquidity. People are induced to conserve on their money holdings through the effects of a higher interest rate. However, over time, the reduction in the money supply causes real GNP to fall, which leads to a reduction in money demand and the interest rate. This is the income effect. In addition, as the aggregate demand curve shifts left, the price level, and therefore price expectations, fall, causing the expected inflation rate to fall--the Fisher or price expectations effect. This causes the interest rate to fall further. Overall, the income effect and the Fisher effect outweigh the liquidity effect and the interest rate falls.

23. d) is the correct answer. These are general conclusions that are derived form the monetarist model and their interpretations of the empirical evidence.

24. a) is the correct answer. As inflationary expectations decline, the expected real interest rate is assumed to increase. This reduces investment demand and causes the credit demand curve to shift left. The increase in the expected real interest rate causes savings to increase--the credit supply curve shifts right. The combined decrease in demand and increase in supply causes the interest rate to decrease.

25. c) is the correct answer. See the answer to question 13.

26. b) is the correct answer. This is the definition of the recognition lag.

27. d) is the correct answer. In this case we can use the formula: Ms growth rate + velocity growth rate = price level growth rate + real GNP growth rate. Substituting in for velocity and real GNP and setting price level growth rate equal to zero we have: Ms growth rate + -3% = 0% + 4%, or Ms growth rate = 7%.

28. c) is the correct answer. Note that a), b), and d) all involve active countercyclical policy, which the monetarists consider to be generally destabilizing. They would argue that the economy will do better if left on its own, and that the best policy is one that increases the stability of the economic environment, e.g., answer c).

29. b) is the correct answer. The Keynesians would argue for a contractionary monetary policy, i.e., one that reduces the money supply. b) will reduce the money supply. c) and d) will cause the money supply to increase.

30. b) is the correct answer. This is one of the primary arguments of the monetarists against the use of active monetary policy. See the discussion in the text concerning the lag in the effect of monetary policy. Statements a), c), and d) are all false.

CHAPTER 34
FISCAL POLICY: A FURTHER TREATMENT

OVERVIEW

In this chapter we develop a detailed analysis of countercyclical fiscal policy. We begin by considering the various combinations of fiscal policy that can be used to offset the business cycle. We then consider the evidence on the effectiveness of countercyclical fiscal policy, as well as questions regarding the magnitude of the effects of changes in fiscal policy. We conclude with a discussion of the concept of a national industrial policy.

In theory, changes in government purchases, transfers, and taxes can be used to alter the level of aggregate demand and offset cyclical fluctuations in the economy. However, because of the government's budget constraint, the impact of a particular policy action will depend on how it is financed. In general, deficit-financed changes in government purchases should have the greatest countercyclical effect. Deficit-financed changes in taxes should also be effective, although less so than changes in purchases. Tax-financed changes in purchases and transfers will have a relatively negligible effect. Spending-financed changes in taxes will, in fact, be procyclical.

Efforts to use countercyclical fiscal policy are subject to a number of problems. First, the problems of a lack of good forecasts and the lags associated with the effects of policy that we discussed in the context of monetary policy apply here as well. Second, enacting and implementing fiscal policy is a time-consuming process. Finally, political pressures often result in fiscal policies that are less than optimal. Automatic stabilizers are an exception to the rule. The income effects of such programs as unemployment compensation and welfare occur automatically in response to changes in the level of economic activity. As such, automatic stabilizers tend to offset fluctuations in the business cycle, making them one of the most effective components of countercyclical fiscal policy.

A number of researchers have addressed the question of the extent to which political pressures influence the business cycle. In particular, it is possible that politicians may manipulate the economy to achieve certain goals, such as reelection, thus creating a political business cycle. Empirical evidence suggests that, at least to some extent, there is a political business cycle.

The empirical evidence on fiscal policy since World War II suggests that with limited exceptions, fiscal policy has not been an effective stabilization tool. Moreover, it appears that in many cases, fiscal policy has been destabilizing. As such, many economists have come to doubt the potential for active fiscal policy to serve as an effective stabilization tool.

In addition to the issue of the effectiveness of countercyclical fiscal policy, there are questions about how powerful fiscal policy actually is over the short run and the long run. Three central issues in this debate are the effects of crowding out and crowding in, the importance of the composition of government spending, and the question of how to measure the expansiveness of deficit-financed fiscal policies.

The extent to which crowding out is a problem depends largely on the actual level of real GNP relative to the natural level of output. When output is substantially below the natural level, crowding out is probably not a problem. In fact, expansive fiscal policy may actually crowd in investment spending when output is low. However, crowding out does become a problem as output nears the natural level. Moreover, over the long run, deficit-financed government spending is likely to have adverse effects on the economy to the extent that it displaces spending in the private sector.

Empirical evidence suggests that effects of fiscal policy also depend significantly on the composition of government spending. In particular, changes in government spending on consumption goods and military investment appear to have little effect on the level of aggregate demand. However, government expenditures on investment in infrastructure appear to have a substantial positive effect on productivity and private investment.

Questions concerning how to measure the degree to which fiscal policy is actually expansionary or contractionary have also been raised. Research suggests that in some cases fiscal policy has been less expansionary that was previously thought. The way in which the government reports its expenditures also makes it difficult to assess the likely effects of specific policies.

Although discussions of fiscal policy generally focus on spending and taxes, some policymakers have suggested that fiscal policy should be expanded to include a national industrial policy. Although there is considerable disagreement as to what constitutes an appropriate national industrial policy, proponents tend to agree that the U.S. manufacturing sector is declining, foreign competition is winning the sales battle in the United States and abroad, and government can do a better job of allocating investment funds than the market. However, there is considerable evidence that can be used to refute each of these arguments, which in turn seriously undermines the argument for a national industrial policy.

KEY GRAPHS AND TERMS

Graphs

As in the previous chapter, the graphical analyses in this chapter employ the standard models developed in previous chapters. Be sure that you understand the issues being analyzed in each graph, and the logic that underlies the shifts and movements along curves that are illustrated in each graph.

Terms

ENACTMENT LAG
IMPLEMENTATION LAG
AUTOMATIC STABILIZER
PARTISAN CYCLE
ELECTORAL CYCLE
NATIONAL INDUSTRIAL POLICY

EXERCISES

1. A decrease in government purchases causes the AD curve to shift to the ________________. If the decrease in spending is matched by an equal decrease in taxes, the tax decrease will cause the AD curve to shift to the ________________. The combined effects of the decreases in spending and taxes will cause the AD curve to shift ________________, causing real GNP to ________________ in the short run.

2. Theoretically, the most effective countercyclical policy actions are ________________-________________ changes in ________________ ________________.

3. List three problems policymakers encounter when they try to use fiscal policy to offset the business cycle.

____

____

____

4. With respect to fiscal policy, the time it takes to develop a specific policy, i.e., a law, is called the ________________ lag, while the time it takes to put a policy decision into effect is called the ________________ lag. Fiscal policy actions that are the result of ________________ ________________ are not subject to such lags.

5. The ideal conditions for the creation of a political business cycle include a relatively ________________ short-run aggregate supply curve that shifts with a ________________, and an aggregate demand curve that is very (responsive, unresponsive) to fiscal policy.

6. An analysis of the available evidence suggests that inflation and real GNP growth are ________________ and unemployment is ________________ during Democratic administrations than in Republic administrations. This effect has been labeled a ________________ cycle.

7. The record of postwar fiscal policy indicates that, in general, fiscal policy (has, has not) been an effective stabilization tool, and that many fiscal policy actions have ________________ the economy.

8. If expansionary fiscal policy is used when the economy is at or near the natural level of output, the most likely result will be ________________ ______________ of investment spending. However, if the economy is operating well below the natural level of output, the same policy may result in ________________ ______________ of investment spending.

9. A given amount of government expenditures on infrastructure appears to have a ________________ effect on the long-run level of income than an equal amount of spending on consumption goods. As such, the ________________ of government spending appears to be as (or more) important as the level of government spending.

10. To the extent that consumers treat government expenditures on consumption goods as perfect substitutes for private consumption goods, aggregate demand ____________________________ as a result of an increase in government purchases of consumption goods.

11. Deficit spending will be (more, less) expansive than tax-financed spending if the public views the bonds sold by the government as part of their wealth.

12. Inflation (increases, reduces) the real value of government debt held by the public. In such a case, deficit spending is (more, less) expansive than it would appear to be.

13. The effect of the accounting practices used by the government is to ________________ the size of the deficit in a particular year. Ceteris paribus, this leads to an (overestimate, underestimate) of the expansiveness of fiscal policy.

14. List three basic arguments made by proponents of a national industrial policy. ________________

____

____

____

Use the figures below to answer questions 15 and 16.

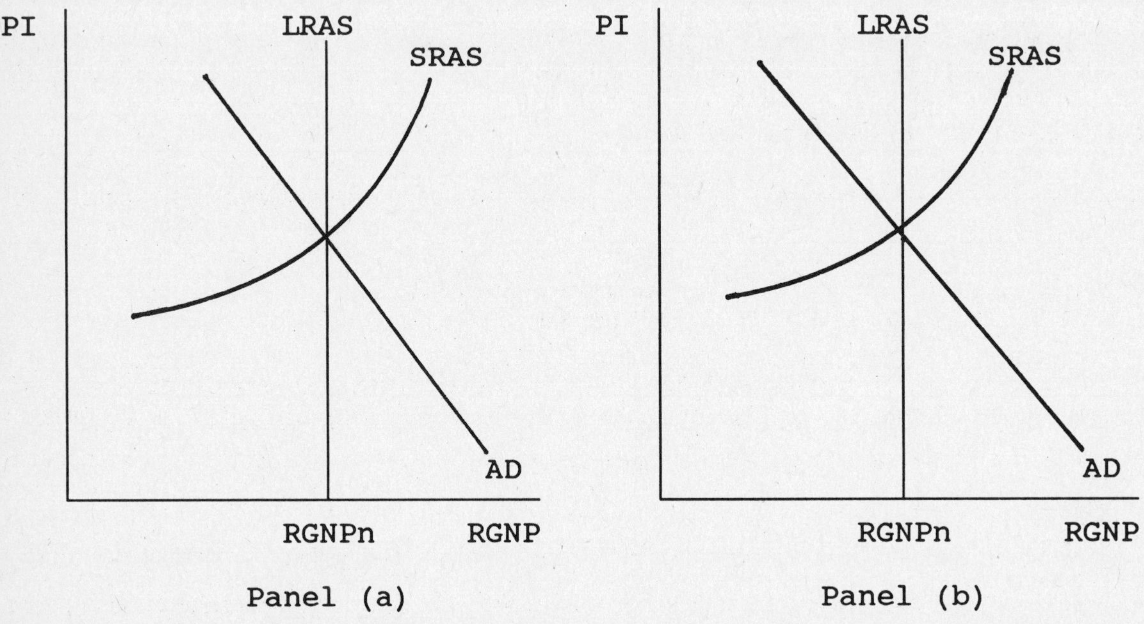

15. In panel (a), illustrate the effect of a significant decrease in the level of aggregate demand curve and label the new aggregate demand curve AD1. Then, using two additional curves, illustrate the relative effects of an expansionary fiscal policy consisting of the purchase of consumption goods that results in crowding out of investment spending. Also illustrate any long-run effects on RGNPn.

15. In panel (b) go through the same basic analysis, but assume that the government increases spending on infrastructure, as opposed to consumer goods, and investment spending is crowded in rather than crowded out. Also illustrate any long-run effects on RGNPn.

REVIEW QUESTIONS

1. Which of the following time lags is associated with discretionary fiscal policy, but not with discretionary monetary policy?

a) the recognition lag.
b) the effectiveness lag.
c) the enactment lag.
d) none of the above.

2. If active fiscal policy is used to offset the price level effect of an adverse supply-side shock, in the short-run this will cause output:

a) to rise, and the price level to fall.
b) to fall, and the price level to rise.
c) and the price level to both fall.
d) and the price level to both rise.

3. Assume that real GNP is currently below the natural level of output. In order to restore full employment output most rapidly, an advocate of active countercyclical fiscal policy would recommend:

a) an increase in government spending, and an increase in taxes.
c) a decrease in government spending, and a decrease in taxes.
b) an increase in government spending, and a decrease in taxes.
d) a decrease in government, and an increase in taxes.

4. The amount of time that passes before a discretionary fiscal policy is actually put into effect is called the ________________ lag.

a) recognition
b) effectiveness
c) implementation
d) enactment

5. If countercyclical fiscal policy is used to bring down inflation caused by excessive aggregate demand, which of the following would a Keynesian consider to be the most appropriate monetary policy for the Fed to follow?

a) decrease the reserve ratio.
b) use moral suasion.
c) decrease the discount rate.
d) sell bonds.

6. Efforts to stabilize the economy through the use of discretionary fiscal policies may turn out to be relatively ineffective due to:

a) a significant lag between the time when a problem is recognized and when a policy is put into place.
b) the existence of political business cycle.
c) the effects of indirect crowding out of investment spending.
d) all of the above.

7. Which of the following statements is correct?

a) Automatic stabilizers overcorrect for fluctuations in economic activity, e.g., they may transform a small expansion into a recession.
b) Automatic stabilizers partially offset fluctuations in the level of economic activity.
c) Automatic stabilizers can be relied on to eliminate completely any fluctuations in economic activity.
d) Automatic stabilizers work to halt inflation, but are incapable of slowing a recession.

8. The primary goal of fiscal and monetary policies is to:

a) balance the budget in a non-inflationary environment.
b) maintain a full employment, non-inflationary level of output.
c) eliminate unemployment at any cost.
d) keep the budget balanced and the money supply stable, respectively.

9. Theoretically (and ignoring the possibility of crowding out), which of the following policy options will be most effective as a means of increasing aggregate demand and the level of real GNP?

a) a tax-financed increase in transfer payments
b) a deficit-financed decrease in taxes
c) a tax-financed increase in government purchases
d) a deficit-financed increase in government purchases

10. Assume that the government decides to cut taxes. However, in order to avoid a deficit, it cuts purchases by an equal amount. The short-run effect of this policy action will be to:

a) reduce Real GNP and the price level.
b) increase real GNP and the price level.
c) reduce real GNP, but increase the price level.
d) increase real GNP, but reduce the price level.

11. Which of the following problems undermines the effectiveness of both fiscal and monetary countercyclical policies?

a) The pressure of having to continually satisfy competing political goals.
b) The long lag time involved in enacting a specific policy.
c) The incentive to manipulate the economy in order to achieve personal goals.
d) The lack of good information on the current state of the economy.

12. In which of the following situations will expansionary fiscal policy be most effective as means of increasing real GNP in the short run?

a) The SRAS curve is relatively steep and wages and prices are very flexible.
b) The SRAS curve is relatively steep and wages and prices are very inflexible.
c) The SRAS curve is relatively flat and wages and prices are very flexible.
d) The SRAS curve is relatively flat and wages and prices are very inflexible.

13. Which of the following statements is correct regarding the existence of a political business cycle?

a) Republican administrations appear to avoid the use of fiscal policy to influence the level of economic activity.
b) Democratic administrations appear to concentrate on the use of fiscal policy to hold down the inflation rate.
c) On average, Democratic administrations encourage more rapid economic growth than Republican administrations.
d) Republican administrations appear to focus on reducing inflation prior to elections, and increasing employment and output in subsequent years.

14. Fiscal policy designed to increase the level of aggregate demand will have the greatest effect when investment spending is:

a) sensitive to changes in the interest rate and insensitive to changes in the level of real GNP.
b) insensitive to changes in the interest rate and sensitive to changes in the level of real GNP.
c) sensitive to changes in both the interest rate and the level of real GNP.
d) insensitive to changes in both the interest rate and the level of real GNP.

15. Ceteris paribus, the long-run outcome of fiscal policy consisting of deficit-financed spending on infrastructure will be:

a) a decrease in the natural level of real GNP and the price level.
b) no change in the natural level of real GNP or the price level.
c) an increase in the natural level of real GNP and a decrease in the price level.
d) an increase in the natural level of output and an uncertain effect on the price level.

16. The results of recent empirical analyses indicate that an increase in government consumption spending:

a) has a greater effect on aggregate demand than the same size increase in private consumption spending.
b) causes aggregate demand to fall.
c) has a greater effect on aggregate demand than government spending on infrastructure.
d) has no direct effect on aggregate demand.

17. The same research referred to in the previous question estimated that the multiplier effect of nonmilitary investment spending is around:

a) 1
b) 2
c) 3
d) 4

18. Assume the public held $2.2 trillion in public debt at the beginning of 1991, during 1991 the government ran a deficit of $220 billion, and the inflation rate during 1991 was 6.2 percent. In this case, the change in the real value of the debt was approximately:

a) an increase of approximately $71 billion.
b) an increase of approximately $136 billion.
c) a decrease of approximately $71 billion.
d) a decrease of approximately $136 billion.

19. Which of the following statements is <u>not</u> correct?

a) If someone sells shares of stock in a company and realizes a rate of return that is equal to the rate of inflation, making them pay a capital gains tax on the profits forces them to incur a loss.
b) The capital gains tax makes it more costly to hire new executives and start new businesses.
c) Opponents of a cut in the capital gains tax argue that such a move will only worsen the government budget deficit.
d) The capital gains tax is only applied to the real increase in the value of an asset, not the nominal increase.

20. Which of the following statements is correct?

a) Given the current understanding of economic policy tools, the economy is essentially depression proof, although not necessarily recession proof.
b) Most economists are concerned that the economy could slip into another depression quite rapidly.
c) Federal deposit insurance has increased public confidence in the banking system and consequently reduced the probability of large-scale bank runs to an extremely low level.
d) A major banking collapse in another part of the world would have no effect on the U.S. banking industry.

21. Which of the following is <u>not</u> an argument that is made in support of a national industrial policy?

a) Government is in a better position than the market to determine the quantities of goods that should be produced.
b) Jobs in the U.S. manufacturing sector are being lost to foreign competitors.
c) Government can do a much better job of allocating investment funds than the market.
d) Foreign competition is winning the sales battle in the United States and abroad.

22. According to the available evidence:

a) the lack of employment growth in the U.S. manufacturing sector has been offset by a substantial increase in productivity.
b) there is nothing to suggest that the U.S. manufacturing industries as a whole are becoming less competitive in the world market.
c) having the government make investment or production decisions wastes most of the information people have about the economy.
d) all of the above.

23. Assume that the government decides to increase the amount of transfers going to the poor and finances the new transfers with an increase in taxes. In this situation the most likely outcome would be:

a) a large increase in real GNP and the price level.
b) a large decrease in real GNP and the price level.
c) a large increase in real GNP and a decrease in the price level.
d) relatively little effect on the level of real GNP or the price level.

ANSWER KEY

Exercises

1. left, right, left, decrease
2. deficit-financed, government purchases
3. 1) Good information on the current state of the economy is scarce (forecasting problems), 2) lags associated with the enactment, implementation and effects of fiscal policy, and 3) the potential for political considerations to override economic considerations in the formulation of policy.
4. enactment, implementation, automatic stabilizers
5. flat, lag, responsive
6. higher, lower, partisan
7. has not, destabilized
8. crowding out, crowding in
9. greater, composition
10. will be unaffected (will not change)
11. more
12. reduces, less
13. overstate, overestimate
14. 1) The U.S. manufacturing sector is declining, 2) foreign competition is winning the sales battle in the United States and abroad, and 3) the government can do a better job of allocating investment funds than the market.
15. The initial decrease in autonomous expenditures will shift the AD curve to the left, causing real GNP and the price level to fall in the short run. The increase in government purchases will shift the AD curve back to the right. However, to the extent that there is crowding out of investment spending, this will offset the rightward shift of the AD curve and it will end up somewhere between AD1 and the AD curve associated with the increase in government purchases of consumption goods. There is no long-run effect on the level of real GNP.
16. The effects of the decrease in autonomous expenditures and the increase in government spending are the same as in the previous question. However, crowding in implies an increase in investment spending, which pushes the AD curve further to the right. Moreover, since the increased government spending is on infrastructure, investment will increase over the long run, causing the productive capacity of the economy to increase. As such, RGNPn will increase over the long run as well.

Chapter 34, Fiscal Policy: A Further Treatment

Review Questions

1. c) is the correct answer. The enactment lag is defined as the amount of time needed to develop a policy and sign it into law. In the case of fiscal policy this can take months. Monetary policy can be formulated literally in a day. Hence, there is no enactment lag with monetary policy. Both types of policy suffer from recognition and effectiveness lags.

2. c) is the correct answer. An adverse supply-side shock causes the SRAS curve to shift to the left, resulting in higher prices and a lower level of output. If fiscal policy is used to offset the price level effect, the result will be a leftward shift of the AD curve. This will put downward pressure on prices but will cause output to fall even further.

3. b) is the correct answer. The idea here is to increase aggregate demand as much as possible. Increasing government spending and decreasing taxes both cause the AD curve to shift right, which causes real GNP to increase.

4. c) is the correct answer. This is the definition of the implementation lag.

5. d) is the correct answer. The appropriate fiscal policy would be contractionary so that aggregate demand is reduced. As such, a contractionary monetary policy is called for as well so as not to offset the effects of the fiscal policy. Decreasing the reserve requirement ratio and the discount rate are both expansionary monetary policies. Selling bonds causes the money supply to decrease, i.e., it is contractionary.

6. d) is the correct answer. These are problems that reduce the effectiveness of fiscal policy. See the text for specific discussions of each problem.

7. b) is the correct answer. Automatic stabilizers work to slow the rate at which income decreases in recessions (unemployment compensation and welfare payments increase), and increases in expansions (unemployment compensation and welfare payments decrease). Thus, they have a dampening effect on the business cycle. However, actual experience shows that they do not completely offset cyclical fluctuations, ruling out answer c).

8. b) is the correct answer. This is a simplified statement of the overall goals of both policies.

9. d) is the correct answer. Government purchases have a larger multiplier effect than government transfers. In addition, an increases in taxes which is intended to finance increased spending puts downward pressure on aggregate demand. Borrowing does not. Hence, theory would suggest answer d).

10. a) is the correct answer. The reduction in taxes causes disposable income to increase, which causes consumption spending, and therefore aggregate demand, to increase. Note, however, that to the extent that the decrease in taxes causes savings to increase, some of the tax cut does not turn into increased spending. The decrease in purchases has a contractionary effect on aggregate demand. Since the decline in purchases affects aggregate demand directly, while the decrease in taxes works indirectly through its effect on disposable income, the purchases effect dominates and the AD curve shifts left, causing output and the price level to fall.

11. d) is the correct answer. a) and c) are problems associated with fiscal policy. See question 1 regarding b). d) is discussed at length in this and the previous chapter.

12. d) is the correct answer. If the SRAS curve is relatively flat, a shift in the AD curve causes output to change by a relatively large amount without altering the price level significantly. The more inflexible wages and prices are, the slower the SRAS curve will be to adjust to a change in the actual price level.

13. c) is the correct answer. This answer is based on recent empirical investigations of the political business cycle. See the discussion in the text regarding this and the other statements.

14. b) is the correct answer. Fiscal policy designed to increase real GNP causes interest rates and real GNP to increase. The more insensitive investment demand is to a change in the interest rate, the less of a problem crowding out of investment spending due to an increase in the interest rate will be. On the other hand, the

more sensitive investment spending is to a change in real GNP, the more crowding in will occur.

15. d) is the correct answer. The increase in government spending causes the AD curve to shift right. However, the fact that the spending is on infrastructure means that private investment spending will increase as well, causing the LRAS curve to shift right, as well as a further shift of the AD curve. Overall, AD, SRAS, and LRAS all increase, causing real GNP to increase. However, because we have a simultaneous increase in both demand and supply, the effect on the price level is uncertain without information on the relative magnitudes of the shifts.

16. d) is the correct answer. This conclusion is based on empirical evidence. See the discussion in the text.

17. d) is the correct answer. This conclusion is based on empirical evidence. See the discussion in the text.

18. a) is the correct answer. The real value of the existing debt declined by $2.2 trillion x .062 = $.136 trillion. The real value of the deficit for 1991 is $.22 trillion/1.062 = $.207 trillion. Adding these two figures together yields a net increase of $.71 trillion ($71 billion).

19. d) is the correct answer. See the Why the Disagreement? box in this chapter for a complete discussion of these issues.

20. c) is the correct answer. See the Does it Make Economic Sense? box in this chapter for a complete discussion of these issues.

21. a) is the correct answer. See the answer to question 14 of the exercises. Note that proponents of a national industrial policy do not suggest that the government should decide how much of different goods should be produced, but rather in which sectors of the economy production will be most beneficial.

22. d) is the correct answer. See the discussion in the text regarding the validity of the arguments in favor of a national industrial policy.

23. d) is the correct answer. The increase in transfers puts upward pressure on aggregate demand, but the increase in taxes puts downward pressure on aggregate demand. Since both changes work through their effects on disposable income and, consequently, consumption spending, they tend to offset each other with the end result that the position of the AD curve is left unchanged.

CHAPTER 35
INTERNATIONAL TRADE

OVERVIEW

In this chapter we consider the theory of international trade. After we show how countries can mutually benefit from trade, we analyze the net benefits from trade in individual markets. We then go on to address the issue of trade restrictions and consider a number of arguments for the erection of trade barriers. We end the chapter with a discussion of the composition of the U.S. balance of trade and how it has changed in recent years.

The theory of international trade is based on the principle of comparative advantage. A country possesses a comparative advantage in a good when its relative opportunity costs of production are lower than the relative opportunity costs in other countries. By specializing in the production of goods in which it possesses a comparative advantage, and then trading with other countries, a country can consume a combination of goods that lies beyond its production possibilities frontier. The terms of trade, which specify the trading ratio between two goods, are determined by the relative demands for the goods.

International trade has the effect of equalizing the price of a good across countries. For example, if the domestic price of a good is lower than the world price it will encourage exports of the good to other countries where the market price is higher, thus lowering the price of the good in other countries, and increasing the good's price in the domestic economy. The opposite effect occurs in the case where the domestic price is higher than the world price.

So long as trade is unrestricted, there will be a net gain in the affected markets. In the case where exports increase, domestic producers gain more than domestic consumers lose. In the case where imports increase, domestic consumers gain more than domestic producers lose. This is not meant to imply, however, that there are not additional costs. For example, there are often adverse employment effects in markets for imported goods. However, evidence indicates that these effects are relatively small and that in fact, more adverse employment effects result from reallocations of production within the domestic economy than across economies.

Although free trade can make economies better off as a whole, trade restrictions are nonetheless frequently employed to alter the flow of goods and services among countries. Trade restrictions generally consist of tariffs--a tax on imported goods--and quotas, which limit the quantity of a good that can be imported during a specified period of time. The general effect of a tariff or quota is to reduce the net benefits from trade. Although domestic producers gain, this gain comes at the expense of a larger loss incurred by domestic consumers. In general, to the extent that trade restrictions are employed, tariffs are preferable to quotas. First, quotas may end up favoring less efficient firms and inferior products. Second, quotas transfer more income to foreign producers than do tariffs.

A number of arguments have been proposed in support of trade restrictions. The infant industry argument contends that new industries need to be protected until they are able to compete effectively on the international market. The cheap foreign labor argument contends that lower-priced labor allows foreign producers to undercut the prices of domestically-produced goods and services. The national defense argument is based on the contention that the economy cannot risk becoming dependent on other countries for its military needs. Finally, it is argued that tariffs can be used as bargaining chips in efforts designed to limit the extent to which trade barriers are actually employed by other countries. In all but the last case, there are strong counter arguments that effectively offset the case for trade restrictions.

The difference between a country's exports and imports--its balance of trade--can be positive (a trade surplus), negative (a trade deficit) or zero. The composition of a country's imports and exports tends to reflect the relative amounts of skilled and unskilled labor and capital that it possesses. Developed countries such as the United States and Japan, which possess relatively large amounts of capital, tend to export more sophisticated manufactured goods and import such goods as textiles. Less-developed countries, on the other hand, possess relatively large amounts of unskilled labor, and as such, tend to export a greater share of items such as textiles. The

United States is a net exporter of agricultural products and capital goods and a net importer of petroleum products, consumer goods, and automobiles. In recent years, the U.S. merchandise trade balance has turned sharply downward.

KEY GRAPHS AND TERMS

Graphs

This chapter employs the model of the production possibilities frontier and the supply and demand model to graphically illustrate a number of key points. Figure 1 uses the PPF to illustrate the benefits of specialization and exchange in much the same manner as was done in Chapter 2. Figures 2 and 3 illustrate the effects of a change in supply on the domestic price of a particular good. In Figure 2 there is, in effect, an increase in supply, which pushes the domestic price down. In Figure 3, the opposite occurs. Figures 4 and 5 use the model of supply and demand and the concepts of producer surplus and consumer surplus to illustrate the net gains from trade. Refer to Chapter 4 for a refresher on these basic concepts. Finally, Figures 6 and 7 illustrate the effects of trade restrictions in a specific market. Once again, the effect in question amounts to a change in supply that in turn alters the market price and quantity exchanged.

Terms

PRINCIPLE OF COMPARATIVE ADVANTAGE
ABSOLUTE ADVANTAGE
IMPORT-COMPETING INDUSTRIES
TARIFF
QUOTA
SENILE-INDUSTRY ARGUMENT
TRADE BALANCE
TRADE SURPLUS
TRADE DEFICIT

EXERCISES

1. When countries possess a comparative advantage in the production of different goods, Specialization and Trade enable them consume beyond their PPFs.

2. A country that can produce a good at lower resource cost than other countries is said to have an absolute advantage, while a country that can produce a good at lower opportunity cost than other countries is said to have a Comparative advantage.

3. Assume that with its available resources, Country X can produce 600 tons of grain or 1200 tons of sugar. Country Y, on the other hand, can produce 800 tons of grain or 1000 tons of sugar. Which country has a comparative advantage in grain production? Country Y Sugar production? Country X Give an example of mutually beneficial terms of trade between X and Y. 1.25S < 1G < 2S or (0.5G < 1S < 0.8G).

4. Assume that the domestic price of good X is higher than the world price of X. In this case, free trade will cause the domestic price of X to decrease, and the quantity purchased to increase. In addition, consumer surplus will increase, while producer surplus will decrease by a Smaller amount.

5. A TARIFF is a tax on an imported good, while a QUOTA is a limit on the quantity of the good that can be imported.

6. The difference between a nation's exports and its imports is called its Trade BALANCE.

7. List the four arguments for trade restrictions that are discussed in the text. infant industry argument, cheap foreign labor argument, national defense argument, tariffs as a bargining chip argument.

Of these four, which one is the most defensible? tariffs as a bargining chip argument.

8. Assume that a tariff is imposed on an imported good that was previously free of all trade restrictions. In terms of gains and losses, the effect of the tariff is as follows: domestic producers gains, domestic consumers lose, foreign producers lose, the domestic government gains, and overall, the domestic economy lose.

Use the figures below, which depict the production possibilities frontiers for countries A and B, respectively, to answer questions 9 - 11.

9. Calculate the relative opportunity costs for the two products in each country.

Country A: 1C = .5 ; 1F = 2 Country B: 1C = 1.33 ; 1F = .75

10. Based upon your answer to 9, which country has a comparative advantage in food production? Country B Cloth production? Country A This suggests that Country A should specialize in the production of Cloth and Country B should specialize in the production of Food.

11. According to the principle of comparative advantage countries should specialize in the production of those goods for which they possess a comparative advantage and then trade with other countries. Assuming that countries A and B specialize in the production of one good each and then trade, which of the following would be considered mutually beneficial terms of trade?

1F = 3C 1F = 1/2C 3F = 1C 1F = 1C

REVIEW QUESTIONS

1. According to the principle of comparative advantage:

a) So long as the absolute price of producing a good is cheaper in one country than another, the country facing the cheaper price should specialize in that good.
b) Countries should specialize in the production of those goods for which the relative costs of production are least.
c) The country with the greatest GNP will have a relative advantage when it comes to specialization and trade with smaller countries.
d) Countries with a relatively small GNP will have an advantage with respect to the benefits of trade.

2. The United States is a major net ____________ of agricultural products and capital goods, and a major net ____________ of consumer goods and automobiles.

a) exporter; exporter
b) importer; importer
c) exporter; importer
d) importer; exporter

3. A tariff can best be described as:

a) a tax imposed on an imported good.
b) a tax imposed on an exported good.
c) a law which limits the amount of a good that can be imported.
d) a government payment to producers of an exportable good.

4. Country A can produce 1 unit of beer in 6 hours and 1 unit of pretzels in 2 hours. Country B can produce 1 unit of beer in 10 hours and 1 unit of pretzels in 2 hours. Which of the following statements is correct?

a) Country A has an absolute advantage in both beer and pretzel production.
b) Country B has an absolute advantage in both beer and pretzel production.
c) Country A has a comparative advantage in beer but not pretzel production.
d) Country A has a comparative advantage in pretzel but not beer production.

5. Based on the information in the previous question, which of the following statements is correct?

a) Country A should specialize in pretzels and Country B should specialize in beer.
b) Country A should specialize in beer and Country B should specialize in pretzels.
c) There will be no mutually beneficial gains from specialization and trade.
d) Both countries should specialize in beer.

6. When the world price of a good is lower than the domestic price of the same good, free trade results in a reallocation of resources:

a) to domestic production of the good, and away from production of the good in other countries.
b) away from domestic production of the good, and to production of the good in other countries.
c) to both domestic production of the good, and production of the good in other countries.
d) away from both domestic production of the good, and production of the good in other countries.

7. Assume, ceteris paribus, that the U.S. government decides to eliminate an existing tariff on French wines. In the U.S. market for wine this will cause:

a) an increase in price, decrease in the quantity exchanged, and increase in the sales of domestic producers.
b) an increase price, quantity exchanged, and sales of domestic producers.
c) a decrease in price, increase in the quantity exchanged, and decrease in the sales of domestic producers.
d) a decrease in price, quantity exchanged, and sales of domestic producers.

Use the following figure, which represents the domestic market for good Z, to answer questions 8 - 10. (Note: Pw indicates world price of Z; Pd and Qd indicate domestic price and quantity of Z.)

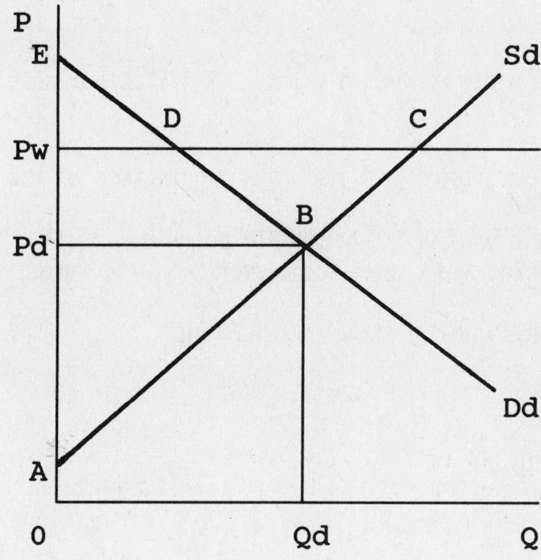

8. Assume that initially there is no trading of Z. In this case, the net gain in the domestic market from production and consumption of Z is the area

a) ABPd
b) EBPd
c) ABE
d) 0EBQd

9. Now assume there is world trade in Z. As a result, producer surplus will increase by the area ________________, and society's net gain will <u>increase</u> by the area ________________.

a) APwC; ABE
b) PwDBPd; PdEB
c) DCB; DCB
d) PwCBPd; DCB

10. As a result of the introduction of world trade, consumer surplus has:

a) increased by the area DCB
b) increased by the area PwCBPd
c) decreased by the area PwED
d) decreased by the area PwDBPd

11. Which of the following statements is correct?

a) Free trade does little to encourage domestic competition.
b) Free trade enables the world economy to achieve a more efficient allocation of scarce resources.
c) Free trade benefits countries only if they possess an absolute advantage in the production of the goods traded.
d) Free trade is of no benefit to underdeveloped countries.

12. Tariffs have the effect of:

a) increasing the potential benefits of specialization and trade.
b) decreasing the well being of consumers.
c) decreasing the sales of domestic producers.
d) reducing the tax revenues of the government.

13. Assume that the domestic price of good X is $10 per unit, while the world price of X is $12 per unit. Assuming there are no trade restrictions,

a) X will be imported to the domestic market, and the domestic price will rise to some average of the current domestic and world prices.
b) X will be imported to the domestic market, and the domestic price will fall below $10 per unit.
c) X will be exported to the world market, and the domestic price will rise to some average of the current domestic and world prices.
d) X will be exported to the world market, and the domestic price will rise above $12 per unit.

14. A quota can best be described as:

a) a law which limits the amount of a good that can be imported.
b) a government payment to producers of an exportable good.
c) a tax imposed on an imported good.
d) a tax imposed on an exported good.

15. Which of the following arguments for trade protection is frequently cited by developing countries?

a) the military-self-sufficiency argument.
b) the infant-industry argument.
c) the cheap-foreign-labor argument.
d) the diversification-for-stability argument.

16. The "Trade Balance" refers to the:

a) difference between the value of the current account and the capital account.
b) difference between the value of a country's exports and and its imports.
c) difference in value between domestic trade and foreign trade.
d) net value of a country's balance of payments.

17. Which of the following statements is not correct?

a) During the 1970s, most U.S. industries that experienced job losses did so due to shifts in domestic demand rather than the effects of international trade.
b) International trade results in an increase in total world output of goods and services.
c) The use of wage subsidies is considered to be a more efficient approach than increased unemployment compensation as a means of helping workers displaced by the effects of international trade.
d) Exports result in a net gain for the domestic economy, while imports result in a net loss.

18. Of the trade restriction arguments listed below, which one may actually contribute to the maintenance of relatively free world trade?

a) the national-defense argument.
b) the infant-industry argument.
c) the cheap-foreign-labor argument.
d) the tariffs-as-a-bargaining-chip argument.

19. Which of the following statement is correct?

a) In 1982, foreign automobile imports accounted for more than 50 percent of the domestic market.
b) It has been estimated that the quotas placed on Japanese car imports in the early 1980s saved approximately 26,000 domestic jobs at a cost of approximately $160,000 per job per year.
c) The quotas placed on Japanese cars in the early 1980s caused the average price of a Japanese car to decline by approximately $2,500.
d) U.S. auto manufacturers took advantage of the quotas placed on Japanese cars in the early 1980s by increasing productivity and negotiating lower wage contracts with their workers.

20. Ceteris paribus, which of the following will tend to move the U.S. trade balance in the direction of a surplus?

a) an increase in the cost of inputs used to produce exports
b) an increase in the level of income in the United States
c) a decrease in the foreign price level relative to the price level in the United States
d) A reduction in the amount of foreign restrictions on international trade

21. With its available resources, Country A can produce 30 units of X or 60 units of Y. With the same amount of resources, Country B can produce 60 units of X or 40 units of Y. Which of the following statements is true?

a) Country A has a comparative advantage in the production of X and Country B has a comparative advantage in the production of Y.
b) Country A has a comparative advantage in the production of Y and Country B has a comparative advantage in the production of X.
c) Country A has both an absolute and a comparative advantage in the production of both X and Y.
d) Country B has both an absolute and a comparative advantage in the production of both X and Y.

22. Referring to the previous question, which of the following would be considered mutually beneficial terms of trade between Country A and Country B?

a) 1Y = 1X
b) 2Y = 1X
c) 1Y = 2X
d) 1Y = 3X

23. If the U.S. government imposes a tariff on German automobiles, in the U.S. market for automobiles this will cause:

a) an increase in price, decrease in the quantity exchanged, and increase in the sales of domestic producers.
b) an increase price, quantity exchanged, and sales of domestic producers.
c) a decrease in price, increase in the quantity exchanged, and increase in the sales of domestic producers.
d) a decrease in price, quantity exchanged, and sales of domestic producers.

24. Which of the following arguments for trade protection would be considered most applicable from the view point of unions?

a) the national-defense argument.
b) the infant-industry argument.
c) the tariffs as a bargaining chip argument.
d) the cheap-foreign-labor argument.

ANSWER KEY

Exercises
1. specialization, trade
2. absolute, comparative
3. Y (grain), X (sugar); anything in the range 1.25S < 1G < 2S (or 0.5G < 1S < 0.8G).
4. decrease, increase, increase, decrease, smaller
5. tariff, quota
6. trade balance
7. 1) Infant industry argument, 2) cheap foreign labor argument, 3) national defense argument, 4) tariffs as a bargaining chip argument, tariffs as a bargaining chip argument
8. gain, lose, lose, gains, loses
9. The relative opportunity cost ratio in Country A is 1F = 2C or 1C = 1/2F. For Country B the relative opportunity costs can be written as 1F = 3/4C or 1C = 4/3F.
10. Country A has a comparative advantage in the production of cloth. Country B has a comparative advantage in food production. Country A should specialize in cloth and Country B should specialize in food.
11. 1F = 1C

Review Questions

1. b) is the correct answer. Comparative advantage is defined as having the lowest relative opportunity cost. As is discussed in the text, so long as countries specialize in goods in which they have a comparative advantage and trade, they can consume beyond their respective PPFs.

2. c) is the correct answer. This is an empirical fact. See the discussion in the text.

3. a) is the correct answer. This is the definition of a tariff.

4. c) is the correct answer. For Country A the relative opportunity costs can be written as 1B = 3P and 1P = 1/3B. For Country B the relative opportunity costs can be written as 1B = 5P and 1P = 1/5B. Hence, the relative opportunity costs of beer production are lower in Country A, and the relative opportunity costs of pretzel production are lower in Country B. See question 1 for the definition of comparative advantage.

5. b) is the correct answer. See the answer to question 1.

6. b) is the correct answer. Since the world price is lower, the good will be imported into the domestic economy and sales will be taken away from domestic producers who will respond by cutting back on production. Foreign producers will increase production to accommodate sales in the domestic economy.

7. c) is the correct answer. Referring to Figure 6 in the text, this is equivalent to starting at a price of Pt and then moving to price Pw. As such, we move down the domestic demand and supply curves. Price falls, total domestic consumption rises to Q*, and domestic production falls from Qt to Qdom.

8. c) is the correct answer. Without trade, the equilibrium price is Pd and the quantity is Qd. In this case the net gain is the sum of producers'

surplus, represented by the area ABPd, and consumers' surplus, represented by the area EBPd. These areas add up to ABE.

9. d) is the correct answer. Producers' surplus is the area bounded by the price line, the supply curve, and the vertical axis, or in this case, PwCA. Thus it has increased by the difference between the old producer surplus--ABPd--and the new producers' surplus. Part of the new producers' surplus--PwDBPd--was formerly consumers' surplus. Hence, the net gain is DCB.

10. d) is the correct answer. See the answer to the previous question.

11. b) is the correct answer. The conclusions of the analysis of comparative advantage and specialization and trade show that b) is the only correct answer. Trade is a win-win situation for all economies, even though there may be costs borne by individuals.

12. b) is the correct answer. As the analysis in Figure 6 in the text shows, consumers are made worse off as a result of tariffs. Price is higher and quantity purchased is lower overall. However, domestic producers are better off since their sales increase relative to what they would be with free trade. Government benefits since a tariff is a tax which results in increased revenues.

13. c) is the correct answer. Since the world price is higher, domestic producers can realize additional profits by selling at higher prices in foreign markets. As they move up their supply curves, price increases. However, the rise in price is bounded by the existing world price of $12.

14. a) is the correct answer. This is the definition of a quota.

15. b) is the correct answer. It is argued that firms in new industries must be protected until they are able to compete effectively on the world market with older, more experienced firms. See the discussion in the text.

16. b) is the correct answer. This is the definition of the trade balance.

17. d) is the correct answer. a) is an empirical fact; see the discussion in the text, which also addresses the point made in c). b) is addressed in questions 1 and 11. To see why d) is an incorrect statement refer to the analysis in Figures 4 and 5 in the text.

18. d) is the correct answer. See the summary of the discussion in the text regarding the alternative arguments for trade restrictions.

19. b) is the correct answer. This is the finding of an empirical study of this issue. See the discussion in the text regarding the quotas on Japanese imports in the 1980s. It addresses all of the statements made here.

20. d) is the correct answer. An increase in the costs of inputs raises output prices, thus reducing the attractiveness of our exports. An increase in income in the U.S. will cause imports to increase relative to exports, as does a reduction in the foreign price level relative to the U.S. price level. A reduction in foreign trade restrictions will enable the U.S. to sell more exports, ceteris paribus.

21. b) is the correct answer. In Country A the relative costs of production are 1X = 2Y, or 1Y = 1/2X. In Country B the relative costs of production are 1X = 2/3Y, or 1Y = 3/2X. As such, A has a comparative advantage in Y, and B has a comparative advantage in X.

22. a) is the correct answer. From Country A's perspective, the range of mutually beneficial terms of trade is 1/2X < 1Y < 3/2X. From Country B's perspective, the range of mutually beneficial terms of trade is 2/3Y < 1X < 2X. Only a) falls into this range.

23. a) is the correct answer. See the analysis in Figure 6 in the text.

24. d) is the correct answer. This one is too obvious to consider further.

CHAPTER 36
INTERNATIONAL FINANCE AND THE OPEN-ECONOMY MODEL

OVERVIEW

In this chapter we examine the financial aspects of international trade. We begin by developing the concept of the balance of payments, which summarizes flows into and out of an economy. We then develop the theory of exchange rate determination, and distinguish between fixed exchange rates and flexible exchange rates. We then go on to consider how the economy responds to various supply and demand shocks in an open economy setting. We conclude with a discussion of the effects of government deficits in the case of flexible exchange rates.

A country's balance of payments summarizes the flows of goods and services and financial assets into and out of the country. The trade balance, i.e, net exports, and net unilateral transfers make up the current account portion of the balance of payments. The capital account summarizes the flows of financial assets into and out of the economy. Strictly speaking, the values of the current account and the capital account must directly offset each other--the balance of payments always sums to zero. However, data collection problems result in a statistical discrepancy that must be accounted for.

The foreign exchange rate measures the price of one currency in terms of another, and influences the levels of net exports and capital flows. The exchange rate is determined by the forces of supply and demand. For example, the exchange rate of Japanese yen for dollars, measured as the number of yen required to purchase a dollar, is determined by the demand for U.S. dollars and the supply of U.S. dollars.

The demand curve for dollars is downward sloping on the assumption that as the exchange rate falls, dollars, and therefore the U.S. goods those dollars can buy, become relatively less expensive. The demand for dollars, i.e, the position of the demand curve, is determined primarily by the real income level in foreign countries, the price level in foreign countries relative to the U.S. price level, and the real interest rate in the United States relative to the real interest rate in foreign countries.

The supply curve for dollars is upward sloping, reflecting the fact that as the exchange rate rises, a dollar buys more foreign exchange and therefore more foreign-made goods. The quantity of dollars supplied increases as the exchange rate rises. The same general factors that affect the position of the demand curve for dollars affect the position of the supply curve for dollars as well.

The equilibrium exchange rate is determined by the interaction of the demand for and supply of the currency in question. An increase in the exchange rate (of foreign currency per dollar) causes the dollar to appreciate, i.e., increase in value. A decrease in the exchange rate causes the dollar to depreciate.

In general, exchange rates can be either fixed--the exchange rate is not allowed to change in response to changes in the forces of supply and demand--or flexible. According to the theory of purchasing power parity, under a system of flexible exchange rates, the exchange rate is determined primarily by movements in relative price levels across countries. The implication of purchasing power parity is that over time, adjustments in the exchange rate will result in equality (or near equality) of the price index for tradable goods across countries.

To the extent that governments attempt to influence the exchange rate, they must intervene in the foreign exchange market. However, attempts to influence exchange rates also affect the domestic economy. This is due to the fact that the money supply is altered in the course of trying to change the exchange rate. In general, efforts to maintain a particular exchange rate target value will affect the price level and/or level of real GNP in one or both of the countries affected by such efforts. Many government's rely on the policy of a managed, or dirty, float, which is intended to offset temporary fluctuations, while allowing the exchange rate to trend up or down to its equilibrium level.

The effects of changes in money demand and money supply, changes in aggregate demand, and supply shocks in an open-economy model differ from the effects of the same changes in a closed-economy model. The effects of specific changes also depend on whether exchange rates are assumed to be fixed or variable. In general, the effects of changes in money demand and money supply will be larger in an open-economy model with flexible exchange rates than in a closed-economy model. However, this affect is reduced in the case of fixed exchanged rates. On the other hand, the effects of changes in aggregate demand and supply are smaller in an open-economy model with flexible exchange rates than in a closed-economy model. However, the effect of such changes become larger with an assumption of fixed exchange rates. One of the implications of these results is that in an open-economy with flexible exchange rates the effectiveness of monetary policy is increased, while the effectiveness of fiscal policy is reduced.

Government budget deficits can also affect exchange rates, and therefore real GNP, through their effect on capital flows. To the extent that the government runs a budget deficit that is financed by borrowing, and real interest rates rise, foreign capital is attracted into the domestic economy. This causes the exchange rate to rise, and therefore net exports fall. The result is a reduction in the growth of aggregate demand and therefore real GNP.

KEY GRAPHS AND TERMS

Graphs

Figures 1 - 4 illustrate graphically the various components of the model of the foreign exchange market and how it is used to analyze the effects of changes in the determinants of the foreign exchange rate. As is the usual case, a change in the price of foreign exchange--the foreign exchange rate--causes a change in quantity demanded and quantity supplied, shown by a movement along the respective curves. A change in any of the other determinants of demand and supply causes the curves to shift. In particular, an increase in the real income level in foreign countries, the price level in foreign countries relative to the U.S. price level, or the real interest rate in the United States relative to the real interest rate in foreign countries causes the demand for dollars to increase--the demand curve shifts right. On the other hand, these same changes cause the supply of dollars to decrease--the supply curve shifts left. As such, the exchange rate increases. Note, however, that the effect on the quantity of foreign exchange is ambiguous.

Terms

UNILATERAL TRANSFERS
BALANCE OF PAYMENTS
BALANCE ON GOODS AND SERVICES
CURRENT ACCOUNT BALANCE
CAPITAL FLOW
EXCHANGE RATE
APPRECIATION
DEPRECIATION
PURCHASING POWER PARITY
INTERVENTION
CONVERTIBLE CURRENCY
ARBITRAGERS
MANAGED (DIRTY) FLOAT
OPEN-ECONOMY MACROECONOMICS
CAPITAL MOBILITY
PAR VALUE
CAPITAL-FLOW SHOCK

EXERCISES

1. A gift or grant for which nothing is received in return is called a ________________ ________________.

2. By construction, the balance of payments always equals ________________.

3. Within the balance of payments, the balance on current account is equal to ________________ minus ________________ plus net ________________ ________________.

4. The current account balance is financed by ________________ flows. When the current account balance is positive, ________________ flows ________________ the economy. When the current account balance is negative, ________________ flows ________________ the economy.

5. Complete the following table, which summarizes the balance of payments for Country X.

1. Exports of goods and services	+$529.8	
2. Imports of goods and services	- ____	
Balance on goods and services	- 111.9	
3. Unilateral transfers (net)	- 14.7	
Balance on current account	- ____	
4. U.S. assets abroad, net (increase)	- ____	
a. U.S. official reserve assets		- 14.3
b. U.S. nonreserve assets		- 73.2
5. Foreign assets in U.S., net (increase)	+ 219.3	
a. Foreign official reserve assets		+ ____
b. Foreign nonreserve assets		+ 209.1
6. Statistical discrepancy	- ____	
Balance of payments	0	

6. The number of units of one currency it takes to buy one unit of another currency is called the

________________ ________________.

7. List the three major factors that cause the demand curve for U.S. dollars in the foreign exchange market to shift. ____

____

____

8. As a result of an increase in the exchange rate of British pounds for dollars, U.S. goods become ________________ ________________ to the British, and the British demand ________________ dollars to buy U.S. goods.

9. List the three major factors that cause the supply curve for U.S. dollars in the foreign exchange market to shift. ____

____

____

10. An increase in the exchange rate (of foreign currency for a dollar) represents an ________________ of the dollar, while a decrease in the exchange rate represents a ________________ of the dollar.

11. According to the theory of ________________ ________________ ________________, a specific amount of currency should purchase the same amount of tradable goods in all countries. As such, to the extent that the price of a tradable good is higher in country A than it is in country B, we would expect to see the exchange rate between country A's currency and country B's currency, measured as the number of units of B's currency it takes to buy a unit of A's currency, ________________.

12. Assume that the U.S. government has decided the fix the exchange rate between British pounds and the dollar at 1.75 pounds per dollar. If the exchange rate rises, in order to push it back to the desired level , the U.S. government must either ________________ the demand for dollars or ________________ the supply of dollars. However, maintaining a fixed exchange rate inevitably affects the ________________ ________________, ________________ ________________ or both in at least one of the two countries involved.

13. The policy of offsetting temporary exchange rate fluctuations, while allowing the exchange rate to trend up or down to its market level is called a ________________ ________________.

14. ________________-________________ ________________ takes account of how the domestic economy is affected by international factors.

15. Under a flexible exchange rate system, a decrease in the money supply causes the interest rate to ________________, which in turn causes the exchange rate to ________________. Consequently, imports ________________ and exports ________________, resulting in a ________________ decrease in real GNP than occurs in the closed-economy model.

16. A decrease in government spending causes the aggregate demand curve to shift ________________ which in turn causes real GNP to ________________. This leads to a ________________ in money demand, causing the expected real interest rate to ________________. Assuming there is a high degree of capital mobility, it is reasonable to expect that the exchange rate will ________________, causing net exports to ________________. As such, the effectiveness of a contractionary fiscal policy is ________________ in an open economy with flexible exchange rates relative to the outcome in a closed economy.

17. In general, changes in real demand and supply have a ________________ overall effect on real GNP under a flexible exchange rate system than a fixed exchange rate system, while changes in money demand and money supply have a ________________ overall effect on real GNP under a flexible exchange rate system than a fixed exchange rate system.

18. To the extent that the government runs a large deficit that is financed by borrowing in the credit market, and assuming inflation is constant or declining, the expected real interest rate ________________. This causes the exchange rate to ________________, which in turn causes net exports to ________________.

Use the figure on the following page, which illustrates the Japanese market for dollars, to answer questions 19 and 20.

19. Determine the equilibrium exchange rate and quantity and label them ER1 and Q1. Define the exchange rate, i.e, explain what it measure in this case.

20. In the figure, illustrate the effects of an increase in the U.S. money supply. What has happened to the equilibrium exchange rate) ________________________ What effect will this have on net exports in the United States? ________________________

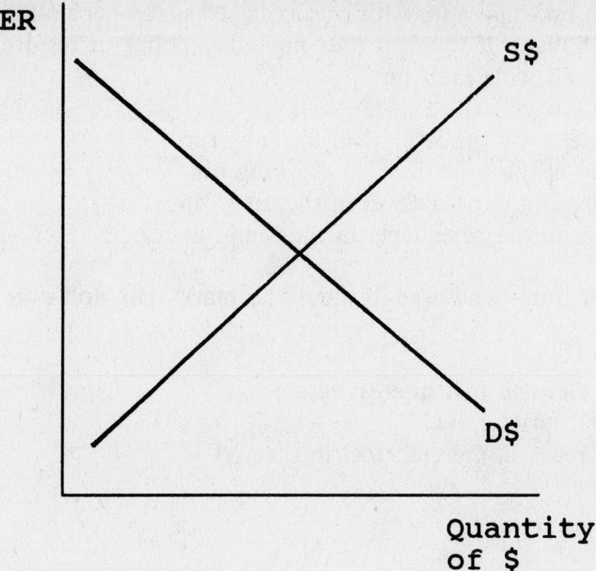

REVIEW QUESTIONS

1. Which of the following statements is correct?

a) A country's balance of payments must always sum to zero.
b) The mercantilist fallacy is that importing is better that exporting.
c) The balance of payments measures the difference between a countries imports and its exports.
d) If imports are greater than exports the balance of payments is negative.

2. In general, given an assumption of a high degree of capital mobility, a system of flexible exchange rates:

a) increases the effectiveness of monetary policy and decreases the effectiveness of fiscal policy.
b) decreases the effectiveness of monetary policy and increases the effectiveness of fiscal policy.
c) increases the effectiveness of both monetary policy and fiscal policy.
d) decreases the effectiveness of both monetary policy and fiscal policy.

3. Assume that the government runs a large budget surplus. Ceteris paribus, and assuming this should cause the expected real interest rate to:

a) fall, the exchange rate to rise, and net exports to increase.
b) fall, the exchange rate to fall, and net exports to increase.
c) rise, the exchange rate to rise, and net exports to increase.
d) rise, the exchange rate to fall, and net exports to increase.

4. Which of the following will cause the supply of dollars in the foreign exchange market to decrease (i.e., the supply curve to shift left)?

a) An increase in the U.S. price level, ceteris paribus.
b) A decrease in U.S. real income.
c) An increase in the exchange rate.
d) An decrease in the U.S. real interest rate, ceteris paribus.

5. Assume that the U.S. government has decided to fix the exchange rate with Mexico at 20 pesos per dollar, but that the exchange rate has increased to 25 pesos per dollar. If the Fed uses monetary policy to restore the exchange rate to its desired level, in the United States this will result in:

a) a decrease in real GNP in the short run, and an increase in the price level in the long run.
b) a decrease in real GNP in the short run, and a decrease in the price level in the long run.
c) an increase in real GNP in the short run, and a decrease in the price level in the long run.
d) a increase in real GNP in the short run, and an increase in the price level in the long run.

6. Which of the following will cause the foreign exchange rate--measured in deutsche marks per dollar--to increase?

a) a decrease in the U.S. real interest rate relative to the German real interest rate.
b) A decrease in the U.S. price level relative to the German price level.
c) A simultaneous increase in U.S. real income, and a decrease in German real income.
d) none of the above.

7. Which of the following statements is correct?

a) Flexible exchange rates tend to worsen the effects of a major import supply shock.
b) An increase in money demand has a greater effect on aggregate demand under a fixed exchange rate system than under a flexible exchange rate system.
c) Fiscal policy is more effective under a fixed exchange rate system than a flexible exchange rate system.
d) Monetary policy is totally ineffective under a fixed exchange rate system.

8. Which of the following will cause the foreign exchange rate--measured in dollars per yen--to increase?

a) a decrease in the U.S. real interest rate relative to the Japanese real interest rate.
b) A decrease in the U.S. price level relative to the Japanese price level.
c) A simultaneous decrease in U.S. real income, and an increase in Japanese real income.
d) all of the above.

9. Purchasing-power parity exists between the currencies of two countries if:

a) one U.S. dollar buys one British pound, or one Japanese yen, and so forth.
b) income is the same in both countries.
c) two countries have the same supply of money.
d) a specific amount of currency purchases the same quantity of tradable goods in all countries.

10. Which of the following would not cause the value of the U.S. dollar to appreciate?

a) a relative increase in foreign prices
b) a decrease in production costs in the U.S.
c) a decrease in U.S. interest rates relative to other countries
d) an increase in tastes and preferences for U.S. made goods

11. From Mexico's perspective, if the exchange rate--measured in pesos per dollar--increases:

a) U.S. goods become cheaper and the quantity demanded of dollars decreases.
b) U.S. goods become cheaper and the quantity demanded of dollars increases
c) U.S. goods become more expensive and the quantity demanded of dollars decreases.
d) U.S. goods become more expensive and the quantity demanded of dollars increases.

12. When the exchange rate between British pounds and the dollar--measured as the number of pounds per dollar--decreases:

a) the dollar appreciates, and the pound depreciates.
b) the dollar depreciates, and the pound appreciates.
c) the dollar and the pound both depreciate.
d) the dollar and the pound both appreciate.

13. According to the theory of purchasing power parity, if the French price level for tradable goods decreases relative to the U.S. price level for tradable goods, the exchange rate--measured in francs per dollar--will:

a) decrease and the dollar will depreciate.
b) increase and the dollar will depreciate.
c) decrease and the dollar will appreciate.
d) increase and the dollar will appreciate.

14. Which of the following statements is <u>not</u> correct?

a) If a country is on the gold standard and runs a trade surplus, gold automatically flows into the country.
b) In order for countries to fix their exchange rates at constant values over long periods of time, they have to coordinate their economic policies.
c) Reliance on a gold standard tends to result in a high degree of price stability.
d) If a country is on the gold standard this means that they are using gold coins as the medium of exchange.

15. The policy of intervening in the exchange market to offset temporary fluctuations in the exchange rate is referred to as a:

a) flexible exchange rate system.
b) fixed exchange rate system
c) arbitrated float.
d) managed or dirty float.

16. Assume that an economy is operating under a flexible exchange rate system, and there is a decrease in the money supply. Over time, this will cause the exchange rate--measured in units of foreign currency per dollar--to:

a) fall, and net exports to decrease.
b) fall, and net exports to increase.
c) rise, and net exports to decrease.
d) rise, and net exports to increase.

17. Under a flexible exchange rate system, an increase in money demand causes the exchange rate--measured in units of foreign currency per dollar--to:

a) fall, net exports rise, and AD shifts right.
b) rise, net exports fall, and AD shifts left.
c) rise, net exports rise, and AD shifts right.
d) fall, net exports fall, and AD shifts left.

18. Assume that in response to a recession, the government decides to increase its purchases of goods and services by way of deficit spending. Assume also that the economy is operating under a flexible exchange rate system, and that there is a high degree of capital mobility. In this case we would expect to observe:

a) an increase in the exchange rate, and an increase in net exports.
b) an increase in the exchange rate, and a decrease in net exports.
c) a decrease in the exchange rate, and an increase in net exports.
d) a decrease in the exchange rate, and a decrease in net exports.

19. Assume there is a decrease in income in foreign countries that results in a decrease in their demand for U.S. exports. Over time, this will cause:

a) the exchange rate to fall, thus moderating the decline in U.S. net exports.
b) the exchange rate to rise, thus moderating the decline in U.S. net exports.
c) the exchange rate to fall, thus worsening the decline in U.S. net exports.
d) the exchange rate to rise, thus worsening the decline in U.S. net exports.

20. Assume that the economy is operating under a fixed exchange rate system and there is an increase in investment. In this case the real interest rate will:

a) rise, causing the exchange rate to rise. This will force the Fed to increase the money supply to restore the exchange rate to its desired level, thus resulting in a further increase in real GNP.
b) rise, causing the exchange rate to fall. This will force the Fed to decrease the money supply to restore the exchange rate to its desired level, thus resulting in a further increase in real GNP.
c) fall, causing the exchange rate to rise. This will force the Fed to increase the money supply to restore the exchange rate to its desired level, thus resulting in a further increase in real GNP.
d) fall, causing the exchange rate to fall. This will force the Fed to decrease the money supply to restore the exchange rate to its desired level, thus resulting in a further increase in real GNP.

21. The ease with which capital flows from one country to another in response to a change in real interest rates is called:

a) the interest elasticity of money.
b) capital mobility.
c) the interest rate equalization index.
d) the capital flexibility index.

22. Ceteris paribus, if the value of the U.S. dollar appreciates relative to the British pound:

a) American wheat will become cheaper in Britain.
b) Net exports by the United States will decrease.
c) British cars will become more expensive in the United States.
d) there will be no effect on the price of imports from Britain.

23. Assume that a country's balance of payments includes the following entries: net increase in U.S. assets abroad = \$117.1, net increase in foreign assets in U.S. = \$204.7, statistical discrepancy = \$11.4, net unilateral transfers = \$10.7, and exports = \$595.2. Based on the this information, the economy's total imports are equal to:

a) \$672.1
b) \$683.5
c) \$694.2
d) \$705.6

24. Which of the following will cause an increase in foreign demand for U.S. dollars (i.e., the demand curve for dollars to shift right)?

a) An increase in the U.S. price level, ceteris paribus.
b) A decease in foreign real income.
c) A decrease in the exchange rate.
d) An increase in the U.S. real interest rate, ceteris paribus.

ANSWER KEY

Exercises

1. unilateral transfer
2. zero
3. exports, imports, unilateral transfers
4. capital, capital, out of, capital, into
5.

1. Exports of goods and services	+$529.8	
2. Imports of goods and services	- 641.7	
Balance on goods and services	- 111.9	
3. Unilateral transfers (net)	- 14.7	
Balance on current account	- 126.6	
4. U.S. assets abroad, net (increase)	- 87.5	
a. U.S. official reserve assets		- 14.3
b. U.S. nonreserve assets		- 73.2
5. Foreign assets in U.S., net (increase)	+ 219.3	
a. Foreign official reserve assets		+ 10.2
b. Foreign nonreserve assets		+ 209.1
6. Statistical discrepancy	- 5.2	
Balance of payments	0	

6. exchange rate
7. 1) A change in the real income level in foreign countries, 2) a change in the price level in foreign countries relative to the U.S. price level, and 3) a change in the real interest rate in the United States relative to the real interest rate in foreign countries.
8. more expensive, less
9. 1) A change in the real income level in the United States, 2) a change in the price level in foreign countries relative to the U.S. price level, and 3) a change in the real interest rate in the United States relative to the real interest rate in foreign countries.
10. appreciation, depreciation
11. purchasing power parity, decrease
12. decrease, increase, price level, real GNP
13. managed (dirty) float
14. Open-economy macroeconomics
15. increase, increase, increase, decrease, larger
16. left, decrease, decrease, decrease, decrease, increase, reduced
17. smaller, larger
18. increases, increase, decrease
19. The exchange rate indicates the number of yen it takes to buy one U.S. dollar.
20. The increase in the money supply will cause the expected real interest rate in the United States to decrease. This will cause the demand for dollars to decrease (the demand curve will shift left) and the supply of dollars to increase (the supply curve will shift right). As such, the exchange rate will fall. This will cause the U.S. imports to decrease and U.S. exports to increase, implying an increase in net exports.

Review Questions

1. a) is the correct answer. This is the result of a country's international budget constraint and the definition of the balance of payments.

2. a) is the correct answer. Under a flexible exchange rate system, a given change in the money supply translates into a larger change in total output than under a fixed exchange rate system. On the other hand, a change in fiscal policy results in a smaller change in total output under a flexible exchange rate system than under a fixed exchange rate system. See the discussion in the text under the heading of open-economy macroeconomics for more details.

3. b) is the correct answer. The budget surplus results in an increase in the supply of credit and a decrease in the demand for credit, pushing the expected real interest rate down. In the foreign exchange market this causes the demand for dollars to fall and the supply of dollars to increase; the exchange rate falls. As such, imports fall and exports increase, causing net exports to rise.

4. b) is the correct answer. a) and d) both cause U.S. demand for imports, and therefore the supply of dollars, to increase. c) causes a movement along the supply curve for dollars. b) causes a decrease in U.S. demand for imports and hence a decrease in the supply of dollars.

5. d) is the correct answer. In order to push the exchange rate back down, the Fed must increase the supply of dollars. This will cause the interest rate to fall, increasing aggregate demand. Real GNP will increase in the short run, which causes the price level to rise over time.

6. b) is the correct answer. a) and c) both cause the supply of dollars to increase and the demand for dollars to decrease, resulting in a decrease in the exchange rate. On the other hand, a decrease in the U.S. price level causes the supply of dollars to decrease and the demand for dollars to increase--the exchange rate increases.

7. c) is the correct answer. Refer to table 2 in the text and read the acompanying discussion in the text.

8. a) is the correct answer. b) and c) both cause the supply of yen to increase and the demand for yen to decrease, resulting in a decrease in the exchange rate. On the other hand, a decrease in the U.S. real interest rate causes the supply of yen to decrease and the demand for yen to increase--the exchange rate increases.

9. d) is the correct answer. This is the definition of purchasing power parity.

10. c) is the correct answer. When the dollar appreciates this means that the exchange rate--measured in units of foreign currency per dollar--has increased. Since a decrease in production costs leads to lower prices, a) is the same as b). In either case, the demand for U.S. exports, and therefore dollars, increases. By the same reasoning, the supply of dollars decreases. Overall, the exchange rate rises. An increase in tastes and preferences for U.S. goods also causes the demand for dollars and hence the exchange rate to increase. However, A decrease in U.S. interest rates causes the demand for dollars to fall and the supply of dollars to increase; the exchange rate falls.

11. c) is the correct answer. An increase in the exchange rate means it takes more pesos to buy a dollar. Hence, it takes more pesos to buy a dollar's worth of U.S. goods. The quantity demanded of U.S. goods, and therefore dollars, decreases.

12. b) is the correct answer. When the exchange rate falls, it takes less pounds to buy a dollar and more dollars to buy a pound. The pound is more valuable in terms of the dollars it buys--it has appreciated. The dollar is less valuable in terms of the number of pounds it buys--it has depreciated.

13. a) is the correct answer. In this case, the supply of dollars will increase and the demand for dollars will decrease. The exchange rate decreases and the dollar depreciates. See the previous answer as well.

14. d) is the correct answer. A gold standard simply means that the value of the currency is tied to the price of gold. Any medium of exchange

will work. See the discussion of the gold standard in the text regarding the other three statements.

15. d) is the correct answer. This is the definition of a managed float.

16. c) is the correct answer. The decrease in the money supply causes the expected real interest rate to rise, which causes the demand for dollars to increase and the supply of dollars to decrease; the exchange rate rises. This causes imports to increase and exports to decrease; net exports fall.

17. b) is the correct answer. An increase in money demand is equivalent to a decrease in the money supply in terms of its effect on the economy. See the previous question and the discussion of this specific issue in the text.

18. b) is the correct answer. The increase in deficit spending causes the demand for credit and therefore the interest rate to increase. This causes the demand for dollars to increase and the supply of dollars to decrease; the exchange rate rises. As noted in question 16, this causes net exports to fall.

19. a) is the correct answer. In this case, the exchange rate will fall. This causes the demand for U.S. exports to increase and the U.S. imports to fall. The decline in net exports is partially offset.

20. a) is the correct answer. The increase in investment implies an increase in credit demand, which causes the expected real interest rate to rise. This causes the demand for dollars to increase and the supply of dollars to decrease, and the exchange rate rises. To bring the exchange rate back down, the Fed must increase the supply of dollars, which leads to a further expansion of aggregate demand and real GNP.

21. b) is the correct answer. This is the definition of capital mobility.

22. b) is the correct answer. When the dollar appreciates, the exchange rate--measured in pounds per dollar--has increased. As such, U.S. exports become more expensive from Britain's point of view and British goods become less expensive from the U.S. point of view. Hence, U.S. imports will increase and U.S. exports will decrease; U.S. net exports fall.

23. b) is the correct answer. This problem can be solved using the following equation: exports - imports - unilateral transfers + net increase in foreign assets in U.S. - net increase in U.S. assets abroad + statistical discrepancy = 0. Substituting in we have \$595.2 - imports - \$10.7 + \$204.7 - \$117.1 + 11.4 = 0. Thus, imports = \$683.5

24. d) is the correct answer. An increase in the U.S. price level and a decrease in foreign real income cause the demand for U.S. goods and therefore the demand for dollars to decrease. A decrease in the exchange rate causes a movement along the demand curve. An increase in the U.S. real interest rate causes the demand for U.S. financial assets and therefore the demand for dollars to increase.

CHAPTER 37
COMPARATIVE ECONOMIC SYSTEMS: THEORY AND EVIDENCE

OVERVIEW

In this chapter we describe alternative economic systems and consider how they answer the fundamental questions that must be addressed by all economies--what, how, and for whom to produce. We begin by comparing market-based and socialist approaches to each question. We then go on to consider arguments for and against each approach. The final section of the chapter consists of a review of the performance of selected economies that comprise a continuum of different economic arrangements.

As we have stated previously in the text, there are three major questions that all economies must address: 1) what and how much to produce, 2) how to produce, and 3) for whom to produce. We have already examined, in considerable detail, how a market economy answers these questions. However, it is worth considering how the alternative to a market economy, i.e., socialism, addresses these questions as well.

With respect to what and how much to produce, markets provide producers with the incentives to respond to consumers' demands. In the pursuit of profits, firms produce those outputs most highly valued by consumers. The quantities of goods produced depend on consumers' willingness and ability to pay and the opportunity costs of production. In a socialist economy, the decision of what and how much to produce is answered through planning. The state owns the factors of production and determines which goods will be produced. However, there are considerable problems with this approach. In particular, it is impossible to coordinate all of the decisions that must be made in a large economy--information costs are a monumental problem. In addition, there are no incentives for workers and managers to cooperate with production plans, let alone produce goods efficiently.

A market economy answers the question of how to produce through the profit motive. Firms seek to maximize profits, which in turn requires cost minimization. Thus, firms use the least-cost method of production. Once again, however, the managers of socialist firms lack such incentives. In addition, because the prices of inputs and outputs do not reflect true opportunity costs, it is not possible to determine the least-cost production methods.

The question of how output is to be distributed is answered on the basis of the income distribution in a market economy. While this outcome is often viewed as promoting inequities, it does create incentives for people to be more efficient and reallocate resources to their most highly-valued uses. Socialism attempts to distribute outputs more equitably by promoting equality of outcomes.

On the basis of efficiency, a market economy is far superior to socialism in its handling of the three major questions. However, proponents of socialism argue that the manner in which efficiency is defined is too narrow. In particular, they maintain that market economies are wasteful to the extant that materialistic motives underlie the pursuit of increased production.

In fact, almost all economies contain a mix of market and socialist elements. As such, economies can be compared on the basis of different general criteria, such as the degree of state ownership of the means of production, the degree of state planning of the economy, and the degree of income distribution carried out by the government. As is indicated in the text, a particular group of countries--such as those considered in the text--will rank differently relative to one another on the basis of these criteria. It is sufficient to note here that very few countries exhibit characteristics that can be consistently categorized as being close to one extreme or the other.

KEY TERMS

CONSUMER SOVEREIGNTY
PRODUCTION PLAN
ENTREPRENEURSHIP
LAISSEZ FAIRE
INDICATIVE PLANNING
WORKER-MANAGED FIRM
ONE-YEAR PLAN
GOSPLAN
MATERIALS BALANCING
GOSBANK
UNDERGROUND MARKET

EXERCISES

1. In a market economy most resources are Privatily owned, while in a socialist economy most resources are state owned.

2. In a socialist economy, the question of what to produce is answered by the State. In turn, how much to produce is decided through the development of a Production Plan. In a market economy, the question of what, and how much, to produce is determined by Consumers.

3. Entrepreneurship refers to the creative management of production.

4. The difficulty of large-scale planning arises from two sources: 1) coordinating production, and 2) providing incentives.

5. With respect to the question of how to distribute output, market economies tend to emphasize equality of opportunities, as opposed to equality of outcomes, while socialist economies stress the opposite.

6. In a competitive economy, input prices reflect the social opportunity cost of production.

7. Indicative planning refers to the situation in which the government sets goals and provides incentives for firms, but allows firms to determine how they will meet those goals.

8. The Soviet state planning commission is called Gosplan, and the Soviet state bank is called Gosbank.

9. The term materials balancing refers to a balance sheet approach to matching available supplies of resources to demands for those resources.

10. In the Soviet economy, producers pay set prices for their inputs and receive set prices for their outputs. However, these prices are accounting prices, not market prices.

11. According to various studies, private individuals in the USSR use Three percent of the available cropland to produce twenty-seven percent of total Soviet agricultural output.

12. List the three factors discussed in the text that appear to impede Soviet agriculture. The inefficiently large size of state farms, the shortage of modern equipment and spare parts, and the lack of incentives for farm workers to be productive.

13. The term perestroika refers to the process of economic restructuring.

14. List the major steps undertaken as part of the Polish economic reforms that were implemented in 1990.
The zlotty was radically devalued and most currency controls were dropped, money supply growth was slowed dramatically, most prices were decontrolled, gov subsidies of state farms were removed, and most restrictions on foreign trade were removed

15. List the three ways in which the French government obtains cooperation with its production plans for the French economy. look

16. Available evidence indicates that the Swedish economic system has greatly (increased, decreased) the incentive to work. However, the Swedish standard of living remains among the (highest, lowest) in the world.

17. From 1961 to 1980, the level of real income in Hong Kong rose at a rate of approximately ___Ten___ percent per year.

REVIEW QUESTIONS

1. The economy of ________________ most closely resembles the model of pure capitalism.

a) the United States
b) Hong Kong
c) France
d) Sweden

2. Of the following countries, in which one is state involvement in the distribution of income and welfare greatest?

a) Sweden
b) France
c) the United States
d) Hong Kong

3. Which of the following statements is not correct?

a) In Marx' view of economic evolution, capitalism would eventually break down and be replaced by socialism and eventually communism.
b) In a socialist economy, the question of what to produce is determined by the state.
c) Socialist and market economies are similar to the extent that both rely on prices to allocate resources to the production of different goods and services.
d) In a socialist economy emphasis is placed on equality of outcome, as opposed to equality of opportunity.

4. A potentially legitimate criticism of market economies is that they:

a) tend to produce some goods that do not make people any better off.
b) lack an effective set of incentives for workers and the managers of firms.
c) fail to take account of the social costs of production in most cases.
d) are generally more inefficient that socialist economies.

5. Which of the following statements is correct?

a) By its nature, materials balancing is a more efficient approach to resource allocation that reliance on markets.
b) The state-determined prices used by firms in the USSR are market prices, not accounting prices.
c) It has been estimated that in the 1980s, less than five percent of the available cropland was used to produce more than 25 percent of the total agricultural output in the Soviet Union.
d) The intent of perestroika is to reinforce the effectiveness of the Gosplan in the Soviet Union.

6. The term "market socialism" refers to the situation in which:

a) firms are allowed to earn a profit in order to have the incentive to produce efficiently.
b) prices are set that reflect the true social opportunity costs of production.
c) production plans are formulated on the basis of how resources are allocated in competing market economies.
d) the government sets input and output prices that reflect its priorities with respect to production.

7. The development and implementation of productions plans run into problems due to the:

a) difficulties encountered in trying to coordinate large scale production.
b) lack of incentives for managers and workers to perform efficiently.
c) the huge data requirements that are encountered in trying to develop such plans.
d) all of the above.

8. Which of the following is considered to be a source of the poor performance of collectivized agriculture in the Soviet Union.

a) the inefficiently large size of state farms
b) the lack of modern equipment and spare parts
c) the lack of incentives for farm workers to be productive
d) all of the above

9. Of the following countries, in which one is the state-ownership of resources greatest?

a) the United States
b) France
c) Sweden
d) Hong Kong

10. Of the following countries, in which one is state planning of the economy greatest?

a) Hong Kong
b) Sweden
c) Poland
d) France

11. Which of the following was not one of the elements in Poland's economic reform package that was implemented in 1990?

a) The money supply was increased to stimulate investment and consumption spending.
b) Most prices were decontrolled.
c) Government subsidies to state firms were removed.
d) Most restrictions on foreign trade were removed.

12. Which of the following statements regarding the effects of the Polish economic reforms is <u>not</u> correct?

a) Inflation initially rose to over 75 percent, but then fell below 5 percent by March of 1990.
b) Workers' real incomes increased.
c) Unemployment increased.
d) There was an increase in the availability of consumer goods.

13. The distinguishing characteristic of the Yugoslavian economy is:

a) worker management of firms.
b) the virtual absence of state ownership of productive resources.
c) the development of detailed production plans that must be followed by all firms.
d) the dominant role of the central government in the workings of the economy.

14. The managers of firms in socialist economies:

a) attempt to minimize the social costs of production.
b) attempt to produce the combination of goods and service most preferred by consumers.
c) lack the information and incentives to produce the economically efficient level of output.
d) have much better production-related information than do managers of firms in market economies.

15. Which of the following statements regarding the French economy is correct?

a) The French economy is based on markets, but utilizes indicative planning to guide the production decisions of individual firms.
b) There is almost no state-ownership of resources in the French economy.
c) Once a production plan is formally developed, all firms are required to follow it as closely as possible.
d) The French economy out-performed most European economies in the 1970s and the 1980s.

ANSWER KEY

Exercises

1. privately, state
2. state, production plan, consumers
3. Entrepreneurship
4. coordinating production, providing incentives
5. opportunity, outcomes
6. social opportunity costs
7. Indicative planning
8. Gosplan, Gosbank
9. materials balancing
10. accounting, market
11. three, twenty-seven
12. 1) The inefficiently large size of state farms, 2) the shortage of modern equipment and spare parts, and 3) the lack of incentives for farm workers to be productive.
13. economic restructuring
14. 1) The zlotty was radically devalued and most currency controls were dropped, 2) money supply growth was slowed dramatically, 3) most prices were decontrolled, 4) government subsidies to state firms were removed, and 5) most restrictions on foreign trade were removed.
15. 1) The French government owns a number of large industrial corporations which it can direct to act according to the plan; 2) the government controls the lending practices of much of the banking sector, and can therefore influence the activities of private firms; and 3) the government can use its taxing and spending powers to influence private activity.
16. decreased, highest
17. ten

Review Questions

1. b) is the correct answer. Of the four countries listed, Hong Kong has the least amount of state-ownership of productive resources. In addition, there is almost no government involvement in production decisions or income distribution.

2. a) is the correct answer. This is an empirical fact. See the discussion in the text.

3. c) is the correct answer. One of the major differences between socialist and market economies is that market economies rely on prices to determine the allocation of productive resources and the distribution of outputs. Socialist economies, on the other hand, replace the price system with central planning in an effort to achieve what they consider a more socially desirable combination and distribution of outputs.

4. a) is the correct answer. It is argued that advertising creates needs and demands for certain goods and services that do not necessarily improve the quality of life or the standard of living. b), c) and d) are not defensible criticisms of a market economy.

5. c) is the correct answer. This is an empirical fact. See the discussion in the text. Materials balancing is less efficient than the market since it does not take account of opportunity costs. In addition, the prices in the Soviet Union are accounting prices. Finally, answer d) is counter to the definition of perestroika.

6. d) is the correct answer. This is the definition of market socialism. See the discussion in the text.

7. d) is the correct answer. Because a production plan replaces the price system as the means of determining what and how much to produce, it must somehow address all of the issues listed here.

8. d) is the correct answer. See the discussion in the text regarding the performance of the Soviet economy.

9. b) is the correct answer. This is an empirical fact. See the discussion in the text.

10. d) is the correct answer. This is an empirical fact. See the discussion in the text.

11. a) is the correct answer. In fact, as is discussed in the text, money supply growth was slowed dramatically as a result of a significant increase in interest rates and a corresponding reduction in loan creation.

12. b) is the correct answer. In fact, real wages fell dramatically. See the discussion in the text.

13. a) is the correct answer. As is discussed in the text, the central government plays a relatively small role in the economy. Although the state owns most of the factors of production, it does not develop production plans.

14. c) is the correct answer. Because prices are not market determined, it is not possible to know what the social opportunity costs of production are, let alone minimize them. In addition, it is difficult to know which goods consumers prefer most. Finally, the lack of the ability to earn profits removes the incentive to minimize production costs.

15. a) is the correct answer. See the discussion of the French economy in the text.

NOTES

NOTES

NOTES